Philosophers of Capitalism

Philosophers of Capitalism

Menger, Mises, Rand, and Beyond

edited by Edward W. Younkins

LEXINGTON BOOKS

A Division of
ROWMAN & LITTLEFIELD PUBLISHERS, INC.
Lanham • Boulder • New York • Toronto • Oxford

LEXINGTON BOOKS

A division of Rowman & Littlefield Publishers, Inc.
A wholly owned subsidary of The Rowman & Littlefield Publishing Group, Inc.
4501 Forbes Boulevard, Suite 200
Lanham, MD 20706

PO Box 317
Oxford
OX2 9RU, UK

British Library Cataloguing in Publication Information Available

Library of Congress Cataloging-in-Publication Data

Philosophers of capitalism : Menger, Mises, Rand, and beyond / edited by Edward W.
Younkins.
    p. cm.
  Includes index.
  ISBN 0-7391-1076-4 (hardcover : alk. paper) -- ISBN 0-7391-1077-2 (pbk. : alk. paper)
  1. Capitalism--Philosopy. 2. Menger, Carl, 1840-1921. 3. Von Mises, Ludwig, 1881-
1973. 4. Rand, Ayn. I. Younkins, Edward Wayne, 1948-
HB501.P4183 2005
330.12'2--dc22   2005011067

Printed in the United States of America

♾ ™ The paper used in this publication meets the minimum requirements of American
National Standard for Information Sciences—Permanence of Paper for Printed Library
Materials, ANSI/NISO Z39.48–1992.

For my parents, who taught me to love liberty, to accept responsibility, to respect reality, and to trust the judgment of my own mind.

Contents

Part III: The Future

Preface

I didn't like his [Ludwig von Mises's] separation of morality and economics, but I assumed that it simply meant that morality was not his specialty and that he could not derive one of his own. At that time, I thought—about both Henry [Hazlitt] and von Mises—that since they were fully committed to laissez-faire capitalism, the rest of their philosophy had contradictions only because they did not yet know how to integrate a full philosophy to capitalism. It didn't bother me; I knew I would present the full case.

—Ayn Rand

By combining and synthesizing elements found in Austrian Economics, Ayn Rand's philosophy of Objectivism, and the closely related philosophy of human flourishing that originated with Aristotle, we have the potential to reframe the argument for a free society into a consistent reality-based whole whose integrated sum of knowledge and explanatory power is greater than that of its parts. In other words, the Austrian value-free praxeological defense of capitalism and the moral arguments of Rand, Aristotle, and the neo-Aristotelians can be brought together, strengthen one another, and result in a powerful, emergent libertarian synthesis of great promise.

After I finished writing my 2002 book, *Capitalism and Commerce*, I came to the realization that virtually all of what I had to say in it fit within the fields of Austrian Economics, Objectivism, or the Aristotelian philosophy of human flourishing. This prompted me to read widely and deeply in each of these fields. The more that I read, the more that I realized that these "schools" had much in common if one looked in the right places.

Ayn Rand's neo-Aristotelian philosophy of Objectivism is the primary impetus and inspiration of the contemporary libertarian movement. Not far behind in terms of their influence are the Austrian thinkers who were political and social philosophers as much as they were economists.

Menger was Aristotelian and had a lot in common with Rand. Mises was off base with his Kantian epistemology, but his excellent deductive use of the action axiom, as shown by Murray Rothbard, could be derived using induction and a natural law approach. I also discovered how Austrian praxeology's emphasis on subjective value and value-freedom are compatible with Rand's objective value and value-relevance. My conclusion was that praxeological economics and Objectivism are complementary and compatible disciplines and that when they are used together to explain reality the case for a free society is strengthened.

Much of this developing model is rooted in the work of Aristotle, who influenced so many thinkers from Aquinas to Locke to the Founding Fathers, to Menger, Rand, and Rothbard, and beyond. The roots of freedom and individualism can be traced back to Aristotle, who acknowledged their moral significance and the value of each individual's life and happiness.

Austrian praxeology (i.e., the study of human action) can be used to make a value-free case for freedom. Such an economic science deals with abstract principles and general rules that must be applied if a society is to have optimal production and economic well-being. Austrian Economics consists of a body of logically deduced, inexorable laws of economics beginning with the axiom that each man acts purposefully. Austrians proclaim the central human element in economic life and search for universal laws that can be expressed in a natural language rather than in mathematical equations and formulas.

The Austrian school is an alternative to the positivistic Neoclassical school that uncritically applies the methods of the physical sciences to the social sciences. The neoclassicals try to make economics look like physics by employing the quantitative approaches of the natural sciences and by searching for quantitative laws, predictive ability, and the statistical significance of changes in variables. Austrians are contemptuous of, and attack, mainstream economists for their pretensions as scientists and for their development of mathematical models that disregard a great deal of human nature and the uncertainty of expectations. Empiricism is appropriate for the purposeless realm of the natural sciences but not for the field of purposeful human action. Because the Austrians see man as a purposeful being who thinks, plans, decides, and acts, they repudiate the neoclassical, positivist, and historical ideas of man as a dependent variable in a system of equations, as a mere quantitative physical object, or as passive objects controlled by history.

Austrian Economics is an excellent alternative way of looking at economics with respect to the appraisal of means but not of ends. Misesian praxeology therefore must be augmented. Its value-free economics is not sufficient to establish a total case for liberty. A systematic, reality-based ethical system must be discovered to firmly establish the argument for individual liberty. Natural law provides the groundwork for such a theory and both Objectivism and the Aristotelian idea of human flourishing are based on natural law ideas.

An ethical system must be developed and defended in order to establish the case for a free society. An Aristotelian ethics of naturalism states that moral matters are matters of fact and that morally good conduct is that which enables the individual agent to make the best possible progress toward achieving his self-perfection and happiness. According to Rand, happiness relates to a person's success as a unique, rational human being possessing free will. We have free choice and the capacity to initiate our own conduct that enhances or hinders our flourishing as human beings. Rand's philosophy of Objectivism is a systematic and integrated unity in which ethics is related to the concept of value, which, in turn, is related to an objective epistemology and a reality-based metaphysics.

Both economists and ethics are concerned with human choice and human action. Human action, the subject of both economics and morality, is the common denominator and the link between economic principles and moral principles. Both economic law and moral law are derived from natural law. Because truth is consistent, it follows that economics and morality are inextricably related parts of one indivisible body of knowledge. Because natural law regulates the affairs of men, it is the task of both economists and philosophers to discover the natural order and to adhere to it. There is an intimate connection between economic science and an objective, normative framework for understanding human life.

It follows that all of the disciplines of human action are interrelated and can be integrated into a paradigm of individual liberty based on the nature of man and the world. A study of human action grounded as a true anthropology of the human person provides insights into both economics and moral truths. Economic and moral principles are part of one inseparable body of thought.

It should not be surprising to find that the discoveries of a truth-based economics and of a moral philosophy based on the nature of man and the world are consistent with one another. There is one universe in which everything is interconnected metaphysically through the inescapable laws of cause and effect. True knowledge must also be a total in which every item of knowledge is interconnected. All objective knowledge is interrelated in some way thus reflecting the totality that is the universe.

Because no field is totally independent of any other field, there are really no discrete branches of knowledge. There is only cognition in which subjects are separated out for purpose of study. That is fine for purposes of specialization, but, in the end, we need to reintegrate by connecting one's specialized knowledge back into the total knowledge of reality. We need to think systemically, look for the relationships and connections between components of knowledge, and aspire to understand the nature of knowledge and its unity.

After a brief introduction, *Philosophers of Capitalism* is divided into the following three sections: (1) Essential Ideas; (2) Scholarly Perspectives; and (3) The Future. The first section consists of three expository essays designed to introduce the readers to the basic arguments of Carl Menger, Ludwig von Mises, and Ayn Rand, respectively. These introductory essays are aimed at the lay reader and are more interpretative than they are critical. Scholars will certainly find my expository approach deficient in terms of the footnote-laden approach of conventional academic debate. These chapters represent a nonspecialist's account of these thinkers' works and ideas. My goal is to make these thinkers' ideas accessible to a great number of readers through the use of clear, nontechnical explanations of their ideas. At the end of each chapter I have included a list of recommended readings for those who wish to study the ideas of a given thinker in greater depth and detail.

The articles included in the section entitled Scholarly Perspectives were published previously in various academic journals. I would therefore like to thank the publishers for permitting me to bring them together in this volume. Although the essays are a diverse lot, they are interrelated and together the contributors provide insight into the depth and breadth of the thought of Menger, Mises, Rand, and others. In any collection of essays, it is common to find disagreements and variations with respect to any thinker's doctrines and this collection is no exception.

The last section of this book looks to the future and to the potential interaction and integration of Austrian Economics and Objectivism into a logical and systematic worldview. In particular, a model is offered that combines Misesian Austrian praxeology and methodology, as rehabilitated by the natural-law-oriented Rothbard, with Rand's Objectivism and the Aristotelian philosophy of human flourishing. An attempt is made to integrate these seemingly disparate areas of thought into a broad natural law and natural-rights-based analytic and normative science of liberty.

Over the last few years, many people have contributed importantly to this work by reading and commenting on all of it, various portions of it, or drafts of my essays containing ideas that appear in it. I am extremely grateful to the following individuals for their useful observations and suggestions and for their help in my efforts to clarify my ideas: Terry Arthur, Charles Baird, Jack Birner, Walter Block, David Boaz, Peter Boettke, Samuel Bostaph, Jurgis Brakas, Bruce J. Caldwell, Eugene Callahan, Rafe Champion, Ricardo Crespo, Paul Cwik, Douglas Den Uyl, Tom DiLorenzo, Richard M. Ebeling, John Egger, Sam Erica, Reginald Firehammer, Fred Foldvary, Arthur Foulkes, Thomas Frecka, Richard Fuerle, Joseph S. Fulda, Roger Garrison, Mark Gordon, Bettina Greaves, Pat Gunning, Homayoun Hajiran, Jeffrey M. Herbener, Stephen Hicks, Randall Holcombe, Hans-Herman Hoppe, Steven Horwitz, Edward L. Hudgins, Matthew Humphries, Candice E. Jackson, Richard C. B. Johnsson, Hubert Jongen, David Kelley, Stephen Kinsella, Peter Kurrild-Klitgaard, Jeff Landauer, George Leef, Roderick T. Long, Tibor Machan, Russell Madden, Uskali Maki, Wendy McElroy, Nigel Meek, Martin Masse, Robert Murphy, Alysha Pannett, Jason Pappas, Neil Parille, Lindsay Perigo, William H. Peterson, Karen Phillips, Ralph Raico, Douglas B. Rasmussen, Adam Reed, Lawrence Reed, Lew Rockwell, David S. Ross, Joseph Rowlands, Larry Schweikart, Chris Matthew Sciabarra, Larry J. Sechrest, Frank Shostak, Aeon Skoble, Mark Skousen, Josef Sima, Barry Smith, Amy Sturgis, Alex Tabarrak, Chris Tame, Thomas C. Taylor, William Thomas, Mark Thornton, Jeffrey Tucker, David Voight, Gary Wolfram, Thomas Woods, Stephen Yates, Andre Zantonavitch, and Gloria L. Zúñiga.

Of course, inclusion in the above list does not indicate endorsement of this book or agreement with the ideas expressed within it. It does mean that each person on the list has assisted me in some way with this current project. Most of all, I am indebted to my secretary at Wheeling Jesuit University, Carla Cash, for her most capable and conscientious help in bringing this book to print.

Finally, in the end, it is only I who can be found responsible for any errors found in this book.

Edward W. Younkins
Wheeling Jesuit University

Introduction

Thus, while praxeological economic theory is extremely useful for providing data and knowledge for framing economic policy, it cannot be sufficient by itself to enable the economist to make any value pronouncements or to advocate any public policy whatsoever. More specifically, Ludwig von Mises to the contrary notwithstanding, neither praxeological economics nor Mises's utilitarian liberalism is sufficient to make the case for laissez faire and the free-market economy. To make such a case, one must go beyond economics and utilitarianism to establish an objective ethics which affirms the overriding value of liberty, and morally condemns all forms of statism.

—Murray N. Rothbard

The power of ideas is great. If we are to educate, persuade, and convert others to free-market thinking, we need to articulate, in structured form, the conceptual and moral foundations of free enterprise. We are obliged to expound a coherent and consistent body of principles that are in accord with reality and that properly reflect and explain capitalism. In other words, we must approach the idea of free enterprise from a philosophical point of view. The survival of free enterprise may be in jeopardy unless people understand its conceptual and moral foundations.

Capitalism is a rational doctrine based on a clear understanding of man and society in which economics, politics, and morality (all parts of one inseparable truth) are found to be in harmony with one another. Capitalism as defined in this book involves that set of economic arrangements that would exist in a society in which the state's only function would be to prevent one person from using force or fraud against another person. This book is concerned with identifying the conceptual foundations of capitalism that are consistent with the nature of man and the world. The development of a conceptual framework is a natural endeavor that is undertaken in most areas that have claims to be called scientific or based on real-world conditions.

This book looks at the feasibility of an integration or synthesis of Austrian Economics and Ayn Rand's philosophy of Objectivism. It will discuss the distinctive approaches of each, their potential interactions, and the possibility of logically tracing their positions back to a set of mutually compatible premises. We will see if it is possible to integrate these schools of thought into a coherent and cohesive worldview. Such an interdisciplinary approach and philosophical perspective must be driven by the demands of truth and must be congenial to free will if it is to make a reasoned case for a free society in which people pursue their lives through reason and trade. The result would be a paradigm or metatheory that integrates and overrides the concerns of each independent worldview into one. The wedding or blending of these traditions will help us attain a deeper understanding of reality which exists as an objective absolute. Such a framework would be in the tradition of a unitary conception of knowledge, and reality would be in accordance with the idea that there is power to truth and to the knowledge of it.

Part 1 of this book consists of three chapters devoted to presenting the essential ideas of Carl Menger, Ludwig von Mises, and Ayn Rand. Part 2 brings together a number of scholarly perspectives on the above thinkers. Finally, in part 3 I look toward the future and the possibility of combining and extending the insights of these champions of a free society. The emphasis in this final section is on how the errors, omissions, and/or oversights made by one theorist can effectively be negated or compensated for by integrating insights from one or more of the others. The remainder of this introductory chapter will provide a brief overview of each of these three sections.

Essential Ideas

The Austrian school of economics places economics on a sound, human basis through its emphasis on actions performed by free, intelligent, creative, and rational agents. Austrian thinkers reject the use of mathematical models, stress the use of words and concepts, and employ the methods of methodological individualism and subjectivism. However, the Austrian school is anything but monolithic, as evidenced by the many disagreements among its members. Authors labeled as "Austrian" cannot be brought together within a unified and coherent analytical framework.

Carl Menger (1840-1921), the father of Austrian Economics, provided the scientific and theoretical foundation for the Austrian tradition toward the end of the nineteenth century. Menger, the founder of the Austrian movement, formulated the concepts and principles which would be continual and elaborated upon by his successors such as Ludwig von Mises (1881-1973) and Murray Rothbard (1926-1995). In this current book I emphasize the Mengerian essence of Austrian Economics as it is developed by these thinkers and exclude the thought of economists such as Frederick A. Hayek (1899-1992), Israel Kirzner (1930-), and Ludwig Lachman (1906-1990) who took Austrian Economics down a very different path. These latter writers have greatly reformulated, altered, and deviated from Menger's original message, principles, and concepts.

Menger presupposed an Aristotelian essentialism about the natural order which includes the realm of economics. Like Aristotle, Menger viewed essences as metaphysical. Menger wanted to investigate essences of economic phenomena such as value, rent, profit, division of labor, and so on. His goal was to discover the invariant laws or principles governing economic phenomena. He said that economics must be constructed according to the model of theoretical science by elaborating exact universal laws. He argued that the status of economics as an exact science is based on the fact that it is possible to develop precise and universal concepts and laws to explain economic phenomena. Menger taught that there are objective laws of nature and that goods had objective properties that made them capable of fulfilling men's needs.

For Menger, the individual is placed at the origin of a proper explanation of economic phenomena. According to Menger, man, himself, is the point at which human economic life both begins and ends. Man, with his purposes and plans, is thus the subject of his own study. He said that the origin of all economic activity lies in the "subjective" values placed by individuals on things that they believe will satisfy their needs.

Menger said that people value because they have needs as living, conditional entities. He explained that subjective values (i.e., based on one's personal estimation) can be viewed as being individual, agent-relative, and perhaps as objective. He noted that people can be mistaken regarding what their needs actually are and they can wrongly believe that a nonuseful thing is a good. For Menger, something is useful because a person thinks it is useful and because the causal relationship between the thing and a need actually exists. Mengerian agents live in a world of uncertainty where errors are possible. People could be mistaken about a good and its properties and its ability to satisfy their needs. He said that they may recognize their error once they acquire better information. People acquire knowledge in order to improve their plans of action. Menger explained that perfect knowledge never exists and that all economic activity involves risk.

Rationality did not imply omniscience to Menger. He explained that people need to learn the causal relationships between things and their properties and the ability of the good to satisfy their needs in order to make a reasonable decision regarding their economic well-being. Menger's concern with causal connections led him to include a means-ends framework at the heart of his conception of economics.

Menger incorporated the peculiarly human elements of purposeful action and uncertainty, the occurrence of errors, the information acquisition process, learning, and time into his economic analysis. He explained that economic activities take place over time and in real time. Menger was the first economist to offer a thorough subjectivist concept based on the personal appraisal of economic actors and to offer a causal-genetic analysis of the emergence of economic phenomena such as money. Menger's Aristotelian essentialism offers a framework of basic and universal principles and concepts that underpins the core of his logic. His nondeterminist view of economic phenomena and use of natural language rather than formal mathematical models changed the essential character of economics.

Mises's goal, like that of Menger, was to formulate a total reconstruction of economics in order to attain for economics the status of a universal theoretical science. Mises continued the research program started by Menger by building time, uncertainty, social cooperation, and process into his system. Building on the work of Menger, Mises rebuilt economics upon the solid foundation of a general theory of human action.

Mises's enterprise was to develop an edifice of irrefutable, coherent, universally applicable, formal economic theory using logical deduction and the sole axiom of human action without employing any other empirical or analytical assumptions. According to Mises, it is possible to deduce the entirety of the logic of economic behavior from the fundamental axiom that individual men act, but that it is impossible to deduce the concrete consequences or details of particular human actions because each person possesses free will. He explains that the universality of human action generates the universality of economic truths. It is possible to discover the essentially true features of human action which he saw as purposeful behavior.

For Mises, the concept of action is universal, intuitive, a priori, and automatically built into each person's mental structure. He deduced a complete system of what he called praxeological laws exclusively from the central introspectively known axiom of human action which he viewed as a law of thought. Mises based all knowledge of the economic system on solely the axiom of action aimed at the satisfaction of human needs.

Misesian praxeological economics is more rationalistic than Mengerian economics, works at a formal level, and assumes that people act in order to achieve goals. Action is determined by the choice of the actor, and economic phenomena are products of individual human action. For Mises, a dissatisfied or uneasy person acts when he believes his action can cause the desired effect in the world. Human action involves causality, time, change, and uncertainty. Real choice involves free will and can only occur in an uncertain environment with respect to the future. Otherwise, it would simply be reaction.

Mises explains that men act in real time, using scarce economic means, directed at ends to be attained in the future. Men, with uncertain and incomplete knowledge, must believe that these actions will make a difference and must act now in order to achieve their ends later. Because their time is scarce and finite, they prefer, ceteris paribus, to gain ends as close to the present as possible. They would rather have goods sooner than have them later.

Mises was dissatisfied with Menger's Aristotelian methodology and value theory. He thought that Menger's subjectivism was not consistent enough and therefore articulated a more thoroughgoing subjectivist position. Because Menger had included the category of imaginary goods in his system, Mises saw Menger as either having objectivist leanings or at least as being inconsistent in his formulations. For a total subjectivist such as Mises, the category, imaginary goods, was suspect. If the character of goods is solely defined by a person's subjective evaluations then how could any good be more imaginary or more real than any other?

Mises's idea of the subjective nature of value takes human ends as the ultimate given. He was not concerned with what or why people value but with how they meet their goals of achieving their values. For Mises, economics is a value-free science of means rather than of ends. Economics is a theory of the consequences of choice and action.

Apriorism is the most problematic and controversial aspect of Misesian praxeology. Mises's praxeological thought has been continued and furthered by his student, Murray Rothbard, who contended that the law of human action could be viewed as a law of reality instead of as a law of thought. According to Rothbard, Aristotelian metaphysics and epistemology are consistent with Mises's action axiom and are able to provide a superior foundation for Misesian praxeological economics. As a consequence, a person would derive the action axiom through induction and deduce the principles of praxeological economics from that axiom. It follows that a man becomes aware of the purposefulness of human action from a combination of introspection and the observation of goal-directed action from the outside.

Austrian praxeological economists speak a different language from that spoken by the neoclassical economists who applied the mechanistic model of physics to the study of human behavior, thereby constructing an unrealistic and nonrepresentative economic model of perfect knowledge and pure competition. Neoclassical economists employ a positivist methodology and reduce scientific proposition to experienced immediate data from which they draw their conclusions. Whereas the neoclassicals assume certainty and full knowledge, describe equilibrium states, and stress empirical testing, the praxeological economists are concerned with the implications of uncertainty and ignorance, describe states of disequilibrium, and reject mathematical methods. The Austrians substitute a conception of the human person as purposeful, creative, and entrepreneurial for the mechanistic and atomistic neoclassical worldview. Austrians, like Objectivists, espouse a critical stance toward neoclassical economics and adopt a strict individualist position and defense of the free market.

Ayn Rand created the broad philosophical system of Objectivism in her novels and essays. Objectivism is her integrated system of thought that defines and explains the abstract principles by which a person must think and act if he is to live a life proper to man.

A coherent philosophical system must have axioms which are irreducible self-evident truths that are implied in all acts of cognition and that cannot be logically refuted. Objectivism is founded on the axioms of existence, identity, and consciousness. More specifically, existence exists, to be is to be something, and consciousness is the faculty that perceives that which exists independent of consciousness. Existence is identity and consciousness is identification. The task of a man's consciousness is to perceive reality, rather than to create it. The denial of any of Objectivism's axioms is illogical because they are implicit in the very act of their denial. The person denying the axiom is forced to use it in his efforts to deny it.

Affirming the primacy of existence, Rand declared that existence is primary and irreducible and that consciousness is a characteristic of human beings by which they acquire awareness of an independently existing reality. Her law of causality states that a thing's actions are determined by its nature. An entity may not act in contradiction to its identity. She explained that reason and free will are features of human nature and that free will is compatible with the law of causality.

Men are beings of conceptual consciousness and reason is man's sole source of knowledge and guide to action. Rand defined reason as the faculty that identifies and integrates the material provided by the senses through the formation of concepts. She maintained the validity of a man's senses (i.e., perceptual realism) and that reason is competent to know the facts of reality.

Rand's metaphysics and epistemology are inextricably interconnected and together they form Objectivism's philosophical foundation. Knowledge is based on the observation of reality. Through both extrospection and introspection, a man pursues knowledge using the methods of induction, deduction, and synthesis. A man forms concepts according to actual relationships among concretes and uses concepts according to the rules of logic. Rand provided a set of rules for deriving valid concepts. She explains that concepts refer to facts, knowledge has a base in reality, that it is possible to define objective principles to guide a man's process of cognition, and that the conclusions reached via a process of reason are objective. Rand contends that it is possible to obtain objective knowledge of both facts and values.

For Rand, essence is an epistemological concept rather than a metaphysical manifestation. An essence is a product of epistemological processes that permit men to group concretes into classes. Her objective theory of concepts, including essences, is integral to her rational epistemology in which concepts are derived from reality. Rand's epistemology, in which concepts or essences are epistemological rather than metaphysical, is arguably superior to the Aristotelian view which sees them as metaphysical.

Rand states that it is only the concept of life that makes the concept of value possible. Life as a particular kind of being is an ultimate end (i.e., an end in itself) for any living being. For a man, living as a rational animal means living by the use of his reason. She explains that reason is a man's only proper judge of value and his only legitimate guide to action. For Rand, what is good is an evaluation made of the facts of reality by a man's consciousness according to the rational standard of value of the promotion of his life.

According to Rand, the concept of value depends upon, and is derived from, the antecedent concept of life. Life, an ultimate goal and end in itself, makes the existence of values possible. Her naturalistic value theory is concerned with what is, in fact, proper or good for human life. Like Menger, Rand espouses a contextually-relational objectivity in her theory of value. Rand contends that it is possible for a person to pursue objective values that are consonant with his own rational self-interest.

Rand's moral theory is based on the Aristotelian idea that the objective and natural end for a human being is his flourishing. Practicing morality will lead to his well-being and happiness, which is the highest moral purpose of his life. A man's need for morality arises from his distinctive nature as an entity with volitional consciousness. Because a person does not automatically perform the actions necessary to meet his needs, it is imperative that he ground his ethical judgments on reason. Adhering to a rational morality enables a person to make the most out of his life.

Rand's *eudaimonistic* account of ethics involves the virtues of independence, integrity, honesty, justice, productiveness, and pride. Life is conditional and requires choosing values, gaining them, and the development of character attributes.

A man must exercise his mind in the service of his life and thus requires the power to act without coercion from others. It follows that men must deal as traders giving value for value through free voluntary exchange to their mutual benefit. A man should not obtain values from others by the use of force and may not institute the use of force against others. Rand explains that a person's rights can only be violated by physical force or fraud and that the proper function of government is the protection of a man's rights. It follows that she views government as the agency that holds a monopoly on the legal use of physical force.

Scholarly Perspectives

Samuel Bostaph's offering deals with the "Conflict of Methods" debate between Carl Menger and the German Historical school. The author's major argument is that conflicting epistemological standpoints underpinned the methodological issues actually debated by the two opposed sides of the controversy. Bostaph explains that neither side clearly and explicitly realized nor recognized that the underlying source of their differences was epistemological in nature. Whereas Menger saw economic law as deductive in origin from "induced" premises, the historicists viewed economic concepts and law as empirical summarization. The author concludes by applauding the virtues, power of mind, originality, and contributions of Menger.

In her chapter, "Truth in Economic Subjectivism," Gloria L. Zúñiga explores the question of whether or not the truth of economic judgments can be determined objectively and, if it can, how truth is made known. In order to attack the question of truth in economic valuation, the author explores how Carl Menger uses the notion of subjectivism both epistemically and ontologically. Zúñiga explains how Menger is able to reconcile the subject-dependent status of economic phenomena with the objectivity of description regarding the nature of such phenomena. She illustrates that Menger's contributions provide us with ideas concerning the ontology of subject-dependent economic objects and an epistemology that is both realist and compatible with a correspondence theory of truth.

Murray N. Rothbard, student of Ludwig von Mises, describes the contemporary neglect of the Austrian school of economics and its policy prescriptions that are diametrically opposite to those proposed by orthodox Keynesian economists. Rothbard details how Mises has supplied us with a complete, correct, and radically divergent paradigm to replace present-day economic orthodoxy. The author calls for a host of Austrian economists who can spread the word of the existence of Mises's true and proper paradigm for economic theory, social science, and the economy itself.

In his chapter, Jeffrey M. Herbener appraises the work of Mises and the Austrian school in the development and promulgation of the economic principles of social progress. His aims are to proclaim the superiority of the Austrian school in formulating the principles of free enterprise and to establish that Mises is the preeminent defender of the free-market tradition. Herbener hails the work of Mises and the earlier Menger but is critical of F. A. Hayek for drifting away from the praxeological method and further and further into error. The author also explains the superior position of Austrian Economics compared to the stances of econometrics and positivism.

In a revised and extended version of his 1990 address to the Ayn Rand Society, Douglas B. Rasmussen examines whether or not Rand's ethics are best interpreted as dependent on a "pre-moral" choice. He argues that such an interpretation undermines Rand's claim to provide a rational foundation for ethics. He suggests an alternative, neo-Aristotelian interpretation of Rand's ethics, which treats "man's survival qua man" as the telos of human choice and takes the obligation to achieve this ultimate end as the result of its being the good for human beings.

Chris Matthew Sciabarra chronicles the ever-growing interest in Ayn Rand's thought. He discusses the explosion of popular references to Rand in music, in the comics, in television series, and so on. He notes that more and more scholarly sessions and works are devoted to Rand's work. She is now discussed in reference works and in textbooks in philosophy, political science, and economics. He details how academic philosophers are now reassessing her thought and viewing her in terms of the larger community of Western philosophy. He demonstrates that, although she did not speak the language of contemporary philosophy and did not write for academic journals, heightened cultural awareness of Rand's ideas and works, and greater and greater attention to them by scholars and academicians, has occurred.

Barry Smith begins by delineating the common Aristotelian underpinning that Carl Menger shared with many of his contemporaries. He then clarifies two alternative approaches to apriorism—the reflectionist and the impositionist approaches. Smith explains that the reflectionist view, which Menger held, is fully compatible with the search for constancies which exist in the underlying structure of reality. According to Smith, the impositionist view holds that the mind imposes its own structure so that a priori knowledge is knowledge of the structure of our own minds. He notes that Ludwig von Mises's great error was to construct an elaborate methodological edifice on an impositionist foundation.

Walter Block discusses and analyzes works by Robert Nozick, Michael Levin, and Ayn Rand, each of whom has criticized anarcho-capitalism, the system in which all goods and services, including courts, police, and armies, would be provided by competing private firms and individuals. Nozick argues that anarcho-capitalism would naturally evolve into limited-government free enterprise without violating the libertarian nonaggression axiom. Levin maintains that the philosophy of Hobbes is correct and requires a government for protection. Rand, in turn, contends that anarcho-capitalism is incoherent. Block considers each of these arguments and rejects each one of them.

In his chapter, Richard C. B. Johnsson reviews the ideas of early Austrian economists and compares them with the ideas embodied in Ayn Rand's philosophy of Objectivism. Johnsson analyzes the value theories of Carl Menger, Eugen von Böhm-Bawerk, and Ludwig von Mises in an effort to understand where the notion of value subjectively originated. The author goes on to present a case that Ayn Rand's ideas regarding value are not essentially different from those of Menger, Böhm-Bawerk, and Mises himself. Johnsson's goal is to offer a possible direction toward the reconciliation of Austrian Economics and Objectivism. His hope is that these two bodies of thought could unite in the struggle for free-market capitalism.

Ricardo F. Crespo's offering maintains that reappraising Austrian Economics in the light of Aristotelian ideas is not only possible but fruitful. Crespo first draws a sketch of the essential features of Austrian Economics. He next argues about the necessity for a thorough analysis of the nature of freedom, and he analyzes Ludwig von Mises's conception of freedom. He then reveals Aristotle's epistemological, social, and economic thought related to the main traits of Austrian Economics. Crespo goes on to provide an account of how the exercise of Aristotelian virtues may be viewed as synergic with economic coordination. He then sketches his proposal for the teaching of economics and the expected consequences of that proposal. Crespo concludes by summing up the content and relevance of Aristotle's contribution.

In his chapter, Larry Sechrest explains that both Murray Rothbard and Adolph Reinach employ a praxeological a priori approach to economic theory and legal theory, respectively. Rothbard takes the praxeological road in economics and it leads him to a pure, laissez-faire, stateless society. Sechrest argues that anyone who, like Reinach, adopts a praxeological method in law, will be led to a similar, anarchistic position. It follows that all law should be civil law, all wrongs should be dealt with as torts, legal redress should be in the form of restitution rather than punishment, and that both legal judgments and law enforcement should be market phenomena. According to Sechrest, praxeology, whether applied to economics or law, implies a polycentric, anarchistic legal structure.

In his contribution, Tibor R. Machan discusses the use of reason in economics and in ethics. He states that neoclassical and Austrian economists understand reason to be the human activity of determining the most effective means to attain a goal. They disparage the prospect of goods being rational versus irrational. Machan notes that in cognitive ethics, however, a goal itself can be considered to be rational or irrational. Machan argues that with the economists' view of reason no nonarbitrary distinction can be made between rational and irrational means. The prospect of repeated variation of one's goals blocks it. What, nevertheless, allows the economists' conception of reason to function as a valid analytical tool is the hidden assumption that some goods (e.g., prosperity, cost cutting, benefit or utility maximizing) are indeed rational whereas others (e.g., selling at lower prices or buying at higher prices than the market dictates or preferring hard labor over leisure) are not. With respect to the criteria of rationality for goals, Machan argues that a broad notion of human flourishing (or happiness or success) turns out to be the standard underpinning the judgment that a goal is rational and ought to be pursued.

The Future: Toward an Integrated Framework

Philosophy provides the conceptual framework necessary to understand man's behavior. To survive a person must perceive the world, comprehend it, and act upon it. To survive and flourish a man must recognize that nature has its own imperatives. He needs to have viable, sound, and proper conceptions of man's nature, knowledge, values, and action. He must recognize that there is a natural law that derives from the nature of man and the world and that is discoverable through the use of reason.

Ultimately, the truth is one. There is an essential interconnection between objective ideas. It follows that academicians should pay more attention to systems building rather than to the extreme specialization within a discipline. By integrating the basic features and essential tenets of Austrian Economics with the natural-law-based theory and moral vision of Objectivism we are able to take positive steps toward an overarching theoretical perspective and truth-based paradigm.

This chapter argues that Misesian praxeology fits within an Aristotelian, Mengerian, Randian, or Rothbardian metaphysical and epistemological framework. It also explains that Rand's view of concepts or essences as epistemological is arguably preferable to the view that they are embedded in entities (i.e., they are metaphysical) that is espoused by Aristotle and Menger. It also maintains that human actions are implicated with ethical standards and that Misesian praxeological economics as a science needs to be connected with a discipline that deals with ends. In other words, value-free economics requires the value-laden discipline of ethics. It needs Objectivism's moral vision that begins in the natural law tradition of individualism.

A sound paradigm requires internal consistency among its components. By properly integrating insights from Austrian Economics and Objectivism we can avoid the errors of rationalism and empiricism and develop a general theory that can be separated from historical circumstances. Such a framework would reframe the argument for a free society and would elucidate a theory of the best political regime on the basis of proper conceptions of the nature of man, human action, and society. This natural-law-based paradigm would uphold each man's sovereignty, moral space, and natural rights. It would hold that men require a social and political structure that recognizes natural rights and accords each person a moral space over which he has freedom to act and pursue his personal flourishing.

Recommended Reading

Butler, Eamonn. *Ludwig von Mises: Fountainhead of the Modern Microeconomic Revolution*. New York: St. Martin's Press, 1988.

Caldwell, Bruce J., ed. *Carl Menger and His Legacy in Economics*. Durham, N.C.: Duke University Press, 1990.

Callahan, Gene. *Economics for Real People*. Auburn, Ala.: The Ludwig von Mises Institute, 2002.

Gloria-Palerno, Sandye. *The Evolution of Austrian Economics*. London: Routledge, 1999.

Gotthelf, Allen. *On Ayn Rand*. Belmont, Calif.: Wadsworth, 2000.

Grassl, Wolfgang and Barry Smith, eds. *Austrian Economics: Historical and Philosophical Background*. London: Crook Helm, 1986.

Herbener, Jeffrey M. *The Meaning of Ludwig von Mises*. New York: Kluwer Academic Publishers, 1992.

Holcombe, Randall G., ed. *15 Great Austrian Economists*. Auburn, Ala.: Ludwig von Mises Institute, 1999.

Kirzner, Israel M. *Ludwig von Mises*. Wilmington, Delaware: ISI Books, 2001.

Machan, Tibor R. *Ayn Rand*. New York: Peter Lang, 1999.

———. *Capitalism and Individualism*. New York: St. Martin's Press, 1990.

Menger, Carl. *Principles of Economics*. New York: New York University Press, [1871] 1981.

Merrill, Ronald E. *The Ideas of Ayn Rand*. Chicago: Open Court, 1991.

Mises, Ludwig von. *Liberalism in the Classical Tradition*. Irvington, N.Y.: Foundation for Economic Education, [1927] 1985.

Peikoff, Leonard. *Objectivism: The Philosophy of Ayn Rand*. New York: Dutton, 1991.

Rand, Ayn. *Capitalism: The Unknown Ideal*. New York: The New American Library, 1967.

———. *Philosophy: Who Needs It*, ed. Leonard Perkoff. New York: Bobbs-Merrill, 1982.

Rothbard, Murray N. *The Ethics of Liberty*. Atlantic Highlands, N.J.: Humanities Press, 1982.

Sciabarra, Chris Matthew, ed. Special Issue on "Ayn Rand Among the Austrians." *Journal of Ayn Rand Studies*. (Spring 2005).

———. *Total Freedom: Toward a Dialectical Libertarianism*. University Park: Pennsylvania State University Press, 2000.

PART I

ESSENTIAL IDEAS

1

Carl Menger's Austrian Aristotelianism

Edward W. Younkins

Theoretical economics has the task of investigating the general essence and the general connection of economic phenomena, not of analyzing economic concepts and of drawing the conclusions resulting from this analysis. The phenomena, or certain aspects of them, and not their linguistic image, the concepts, is the object of theoretical research in the field of economy.

—Carl Menger

Carl Menger (1840-1921) began the modern period of economic thought and provided the foundation for the Austrian school of economics. In his two books, *Principles of Economics* (1871) and *Investigations into the Method of the Social Science with Special Reference to Economics* (1883), Menger destroyed the existing structure of economic science, including both its theory and methodology, and put it on totally new foundations. Menger was an immanent realist who said that we could know what the world is like through both common sense and scientific method. Strongly opposed to historicism in the social sciences, Menger was committed to finding exact laws of economics based on the direct analysis of concrete phenomena which could be observed and characterized with precision. He sought to find the necessary characteristics of economic phenomena and their relationships. He also heralded the advantages of verbal language over mathematical language in that the former can express the essences of economic phenomena, which is something that mathematical language is unable to do.

Menger viewed exchange as the embodiment of the essential desire and search to satisfy individual human needs. It follows that the intersection between human needs and the availability of goods capable of satisfying those needs is at the root of economic activity. Emphasizing human uncertainty, error, and the time-consuming nature of economic processes, Menger was concerned with the

15

information content of economic choices and the process of acquiring information in order to increase the well-being of economic actors.

He demonstrated that both the methodology and the labor theory of value of the classical economists were wrong. In place of the labor theory of value, Menger created the system of value and price theory that makes up the core of Austrian economic theory. He is probably best known for developing the logical foundations of marginal utility theory and for arguing that social institutions (e.g., money) are the undesigned results or outcomes of individual human preferences and choices.

This chapter is primarily and systematically based on Menger's two books. Its purpose is to provide to the general reader an essential and accurate introduction to Menger's theoretical system.

The Marginalist Revolution

Carl Menger is perhaps best known for his development of marginal utility theory. One of the three pioneers of marginal utility theory, Menger formulated and codiscovered marginal utility theory simultaneously with, and independently of, Jevons and three years ahead of Walras. Jevons and Walras concentrated on marginal utility as the mathematical concept of the first derivative of a total utility function. They were responsible for introducing the mathematization of subjective preferences in economic analysis.

Contrariwise, Menger's concept of marginal utility was an implied ordinal ranking of utility rather than the first derivative of some idea of total utility. Menger does not attempt to mathematically simplify by assuming continuity, divisibility, or a perfect market. Greater realism and generality can be attained when economic propositions are not confined by implicit assumptions of continuity and differentiability of functions. Menger emphasized variable elements such as needs and wants instead of more stable factors such as labor costs and production costs.

Menger stressed the role of subjective evaluation with respect to the principle of marginal utility. Whereas Jevons and Walras were concerned with equilibrium, Menger was interested in process. Menger extensively developed the subjectivist dimensions of the marginalist revolution. He did this by emphasizing an individual's subjective satisfaction, the subjectivity of decisions, the limitations of knowledge, the uncertainty of choices, and the possibility of error. He also employed the time dimension in connection to the study of economic quantities necessary for the satisfaction of wants. It was more important for Menger to comprehend the meaning of individual choices than to artificially calculate the intensity of their choices.

According to Menger, goods are valued because they help to appease some human need or want. A given unit, quantity, or amount of a particular good will satisfy a person's most intense need or desire. After each unit consumed or used, a man's need or desire may be less intense. Each increment of that specific good available to him will be less valuable in his eyes. The value of goods are mutually interdependent in a given location and the exchange value of a certain increment of each product or service will be determined by the relationships between the aggregate amount available and the intensity of the human need or desire that it meets. The economic value of goods hinges on their respective quantities in relation to the human needs and desires they are expected to meet.

The Evolution of Institutions: The Case of Money

Menger's emphasis on methodological individualism and the compositive method led him to the significance of the unintended consequences of human action. He recognized that the relevant unit of inquiry is acting and purposive man and searched for general patterns of social development that arose as a consequence of human action in a world of scarcity. Menger grounded his analysis on the experience of the valuing individual and concentrated on explaining the process through which individual valuation set in motion the competitive discovery process of the market. He explained how market phenomena emerge as unintended consequences of subjective valuation processes and demonstrated how institutions which serve everyone can come into existence without a common will overseeing their establishment. Menger searched for compositive interpretations for the existence of social and economic institutions rather than accounts which focus on how specific institutions have been intentionally designed for special purposes.

For Menger, the individual is the unit of analysis because it is only at the individual level that meaning can be assigned to actions. His methodological individualism is not atomistic. On the contrary, it treats individuals not as independent and isolated but instead as members of various types of complex relational systems. For Menger, it is the impact of actions of individual persons that determines the course of human events. Institutions emerge as the unintended consequences of choices by individuals pursuing their personal interests. Economic phenomena are the results of interactions of the thoughts and actions of countless individuals. Menger was a pioneer in providing theoretical support for the evolutionist concept of social processes.

Causal-genetic analysis is part of the Mengerian heritage. His search for causal-genetic explanations ruled out the use of mathematical techniques because Menger sought causal explanations whereas mathematical economics is limited to providing functional relationships. Menger's concern with the nature of economic phenomena prompted him to pay attention to the reasons and origins for their existence. His essentialism led him to repudiate mathematical models and the interdependent determination of economic variables. Through causal-genetic analysis Menger sought to discover relationships of cause and effect and to explain the emergence, change, and development of organic institutions over time.

Menger's theory on money forcefully illustrates the essential role he assigned to the principle of methodological individualism. His theory begins with the idea that valuation arises from subjective perceptions of individuals and ends with money as an emerged social institution. Menger's theory of the origin of money is an evolutionary explanation of a spontaneous process in which direct exchange via barter transforms into indirect trade with an institutionally established medium of exchange. He illustrates how the money universal is an institutional form that is a product of a spontaneous social process relying on the entrepreneurial and economizing actions of individuals. Human action begins a discovery process that results in the creation of the institution of money that none of the actors intended. The composite outcome of individuals' economizing activities is shown by Menger to be the establishment of a generally accepted medium of exchange despite the fact that no one intended to create money by engaging in indirect exchange.

Menger's causal history of money starts with the state of barter economy which permits exchange but with great difficulty. A barter economy is a natural system of exchange in contrast to a monetary system. People who want to trade first try barter, but the difficulty or impossibility of finding the requisite double coincidence of wants between individuals poses a huge problem. In the course of time, some individuals realize that they will be more able to make trades if they accumulate goods that other people want. These agents who acquire goods that have greater subjective value to many other people will make a greater number of exchanges and make them more easily and thereby make themselves wealthier. In the beginning only a small number of actors recognize the advantage of indirect exchange, the process of exchanging their goods for more marketable commodities. Other people will adopt the same behavior as they observe and imitate the successful behavior of these first individuals. They too will begin to attempt to use those same goods as a medium of exchange. Less saleable goods are surrendered for those of greater saleability. The most saleable of all goods eventually becomes money. It follows that money will appear progressively via a spontaneous learning process that is a product of individual interactions of people following their self-interest and their personal plans of action.

Menger explains that people will trade to obtain the goods they want to consume and that they prefer to make the requisite trades as easily as possible. It follows that people will progressively learn to choose more and more marketable commodities to advance to indirect exchange. As the number of desired media commodities dwindles, the demand for each of the remaining ones increases, making each of them more desirable as a medium of exchange. This narrowing process continues until the number of commodities used as a medium of exchange is reduced to one (or perhaps two) goods that are subjectively highly desired and that can fulfill the minimal physical requirements of money. Menger explains that gold was selected as a generally accepted medium of exchange because of its physical real essence and not by mere chance. The real essence of gold, based on its various properties, is at least partly responsible for its choice as a medium of exchange.

The economic interests of individuals combined with their increasing knowledge leads them to exchange their goods for more marketable ones without any prior agreement, legislation, or consideration of the common good. Money emerges from an invisible-hand process. It is the result of human action but not of human design. The institution of money is an unintended consequence of human action. Money results from an ongoing learning process.

Menger is an essentialist who discusses the real essence of money. He explains that money is measure of price rather than a measure of value and that it is the only commodity by which all the other commodities can be evaluated without using roundabout procedures. He illustrates how money, as an economic universal, is embodied in the many money particulars. Specific exemplifications of money have the capabilities, tendencies, and powers they do by virtue of money's real essence. The specifics of a particular manifestation of money are the result of human design, whereas the universal of that and all other appearances of money is due to a spontaneous social process in which economizing individuals notice that some goods are more marketable than others. Menger emphasizes the subjectivity and knowledge of the individual regarding his needs and wants and the ability of objects to satisfy them.

Menger studies the essence (or nature) of economic phenomena such as money. He explains that any particular instantiation of money is contaminated because it is not merely a manifestation of characteristics and tendencies that inhere in the money universal, but includes other specific factors of time and place as well. These other factors are omitted in the process of abstraction and isolation in which the idea of money as an economic universal was constructed.

Menger's account of the origin and evolution of money is a prime example of his conception of the spontaneous emergence of organic institutions As complex economic phenomena. Institutions thus result from a decentralized trial-and-error process in which the behaviors that best systemize and harmonize actions of individuals within society have a tendency to predominate. Institutions emerge from a social process resulting from numerous human actions and initiated by creative and successful individuals who, in their peculiar historical circumstances of time and place, are able to discover before others that they can achieve their goals more easily if they follow certain behaviors. Through an unconscious social learning process, other members of society imitate the actions of these innovators. As a result, institutions, or guided behaviors, which enhance life in a social setting, emerge.

Menger's Aristotelian Background

Carl Menger was an Aristotelian although not a pure one. He read Aristotle and studied the works of Franz Brentano (1838-1917), a contemporary of Menger at the University of Vienna, who taught Aristotelian philosophy there. Brentano has been considered to be the leading Austrian philosopher of the late nineteenth century. He is widely credited with reviving the study of Aristotle at the University of Vienna. It is no wonder that Aristotelian philosophy and language filtered into Menger's thinking.

Aristotle was a this-worldly philosopher and scientist whose observations of the biological world led him to endorse realism, knowledge based on experience, and experience-based reasoning. For Aristotle, an immanent (or naïve) realist, what is general does not exist in isolation from what is individual. The existence of universals is thus dependent on the existence of particulars. Universals exist in the particulars that instantiate them. Aristotle holds that universals do exist, but not separately from the particulars. His view is that the one exists only as instantiated in the many. For Aristotle, the immanent realist, both universals and particulars are real. Individual concrete entities exist in reality and universals exist only in particulars in the form of essences. In this way, Aristotle weds universals to objects. The universal and the particular are indivisible in reality and are separable only in analysis and thought. All things are a composite of a "this" and a "such." Each object is an individual of a certain class. Aristotle distinguishes between matter and form. The matter is the individualizing and unique-making element or aspect. The form is the universalizing element that makes it a member of a particular class. Forms are joined to objects.

Aristotle's view is that concepts refer to essences that are within the concretes of the external world. An essence is an object's nature. It is made up of the invariant characteristics inherent in a thing. An essence is in an object from the time the entity is a potentiality all the way to its becoming and being an actuality. Aristotle explains change as matter getting restructured and as requiring identity. An object that changes is what it is, the thing that it changes into is what it is, and the change process itself is what it is. Change is the actualization of potential. It follows that the world of particulars and changes in particulars is rationally explainable. Change is the capacity to grow into something and is thus the actualization of potential.

Aristotle explains that a thing's essence is in the object from the time an entity is a potentiality all the way to its actuality. Since universals exist only in particulars, we cannot apprehend the universal except through apprehension of the concrete. Matter is the underlying substratum in which development of form occurs. Aristotle is an "ontological essentialist" who defines essence as embodying the actual metaphysical nature of things. Essences exist in the world independent of the mind and are what a person's mind refers to when it forms concepts.

Knowledge is a natural process in the real world. Aristotle explains that it is natural for an animal with rational consciousness (i.e., man) to actualize its potential. This potential involves the ability to understand intelligible or law-governed structures and changes. It also includes the ability to apprehend that there are intelligibly impossible changes. Aristotle teaches that the world encompasses both material and mental aspects and exists independently of our reasoning and thinking activities. In addition, there are certain essences in the world as well as knowable laws, structures, and connections governing them. He explains that there are no contradictions in nature (i.e., in reality). By a contradiction he means being both x and not x at the same time and in the same respect. Also, Aristotle emphasizes individual human action in his *Nichomachean Ethics*, thus inventing the concept of methodological individualism—the notion that collective entities such as states, communities, or classes are reducible to individuals in relation with one another. Furthermore, he emphasizes deductive reasoning in which a person begins with self-evident axioms and deduces from them.

In the *Topics*, Aristotle provides his philosophical analysis of human ends and means. He explains that means or instruments of production are valuable because their end products are useful to people. The more useful or desirable a good is, the higher the value of the means of production is. Aristotle then goes on to derive a number of economic ideas from axiomatic concepts, including the necessity of human action, the pursuit of ends by ordering and allocating scarce means, and the reality of human inequality and diversity.

Aristotle explains that actions are necessarily and fundamentally singular. For Aristotle, the individual human action of using wealth is what constitutes the economic dimension. The purpose of economic action is to use things that are necessary for life (i.e., survival) and for the Good Life (i.e., flourishing). The Good Life is the moral life of virtue through which human beings attain happiness.

Given that human actions are voluntary and intentional, it follows that action requires the prior internal mental acts of deliberation and choice. Human beings seek to fulfill their perfection via action. Observing that human nature has capacities pertaining to its dual material and spiritual character, Aristotle explains that economics is an expression of that dual character. The economic sphere is the intersection between the corporeal and mental aspects of the human person.

Aristotle makes a distinction between practical science and speculative science. He states that practical science is concerned with knowledge for the sake of controlling reality. It studies knowledge that may be otherwise (i.e., contingent knowledge). Practical science studies relationships that are not constant, regular, or invariable. Aristotle classifies economics as a practical science. On the other hand, Aristotle sees speculative science as yielding necessary, universal, noncontingent truths. Speculative science generates universal truths deduced from self-evident principles known by induction. The goal of speculative science is knowledge for its own sake. Mathematics and metaphysics are speculative sciences for Aristotle.

Aristotle teaches that economics is concerned with both the household and the polis and that economics deals with the use of things required for the good (or virtuous) life. As a pragmatic or practical science, economics is aimed at the good and is fundamentally moral. Because Aristotle sees that economics is embedded in politics, an argument can be made that the study of political economy begins with him.

For Aristotle, the primary meaning of economics is the action of using things required for the Good Life. In addition, he also sees economics as a practical science and as a capacity that fosters habits that expedite the action. Economics is a type of prudence or practical knowledge that aids a person in properly obtaining and using those things that are necessary for living well. The end of economics as a practical science is attaining effective action.

Aristotle explains that ontologically the operation of the economic dimension of reality is inextricably related to the moral and political spheres. The economic element is integrated in real action with other realms relating to the acting human person. The various domains mutually influence one another in an ongoing dynamic fashion.

Aristotle explains that practical science recognizes the inexact nature of its conclusions as a consequence of human action which arises from each person's freedom and uniqueness. Uncertainty emanates from the nature of the world and the free human person and is a necessary aspect of economic actions that will always be in attendance. Aristotle observes that a practical science such as economics must be intimately connected to the concrete circumstances and that it is proper to begin with what is known to us.

Aristotle's this-worldly intrinsicism says that universals exist in particulars and that men can abstract or intuit the essences or universals out of the particulars. Aristotle wants to ground his theory of concepts in the facts of reality but is not fully explicit with respect to methods by which essences get imprinted on a man's mind. He does see man as scientifically looking at reality, gathering instances, isolating and classifying phenomena, detecting similarities, discerning patterns and regularities, and obtaining essences upon which concepts and laws are constructed. Aristotle refers to this process as intuitive induction.

Aristotle sees a universal teleology or purposiveness in which everything in the universe is goal-directed and striving to actualize its essence. For Aristotle, an object actualizes its distinctive essence when it achieves an identity of formal and final causation. Man, as a rational being with free will, should strive for his own perfection. By achieving his fulfillment and all-around development he will attain happiness or *eudaimonia*. It follows that in ethics a man should choose actions that are proper to man qua man.

Aristotle thinks that it is possible to conduct rational research with respect to value. He sees practical science as an essentially evaluative or moral science. A practical science is ethical to the extent that it takes into account the ethical aspects of the subject being studied.

Aristotle regards reality as ordered and teaches that order with respect to human affairs is a project or effort through which people aspire to happiness through the cultivation of virtues. He asserts that the end of politics is the good for man. According to Aristotle, the virtue of prudence is personal, freely pursued, and changeable according to situations. A prudent action for one individual may not be a prudent action for another person. Nevertheless, according to Aristotle, the integration of freely made prudent and varying actions results in social coordination. He believes that economic coordination is attainable when persons prudently choose and undertake economic transactions with others. Aristotle believes that human flourishing requires a life with other people.

Aristotle teaches that people acquire virtues (i.e., good habits) through practice and that a set of concrete virtues can lead a person toward his natural excellence and happiness. Aristotle views economic activity as a means of coordination through which persons will have the opportunity to obtain the external goods necessary to attain happiness. Morally good habits promote stable and predictable behavior and foster coordination in an imperfect world. Habits, natural dispositions created through the repetition of actions, underpin virtues.

Franz Brentano, who overlaps at the University of Vienna with Menger, helps to make the axiomatic-deductive method available to Menger. Brentano believes that philosophy should be carried out in a rigorous scientific manner and thinks that we could know the world in both its general and individual aspects. For Brentano, strict universality is a necessary condition for any genuine scientific theory. He distinguishes between acts of consciousness and their objects and believes that the laws governing mental and physical phenomena provide objective principles for both the science of logic and for ethics. He explains that these laws do not express purely epistemological interconnections that are imposed on external phenomena. The laws of consciousness are not completely mental or analytic. The world is real and is not created by the mind. Brentano views the mind as clearly distinct from the external world and distinguishes acts of consciousness from their objects.

For Brentano, thinking is a mental action or doing of an individual. His name for thinking is intentionality. He explains that an intention is a mental going out toward, or grasping of, an object. The object of such an intention could be either a physical object or a mental object (i.e., an idea). Intentionality is a form of an individual's relational contact with reality. He explains that valuation is implicit in all actions and that the act of valuation cannot be separated from the individual.

Brentano sees the compositive method as leading to certain or apodictic knowledge. The compositive method involves the analysis of a given subject into simple basic elements and the investigation of the systematic approach through which these parts could be combined into wholes. Brentano thus rejects the German Historical school's doctrine of internal relations that holds that everything is inextricably bound with everything else and that nothing can be studied individually and separately.

Metaphysics and Epistemology

Menger sees the world, which includes both physical and mental aspects, as existing independently of our reasoning and thinking activities and as organized in an intelligible fashion. We can know what the world is like due to its conformity to laws that are accessible to reason. Menger is an immanent realist who says that we can know what the world is like both via common sense and through the scientific method. Menger's Austrian Aristotelianism is a doctrine of ontology that informs us what the world is like and what its objects, processes, and states are. His commonsense realism says that we have access to what is real through our everyday experiences. Menger argues that there is one reality knowable by rational means and that all things are subject to the laws of cause and effect. Laws of causality have an ontological or metaphysical reality—how a thing acts is determined by what a thing is. Entities in reality act according to their natures. An object necessarily tends to behave in a particular way by virtue of its real essence.

According to Menger, there are intelligible a priori essences or natures existing autonomously in reality. Because these essences and essential structures are knowable, corresponding laws of and connections between these structures are able to be comprehended. These essences and the laws governing them are manifested in the world and are strictly universal. These tell us what kinds of relations can exist between various components of reality. Menger sees intelligible law-governed change in the particulars of the world. The essences or laws are precisely universal in that they do not change and in that they are capable of being instantiated in all cultures and at all times. For Menger, theory must relate to knowledge that must endure and extend in time beyond immediate and present knowledge. The essences relevant to the various different aspects or levels of reality make up a graphic representation of structural parts. Reasoning using essences or universals as simple conceptual elements will proceed according to the nature of objects and will deduce conceptual systems of causality consonant with the causality of the real world.

Menger's essentialism holds that general essences do not exist in isolation from what is individual. Universals are said to exist only as aspects of specific objects and phenomena that are not directly observable in pure form. Every experience of the world involves both an individual and a universal or general aspect. According to Menger, we can know what the world is like in both its individual and general features.

A realist about universals, Menger observes that they exist in reality and that they are attributes shared by many particular objects. The particulars are individual whereas the universals are general. In order for the universals to be phenomena of conceptualization, they have to be abstracted from empirical reality. Essential or necessary characteristics of an object are those of its real essence. A depiction is concrete if it concerns particulars and is abstract if it is about universals. Only particulars have the capacity to act. Universals not only do not possess the power to act, they cannot exist without the particulars.

Menger believes in the knowability of general laws. However, he says that our knowledge of the general aspect of experience is in no way infallible. There may be difficulties in gaining knowledge of essential structures and converting such knowledge into the form of a strict theory. Despite the existence of problems and obstacles, he says it is possible for our knowledge of essential structures and laws to be exact and that our knowledge will in all probability exhibit a progressive improvement.

For Menger, these structures are a priori categories in reality that possess an intrinsic simplicity and intelligibility that makes them capable being apprehended in a straightforward manner. The nature of objects in the world can be read off directly through both external observation and introspection. Menger acknowledges the existence of both intelligible (i.e., law-governed) structures and structures of accidental association that can be comprehended.

Menger follows Aristotle in saying that all knowledge about the world begins with induction. He reasons that we can actually detect essences in reality through repeated observations of phenomena, which reveal certain similarities according to which objects would be grouped into types or classes via a process of abstraction. Induction involves inference from experience and going from the particular to the general. It follows that even deductions are ontological since they are based on metaphysical reality. Deductions are made from inductively known facts and premises. They are based on reality and are not purely a priori mental categories. Introspection is an ingredient in Menger's epistemology. He says that introspection gives people access to some limited useful and reliable knowledge about other human persons and their experiences, such as the experience of making choices. Menger's epistemology makes use of the internal perspective on human action that people share because of their common humanity. He says that introspection should be included in a legitimate epistemology because we live in a world inhabited by other human minds as well as our own.

Menger's doctrine of ontological individualism states that there are no "social organisms" or "social wholes." Explanations of such social phenomena are traceable to the ideas and actions of individual persons. He explains that the individual precedes the state and other collective bodies both chronologically and metaphysically.

Menger's view is that man has no innate ideas but does have the ability to reason. Man begins uninformed and becomes ever more knowledgeable about the world. Although he espouses that man has free will, he displays what might be regarded as deterministic overtones in his belief in the existence in human nature of fundamental common influences of, or motives for, human behavior, including the economic, moral sentiments, altruism, and justice. Menger observes that the impulse for one's economic self-interest is man's primary and most common trait. He says that man is ingrained with a drive for self-interest in a healthy sense, rather than in a Hobbesian one. According to Menger, the individual, although desiring to satisfy his needs, is not directly driven or determined by them.

Menger's rational egoism recognizes that value is grounded in human needs and their satisfaction. Man's physical and intellectual needs derive from genuine needs of the species. Equating self-interested behavior with economic behavior, Menger says that men do, and should, rationally seek to attain economic advantages or gains for themselves. He is finding a basis for economics in biology. Man's metaphysical and biological needs are not arbitrary and must be met if he is to survive and prosper. Rational self-interested behavior is thus viewed as good behavior.

Rationality does not imply omniscience. Menger explains that men are born into ignorance and that their primary enterprise is to learn the causal connections between objects and the satisfaction of their needs in order to make rational decisions regarding their well-being. Economic life is constructed around the acquiring of knowledge. Menger portrays rational, economic man as an uncertain being who gradually gains the knowledge and resources necessary to attain his ends. He also explains that economic progress is caused by the growth in knowledge.

Economic Goods

Menger explains that all things are subject to the law of cause and effect and that if one passes from a state of need to a state in which the need is satisfied then sufficient causes for this change must exist. Accordingly, useful things are those that can be placed in a causal connection with the satisfaction of human needs. The satisfaction of human needs is the final cause in Menger's exact theory and the driving force of all economic activity. Human needs are the beginning and the end of human activity because nothing would take place without human needs and the requirements of satisfying them. By conceptualizing the law of cause and effect, man recognizes his dependence on the external world and transforms it into the means to attain his ends. Man thereby becomes the ultimate cause as well as the ultimate end in the process of want satisfaction.

After discussing the properties of a useful object, he proceeds to discuss those of a good, and then of an economic (or scarce) good. According to Menger, a thing becomes a good or acquires a goods-character if all four of the following conditions are simultaneously present: (1) a need on the part of some human being; (2) such properties that render the object capable of being brought into a causal connection with the satisfaction of this need; (3) knowledge of this causal connection on the part of the person involved; and (4) command of the thing sufficient to direct it to satisfaction of the need. Goods are those elements of the external world that are integral to the causal process of want satisfaction and upon which action operates. Goods exist only to serve human satisfactions. Goods can be divided into material goods and useful human actions (e.g., labor services).

Menger's explanation of goods relates them back to human needs and human nature. Linking the idea of utility to biology, Menger believes that human wants are to a great extent determined by physiological needs. He sees the biological foundations of human needs as the key to integrating economics with material reality. People can comprehend the goal of much activity in terms of its relation to an organism's biological needs. Through the study of biology and physiology, Menger formulates a theory of needs to complement his theory of value. A person's biological and intellectual needs have to be met and satisfied if he is to survive and prosper. Menger thus emphasizes the biological and the choices people make beyond the purely biological.

According to Menger the combination of the views an individual holds about things as economic objects and the laws describing the categories to which economic objects are members is what makes an object economic. In order for something to be an economic good: (1) the judging subject must perceive an object as scarce; (2) the thing must be evaluated in relation to needs known to the self-interested judging subject as urgent; (3) the judging subject must perceive a causal connection between the object and the fulfillment of a mediate or immediate end; and (4) the subject must believe that he has a feasible command of the thing sufficient to be able to direct it to the satisfaction of an end.

For Menger, the nature of the world and the scarcity of its natural resources, combined with human nature and people's desires for greater satisfaction of their wants, circumscribe the fundamental nature of the economic world. Menger defines economics as the science which examines the laws of cause and effect which control the processes through which goods satisfy human needs. He meditates on the nature of human striving to satisfy wants and deduces its immediate implications. Through this process, Menger discovers that the laws of human needs are entirely sufficient to explain the basic facts regarding all the phenomena of the exchange economy. He envisions the economy as a system driven by the valuations and choices of consumers.

The idea of scarcity underpins Menger's analysis of economic goods and economic value. Every choice involves scarcity. Dealing with scarcity is an essential feature of the human condition that necessitates the allocation of means to attain ends. Economic judgments include evaluations aimed at choosing among known alternatives. Menger calls choosing "economizing."

Economic judgments that a person makes indicate the degree to which he believes an object may satisfy his needs. Menger's economic object is thus a subject-dependent entity in the sense that the manner of its existence depends upon its being perceived as economic by the agent. The economic character of a good cannot be determined in the absence of a mind judging or perceiving the significance of an object in relation to an end.

Whereas the judgment regarding an economic entity is subjective, its truth or untruth can be determined objectively via a realist economic ontological theory of truth involving the correspondence of facts about the object with the judgment that is made. What decides the truth in economic judgment is the correspondence between expectations and their instantiation in facts. The fulfillment of a person's expectations is based on the facts, of which some are intrinsic properties of the object. Although the truth or falsity of an economic judgment can be settled objectively based on facts in the world about the object in its role as an economic good and their correspondence to the agent's expectations, it is clear that no one except the acting subject could make the verdict.

Menger thus demonstrates that economic subjectivism can be compatible with philosophical realism. Economic judgments depend on men's minds for their existence but not for their truth. Menger reconciles the subject-dependent character of economic phenomena with objectivity of representations regarding the nature of these phenomena. An economic object is a subjective entity because its existence is contingent upon its being viewed as economic by a subject. However, its truth can be judged objectively by the correspondence of the judgment with the facts of reality.

Menger emphasizes and expresses the causal interplay between the subjective and objective aspects of action. In his theory of goods, or general theory of the good, there must be a belief or opinion by the agent that there is a causal connection between the object and the satisfaction of the human need under consideration. Menger thus even contends that imaginary goods may derive a goods-like character from attributes they are imagined to have or from needs merely fantasized by men.

What makes something an economic good is a combination of the views a person has about objects as economic goods and the exact laws governing the categories of economic objects. The term economic goods applies to both material objects and to intangible ends that almost always have tangible things as mediate ends.

Noneconomic goods are available in superabundance in that the quantity available exceeds the amount necessary to satisfy all human wants for them. On the other hand, economic goods are those available in a quantity insufficient to totally appease all human wants for them. Menger explains that there is an objective relationship between how much of a good could be used to satisfy all needs and how much of the good exists. An economic good exists when the total demand for it is greater than the amount in supply. The existence of an economic good leads to economizing or making the best use of available but scarce resources. The economic or noneconomic character of goods is not inherent in them or in any of their properties. Rather, a good achieves economic character when it enters into the quantitative relationship of scarcity and loses it when it is no longer scarce. Goods are thus able to change economic character.

According to Menger, all market transactions and every act of production are set in motion by consumer preferences. In fact, Menger attempts to construct economics using the human person as the creative actor and starting point of all social processes. Specifically, Menger sees the purpose of the study of economics as to understand the conditions under which men engage in activity directed to the satisfaction of their needs.

Menger perceives a causal connection between goods. He sees that goods of the lowest order, consumer goods, have a direct causal connection with the satisfaction of needs. Goods of higher order or factors of production have only an indirect causal connection with men's needs. People produce for the sake of goods that can be consumed.

Goods desired and available for consumption or direct use are termed goods of the first order. Goods of the second order consist of raw materials and other factors necessary to produce goods of the first order. In turn, factors required to produce goods of the second order are called goods of the third order, and so on. Goods of higher order do not possess intrinsic value but derive their goods—character from that of the corresponding goods of lower order which they cooperate in producing. Menger thus theorizes based on a process of action including a series of intermediate steps beginning with the production of economic goods of a higher order and ending when the final consumer good is attained.

Menger stresses the importance and implications of time and uncertainty in the production process. Because production occurs in real time it is necessary to anticipate the future, which is uncertain. All economic activity implies risk because perfect knowledge does not exist. Menger sees risk and uncertainty in the time-consuming nature of economic processes. It takes time to produce and producers cannot know with certitude what market conditions will exist when the final product is ready for sale. The ideas of time and causality cannot be separated. A change process such as productive action takes time and is inherently uncertain.

Causal productive processes are planned and carried out by economizing individuals who in social situations become increasingly perceptive of, and attentive to, their economic interests. With respect to economic goods, people economize them in order to satisfy their wants for them as fully as possible. Economizing, the purposive behavior of action, involves evaluating and arraying wants for goods according to their greatest importance or urgency and then deciding to assign units of a good to those uses that meet the most important wants. Menger's economizing man allocates scarce means in order to achieve his most highly valued ends.

Menger explains that the entrepreneur is an economizing man who initiates and directs an uncertain causal process. The entrepreneur's activities include the set of functions essential for mobilizing the production process. His most important mission is to visualize and predict future wants, gauge their relative importance, and attain knowledge of potentially available means. Menger recognizes that knowledge is limited and that the acquisition of knowledge is the cause of wealth. He is especially concerned with improved resource use as a result of enhanced knowledge of production processes. Evidencing a belief that knowledge is power, Menger maintains that economic life is constructed around the gaining of knowledge with respect to the causal relationship between objects and satisfactions, the relationship between goods of a higher order and goods of the first order, economic opportunities and situations, and so on.

Mengerian economics is concerned with goods, expectations, knowledge, and property. The notion of property is inherent in the idea of economizing. In fact, Menger's vision assumes a given structure of property rights and property laws. Because various individuals will attain different degrees of success, it is necessary to protect individuals in the possession of goods against possible acts of force and fraud. The basis for protection of ownership lies in the fact that some men will have interests opposed to those of the current possessors of property.

Menger contends that markets will express consumer sovereignty in the absence of errors, aberrations, and departures from the carefully defined assumptions of his theoretical system. Of course, in the real world, consumers may be mistaken regarding what is actually in their own best interests. In addition, there may be complicating considerations regarding the protection of property rights and proper functions of the state.

Value Theory

Menger states that goods have no inherent or intrinsic value in themselves and that their value is not related to the amount of labor expended in producing them. He contends that the labor theory of value held by Adam Smith and other classical economists is wrong. Menger observes that the so-called "objective" approach of adding up various costs, the most important being labor, is vague and produces contradictions. The classical labor or cost-value theory is called "objective" because it is based on the costs that go into making the object. In actual fact, it is a theory of intrinsic or inherent value. A keen observer of reality, Menger, who worked as a commodities analyst and reporter, recognizes that prices often have no relation to the labor added to particular goods. He notes that the price of a finished product might bear no resemblance to the costs of production because the two represent market conditions at very different periods of time. He also sees that a price can be seen as objective only in the sense that it is an objective magnitude of a numerical value that can mutually be agreed upon.

Menger explains that value is a judgment made by economizing individuals regarding the importance of particular goods for maintaining their lives and well-being. A person assigns value to a good based on the end it enables him to achieve. Applying the concept of intentionality to economic value, Menger stresses that only individuals value and act. His value theory incorporates an analysis of natural human behavior. His theory focuses on individual action itself, rather than on the social phenomena that develop out of individual action. A value must require action in order to be reached. Value in every case is a function of valuing acts of an individual given his own particular context. Individual judgments are acts of preference or evaluation.

Menger seems to want to find a basis for economic value in biology. He explains that economic goods have value because of their ability to fulfill human needs and wants. Like Aristotle, he views goods as the means of life, well-being, and need satisfaction. Self-interested behavior (i.e., attaining goods) is economic behavior and is good behavior. The value of a good is a necessary consequence of the knowledge that the maintenance of one's life and well-being depends upon the control and use of that particular good. Value derives only to the extent that a product satisfies a human need or want. Menger recognizes that value originates in a relationship between man and his survival requirements. Value arises out of a relationship between human beings and what they require for their survival and well-being. Human beings must value because they have needs as living, conditional entities.

Menger accounts for value in terms of the satisfaction of human needs and wants. Value is "subjective" in the sense that it stems from a personal estimation of products and attributes of products with respect to the satisfaction of a man's needs. These needs are not arbitrary. They are real needs the satisfaction of which forms the basis of valuation.

The value of goods emerges from their relation to our needs and is not inherent in the goods themselves. Nor is value merely in a man's mind independent of reality. While most accounts reduce value to either some intrinsic property of things or to the mind, Menger demonstrates that value results from an interplay between a man's conceptual consciousness, human needs, and the physical ability of goods to meet those needs. Value is not in man alone nor inherent in the goods themselves. Value is a necessary consequence of economic activity. Goods are the objects of a person's economizing and valuation.

Value must be in a man's mind but also must be based in reality. While Menger recognizes that value does not exist outside the consciousness of a human being, he also does not disregard the realm of external reality. For value to exist, consciousness must recognize a connection between means and an end in reality. A value must be to a particular valuer in his unique and specific context for an end to which the value is a means. A person's life is seen by Menger as the ultimate end of valuation and action. Life requires action and is an end in itself—an end which is not a means to any further end. Men must act to reach values in order to survive.

What a man needs depends on the facts of his nature and on the facts of things in reality. Menger recognizes that there are facts of economic reality. Values are not subjective, arbitrary, nor intrinsic but are objective when a person's wants correspond to the objective state of affairs. Menger understands that the process of want satisfaction is not entirely cognitive and internal to the human mind, but dependent on the external world and upon the law of cause and effect. For value to exist, there must be a connection in reality grasped by consciousness with respect to means and ends which support a particular man's life. Knowledge in the form of a means-end relationship grasped by reason is a precondition for value. The evaluation of facts is necessary for the creation of value. In this sense, values can be said to be "products" of the mind. In addition, values can only be said to be "subjective" from the perspective that the evaluation of a causal connection with the satisfaction of an end is performed by an individual subject's consciousness. Subjective conditions of satisfaction are elements in the very causal series that includes objective states of reality.

In a larger sense, values as depicted by Menger are not subjective (i.e., arbitrary) nor inherent but are objective. Unfortunately, because the label "objective value theory" had already been attached to the labor theory of value, Menger's new value theory was eventually accorded the mistaken label of subjective value theory. Menger's theory explains the inextricable ontological connection between the realm of cognition and the sphere of objective causal processes that results from valuation and economizing. Value is a judgment made by economizing individuals regarding the importance of things for maintaining their lives and advancing their well-being. A person's judgment of value can be said to have been objectively made when it derives from knowledge based on the facts of the reality and on reasoning in accordance with the laws of logic.

Menger equates self-interested or selfish behavior with economic behavior. He says that it is proper for an individual to attain economic advantages or gains for himself. The satisfaction of one's needs constitutes economic activity. It follows that to act uneconomically means acting against one's own self-interest.

He explains that a person values most highly what he needs most highly and that value is the importance a person assigns to objects of the external world with respect to his well-being. According to Menger, value is the importance that individual goods or quantities of goods have for us because we are conscious of our dependence on the command of them for the satisfaction of our needs. The value of all goods can be seen as the imputation of the importance of satisfying our needs to economic goods. In the end, it is man's life that is the standard of economic value.

Because of the scarcity of available means such as time, labor, and resource goods, individuals must choose which ends to try to satisfy. Menger demonstrates that it is the consumer evaluation of output that tends to be reflected in the prices of inputs. Both resource goods and producer goods are valued according to the value of the ends they seek, which are sequentially determined by the consumers. In other words, the value of goods at earlier stages in the production process is derived from the values to consumers of the product at later stages. Economic value thus derives from the valuing acts of ultimate consumers.

Consumer goods (i.e., goods of the first order) are valued only because people are aware of their dependence on particular quantities of these goods for the satisfaction of their specific needs and wants. The value of goods of higher order (e.g., capital goods) is derived from or determined by the prospective value of goods of lower order which they produce. The factors of production that cooperate in producing consumer goods have no immediate connection with the satisfaction of human needs and wants, but through the causal production process they do contribute to the process of need and want satisfaction. The value of higher order goods is thus dependent upon the expected value of goods of lower order that they produce. Valuations are communicated upward through the economic system to goods of higher order, determining how higher order goods are allocated among industries and products and how they are valued and compensated. Menger refutes the labor theory of value when he points out that costs of production are simply the aggregate of the prices paid for various types of higher order goods and that it is impossible for the prices of consumer goods to be determined by the costs of production, which themselves are ultimately determined by the prices of the consumer goods.

According to Menger, because of time lapses inherent in production, the value of goods of higher order is determined by the prospective value of the product. A change process, such as production, takes time and is inherently uncertain.

In addition, Menger preferred a time preference theory of interest as opposed to a productivity theory of interest. The rate of interest is simply the market's reflection of time preference. Menger presents interest as a phenomenon of exchange. It is the expression of individual preference for present goods as compared to future goods. Positive time preference is seen as a necessary and sufficient condition for the emergence of the phenomenon called interest. For a producer, Menger sees the ownership of capital goods as equal in present value to the holding of a supply of future consumption goods. The difference between the present value and future value represents interest. In other words, Menger explains that the total present value of all complementary goods of higher order required for the production of a good of lower order or first order is equal to the prospective value of the product. However, he goes on to more specifically say that it is necessary to include not only goods of higher order required for production but also the services of capital and the activity of the entrepreneur. It follows that the present value of the technical factors of production is not equal to the full prospective value of the product, but acts so that a margin for the value of the services of capital and entrepreneurial activity can result.

As observed earlier, Menger distinguishes between the value of a thing and the thing itself. He also points out that only concrete things are available to economizing individuals. The articles that exist objectively are, without exception, specific things or quantities of things and their value is invariably something fundamentally different from the objects themselves.

In reality, there are only concrete wants and concrete goods. It follows that only actual units of a good are relevant to human valuation and choice. Menger explains that the want for any good is really a succession of wants for a discrete unit of the good. Implied in the concept of human action is the personal ranking of different satisfactions expected to be obtained from a particular unit or a definite quantity of a good.

Menger's value theory depends upon both the objective and subjective elements influencing supply and demand. Objectively, there is an exact quantity of a particular good in existence. From a subjective standpoint, a good is demanded by individuals in society with the first units being valued most highly and the last ones being valued least highly by each particular person. Regardless of which specific unit of a person's supply is removed, he will economize by deciding to reallocate the remaining units in order to satisfy his most important needs and wants and to do without the satisfaction of only the least important needs and wants of those formerly satisfied by the more plentiful supply.

Menger's theory views the value of all goods and services precisely in terms of how much satisfaction will be foregone without them. It is the least important satisfaction that is dependent on an item of the person's supply of a good. This is known as marginal utility. It is because of the reverse working of the idea of diminishing marginal reliability that as a shortage becomes larger the higher the value of the good in question rises. As unmet needs and wants increase, so does the per-unit value of the required goods.

Theory of Price

Menger explains how market prices emerge as unintended consequences of subjective evaluation processes. His theory of price is a theory of price formation, rather than of price determination, that is concerned with market processes and not with mathematical equilibrium. Menger seeks to establish a causal link between the values underlying consumers' choices and the objective market prices used in the business world. He wants to anchor his theory of price formation and monetary calculation in a realistic general theory of human action that includes an economic theory based on the activities and choices of consumers. He sees prices as the objective manifestation of causal processes intentionally entered into and aimed at the satisfaction of human wants. Prices are thus determined by the valuations of market participants.

Menger's goal is to discover the laws of price formation which he sees as the specific attribute of the market economy. He believes that all characteristically economic events can be understood within a framework of price formation. In the market economy, exchange is purposefully undertaken as part of the causal process of want satisfaction. Prices are formed during individual acts of exchange that take place within this process.

Menger builds his theory of price on the basis of the law of marginal utility. He explains that marginal utility is the active ingredient in determining the prices of goods of all orders. Menger perceives that the consumer evaluation of output tends to be exhibited in the market prices of the pertinent inputs (i.e., higher-order goods).

The cause of a transfer is the willingness to satisfy needs. The exchange takes place because each involved party values the goods owned by the other more highly than he values his own goods. People will consider a mutual transfer only when they judge their needs to be better satisfied with the transfer than without it. The limit to the exchange is arrived at when one of the two negotiators has no additional quantity of goods which he values less than a quantity of another in the hands of the second bargainer. Exchange continues as the two parties rank the values of the goods in inverse order. Exchange ends when the two parties have dissipated the mutual benefits garnered through trade.

Menger's theory of price explains the limits of economic prices and does not try to determine equilibrium prices. A price agreed upon by the bargainers reflects one objective measure among a range of possible magnitudes at which the buyer and seller may have been willing to exchange. Price formation occurs between limits set by the participants. Whereas one bargainer will sell his goods for a certain minimum price, the other will pay up to a specific amount for that same good. It follows that the alleged value subjectively evaluated by each of the agents is not equivalent to the price at which it may be selling. Price is simply an objective and perceptible magnitude of numerical value that can be measured with exactness.

Menger refutes the classical view that, at least in the long run, price is determined by the production costs, including labor cost, long considered to be the most important cost. When he worked as a commodities analyst and reporter, he observed that conventional classical value and price theories did not function to explain actual prices and price changes of various material and non-material goods. He saw that prices frequently bore no relation to the labor added to them. There was a stark contrast between the factors identified by the classical economists and those that experienced market participants believed exerted the greatest influence on prices.

Menger concludes that prices result from both subjective and objective criteria emanating from the demands of individuals and the real physical characteristics and supplies of corresponding goods. Purposeful actions undertaken to satisfy human wants determine prices, resource allocation, and income distribution in the market economy.

He distinguishes between economic prices and real prices. Menger explains that economic prices are those that would prevail in the absence of error. Economic or correct prices would exist only when individuals acted in their own best economic interests, people have complete knowledge of their goods and their means of attaining them, they understand the economic situation, and they possess the freedom to pursue their goals. Real prices differ from economic prices. Entrepreneurial errors and other aberrations and inefficiencies in the real word result in an array of noneconomic (i.e., real) prices in place of economic prices.

Menger assumes that in the long run real or market prices will tend toward economic prices. He views economic prices as the benchmark for judging the deviation of real prices and as the goal toward which civilization is progressing. As people's knowledge increases, real prices will more closely approximate economic prices.

The German Historical School

Menger's methodological views opposed those of the German Historical school. Unlike the German historicists, who excelled in the production of detailed investigations of social and economic conditions, Menger set forth the case for formal theoretical economics.

The German Historical school flourished between approximately 1840 and World War I and emphasized field studies and concrete-bound historical empiricism. The historicists regarded economics as a practical and historical discipline and formed a methodological approach with the intention of highlighting empirical regularities. This school denied the existence of economic laws that are the same for all people at all places and at all times.

The German historicists were complicit with the socialist state. Their pragmatism led to their socialism. Heavily nationalistic, much of their research was used to support interventionist, mercantilist, and protectionist legislation of the state. In essence, the historicists were propagandists for the state and defenders of Bismarck, the founder of the welfare state. They held an organic view of the state, in which the individual is merely a cell in the social body.

Preoccupied with data and history, the German historicists totally excluded theoretical economics from their institutions of higher learning. Their goal was to investigate phenomena in their full empirical reality through the study of all sides of certain phenomena. Through their holistic and empirical orientation, they applied the descriptive historical method to the data of history. Unfortunately, for them, there were no graspable laws of historical development.

The historical sciences such as statistics and history merely study individual and concrete phenomena and their relationships with one another. It follows that the Historical school only attains knowledge of an empirical variety that may be valuable but only in its appropriate context. Any historical "laws" would likely be "short run" and descriptive of the processes of particular economies. Unable to claim universality, these laws would be relative in time and space and would be discovered through intertemporal and interspatial comparisons between nations, societies, social institutions, and social processes.

The historicists would observe, describe, classify, and contrive concepts for particular situations. Their goal was to observe and describe short-run, empirically derived uniformities in the sequence of phenomena. Any economic laws constructed by the historicists would be relative to, or depend upon, the context within which they were discovered. It follows that the idea of causality for the historicists is related to the worldview of Humean nominalism.

Menger observed that the Historical school was not wrong in declaring that every situation had a different historical setting and that such dissimilarities and distinctions should be taken into account. For practical economic policies it was essential to recognize historical differences. Menger said that there could be more than one method to understand economic reality and to generate economic theory. He explained that the historical, the realistic-empirical, and the exact approaches are three of these methods. He noted that each area should be investigated by the methods relevant to research for the specific phenomena under study and appropriate to the goals pursued. Along with the historical, the experience of everyday life was important to Menger's economics in its exact orientation.

The historicists believed that their research did not require theory. Menger, on the other hand, recognized that even historical research needed a theoretical underpinning, with respect to its pursuit of classificatory understanding. Classification methods in historical research not only required, but also presumed, a conceptual viewpoint. In order to properly study historical phenomena, a researcher had to employ some type of classificatory cognitive method.

Menger tends to be somewhat vague in explaining specifically the manner in which the empirical and exact methods are related to one another and how they differ from each other and from the historical method. Very basically and simplistically, it can be said that the historical method attempts to avoid abstraction from the empirical assumption and tries to investigate concrete phenomena in their full empirical reality. In contrast, and to different degrees, both the realistic-empirical and exact methods abstract from phenomena in their total empirical reality. Both are concerned with certain sides of phenomena. These sides are motives, influences, or basic tendencies of human beings and include economics, moral sentiments, altruism, and justice.

The realistic-empirical approach in economics studies economic human behavior to the exclusion of the other sides or aspects of human existence. Although this approach isolates a solitary side or aspect, it still does not investigate a phenomenon in pure form. There still exist disturbing factors such as ignorance, error, external coercion, and the extent to which individuals are influenced by various other basic motives or drives. Real economic phenomena are isolated from other fundamental motives without abstracting from disturbing factors. It follows that realistic-empirical theory is subject to exception and change over time. In other words, real types have the status of particulars.

Exact types differ from real types in that they abstract from all empirical peculiarities and spatiotemporal circumstances of the phenomenon being studied. Economics, as an exact theoretical discipline, isolates from other fundamental aspects and abstracts from disturbing factors. It follows that the results of exact theory and research are true only with certain assumptions. In the exact approach essential relationships hold because of the presupposition that the phenomena is free of all disturbances.

According to Menger, statistics and numbers can give us the end results of economic activity but cannot provide us with the explicit reasons why the behavior occurred, the circumstances under which the same behavior will take place again, or how the results could be changed.

Menger wanted to avoid the fallacy of misplaced quantitative exactitude. He argued and insisted that the function of economics was not merely to study and investigate relationships among specific magnitudes of economic phenomena, but instead to study the essences of things such as the ideas of value, rent, profit, entrepreneurship, division of labor, etc.

Menger understood the deeper implications of the Historical school's emphasis on radical empiricism through which it avoided abstraction in favor of the immediately empirically given. He saw that the logic of the historical approach led to the conclusion that everything is relative and that every situation was unique. Because no generalizations could be made, the purpose of the social sciences, including economics, was thereby invalidated. If the historicists carried out fully their goal of investigating phenomena in their total empirical setting, then it would not be feasible for anyone to attain knowledge.

The vicious debate between Menger and the German historicists was known as the *Methodenstreit* or the War of Methods. Menger and the historicists had basic and major conflicts in the metaphysical and epistemological underpinnings of their contrasting respective methodologies. Menger's abstract-theoretical approach was largely based on Aristotelianism whereas the Historical school's was based on Humean nominalism. It is hard to say who won this battle. On the one hand, Menger is still read today while the historicists are not. On the other hand, the interventionist methods advocated by the historicists are still very much evident today. For example, today's neoclassical economists such as Milton Friedman and his Chicago allies of liberty ironically have adopted a social engineering approach that leads them as analysts to the promotion of interventionist prescriptions to problems. The paradox is that these libertarian empirical economists attempt to justify supposedly more libertarian policies which are oftentimes in opposition to the philosophy and essential principles of liberty. These libertarian social engineers view the prime object of their positive economics as the making of ever more accurate predictions. Their pragmatism rejects introspection and the realism of assumptions as a way of assessing theory. What matters to them is whether or not their predictions conform to empirical evidence. These instrumentalists make judgments about policy on the basis of empirical evidence. This approach can lead economists to give advice based on absurd theoretical constructs.

Methodology

Menger began the bitter conflict known as the Methodenstreit with the 1883 publication of his *Investigations into the Method of the Social Sciences with Special Reference to Economics*. This was twelve years after he published his *Principles of Economics*, the book that made him famous and enabled him to attain a prestigious chair of economics at the University of Vienna. In *Investiga-*

tions Menger elaborated upon the methodology he had originally presented in *Principles of Economics*. In *Investigations* he offered a written argument against the German Historical school's idea of economics as a historically based discipline to be studied solely by the application of concrete-bound empiricism. In addition, he denied the existence of any essential differences between the natural and the social sciences. In contrast, the Historical school assumed that the natural sphere was governed by strictly universal laws, but that the search for such laws in the social realm would be futile. For the German historicist, economic theory did not possess the scientific nature of the natural sciences.

Menger sought to develop a categorical ontology of economic reality in an Aristotelian sense. His causal-genetic method was rooted in Aristotelian metaphysics and epistemology. Menger thereby destroyed the existing structures of economic thought and established economics' legitimacy as a theoretical science. Menger advanced an ontology of economic objects by providing a description of the exact laws of economic phenomena. In the absence of exact laws, there could not be a science of economics and without empirical realism, economics could not be termed a social science.

Menger argues that exact theory, theory based on a few evident axioms, is possible in economics. He reasons that there are specific pure and simple categories which are universal, capable of being exemplified in principle in every economy, and able to be understood as universal by economic theorists. He goes on to say that exact laws are the propositions that express the relationships among these categories. These exact laws are not laws of mathematical precision, but instead are laws which follow inexorably from the essential nature of the elements involved. These laws are changeless and invariably true regardless of time and place. Exact laws are the propositions expressing universal connections among essences. Menger's exact method is limited to essences and to elementary and rationally intelligible essential connections only.

Unlike the historicists, Menger acknowledged the coexistence of different but complementary approaches to economics. Study for the sake of knowing the individual aspects of economic phenomena is the province of economic history and statistics. The goal of attaining knowledge of the general aspects of economic phenomena belongs to the field of theoretical economics. While he insisted on the need for theoretical reasoning, Menger also explained the need for and relationship between the realistic-empirical tendency and the exact tendency in economics and the other social sciences. He argued that the exact orientation in theoretical research has a proper place next to a realistic-empirical orientation to theoretical research. This is because experience of the world in each and every instance involves both a general and an individual aspect. Men understand a concrete phenomenon in a specifically historical way through the investigation of its individual processes of development. A concrete phenomenon is understood in a theoretical way when it is recognized to be a distinctive case of a particular regularity in the succession or in the coexistence of phenomena. It follows that theories, laws, and strictly universal statements are necessary for both historical and theoretical explanations. Economics as a theoretical science provides knowledge that transcends immediate particular and tangible experience.

Menger thus maintained that both empirical and exact theories are descriptive of reality. Each method produces theories that differ in the degree of absoluteness or strictness from the other.

For the German historicists, only a historical approach would enable empirical regularities to be incorporated into theory. Menger clashes with this approach when he observes that there are no graspable laws of historical development. He says that no theories may be extracted directly from history, but contrariwise, theory is required in order to interpret history properly. Menger adamantly declares that the Historical school is mistaken when it claims that the historical method is able to produce universally valid laws and that the truth of empirical laws is more legitimate than the truth of exact or theoretical laws.

In his methodology, Menger stressed that economics is a science by demonstrating that there are economic regularities and that the phenomena of economic life are ordered strictly in accordance with definite laws. Insisting on the exactness of economic theory, he used the language of the pure logician when he analyzed relationships between variables. It is the knowledge of exact laws (i.e., those subject to no exceptions) which comprises scientific knowledge and scientific theory. Exact theory is developed by searching for the simplest, strictly typical elements of everything real.

Menger looked for the essence of economic relationships. He delved for those features which must be present by the nature of the relationship under study. He held that there are simple economic categories which are universal and capable of being understood as such. Exact laws are propositions expressing the relationships among such categories. There are certain elements, natures, or essences in the world as well as connections, structures, and laws regulating them, all of which are precisely universal. Menger's term, exact laws, refers to propositions expressing universal connections among essences. A scientific theory consists of exact laws. For Menger, the goal of research in theoretical economics is the discovery of the essences and connections of economic phenomena. The aim of the theoretical economist is to recognize general recurring structures in reality. According to Menger, the universals of economic reality are not imposed or created, but rather are discovered through theoretical efforts. Economics, as an exact science, is the theoretical study of universals apprehended in an immanent realist manner. Theoretical economics understands economic universals as real objects that the mind has abstracted from particulars and isolated from other universals with which they coexist. If a person has an idea of the essence of something, he can explain its behavior as a manifestation of its essence. In other words, the manner in which objects act depends upon what those objects are. Menger's theoretical framework deals with the intensive study of individual economic units and the observation of how they behave.

Menger distinguishes between the realistic-empirical orientation to theory and the exact orientation to theory. Whereas the realistic-empirical branch of economics studies the regularities in the succession and coexistence of real phenomena, the exact orientation studies the laws governing ideal economic phenomena. He explains that realistic-empirical theory is concerned with regularities in the coexistence and succession of phenomena discovered by observing actual types and typical relationships of phenomena. Realistic-empirical theory is subject to exceptions and to change over time. Theoretical economics in its realistic orientation derives empirical laws that are valid only for the spatial and temporal relationships from which they are observed. Empirical laws can only be alleged to be true within a particular spatiotemporal domain. The realistic orientation can only lead to real types and to the particular. The study of individual or concrete phenomena in time and space is the realm of the historical sciences. According to Menger, it is the aim of the practical or historical sciences to discover the principles, policies, and procedures that are needed in order to shape the phenomena according to predetermined goals.

The aim of the exact orientation of research is the determination of strict laws of phenomena. Exact economic laws are established through a precise understanding of the way typical economizing individuals react to given situations. Menger insists on the precision and exactness of typical behavior. He maintains that once it is acknowledged that rational behavior is the typical behavior of economizing individuals, economists can logically derive theorems that will make up what Menger terms an exact and absolutely true theory. For Menger, theoretical research seeks to identify the simplest and strictly typical elements of everything real.

Menger's view implies that economic reality manifests certain simple and intelligible structures. Economic reality is constituted in intelligible ways out of structures depending upon human thought and action. The individual and his behavior are the most basic elements by means of which Menger explains economic phenomena and derives universal laws. Mengerian economics is built on the basis of the idea that there are, in the realm of economic phenomena, indispensable structures to every economic action that are manifested in every economy. Economic universals involve economizing action on the part of individuals. These universals of economic reality are discovered through theoretical efforts and are not arbitrary creations of the economist.

Menger's understanding of economic theory is essentialist and grounded in Aristotelian metaphysics. His causal-realistic economic method is a search for laws about actual, observable events. It follows that Menger's economics is actually a theory of reality. Menger is concerned with essences and laws manifested in this world. For Menger, as well as Aristotle, what is general does not exist in isolation from what is particular. Menger's theoretical economics studies the universal aspects of particular phenomena. These economic universals are said to exist only as instantiated in specific economic actions and institutions. For Menger, the goal of theoretical research is to discover the simplest elements of all things real which must be apprehended as strictly typical merely because they are the simplest. Of course, it is not an easy matter to discover those structures and to construct workable theories about them. There may be huge difficulties in gaining knowledge of essential structures and in converting such knowledge into the organized system of a strict theory.

Menger's theoretical economics is an exact science that investigates exact types and exact laws. Whereas exact types can be seen as first-order universals, exact laws may be viewed as second-order universals which are concerned with connections between and among exact types. These connections can be seen as involving real necessities. Because first order universals (such as economizing action, value, money, division of labor, sales, rent, profit, etc.) are what they are, their interrelations inevitably are of certain types. Menger contends that economists must study the essences and relations or connections between such economic phenomena.

Menger denies that exact laws supply knowledge simply for its own sake. He contends that even exact laws assist people in controlling and predicting reality, thereby enabling them to live more successfully. According to Menger, even exact laws are practical in helping us to control and enjoy our existence. They are practical primarily because they are exact. Exact laws contribute to our understanding of the real world. In other words, both the realistic and exact orientations are means for understanding, predicting, and controlling economic phenomena. These two orientations allow people to understand the whole sphere of economic phenomena, each contributing in its own characteristic fashion.

Menger finds it necessary to justify inductively the basic causal categories that are arrived at by the analytic part of scientific method. The scientist needs to learn to recognize the general recurring structures in constantly changing reality. He says that theoretical knowledge is gained only by apprehending the phenomenon in question as a special case of a particular regularity in the succession or in the coexistence of phenomena. Economic reality manifests specific simple intelligible structures which the economic theorist is capable of grasping.

Menger endeavors to develop a categorical ontology of economic reality which he says cannot be attained through any mere inductive enumeration of cases. Exact laws are not simply derived from empirical inquiry. He states that they can be scientifically authenticated but not through the tabulation of approximate statistical data based on a finite number of observation statements. Of course, Menger's exact theory is necessarily partially based on empirical inquiry that reveals what is typical about economic behavior. After what is typical is discovered, logically derived theories are thus developed from the typical elements to construct a strictly exact and true theory. These theories make up the form which expresses the essences of economic phenomena. Such theories are developed via a process of introspection or internal reflection as part of a logical process based on deductive reasoning from inductively-derived concepts.

It is apparent that Menger recognizes the difference between empirical knowledge and strict empiricism as a method. Although empirical knowledge originates from the use of a person's senses, it also necessitates the use of one's reason to interpret and analyze the data supplied by the senses. All knowledge can be said to be empirical in the sense that it begins with observed experience of external reality. On the other hand, strict empiricism or positivism states that a person is incapable of knowing the essence of a class of entities and therefore can only know the particular concrete entities they study. It follows that the approach of the empiricist with respect to the verification of knowledge must be continual testing to find out if past relationships between entities still hold.

Menger says that we can find regularity all around us and that, through common sense and scientific reasoning, we can reduce complex abstractions down to their simplest elements which are strictly typical and from these we can build exact laws. He explains that the main goal of theoretical activity is to search for laws and to propose theories and strictly universal statements.

In explaining the transition from particulars (i.e., real types) to universals (i.e., exact types), Menger contends that it is acceptable to omit principles of individuation such as time and space. In order to derive exact laws it is first essential to identify the essential defining quality or essence in individual phenomena that underpins their recognition as representations of that type. Menger thus seeks the simplest elements of everything real (i.e., the typical phenomena) in solving the problem of universals or concepts. To find the simplest elements, a person must abstract from all particular spatiotemporal circumstances.

Experience, reason, and insight are critical and essential to have a science of economics. Exact laws involve introspection and an act of mental effort based on inductive and deductive processes of logic. However, these exact laws are not constructions of the mind but rational descriptions of eternal configurations and regularities in real economic life. Menger believes that general connections or typical relationships between economic phenomena can be apprehended in an exact sense as exact laws. He maintains that the regularities in the coexistence and succession of phenomena discerned through the exact approach allow for no exceptions because of the process of cognition through which they are discovered. In his search for economic laws, he aspires to isolate them and to utilize the simple elements so acquired to deduce more complicated phenomena from the simplest. The exact orientation reveals to us the simplest and strictly typical constitutive factors of phenomena. Exact laws, laws of complicated phenomena which are built up out of simple elements, result from the exact orientation. Exact laws are rarer than empirical laws and are laws without exceptions and are exact for all times and places. They are validated in reality, but not with formal empirical testing. Strictly universal theories can only be constructed at the expense of empiricism. Menger says that it is a methodological absurdity to assume that an economist can test conclusions derived from exact laws by means of empirical evidence. Conclusions arrived at through the exact orientation cannot be corrected or altered by evidence produced through the empirical approach.

Menger states that the results of exact research are true only under certain assumptions which in reality may not always be present. His theoretical system applies only to problems stated under carefully defined presuppositions. In fact, an abstract statement or pure type of relationship found through the exact orientation may be considered realistic and representative of objectively existing facets of the economy even if the pure type does not have an exact ontological correlate. Because of disturbing factors in reality, there is no guarantee that a pure type can be studied in pure form in empirical reality. Menger's argument for an exact orientation of theoretical research is independent of empirical testing. However, his theoretical research does establish the existence of strictly typical elements by means of an only partially empirical-realistic analysis which does not then consider whether or not these elements are present in reality or independent phenomena. The empirical search is only a limited one because it is irrelevant to see if the considered elements are pure or if they are mixed with disturbing influences. Menger's exact theory applies only if the elements are pure because such flawlessness or completeness is presupposed by his approach. It follows that a theoretical understanding of concrete phenomena cannot be achieved through mere inductive enumerations of cases that are subject to contaminating influences. Whereas exact economics makes us aware of the laws holding for an abstractly conceived economy, an empirical-realistic economy makes us aware of the regularities in the succession and coexistence of real but isolated economic phenomena in their full empirical reality thus containing numerous elements not emergent from that abstraction.

According to Menger, theoretical sciences in their exact orientation abstract from disturbing factors such as error, ignorance, and external compulsion. Accordingly, Menger's exact laws rely on the following definite presuppositions, which in reality do not always apply: (1) people tend to be selfish, egoistic, or self-interested; (2) people tend to be rational; (3) people have full, complete, or perfect knowledge of the economic situation with which they are confronted; and (4) people are uninfluenced by error, ignorance, and external compulsion (i.e., they are free and uncoerced by government). There can be exact laws to the extent that individuals are rational, self-interested, informed, and free. For example, Menger would contend that an essential relationship necessarily exists between needs, values, and prices unless the relationship is hindered by disturbing factors, such as government interference through price controls. When Menger's four conditions exist, we can have exact laws and economic prices. In their absence, the best we can have are real prices. For a realist like Menger, the only way to arrive at essences from a succession of concretes is to conceive of an abstract world that holds to his four conditions. There are no guarantees that exact laws will correspond to empirical laws given the actual relationships which the world of phenomena offers to us. History occurs with theory and consists of the numerous empirical facts that form matter in an Aristotelian sense.

According to Menger, the variance or divergence between the theorems of exact theory and the results of empirical studies is not a distinguishing characteristic of economics and the other social sciences, but instead, also pertains to the natural sciences. In physics, the actual movements of bodies do not conform to the theories of pure physics just as in economics exact theory does not exactly correspond to the observed behavior of economic actors.

Menger's scientific realism involves the use of isolation and abstraction. During the process of isolation, the economist selects a limited set of elements from a total situation or task environment and excludes the other elements from mental analysis. Isolation, a subset of abstraction, involves the separation of a universal attribute of the object of study from its other characteristics. Exact theoretical sciences study solitary particular sides of phenomena and abstract from disturbing factors.

Menger identifies fundamental motives for human behavior including economy, moral sentiments, altruism, and justice. He thus isolates or delineates the boundaries between corresponding scientific disciplines such as economics, ethics, social philosophy, and justice. Each of these disciplines would study the behavior of human beings from one of these viewpoints while excluding the others. In addition, within each discipline, the functioning of any one basic human drive or motive could be studied by abstracting it from disturbing factors which are present in the real world. Mere isolation does not guarantee that a factor can be studied in pure form. To study it in pure form, one must abstract from other factors which restrict the total operation of that single factor.

With respect to economics as an exact theoretical science, Menger abstracts from disturbing factors such as error, ignorance, the presence of external force, and the extent to which an individual is influenced by the various fundamental motives for human behavior. Economics as an empirical discipline would isolate economics from other fundamental motives but would not abstract from disturbing factors. However, economics as an exact theoretical discipline would isolate and abstract economics from other fundamental motives and from disturbing factors. The exact method is concerned with isolated aspects of ideal phenomena.

Conclusion

Menger's work will stand out and be applauded throughout many future generations. His realistic and systemic perspective and metatheoretical framework with respect to his exact theory of economics has supplied us with a type of philosophy of economics. Menger laid the groundwork for the Austrian school of economics with his methodological innovations of individualism and ontological essentialism. His Aristotelian approach was to discover the essence or real nature of economic phenomena. He was committed to the doctrine of the strict universality of laws in addition to the ideas of exactness, preciseness, and concreteness in economics as a social science. His theoretical economics investigated the general essences and general connections of economic phenomena. Menger thus was able to demonstrate that the phenomena of economic life are ordered strictly in accordance with definite laws.

Menger constructed economic principles from the human need to satisfy material and other ends and observed that the attempt to provide for the satisfaction of a man's needs is synonymous with his efforts to provide for his life and well-being. This attempt is the most critical of human projects because it is the prerequisite and underpinning of all other human achievements.

Human beings have needs and wants embedded in their nature. These needs and wants are reflected in the actions of human agents to satisfy them. Menger's theory of needs and wants can thus be viewed as a combination of biology and teleology. The maintenance of human life and human well-being is the end or telos of economic activity. A given person's needs and wants are determined for each economic agent by his human nature and his individuality. While some needs are biologically and genetically linked to sustaining human life in general, other needs of a given person are relevant to the individual facticity of the agent, including his potentialities and previous development.

Menger viewed the purpose of economic activity as the satisfaction of human needs. He thus concluded that the ontological foundations of economics were concerned with phenomena generated by the plans and actions of individuals in satisfying their material and other essential needs and wants. Economic phenomena were products of individual human action. Relevant human activity was deliberate, purposeful, and self-concerned. Menger saw a relationship between individual interests and the naturalness of action and economic phenomena. For Menger, both needs and goods had a natural foundation. The essence of all economic concepts emanated from the aspiration to satisfy one's needs and wants.

Aristotelian philosophy was the root of Menger's framework. His biologistic language went well with his Aristotelian foundations in his philosophy of science and economics. Menger demonstrated how Aristotelian induction could be used in economics. In addition, he based his epistemology on Aristotelian induction. Menger's Aristotelian inclinations can be observed in his desire to uncover the essence of economic phenomena. He viewed the constituent elements of economic phenomena as immanently ordered and emphasized the primacy of exactitude and universality as preferable epistemological characteristics of theory.

Like Aristotle, Menger thought that the laws governing phenomena of thought processes and the natural and social world were all related as parts of the natural order. In other words, the knowability of the world was a natural condition common to the various aspects of the external world and the human mind.

Menger wanted to emulate the accomplishments of natural scientists by maintaining, as far as was practicable, the same standards of methodology and epistemology that existed in the natural physical sciences. He recognized economics as a science with multiple dimensions of inquiry (i.e., exact and realistic-empirical) that could pattern itself after the natural sciences with respect to its analytical formality and the universal relevance of its abstract arguments. Menger's goal was to establish the legitimacy of economics as a theoretical science by developing a complete, consistent, and realistic theoretical foundation for comprehending economic activity.

Menger's theory of needs and wants is the link between the natural sciences (particularly biology) and the human sciences. He established this link by describing the final cause of human economic enterprise as an aspect of human nature biologically understood. He analyzed economic activity based on a theory of human action and sought to identify the systemic rule-governed aspects of human action. His theory emphasized individual perception, valuation, deliberation, choice, and action.

Menger's theory of value essentially states that life is the ultimate standard of value. According to Menger, human life is a process in which a person, given his needs and the command of the means to satisfy them, is himself the specific location where human economic life both originates and ends. Menger thus introduces life, value, individual preferences that motivate people, and individual choices into economics. He thus essentially agrees on the same standard of life as the much later Ayn Rand. Value is a contextual judgment made by economizing men. Value is related to the existential state of the individual and the ability of the good in question to change that state in a manner desired by the person.

The foundation of Menger's value theory is a theory of human action which involves a theory of human knowledge. He believes that men can understand the workings of the economy; Menger's goal is to establish economic theory on a solid foundation by grounding it on a sound value theory. To do this he consistently incorporates his methodological individualism in his theory of value.

As a supreme advocate of individualist methodology, Menger recognizes the primacy of active individual agents who generate all the phenomena of the social sciences. His methodological individualism is an ontological doctrine that reflects the real structure of society and economy and the methodological and ontological centrality of the human agent.

It follows that social development is constructed from individual action. Social wholes are the result of the combined intended and unintended consequences of the deliberations and actions of individuals. His new theory of the origin and development of social institutions sees social bodies as the product of individual choices and social order as derivative from a complex of individual actions which are combined into ever more complex social phenomena. Menger has thus provided us with a better understanding of large-scale social formation in which reason is necessary to understand social processes that are genetically built on the satisfaction of needs.

Menger's ontologically founded essentialist theory developed economics as a formal theoretical science that has the purpose of understanding the real world. Not only did the Aristotelian Menger establish the premises for a new conceptual framework in economics and the social sciences, he also successfully criticized positivist doctrines of science, the notion that knowledge of the nature of economic phenomena can be gained via mathematical methods, the claim that theoretical knowledge of human affairs can be derived from history, and the role of rationalistic knowledge in human concerns. In short, Menger brilliantly demonstrated the possibility of economics.

Recommended Reading

By Menger:

Principles of Economics. New York: New York University Press, [1871] 1981.
Investigations into the Method of the Social Sciences with Special Reference to Economics. New York: New York University Press, [1883] 1985.

On Menger:

Alter, Max. *Carl Menger and the Origins of Austrian Economics.* Boulder, Colo.: Westview Press, 1990.
Birner, Jack. "A Roundabout Solution to a Fundamental Problem in Menger's Methodol-

ogy and Beyond." *Carl Menger and His Legacy in Economics,* edited by Bruce J. Caldwell. Durham, N.C.: Duke University Press, 1994, 241–61.

Blaug, Mark, ed. *Carl Menger.* London: Edward Elgar, 1992.

Bloch, Henri-Simon. "Carl Menger: The Founder of the Austrian School." *Journal of Political Economy* 3 (1940): 428–33.

Bostaph, Samuel H. "The Methodological Debate between Carl Menger and the German Historicists." *Atlantic Economic Journal* 4 (1978): 11–15.

Caldwell, Bruce J., ed. *Carl Menger and His Legacy in Economics.* Durham, N.C.: Duke University Press, 1990.

Gloria-Palerno, Sandye. *The Evolution of Austrian Economics.* London: Routledge, 1999.

Grassl, Wolfgang and Barry Smith, eds. *Austrian Economics: Historical and Philosophical Background.* London: Crook Helm, 1986.

Hicks, J. R. and W. Weber, eds. *Carl Menger and the Austrian School of Economics.* Oxford: Clarendon Press.

Jaffé, William. "Menger, Jevons, and Walras Dehomogenized." *Economic Inquiry* 4 (1975): 511–21.

Kirzner, Israel M. "The Entrepreneurial Role in Menger's System." *Atlantic Economic Journal* 3 (1978): 31–45.

Mäki, Uskali. "Mengerian Economics in Realist Perspective." *Carl Menger and His Legacy in Economics,* edited by Bruce J. Caldwell. Durham, N.C.: Duke University Press, 1990, 289–311.

Milford, Karl. "Menger's Methodology." *Carl Menger and His Legacy in Economics,* edited by Bruce J. Caldwell. Durham, N.C.: Duke University Press, 1990.

Moss, Lawrence S. "Carl Menger's Theory of Exchange." *Atlantic Economic Journal* 3 (1978).

Oakley, Allen. *The Foundations of Austrian Economics from Menger to Mises.* London: Edward Elgar, 1998.

Smith, Barry. "Aristotle, Menger, Mises: An Essay in the Metaphysics of Economics." *Carl Menger and His Legacy in Economics,* edited by Bruce J. Caldwell. Durham, N.C.: Duke University Press, 1990, 263–88.

———. *Austrian Philosophy: The Legacy of Franz Brentano.* LaSalle, Ill.: Open Court, 1994.

Vaughn, Karen I. "The Reinterpretation of Carl Menger: Some Notes on Recent Scholarship." *Atlantic Economic Journal* 3 (1987): 60–64.

2

Misesian Praxeology as the Path to Progress

Edward W. Younkins

Economics is a theoretical science and as such abstains from any judgment of value. It is not its task to tell people what ends they should aim at. It is a science of the means to be applied for attainment of ends chosen, not, to be sure, a science of the choosing of ends. Ultimate decisions, the valuations and the choosing of ends, are beyond the scope of any science. Science never tells a man how he should act; it merely shows how a man must act if he wants to attain definite ends.

—Ludwig von Mises

Ludwig von Mises (1881-1973), the Austrian philosophical economist and social thinker, is one of our most passionate, consistent, and intransigent intellectual defenders of capitalism. This chapter provides a systematic survey and overview of Mises's ideas, which are most fully expressed in his 1949 magnum opus, *Human Action*, one to the most uncompromising and vigorously reasoned arguments for capitalism that has ever appeared. Mises defends the free society and private ownership on the grounds that such ownership is the most desirable from the perspective of human happiness, freedom, peace, and productivity. Mises speaks of individual sovereignty, the limitation of the state, the necessity of a gold standard, cooperation in society through individualism, world peace via free world trade, and so on.

Mises's works are increasingly receiving serious attention from scholars. We may now be entering the "Age of Mises" with respect to economic education, as his writings are currently being recognized as great contributions in the intellectual battle of ideas. Not only are Mises's ideas gaining in influence, many believe that they are essential to the preservation of material civilization. It follows that they deserve to become required reading in every college and university curriculum. His books (particularly *Human Action*) remind one of the works of the great eighteenth-century philosophers. *Human Action* should become a primary work for anyone who believes in freedom, individualism, and the free-market economy. If Mises's works are read widely enough, his efforts to preserve civilization and to defend human freedom may succeed.

From Historicist to Praxeologist

Mises began his career as an economic historian in the German Historical school. His enthusiasm for the historical approach waned when, at age twenty-two, he read Menger's great polemic against the German Historical school, *Principles of Economics*, and was convinced that although historical research was important and needed, there are factors which could not be grasped by the historicists' empirical field studies and archival research. He soon realized that economic history could not produce economic laws or principles and that historicism simply supplied pure propaganda for the welfare state.

Menger had contended that the purpose of economic theory is to elucidate causal-genetic explanations of market phenomena. Mises was dissatisfied with Menger's Aristotelian methodology, which for Mises was too closely related to reality. Menger had based his method on realism and had explained in detail two orientations or ways to know reality—the realistic-empirical orientation and the exact orientation. Mises argued that concepts can never be found in reality. He wanted to study and develop pure theory and maintained that "theory alone" could provide firm guidance. Mises wanted to construct a purely deductive system and was searching for a foundation upon which to build it.

The historical school could only offer limited help to Mises in his endeavor. The theory of understanding and the concept of ideal types developed by Max Weber, a prominent German historicist and sociologist, provided Mises with some useful instruction, but Mises found his method to be insufficiently idealistic. Although he generally admired Weber's work, Mises concluded that Weber's interpretation of economics as involving historical ideal types was not acceptable.

Weber explained that an ideal type is constructed by the one-sided accentuation of one or more points of view and by the synthesis of a great many different and distinct phenomena that are arranged according to these one-sidedly emphasized viewpoints into a unified analytical construct. There may be many ideal types because an entity has a variety of attributes or there are various viewpoints regarding the entity. For Weber, the ideal type is to be derived inductively from the real world of social history. Pure or ideal types are derived from historical reality and are one-sided exaggerations of the essence of what occurs in the world. The adjective "ideal" refers to an idea or concept and not to perfection. The delineation of the typical features of a historical period is what makes ideal types possible.

Weber's ideal types are abstract, arbitrary models of acting man with only the ideal type of rational action pertaining to Weber's ideas on economics. Weber's propositions in economic theory fall into the category of rationalizing reconstructions of certain types of behavior. This involves the study of the ways in which people would act if they were driven by purely economic motivations. Weber's idea of economic man is a product of history. His views differ from Menger's views in that Weber's point of departure is a particular historical and actually existing national economy or a part thereof that is restricted to a specific geographical area.

Mises observes that Weber erroneously saw only some human actions as being rational. Weber differentiates "purposive-rational" actions in which a person uses means to attain ends from "valuational" action which he states do not possess a means-ends structure. He asserts that valuational actions are guided by conscious belief in the intrinsic value of a mode of conduct. Weber contends that valuational actions are pursued purely for their own sake and independently of their consequences. Mises refutes Weber by explaining that both rational and valuational behavior display a means-end structure. In other words, all action involves the use of means to achieve ends.

Weber's ideal type is a mental construct gained through abstraction. It is a conceptual tool that does not correspond to concrete reality and that is always one or more steps away from concrete reality. Weber's theory is concerned with rational economic actions of a type that is hardly ever found to exist in empirical reality. Ideal types permit a researcher to construct hypotheses connecting them with the conditions that accompany the phenomenon into importance or with consequences that stem from its appearance. Weber developed his ideal-type methodology for use in interpretive sociology as a bridge between history and theory.

Weber's interpretive sociology employs ideal types to understand events. Such understanding is historical because the interpretation of meanings is specific to time and place. Understanding requires a special subjective intuition on the part of the historian to apprehend the specifics of a situation. Mises observes that understanding can therefore never yield results that must be accepted by all people. He views Weber's ideal types as conceptual tools of historical rather than of theoretical investigation. Weber's interpretation of meanings is historical and not scientific. Mises is not against the use of understanding in history because, of course, history requires presuppositions in the form of the subjective perspective of the researcher. He sees that historical case studies do have some pedagogical value.

Mises was searching for a theoretical foundation that could not be questioned or doubted. He wanted to find knowledge of logical necessity. He also wanted to escape from the concrete-based empiricism of historicism. His mission became to look inward in order to deduce a system that was logically unobjectionable. He wanted to find laws that could only be verified or refuted by means of discursive reasoning.

Mises makes a distinction between understanding and conception. His description of understanding is based upon Henri Bergson's idea of intuition.

The understanding that Mises discusses is essentially that of Weber and of members of the German Historical school. Whereas understanding is intuition, conception for Mises was ratiocination. The substance of an action is disclosed by the a posteriori insights of understanding and the form of action is revealed via the a priori logic of what Mises calls praxeology. Conception of a priori concepts of human action provides the framework for understanding specific actions. Conception involves knowledge understood prior to experience. To find such knowledge, Mises needed a Kantian base which will be discussed in depth later in this chapter.

Mises's axiom of action, the universal introspectively known fact that men act, was the foundation upon which Mises built his deductive system. Action, for Mises, is the real thing. Mises says that action was a category of the mind, in a Kantian sense, that was required in order to experience phenomenal reality (i.e., reality as it appears to us). The unity found in Mises's theorems of economics is rooted in the concept of human action. Mises's economic science is deductive and based on laws of human action that he contends are as real as the laws of nature. His praxeological laws have no spatial, temporal, or cultural constraints. They are universal and pertain to people everywhere, at every time, and in all cultures.

Mises Reconstructs Menger's Value Theory

Mises was not only dissatisfied with Menger's Aristotelian methodology, he was also critical of Menger's value theory. He thought that Menger used unclear language to describe value theory and that Menger carried over ideas from classical liberalism's theory of objective value. According to Mises, Menger makes statements that are incompatible with the basic principles he advanced. He says that Menger was inconsistent in elaborating his ideas and contended that Menger did not pursue subjectivism consistently enough. Mises therefore set out to correct or rehabilitate Menger's theory of value.

Remember that Menger's value theory eventually was labeled subjective value theory because the description of objective value theory was already assigned to the classical liberals' labor theory of value. Mises was convinced that Menger actually meant Misesian subjectivism despite the fact that Menger described his "subjectivism" as more of an objective value approach. Menger understood that values can be subjective, but that men should rationally seek objective life-affirming values. He explained that real wants correspond with the objective state of affairs. Menger distinguished between real and imaginary wants depending upon whether or not a person correctly understands a good's objective ability to satisfy a want. Individuals can be wrong about their judgment of value. Menger's emphasis on objective values is consistent with philosophical realism and with a correspondence theory of truth.

Menger does trace market exchange back to a person's subjective valuations of various economic goods and observes that scales of value are subjective and variable from person to person and subject to change over time. There are certainly subjectivist features in Menger's economic analysis which is founded on his methodological individualism. Methodological individualism implies that people differ and have a variety of goals, purposes, and tastes. Subjectivism is therefore inherent in a principled and consistent understanding of methodological individualism.

Menger explains that objective value originates in a relationship between a man's consciousness (i.e., reason) and his survival requirements. To have an objective value a man's mind must grasp the relationship between the facts of existence and his life. He points out very clearly that a person can be mistaken with respect to their judgments of economic value. Consciousness can be wrong regarding what a man's authentic needs really are, the actual relative importance of his needs, and the products or services that truly seem to meet his needs. Menger also states that it is only the evaluating subject who can make the determination that his judgment was wrong.

Some of Menger's propositions and concepts are incompatible with Mises's brand of subjectivism. Mises did not believe that Menger really meant what he asserted about objective wants corresponding to an objective state of affairs. In other words, Mises thought Menger actually meant values that are purely subjective. Mises is an absolute subjectivist who contends that all values emanate from the consciousness of the valuer.

Mises uses the term "value" in a completely nonnormative, non-philosophical manner. He insists that economic theory does not incorporate any idea of a correct preferential ordering among goods and services. His subjectivism emphasizes the private personal character of preferences, costs, and benefits. Mises's praxeology does not pass judgment on action. It simply explains market phenomena on the basis of a given action and not on the basis of right action. For Mises, to state that an object has value is merely to state that it is the goal of a personally chosen course of action. The Misesian sense of value is purely formal and indicates nothing about whether or not an end (i.e., a value) is in fact valuable. Values are embedded deeply in personal, subjective acts of valuation and depend upon the personal assessment and reaction of an individual to the choices available.

For Mises, an economist deals with subjective factors in the form of the meanings of events and objects for individuals. Economic events are thus the outcomes of valuations. Misesian economic science is therefore free from the value judgments of an economist who must take the value judgments found in the marketplace as his given data. An economist, in his role as economist, does not approve of or denounce individuals' ends. He does nothing more than ask if the means chosen are appropriate for their purposes. Men act and choose according to their hierarchy of values. The foundation upon which the hierarchy is based is irrelevant to Misesian praxeological economics.

Mises's reinterpretation of Menger's value theory added to the confusion caused by its mislabeling as a theory of subjective value. Weber added to the misunderstanding when he began replacing the often-used phrase "Menger's theory of subjective value" with his formulation of "Menger's subjective theory of value," thus switching the subjectivity from an individual's values to the province of the perspective of a given historian, sociologist, or scientist.

Despite the differences between Menger and Mises, they certainly agreed that the best available political system is found in a free society that permits all of its members to attempt to attain their subjective ends or values. The satisfaction of individuals' ends, values, and needs can best be accomplished via a system of market cooperation.

Mises's Kantian Influences

In order to understand Mises's economics, one needs to be familiar with his philosophical theory of knowledge (i.e., his epistemology). Epistemology is the study of (1) what man is capable of knowing; (2) how man can attain knowledge; and (3) the validity of his knowledge. The first 142 pages of Mises's 889-page magnum opus, *Human Action*, are concerned with epistemological issues.

Mises's epistemological ideas are influenced by Immanuel Kant (1724–1804) and by neo-Kantians Max Weber and Morris Cohen. Not a strict Kantian, Mises modifies and extends Kant's epistemology. However, he does make use of Kant's main terminological and conceptual distinctions and basic insights into the nature of human knowledge. It follows that, in order to understand Mises, we must first study and comprehend Kant's epistemology.

The major philosophical problem as seen by Kant was to save science by answering skeptic David Hume (1711–1776), who declared that man's mind is only a collection of perceptions in which there are no causal connections. Hume argued that all knowledge is from experience and that we are incapable of experiencing causality. He explained that causality, as well as entities, are only true by association and customary belief. Causality is simply man's habit of associating things because of experiencing them together in the past. Necessary connections between objects or events are not implied by experiences of priority, contiguity, and constant conjunction.

Hume contended that experience does not give us necessity or mustness. He said that things are contingently true, but that they could be otherwise. We can imagine them being different than what we have experienced in the past. Just because something occurred in a certain way in the past does not mean that it has to occur in the same way in the future. Without necessity, our knowledge about the world is merely contingent. We cannot say with certainty that there are objects, identity, causality, order, and other laws of reality. Hume's conclusion was that we are forced to be skeptics. Science is thus wiped out at its foundation because science deals with causal connections.

Kant wanted to limit Hume's skepticism and rescue science from it. As we shall see, Kant's solution is to argue that order is the mind's contribution to the way we experience the world. The mind supplies order and structure to empirical stimuli. The human mind receives sensory stimuli and organizes, structures, and synthesizes them to give us our perceptual experiences. The mind has an inescapable set of innate and subjective processing and ordering powers and devices through which it structures or filters what it receives from reality. The world that men perceive and act in is thus a product of mechanisms inherent in the structure of human consciousness.

Kant says that we don't need more content (i.e., sense data) from the world. Rather, what we need to do is to organize, structure, and synthesize the disintegrated world of David Hume. Kant declares that consciousness makes synthesis necessary and possible by performing the synthesis itself. The mind processes discrete sense data before it reaches a man's perceived level of awareness. The necessity we see in reality is put there by consciousness through its own processes. The idea that the mind creates necessary relationships is what he called his Copernican Revolution in epistemology. Instead of the mind corresponding to reality, the world must conform to the mind's rules. For Kant, the mind's role is no longer to identify but instead to create necessary connections. Preconscious, automatic, nonvolitional processes built into the mind impose order and create relationships. As a result, our experiences will always be orderly, structured, and systematic.

How does Kant attempt to prove his radical new theory? He begins by distinguishing between analytic a priori knowledge and synthetic a posteriori knowledge. Analytic judgments are made when the predicate of a proposition is known through the analysis of the subject. A priori means independent of experience. Analytic a priori truths are logical, necessary, and certain but tell us nothing about the sense world. Synthetic a posteriori knowledge tells us about the world but does not give us necessity or causality. Such knowledge is from sense experience and is therefore contingent knowledge that we can imagine being different. Knowledge about the world is only contingently possible rather than necessary. Experience does not give us necessity or mustness. The empirical method (i.e., observation) tells us about the world by bringing together a subject and a predicate but does not supply us with necessary truths.

Logic and observation are man's two sources of knowledge. Formal logic is sufficient to determine the truth or falsity of analytic propositions. Propositions are a priori if observations are not necessary and are a posteriori when observations are required. According to Kant, synthetic a priori propositions actually exist and are the only propositions whose truth-value can be definitely established. As we shall see, Mises also subscribes to this claim.

In order to save science, Kant needed to create a method to establish mustness and necessity and to validate truth. What he needed was synthetic a priori truths—necessary and factual truths about the world.

Analytic a priori knowledge gives us certainty without facts and synthetic a posteriori knowledge gives us facts without certainty. Realizing man's need for certainty about the world of objects, Kant set out to prove the existence of synthetic a priori knowledge.

Kant maintains that truth follows from self-evident axioms. They are self-evident when a person cannot deny their truth without self-contradiction. There exist logically certain axioms, which cannot be refuted by reason or logic because these tools already presume their existence. In other words, when trying to deny these axioms one would really be implicitly acknowledging their truth.

Kant contends that these axioms can be identified by reflecting upon and understanding ourselves as knowing subjects. They can be derived from a man's inner experience. The truth of the derived synthetic a priori propositions would be understood as necessarily true, unlike observational experience, which only shows things as they happen to be and not as they must be.

Kant states that if there is certainty it must be supplied by consciousness. He postulates that we have a problem of synthesis rather than of content and that necessity comes from consciousness. He therefore takes a look at sense experiences and asks if there are any things that are always there. If there are things that are always there, they must be there and must be provided by consciousness. Are there necessary ways to perceive the world and what are they, and are there necessary ways to conceive the world and what are they? These ways need to be deduced—we can't experience them because they are prior to experience. We need to find the mind's contribution to each of the above. If we can find necessity in experience it must be from the subjective world and be mind-contributed.

At the perceptual level, we find space and/or time to always be present in our experiences. Space and time are always a person's form of outer experience (extrospection) and time is always a person's form of inner experience (introspection). Space and time are necessary issues of form rather than of content and are not derived from sense experience. Kant concludes that space and time are a necessary part of the way we perceive the world of fleeting sensations. Men always have experiences here and now and recall them there and then. Space and time are therefore inborn elements of one's sensing power. The senses furnish the raw materials of knowledge and the mind arranges knowledge according to its own nature. Space and time are necessary, inescapable, subjective a priori mental forms that organize and condition the perception of things.

Kant next turns to the conceptual level, where he derives the categories that guide the synthesis of sensory fragments into wholes. Recognizing that he has already proven that space and time are necessary forms of perceiving, Kant asks whether space and time require certain categories of conceptualization. He reasons that the fundamental categories must be observed in the kinds of judgment that the human mind is capable of making.

What do space and time presuppose? They presuppose the existence of objects. Kant proposes that all perception and all thought presupposes the existence of mental categories. One's awareness of the world comes from synthesizing categories, providing apprehension of things. With respect to intellection proper, Kant derives categories such as entity, causality, quantity, quality, etc.

Through reason, logic, and science, Kant explains that the mind is able to know things as they appear, but it cannot obtain knowledge of reality. For Kant, the world consists of two opposing realms—true reality (the noumenal realm) and the world of appearances (the phenomenal realm), which is a creation of man's consciousness. Kant declares that the world that we can know is mind-constructed and that any necessary order is in the subjective world. We don't know what is in the objective world.

Kant's epistemological dualism leads to abject skepticism. Knowledge of the noumenal world is not possible. According to Kant, the mind creates the phenomenal world but cannot know the noumenal world, the world in itself. This leads one to ask how Kant knows that the noumenal world even exists, if it can't be known. For Kant, belief in the noumenal world must be an act of faith. Reality is out-of-bounds. Metaphysical knowledge is impossible. Such knowledge is denied by Kant in order to make room for faith.

According to Kant, the mind can get beyond sense experience only through postulates that are based on a nonrational faith. These postulates are that a man has free will, the soul is immortal, and God exists. Kant has limited science to the phenomenal realm in order to open the noumenal realm to faith and intuition.

Kant's philosophy constitutes an all-out attack on the mind's ability to know reality. Man is denied access to the noumenal world. The mind is trapped in its own logical way of thinking. Kant's impositionist view is that the content of man's knowledge reflects certain structures or forms that have been subscribed or imposed on the world by the mind of the knowing subject. This knowledge is never directly of reality itself but instead reflects the logical structures of the mind and reflects reality only as shaped, formed, or filtered by the human mind.

According to Kant, there is only one type of human mind and human logic, which is universally the same. Each person has the same categories and thus constructs the world in the same way. As members of the same species, we each have the same processing apparatus.

Kant believes that man's categories are universal and unchangeable. For Kant, there is one universal collective. His followers break the collective into subgroups. Each little collective is said to create its own reality. Marx claims that the categories differ among economic subgroups. Multiculturalists believe that groups create their own reality based on race, gender, ethnicity, sexual preference, etc. Each group has its own logic, its own reality, its own truth and falsity, and its own right and wrong.

Like Kant, Mises believes that the human mind understands the world only through its own categories. However, Mises is not a pure Kantian. Unlike Kant, Mises does not attempt to make a transcendental argument to derive the categories. He merely says that there is a group of common categories lodged in men's minds through which they grasp that which exists. What Mises considers as critical in Kant is his conviction that reason can supply universal and necessary knowledge.

Mises also disagrees with Kant regarding freedom of the individual. Kant conceives of the noumenal or real self as possessing free will and of the phenomenal self as being determined by the rational desire for happiness. Mises views freedom as the use of reason to attain one's goals. Assuming as little as possible, Mises says that we should assume people to be free and rational actors in the world as we perceive it since we have no certain knowledge of any determinants of human action. Mises is a metaphysical and cosmological agnostic regarding materialist or spiritual explanations of mental events.

Mises extends Kant by adding an important insight. Kantianism has been viewed as a type of idealism due to its failure to connect the mind's categories to the world. Mises further develops Kantian epistemology when he explains that the laws of logic affect both thought and action. He says that we must acknowledge that the human mind is a mind of acting persons and that our mental categories have to be accepted as fundamentally grounded in the category of action. Mises states that when this is realized, the notion of the existence of true synthetic a priori categories and propositions can be accepted as a realistic, rather than as an idealistic, philosophy of knowledge. The mind and physical reality make contact via action. Mises believes that this insight fills in the gap between the mental world and the outside physical world. Mises thus contends that epistemology depends on our reflective knowledge of action.

Mises considers the law of human action to be a law of thought and as a categorical truth prior to all experience. Thinking is a mental action. For Mises, a priori means independent of any particular time or place. Denying the possibility of arriving at laws via induction, Mises argues that evidence for the a priori is based on reflective, universal inner experience.

Unlike Menger, the father of Austrian Economics, Mises did not believe that the essential defining qualities or essences existed in individual phenomena that made possible their recognition as representatives of that type. If he had held to the notion that there are certain ontological, a priori, and intelligible structures in the world, then he may have considered the law of human action to be a law of reality rather than a law of thought. An a priori in reality would not be the result of any forming or shaping of reality on the part of the experiencing subject. Rather, essences or universals would then be said to be discerned through a person's theoretical efforts.

It is hard to see how Mises could contend that a priori knowledge of action is gained exclusively through introspection without any external observation. Perhaps it would have been better if he had said that economic theory is based in part on introspection. He could have argued that sense data alone could not reveal to a person the essential purposefulness of human action. The action axiom could then be depicted as derived from a combination of both external observation and introspection.

Natural Sciences versus Human Sciences

Despite the singularity of the logical structure of human thought, Mises explains that people have access to two separates spheres of scientific thought—the science of nature and the science of human action. Whereas the natural sciences are the experimental sciences, the science of human action includes praxeology and history. Humans experience both the external world of natural phenomena and the internal world of thought, values, and feelings. Mises observes that we approach the subject matter of the natural sciences from the outside and the subject matter of the human sciences from within. He says that we are unable to reduce conscious and intentional human action to the physicalist methods of the natural sciences. Whereas nature reacts, humans act. Mises thus declares the need for a methodological dualism—one methodology for the external world of chemical, physical, and physiological phenomena and another one for the internal world of purposeful action. The natural sciences are distinct and separate from the human sciences. Because, in of the natural order, objects do not choose their behavior, it follows that there exist causal regularities and constant relationships between them. In the human sciences, there is only the regularity of the logical structure of the human mind. There is a major difference between the laws of nature and teleology (i.e., purposeful action). Study of the logic of human action is essentially different from the method used by scientists to gain knowledge about the physical world.

The inanimate matter of the external natural world can be measured, quantified, and systematized based on hypotheses, observations, and experiments. It follows that empiricism and pragmatism are correct approaches for the natural sciences. Experimental sciences are based on the assumption of constant relations (i.e., the same results occur when the same conditions exist). Mises finds strict regularity in natural phenomena. In the physical world, the objects of study consist of phenomena of constant relations. Mises concludes that positivism is the correct methodology for the natural sciences. In the natural sciences we can only hypothesize, test quantitatively, and draw tentative conclusions that may later be falsified. We do not know the consequences in the natural sciences until we attempt something and then observe what occurs. Even after observing specific outcomes over time, our predictions will continually and permanently be merely hypothetical. The best we can achieve is a never-ending trial-and-error process in which our knowledge can be progressively and incrementally improved. Within the natural realm, there are constant relations among magnitudes, which men are able to discern with a reasonable degree of precision.

Mises observes that social processes cannot be controlled and manipulated like inanimate material in laboratory experiments. Social processes have their basis in, and can be traced back to, the actions and reactions of individual persons. In the human sciences, people have the ability to understand the nature and causes of the social processes. The social scientist is a human being and thus can make use of a source of knowledge unavailable to the natural scientist. Through introspection, the social scientist can understand the meaning of human action. He can grasp the meaning that the actor has ascribed to his action.

Mises declares that the two main branches of the human sciences are praxeology and history. Praxeology is the study of what is universal about actions and history is the study of what is specific about them. Whereas praxeology studies the formal relationship of ends and means, history examines the content of means and ends. Mises separates the domain of knowledge into conception, the mental tool of praxeology, and understanding, the mental device of history. Like the natural sciences, history deals with the past. Praxeology deals with what is universal and necessary in the actions of individual men. Not a historical science, praxeology is a systematic and theoretical science, whose subject matter is the concept "human action" and its implications, whose methods are a priori and purely logical, and whose principles are eternally and apodictically certain and objective. History, on the other hand, deals with data that is unique and complex, uses methods that are partially a posteriori and partly a priori, and makes judgments that are approximate and tentative. Through the above distinctions, Mises has created a dualism between a priori praxeology and a posteriori history.

Misesian Praxeology

According to Mises, axioms are facts which all humans must presuppose are certain. He states that axioms do not arise from observations but emanate only from reflective understanding (i.e., introspection). A human being can look within himself and discern the logical and formal attributes of his own mental processes. By understanding the logic of his reasoning process, a man can comprehend the essentials of the reasoning process of all men. Mises thus contends that all men, regardless of their class or race, possess the same logical structure of thought and therefore can and do make the same logical inferences during the reasoning process. People share a common logical structure and thus can understand and communicate with one another. Mises contends that men's minds are equipped with the same set of tools for apprehending reality and that these tools are possessed prior to experience.

Mises states that his action axiom, the proposition that men act, meets the requirements for a true synthetic a priori proposition. This proposition cannot be denied because the denial itself would necessarily be categorized as an action. Mises defines action as purposeful behavior. He explains that it cannot be denied that humans act in a purposeful manner because the denial itself would be a purposeful act. All conscious human action is directed toward goals because it is impossible to conceive of an individual consciously acting without having a goal. Reason and action are congeneric. For Mises, knowledge is a tool of action and action is reason applied to purpose. When people look within, they see that all conscious actions are purposeful and willful pursuits of selected ends or objectives. Reason enables people to choose.

Human actions are engaged in to achieve goals that are part of the external world; however, a person's understanding of the logical consequences of human action does not stem from the specific details of these goals or the means employed. Comprehension of these laws does not depend on a person's specific knowledge of those features of the external world that are relevant to the person's goals or to the methods used in his pursuit of these goals. Praxeology's cognition is totally general and formal without reference to the material content and particular features of an actual case. Praxeological theorems are prior to empirical testing because they are logically deduced from the central axiom of action. By understanding the logic of the reasoning process, a person can comprehend the essentials of human actions. Mises states that the entirety of praxeology can be built on the basis of premises involving one single non-logical concept—the concept of human action. From this concept all of praxeology's propositions can be derived. Mises contends that the axiom of action is known by introspection to be true. In the tradition of Kant, Mises argues that the category of action is part of the structure of the human mind. It follows that the laws of action can be studied introspectively because of aprioristic intersubjectivity of human beings. Not derived from experience, the propositions of praxeology are not subject to falsification or verification on the basis of experience. Rather, these propositions are temporally and logically prior to any understanding of historical facts.

Praxeology studies only purposeful, chosen human actions without regard to the action's motives or causes, which are the objects of study of psychology. Mises's position is that we must treat human beings as free and rational actors because we do not know how or if action is determined. Mises says that although human thought and action are affected by a person's facticity (i.e., his physiological inheritances and past experiences), we do not know how or to what extent his thought and actions are influenced by these factors. He states that all human actions involve choice and that the principles of choice are valid for every human action without consideration of underlying goals, motives, or causes. Each human being has internal purposes, ends or goals that he attempts to attain and ideas about how to attain them. Valuation reflects the internal scale of preferences of the acting person. Separate individuals value the same things in different ways and valuations change for the same individual with changing conditions and over time. Every human activity is engaged in under the motivating power of human values.

Mises explains that every person is a constant valuer who attempts to improve his position, uses means in his attempts to attain his ends, estimates his costs, and chooses his course of action, which ultimately results in either a success or a failure. Every human action can therefore be viewed as a purposeful attempt to substitute a more satisfactory state for a less satisfactory one. The existence of an unsatisfactory state presupposes scarcity and the choice between different alternatives. The aim, goal, or end of any action is relief from a felt uneasiness. Put another way, humans act purposefully to increase their happiness. The sought-after end of every action is the exchange of a better state of affairs for the current state.

Action is purposeful behavior where a person with limited knowledge uses means to attain a desired end, and this relation is influenced by logical laws. Means are used as effectively as possible to attain an end. Acting persons understand that they are employing limited means to attain goals. Every action has a cost and a potential gain. Man, as conscious being, finds some aspects of his condition wanting, imagines ends that he would like to achieve, and perceives means and methods to attempt to attain them. Confronted with the necessity of selecting from among desired goals, he uses his means to pursue the goals to which he has assigned the greatest importance. Implicit in the necessity of choice is scarcity. All action entails choosing one thing instead of another. All means, including time, are scarce. Means have multiple uses, so decisions have to be made regarding the best way to use them. A person must also choose among the ends for which scarce means could be applied. Choosing reflects man's free will, reason, and subjective evaluations regarding the continual removal of felt uneasiness. Each person is a purposeful and rational subjective valuer whose ends, means, thoughts, and actions are integrated into cause-and-effect relationships.

All action requires giving up the most highly valued alternative that is not pursued. The alternative foregone represents the opportunity cost of the action. At the moment of action, a person is also choosing what his options are. He identifies for himself which alternatives are worth pursuing. Mises views action as the determination of both what the feasible alternatives are and the ranking of their relative desirability. His vision is of each individual arranging all of one's innumerable possible ends and means in a series and ranking them according to his own scale of preference. Choices do not simply reflect the subjective preferences of the agent among given alternatives. Rather, the choice manifests the actor's subjective judgment regarding the range of alternative courses of action available and with respect to the likelihood of the outcome of each alternative. Human action emphasizes purposefulness in an open-ended future world of uncertainty. It follows that decisions are made that will maximize the perceived probability of the achievement of one's purposes. Each person, therefore, attempts to influence the degree of uncertainty about what the future might hold for him. Mises thus includes an entrepreneurial element in human choice. He perceives individuals as purposeful agents who are alert to opportunities as well as to threats. Mises views human action as essentially entrepreneurial and sees each person, to some degree, as an entrepreneur. Acting includes the discovery of opportunities and the exploitation of those opportunities.

Mises explains that causality is a prerequisite of action and that the mind comprehends phenomena in a cause-and-effect manner. He states that there exist discoverable causal relationships in the world that can bring about desired effects if they are taken advantage of by human actors. To act means to intervene at some earlier point in order to effect some later outcome. Human action originates change and continuous alteration of the world.

Economics as Praxeology

For Mises, economic behavior is simply a special case of human action. He contends that it is through the analysis of the idea of action that the principles of economics can be deduced. Economic theorems are seen as connected to the foundation of real human purposes. Economics is based on true and evident axioms, arrived at by introspection, into the essence of human action. From these axioms, Mises derives logical implications or the truths of economics.

Mises's methodology thus does not require controlled experiments because he treats economics as a science of human action. By their nature, economic acts are social acts. Economics is a formal science whose theorems have no formal content and whose propositions do not derive their validity from empirical observations. Economics is the branch of praxeology that studies market exchange and alternative systems of market exchange.

Mises insists that the core propositions of economics are based on methods distinct from those of the natural sciences, including the natural science of experimental economics. He says that "economists" who claim to do science based on the model of physics and chemistry disregard the distinctive nature of economics as a social science. Mises is opposed to the positivist method in which the role of economic theory is to observe quantitative statistical regularities of human economic behavior and then to conceive of laws which would then be used to make predictions and which would be tested based upon additional statistical evidence. Mises explains that statistical data does not provide any universal laws and is limited to indicating particular trends and thus can be used to predict the future only in a qualified and minimal way. He warns that the positivist method is congenial to the idea of economics as planned and governed by social engineers who would deal with human beings in the manner that technology and the physical sciences permit engineers to deal with physical objects and inanimate matter. By contrast, the laws of economics are logical, rather than empirical, relationships that are not open to quantitative prediction or verification. Unlike inanimate objects, men have free will, the ability to choose, and the capacity to imagine and pursue new possibilities.

Mises explains that in economics the unit of analysis is individual human action, which we can know from within. Mises's study of the human sciences is based on his methodological individualism. He argues that all theorems of economics must be properly predicated upon the supremacy of the reasoning individual. People choose how to act. Mises argues that it is only at the level of the individual that an observer can assign meaning to social action. He explains that it is only individuals and their actions that provide meaning to social arrangements. Only individuals have purposes and plans and act by organizing the means at their disposal to attempt to attain the desired goals. Methodological individualism is the best method to discover the principles on which a group of people interact. All social processes are derived from the choices and actions of individuals taking part in the social and market order. Individuals cooperate with other people because such cooperation enables them to attain their own desires better than solitary action would. Mises is not an atomistic individualist. In his system of thought he views man as a social being. Most of the time, human purposes can be fulfilled only by the concurrent fulfillment of the purposes of others. Mises's individualism is a philosophy of social cooperation.

Misesian economics recognizes that ends are subjective. Therefore, human action is the ultimate given and cannot be reduced to further causes. All action must be viewed as rational from the point of view of economics because it cannot be analyzed further. For Mises, to be rational is to engage in purposeful behavior. Mises explains that value is the perceived usefulness of a good or service for the attainment of an end. Economic values are subjective, existing within the minds of acting individuals. Values express a ranking or ordering of alternatives. These values cannot be measured or calculated, but each man has a scale of values through which he ranks every possible alternative ordinally.

Contending that determinism has no use in the study of economics or other praxeological sciences, Mises says that we must assume that the mind operates autonomously and that each individual possesses free will. He explains that we do not know how external events affect human thought and value judgment. Avoiding any propositions regarding metaphysical, cosmological, or religious constructs, he argues that any such theories that assign specific causes to thought and values must be dismissed. Mises is agnostic regarding the nature of human nature and the world. Rather than disdain spiritual goods, he is merely not sure about them. He says that metaphysical arguments cannot be used to dispute economics because human beings cannot know the ultimate truth.

Mises's use of apriorism in economic theory clearly differentiates him from mainstream economists. Through the use of abstract economic theorizing, Mises recognizes the nature and operation of human purposefulness and entrepreneurial resourcefulness and identifies the systematic tendencies which influence the market process. Mises's insight was that economic reasoning has its basis in the understanding of the action axiom as a true synthetic a priori proposition. He says that sound deductions from a priori axioms are apodictically true and cannot be empirically tested. Mises developed through deductive reasoning the chains of economic theory, based on introspective understanding of what it means to be a rational, purposeful, and acting human being. The method of economics is deductive and its starting point is the concept of action.

According to Mises, all of the categories, theorems, or laws of economics are implied in the action axiom. These include, but are not limited to: subjective value, causality, ends, means, preference, cost, profit and loss, opportunities, scarcity, choice, marginal utility, marginal costs, opportunity cost, time preference, originary interest, association, and so on.

Mises maintains that all economic reasoning rests on (1) an understanding of the categories of human action and the meaning of a change taking place in phenomena such as knowledge, values, preferences, means, ends, costs, etc., and (2) the logical deduction of the consequences which would emerge from the accomplishment of some particular action or of the outcome which would arise from a specific action if the circumstances were altered in some specific way. Economics identifies consequences using its concepts of subjectively perceived values and costs.

Economics is the study of all men's aims and the means they use to try to attain their aims. Individuals have purposes and plans and act by arranging the means available to them to achieve the ends sought. These ends always involve the satisfaction of some subjective desires of men who are constantly choosing, rejecting, and acting. A means is what serves the attainment of an end. To act means to intervene at some earlier point in order to cause some later result. It follows that every actor presupposes and acknowledges the existence of causality.

Mises argued that all human action is motivated by personal desires and discomfort. There must be a felt uneasiness, an imagined preferable stage of affairs, and the belief or expectation regarding the availability of means and methods to bring the preferred state of affairs into existence. The function of man's reason is to acquire knowledge to enable him to proceed in his endeavors to remove uneasiness. Humans act because they believe their action will result in a state of affairs more desirable to them.

The aim, goal, or end of an action is the result sought by it. A means is what the acting individual uses in his attempts to achieve his end. A good is any means or ends—it is whatever an individual desires. Mises distinguishes between a consumer good which itself promotes satisfaction to the individual and a producer good which must be combined with other goods to produce a consumer good. Production is the use of human reason to direct resources for the achievement of human ends.

Acting is choosing. To select an end is to choose it from an array of alternatives. To attain an end one must use means appropriate to its accomplishment. Choosing involves making trade-offs and weighing costs and benefits. The price of any action is that which is given up. Mises says that the cost is the value of the price paid to the individual paying the price. People buy and sell only because they appraise what they are giving up as less than what they are receiving. The profit (gain), loss, or net yield of an action is the difference between the cost of an action and the value of the end attained by the acting person. Success or efficiency is subjective and must always be measured in relation to the individual's chosen end. Profits and losses inhere in all actions of all individuals and are purely subjective and ordinal.

Man decides on the basis of marginal utility. Most decisions are incremental, rather than categorical, and are made at the margin. An important implication of human action is the law of diminishing marginal utility that says that, as a person obtains successive units of a good, he assigns that good to a lower priority. Mises demonstrated that marginal utility is purely an ordinal ranking in which a person lists his values by preference without assigning any unit or quantity of utility.

The idea and reality of time cannot be separated from the human condition. Time is limited and must be economized and allocated like other scarce resources. All other things considered to be equal, the satisfaction of a want or need in the nearer future is preferable to its satisfaction in the more distant future. Time preference is an unqualified requisite of human action. The concepts of human action, change, and time are inextricably related. Unlike some other resources, time cannot be reversed. When time is used for one purpose it cannot be reallocated to another purpose.

The idea of time preferences manifests itself in Mises's notion of originary interest, which is the discounting of future goods against present goods. The originary (or neutral) rate of interest is the product of the higher valuation of current goods as compared with future goods. It is the ratio between prices of present goods and future goods. The originary rate of interest is independent of the money supply.

The Market Process

Mises explains that economics is a specific science derived from the insight that all social processes stem from the choices and actions of individuals participating in the social and market order. The market is a social process that derives from conscious, cooperative, and purposeful individual exchanges. The configuration of the market at any point in time can be explained by the human values and choices which led to economic exchanges. The fundamental rule of the market is mutual agreement and voluntary exchange of individuals cooperating under the division of labor.

Market processes are stimulated by the discoveries made by imperfectly informed market participants who exhibit purposeful behavior in an open-ended, uncertain world. The future consequences of a person's actions are never given to the actor but must be conjectural in a speculative world. The market process consists of continual discoveries, opportunities, and corrections which tend to be sensed, exploited, and made in a free market. It is the interminable discoveries of entrepreneurial opportunities that make up the market process. The fundamental component of the market process is the profit-motivated activity of entrepreneurs, who act in the face of uncertainty. The function of the entrepreneur is to discover and correct maladjustments in economic decisions and market prices. The entrepreneurs' profit or loss is due to his success or failure in adjusting his activities so as to best serve consumers. The entrepreneur perceives a correlation between market maladjustments and profit opportunities.

The continuous flow of corrective discoveries sets equilibrating, corrective entrepreneurial adjustments in motion. Although the market is never actually in equilibrium, the continuous market process of entrepreneurial discoveries has an equilibrating nature.

The market process is a competitive process through which profit incentives induce competing producers to find better ways of serving consumers. Consumer sovereignty is experienced through competition for entrepreneurial profits. According to Mises, every commodity competes with every other commodity. It follows that prices are mutually interdependent phenomena that are connected in a dynamic competitive process. In fact, Mises's insight is the idea of the interconnectedness of all economic phenomena.

Without market prices to convey information to decision-makers there would be no competition and no profit-or-loss system. Competitively determined market prices permit individuals to assess the relative value of scarce means in competing applications. Market prices are used to discover the relative values of alternative uses of goods and services. Through these prices, the market enables the means at people's disposal to be applied to the most highly valued uses. The pricing process, a social process, is accomplished through the interaction of all valuers within the society. It is the complex of interrelationships of prices that makes up the social aspect of the market.

The social function of the price system is to promote the use of knowledge in society by making calculation possible. Calculation is necessary for a person to determine the best allocation of his scarce resources. Exchange ratios between commodities are fleeting and perpetually changing. The market and money are prerequisites for the mental tool of rational economic calculation. Prices are expressed through the common denominator of money. Rational economic calculation depends on the shorthand signals of market prices to make decisions regarding the alternative uses of scarce resources.

Mises's Utilitarianism as Social Cooperation

Mises's utilitarianism is a priori by nature. He deduces the idea that individuals cooperate because work performed under the division of labor is more productive than work done in isolation. Not only are men innately unequal in their ability to perform various types of labor, nonhuman factors of production (i.e., natural resources, raw materials, and climatic conditions) are unequally distributed around the world. Also, there are many endeavors which simply exceed the capacities of any one person. Mises proclaims that the discovery that higher productivity results from a division of labor is one of the greatest achievements of mankind. Cooperative action based on the division of labor recognizes and gains from the innate inequality of persons and increases the output per unit of labor expended.

In effect, Mises extended Ricardo's Law of Cooperative Advantage. Ricardo had illustrated the profitability of division of labor to all market participants, even in the case where one individual is more productive in every instance and respect. For Mises, the law of cooperative advantage becomes the law of human association, through which each person finds his most profitable niche in the collaborative activities of production and exchange. Mises argues that social cooperation under the division of labor is the fundamental source of man's success in the quest for survival and flourishing and in his efforts to improve his material conditions. Social cooperation is deemed to be essential to individuals' accomplishments of their own diverse and freely chosen pursuits. According to Mises, social cooperation is essential to the survival and prosperity of the human race.

Mises views society as the concerted action or cooperation of individuals that is a product of their conscious and purposeful behavior. A product of human reason and volition, society is the total complex of mutual relations created by collaborative action for the attainment of individual ends. Human society is a rational phenomenon because it is through reason that people are able to grasp the benefits of social cooperation, which results when people are free to know, choose, and act. Human society is an association of persons for cooperative action, resulting in greater productivity and mutual benefits. Mises contends that the recognition of the mutual benefits resulting from specialization was the origin of society and the beginning of the development of civilization. The gain which a society of social cooperation provides is the basis for its origin and persistence of existence.

Mises teaches that social cooperation is a more effective and efficient means to attain one's self-interest than is social conflict. Conflicts are naturally resolved through the division of labor and the substitution of economic competition for biological or Hobbesian competition. What makes friendly relations possible and preferable is the high productivity of the division of labor, which eliminates conflicts of interest. Mises wanted men to have the chance to pursue their happiness successfully. That chance presupposes social cooperation, meaning a peaceful and secure society in which individuals can interact to their mutual benefits while seeking their own diverse projects, specializations, and forms of flourishing.

Mises contends that prosperity is expressed by the fulfillment of diverse human purposes. His ultimate concern is the survival of the human race, which he views as prosperity in the broadest sense. Mises maintains that social cooperation is required for the achievement of human prosperity and happiness. Mises's utilitarian benchmark to be applied to social institutions, law, and moral codes is effectiveness with respect to human welfare. Mises's utilitarianism focuses on outcomes or consequences. It follows that political legislation and moral rules are to be judged based on their consequences or effects. Mises offers the proposition that one must judge legislation according to its logically deduced probable consequences. Rules, therefore, derive their value as preconditions to social cooperation.

According to Mises, social institutions, law, and normative rules of conduct are the outcomes of an evolutionary process and the product of efforts by individuals to purposively and rationally adapt their behavior to the demands of social cooperation under the division of labor. In Mises's view, the type of society we live in is a product of reason and choice. Through the deliberate use of reason people grasped the idea that the division of labor is the essence of society, and they consciously used that idea to improve their welfare. The idea of the division of labor has been progressively extended and intensified over time to include ever-greater numbers of individuals and groups and to achieve an ever-increasing variety of individual goals. Mutual prosperity is increased through the facilitation of social cooperation. By taking advantage of individual circumstances and talents through specialization the total quantity and quality of the output of society can be increased.

Mises emphasizes that priorities are those of individuals. It is individual men who endeavor to advance their priorities and to attain prosperity. For individual persons, social cooperation is a means to attain all of their ends. Through specialization and division of labor the independent individual becomes a social being. Mises maintains that only a system based on freedom for every person elicits the greatest productivity of human labor and is in the interest of all individuals. It follows that Mises assigns importance to social cooperation achieved impersonally through the free market process. Free markets promote prosperity by allowing individual purposes to be fulfilled. An act of exchange achieves prosperity by simultaneously fulfilling the purposes of both involved parties. Free markets permit and enable men to achieve their own goals through mutual cooperation and exchange. Mises's defense of individual freedom is on the consequentialist grounds that freedom leads to good results. Mises's kind of individualism is thus utilitarian individualism.

Mises distinguishes between social cooperation based on freely made contracts and social cooperation based on subordination. If social cooperation is voluntary, it is contractual, and if it is based on subordination and command it is hegemonic. Mises favors contractual social cooperation because the maximization of individual free choice is a means to achieve greater prosperity for everyone in society. Any interference with the free market is interference with the freedom of human choice and action. Mises thus concludes that the free market and the social order based on it comprise the only viable system of social cooperation and division of labor. He argues that men's potential for cooperation depends upon freedom, peace, private property, individual rights, limited government, and inequalities of wealth, income, talents, and natural resources.

Utilitarianism is based on the notion that happiness (i.e., human flourishing) is good and that suffering is bad. Utilitarianism favors institutions, laws, rules, and traditions that underpin the types of society that permits people to make satisfactory lives for themselves. Such institutions and practices facilitate cooperation among persons as they pursue their diverse specific goals. Utilitarianism views social cooperation as valuable to human life.

Mises maintains that the survival of the human race hinges on the recognition and application of economic truth. He sees economic knowledge as a necessary condition for the continuing existence of human civilization. It follows that the goal of economic inquiry is the promotion of the survival of the civilized human race. For Mises, economic theorizing and evaluation are deductive, stable, definite, and totally unaided by experience. He insists upon the purely aprioristic and scientific character of economics.

Mises was a passionate advocate of the free market while at the same time insisting upon the value-neutrality of economics and the economist. He believed that it was possible and desirable to have a clear-cut boundary between an economic scholar's analysis and his personal and political value judgments. For Mises, economics is a neutral or value-free theoretical science. Such ethical neutrality means that economics is concerned with deductively tracing the consequences of market activities and economic policies. Economics, like any scientific project, must be conducted in a manner severed from the investigator's motivations, values, beliefs, and preferences. Mises was truly a philosopher of economics who wanted to systematize and make explicit the nature of economics.

Mises explains that economic theory examines the efficiency and effectiveness of the means selected to attain chosen ends. Since action pursues definite chosen ends, it follows that there can be no other standard for evaluating actions but the desirability or undesirability of their effects. The given purpose of economics is to preserve the order of social cooperation and social harmony. This is done by deducing the outcomes of purposive actions undertaken within the framework of the division of labor. Actions, institutions, laws, and so on are correct if they sustain social cooperation, which is a precondition of the happiness of individuals within society. In the other words, social cooperation facilitates and contributes to human flourishing and happiness.

Mises contends that economics is the foundation for politics, even though economics itself is value-free and apolitical. He explains that the political doctrine of classical liberalism is a direct application of the scientific findings of economics. Mises's case for classical liberalism is a utilitarian one because when an economist proclaims that a certain economic system or policy is bad he is saying that it is inappropriate to the desired goal. In assessing an economic doctrine, one only has to ask if it is logically coherent and if its practical application will enable people to attain their desired goals. Mises's concern is whether policies and institutions serve or undermine social cooperation and individuals' happiness. He thus sees classical liberalism, a political doctrine, as an application of theories developed by praxeology and based on rational economics. According to Mises, classical liberalism is a coherent theory of man, society, and the institutional arrangements required to provide social harmony and cooperation.

Mises maintains that sound, value-free economic reasoning leads a person to favor laissez-faire economic systems. He deduces the nature and outcomes of human cooperation in a market economy based on private property and the division of labor and compares these with the means employed and outcomes achieved under alternative systems such as socialism and interventionism. As an economist, he employs the logic of praxeology to work toward his goal of comparing systems with regard to their capacity to attain ends. He thus advocates the market economy because economic reasoning shows that it best enables people to achieve their chosen ends.

Mises explains that well-intentioned government interventions interfere with the tendency of the free market to respect the sovereignty of the individual. Interventionist policies will fail to attain their objectives, generate unintended and undesirable results, and lead to further government controls. Interventionism involves regulations and controls that divert production from the projects that would have been undertaken if people were free to follow their own judgments. These interventions reduce the standard of living by disturbing the division of labor.

Mises observes that it is impossible to have rational central planning under socialism. This is the basis of his epistemological case against socialism. Without market-based prices, decision-making by central planners would be irrational and arbitrary. Because of the elimination of market-based prices, a fully centralized planned economy would be unable to allocate resources rationally. Socialism, even more than interventionism, obstructs the operation of market processes, thereby decreasing the rationality in the social system.

According to Mises, socialism is inherently unworkable, destroys individual motivation, and suppresses the means of economic calculation. Economic calculation through the use of market prices is a logical precondition for the existence of society. Reason and society develop together and it is impossible to have a society without calculable action. The rational calculation of costs and benefits is the basis for economic efficiency. Socialism lacks this means to calculate and thus has to resort to irrationality.

Monetary calculation is a tool of action. Mises defines catallactics as the analysis of actions which are performed on the basis of monetary calculations and prices. It is prices, articulated through the common denominator of money, that makes economic calculation possible. The free market permits economic calculation—the mental tool that allows the development and evolution of the system of division of labor. It is through the system of division of labor that men are able to improve their earthly existence.

Socialism destroys the incentive of profits and losses, private ownership of property, and the benefits of competition. Mises explains that there is room for everyone in the market economy, even those with unexceptional abilities. He specifies that the function of competition is to designate to every member of a social system that position in which he can best serve. Competition is a method for choosing the most able men for each task. The competitive process is characterized by an absence of artificial barriers to entry (i.e., government-granted monopoly privileges). Competition requires freedom of entrepreneurial entry.

Mises insisted on the value freedom of the theoretical character of economics. He sees economics as a theoretical science that abstains from any judgment of value. For Mises, economics simply judges whether a specific policy will attain the ends that the proposer of the policy has in mind. Economics merely asks, given certain ends, how can those ends be best achieved? Mises sees no logical contradiction between himself (or any other economist) as objective scientist and rational agnostic and, on the other hand, as an advocate of classical liberalism and denouncer of protectionism, antitrust policy, price-fixing, etc., based on the conclusions of economic science.

Mises explains that a policy is bad when it can be deduced to generate results which are inconsistent with the objectives intended for the policy by the policy-proposers themselves. He illustrates that statist interventions in the market bring about consequences which are worse than the state of affairs they were meant to improve. He demonstrates with deductive logic that every political intervention hurts some individuals and makes society less prosperous.

Mises contends that the reasoning of a value-free economics could be used to demonstrate that interventionist and socialist policies cannot attain a goal that their proponents are explicitly or implicitly attempting to accomplish—the goal of progress with respect to the material well-being of individuals in society. Realizing that social progress depends upon the construction and acceptance of a proper ideology of social life, Mises endeavors to formulate a theory of society that is as value-free and objective as possible. As a scientist and economist, Mises logically analyzes the ends of specific ideologies and the means available to attain these ends. The goal of his economics is to identify incorrect and correct views about how individuals in society can achieve their ends. His value-neutral economic science identifies free markets as best. Laissez-faire economics leads to progress and prosperity and lessens the incentive to go to war. Mises's evaluation of laissez-faire is an approval of the system of private property and voluntary social cooperation. It follows that, as a political ideology, classical liberalism is not neutral with respect to the values and ends sought by human actors.

According to Mises, government is a necessary prerequisite for a free market society. The free market requires an institutional framework that identifies and protects individual rights. This framework includes private property, freedom to contract, and government monopoly of coercion. As the monopoly of violence in society, government maintains peace and enforces rules so that individuals can cooperate and enjoy the benefits of that cooperation. Although Mises saw a role for government, he vehemently maintained that the exercise of state function conveys no innate dignity, virtue, or prestige.

Mises's utilitarianism starts with the goal of human flourishing and moves to social cooperation and the existence of individual rights. It does not explicitly include natural law, which Mises thinks is unnecessary and problematic and which he equates with intuitionism. Mises says that he is agnostic with respect to the nature of human nature. With regard to individual rights, he says that there exists a private domain in man which should not be regulated or violated. This realm constitutes what is deepest, highest, and most valuable in the individual human being.

Although he says he rejects natural law, Mises's approach to justifying the free society has a great deal in common with natural law constructs. The life-affirming rules for social cooperation and for interpersonal conduct that he deduces seem to be based on the essential nature of human life. For Mises, the reason or goal for this system of rules is to maintain and promote social harmony and human life. These rules for the protection of individual rights are essential for social cooperation on the part of rational human beings with free will. In the end, Mises's utilitarianism appears to be based, at least implicitly, on a principled, categorical, natural-law-like framework.

Theory of Money, Interest, and the Business Cycle

Mises's praxeology connects individual subjective values to price determination and links the supply and demand for money to marginal utility theory and to the value of money. His theoretical explanation for the value of money is the same explanation that he uses to account for all commodity market values. In other words, he demonstrates that the purchasing power or price of the monetary unit is determined on the market. The interaction between the demand for money and the quantity of money available determines its price.

Mises demonstrates how money emerges from the domain of directly exchanged commodities. He explains how the unique value of money originates on the free market when a specific commodity is no longer valued only as a consumer good or a producer good but also as a medium of exchange. From that point on the value of that commodity consists of its subjective value for its use as an ordinary good and the subjective value for its use as money. Money is thus the most marketable good. It is acquired with the intention of spending it at some later point in time. Mises states that the demand for money is a demand for maintaining cash balances and that the marginal utility of the monetary unit determines the strength of the demand for cash balances. He explains that the present valuation of money is derived from its objective exchange value in the preceding period and deduces that all changes in the demand for, or supply of, money generates revisions in the value of the medium of exchange. Mises rejects the idea of neutral money.

Mises says that we must begin with the particular individuals whose specific new demand for, or new supply of, money originates the process resulting in a changed value of money. The effects of the particular change in the demand for, or supply of, money work through the economy in a temporal-sequence series of actions, ending with an increase or decrease in the general purchasing power of the monetary unit. Any change in market conditions begins in the circumstances and cash holdings of one or more persons. Mises developed a dynamic sequence analysis to demonstrate the temporal sequence through which diverse purchasing powers of the monetary unit over time are interrelated and to illustrate the way changes are effected in the general purchasing power of money through increases or decreases in the demand for, or supply of, money.

Time preference relates to the distance in the future of an object of evaluation from the point in time at which the object is appraised. Time preference is a praxeological category or theorem arising deductively from the axiom of human action. Mises contends that a positive time preference (i.e., preferring something sooner rather than later given that all other factors are equal) is a categorical requirement of human action. Mises explains that interest is the economic expression of positive time preference. Originary interest is the product of the preferences of current goods as compared with future ones. According to Mises, originary interest is unconnected to the money supply.

Mises explains the process through which changes in the quantity of money generate relative price changes, modify the allocation of resources among market sectors, redistribute wealth, distort interest rates, and cause business cycles. He does this by tracing the sequence of events by which changes in the money supply transmit from individual to individual and from sector to sector.

Mises begins by distinguishing between commodity credit and circulation credit. These were often called transfer credit and created credit, respectively, by other writers. Commodity credit is based on fully backed resources. Circulation credit is not fully backed by reserves. Like money certificates, fiduciary media are money substitutes (i.e., claims to a definite amount of money, payable and redeemable on demand) that circulate indefinitely. Mises defines fiduciary media as the amount of money-substitutes against which debtors do not keep a one hundred percent reserve of money proper. Unlike fiduciary media, money certificates are money substitutes that are totally backed by the reservation of corresponding amounts of commodity money. Banks can increase the quantity of less-than-fully-covered money substitutes with no associated and necessary decreases in the quantity of commodity money remaining in circulation. This is accomplished by giving loans to borrowers without a corresponding increase in commodity money deposits in their institutions. Circulation or created credit results in the borrower receiving an amount of money substitutes with no corresponding sacrifice being made by another person in the economic community.

Through its ability to expand the money supply, the monetary authority is able to create credit for lending purposes. As we will see, this introduction of created credit makes the business cycle possible. According to Mises, the source of the business cycle problem can be found in the expansion of the money supply. He explains that created credit represents added units of the medium of exchange with no corresponding decrease in consumer demand for goods and sources which typically comes after decisions to save more. Credit creation by the banking system thus can exceed the constraints by which investments would be limited to actual savings. An increase in the supply of money necessarily dilutes its purchasing power. As banks expand the money supply and make new loans, they push the rate of interest below the natural rate of interest. Present-day governments follow easy money policies, unfortunately but unavoidably leading to recurring periods of boom and bust.

Mises observes that an increase in the supply of money will have a tendency to lower its value, but that the extent of the decline in value (or even whether it declines at all) is contingent upon changes in the marginal utility of the monetary unit as perceived by individuals. He also explains that increases (or decreases) in the quantity of money are not accompanied by simultaneous and proportional changes in all prices. This is because the increase of money is introduced at one point in the economy with prices rising as the new money spreads throughout the economy. The demand for goods and services starts to rise because of the increase in the money supply, but not all demands will increase in the beginning or at the same time. Mises illustrates the manner in which a change in the supply of money will bring about changes in the relative income and wealth situations of individuals, alter the structure of relative prices, and modify the allocation of resources among various sectors of the economy. Only slowly will the changes in the purchasing power of money work its way throughout the whole economy. Mises demonstrates that inflation is essentially a process of taxation and redistribution of wealth. He explains that the primary appeal of inflation is that not everyone receives the new money at the same time and to the same extent. Those who receive the increase in the supply of money earlier are able to buy more goods and services before the total inflationary effect on the economy has taken place. People affected later will end up paying higher prices for many of their purchases. The incomes of the favored recipients of the new money go up before many prices have risen. The unfortunate parties who receive the new money toward the end of the sequence (or those on fixed incomes who receive none of it) lose because the prices of their purchases increase before they can benefit from the increased income, if they can benefit at all.

In the first stage of the inflation process the prices of only those goods and services for which the initial individuals have a large demand begin to increase. Those who sell those goods and services have more money and, in turn, increase their purchases of goods and services. This process will continue until, at its completion, prices in general will be higher but each price will have been influenced by the monetary increase in a specific sequence, at different times, and to varied extents. The end result is that the relative price structure in the economy will have been changed. This restructuring of relative prices affects the demand for, and allocation of, resources among the diverse sectors of the economy. Income and wealth are thus redistributed among groups and individuals who are in essence winners and losers in the sequential-temporal process that springs from changes in the supply of money.

Only the prices of those goods and services demanded by the first beneficiaries of the inflation go up at the outset. Later, the prices of other goods are raised as the increased supply of money works its way step-by-step through the whole economy. Since all commodities are never affected simultaneously, the prices of all the goods and services will not have gone up to the same degree. The groups that make and sell goods and services that increase in price initially profit from the inflation. They enjoy higher incomes in the infancy of the inflation and are able to purchase goods and services at lower prices, which are still based on the previous stock of money. Individuals and groups whose incomes do not change during the inflation process are compelled to compete in their purchasing endeavors with those who are obtaining inflated incomes.

Banks have the ability to set the money rate of interest below the natural rate of interest. In the absence of the gold standard, or similarly under a fractional gold standard, government and central banks allow or endorse an artificial lowering of interest rates. This artificial lowering is effected through monetary expansion. Combining the depository and lending functions, the banking industry is able to pyramid the supply of money substitutes in the guise of loans, surpassing the previously existing supply of money substitutes that represented claims on demand by depositors of commodity money. The result is that some segment of the banks' outstanding money substitutes would not be totally backed by existing resources if enough possessors of money substitutes were to demand payment within some limited time period.

Mises explains how the monetary changes introduced via the banking system not only distort interest rates but also generate business cycles. The artificially lowered interest rates stimulate the demand for bank loans over and above the amount of real savings available for lending. This demand is met with inflationary increases in the quantity of money and credit.

The initial recipients of the newly created funds begin or expand business ventures. When the interest rate is artificially lowered, business invests the money in long-term projects and capital investments. The investment borrowers thus bid resources away from the production of consumer goods and shorter-term investment projects to start or expand projects with longer time horizons. In other words, resources are transferred into earlier orders of investment. Resources are drawn from other uses that would have been preferred by consumers, who are deprived of a greater value of immediate consumer goods. This aberration of entrepreneurs' production plans has many consequences.

When the borrower offers higher prices for the required factors of production, he siphons them away from alternative uses. The effect of newly created credit then transfers to those factors of production in the form of higher money incomes. When workers and others receive the new money, they will spend it in their previous proportions because their time preferences will have remained the same. This increased money demand for goods and services will cause prices of consumer goods to increase. Of course, because of the previous reallocation of resources away from consumer goods production and into long-term investment projects, the amount of consumer goods available is less than it would have been. This, in turn, accentuates the price upswing. As a result, consumer goods manufacturers and providers increase their demand for factors of production to attract them back to the consumer goods industry and into investment projects with short-term completion periods.

The original receivers of the created credit will find it challenging, or even impossible, to finish their long-term endeavors because of the increasing costs that stem from others' efforts to attract factors of production back to the consumer goods areas. Their demand for additional loans causes the market rate of interest to increase and an even greater predicament occurs. The expansion phase of the business cycle is thus replaced by the depression stage. The failure of some unsustainable projects and businesses is unavoidable because people will have not been saving a sufficient amount to buy (finance) the higher-order investments. The crisis can only be solved by means of a readjustment of the production process, through which the market liquidates the malinvestments and moves back to the consumption-investment ratio desired by consumers. Mises concludes that, in the long run, the only way progress and increases in the standard of living can be achieved is through capital formation, which includes the processes of saving and investment. He also deduces that the causes of business cycles are government mismanagement and manipulation of money and credit.

Conclusion

As we have seen, Mises has constructed a monumental, overarching, systematic, and comprehensive conceptual framework that attempts to elucidate the timeless, immutable laws that guide the world and human behavior. Mises's logical thinking and critical analysis led to his passionate defense of capitalism and a free society. As a Renaissance man, Mises integrated his profound theories of scientific methodology, political science, history, the social sciences, and so on, in his various writings and especially in his magisterial work, *Human Action*. Mises's unification of related disciplines was accomplished by means of his methodological individualism.

The foremost economist of the 20th century, Mises inspired the rebirth of classical political economy. He is without doubt one of the most prolific and important contributors to men's understanding of the nature and processes of economics. His invaluable contributions have been in many economic fields, including but not limited to methodology, market processes, comparative economic systems, monetary theory, business cycle theory, capital theory, and market structure theory.

Many believe that Mises is on questionable grounds with his extreme aprioristic position with respect to epistemology. However, his praxeology does not inevitably require a neo-Kantian epistemology. It is not inextricably tied to an aprioristic foundation. Other epistemological frameworks may provide a better underpinning for free will and rationality. For example, Misesian praxeology could operate within an Aristotelian, Thomistic, Mengerian, or Randian philosophical structure. The concept of action could be formally and inductively derived from perceptual data. Actions would be seen as performed by entities who act in accordance with their nature. Man's distinctive mode of action involves rationality and free will. Men are thus rational beings with free will who have the ability to form their own purposes and aims. Human action also assumes an uncoerced human will and limited knowledge. All of the above can be seen as consistent with Mises's praxeology. Once we arrive at the concept of human action, Mises's deductive logical derivations come into play.

Murray N. Rothbard, student and follower of Mises, agrees that the action axiom is universally true and self-evident but has argued that a person becomes aware of that axiom and its subsidiary axioms through experience in the world. A person begins with concrete human experience and then moves toward reflection. Once a person forms the basic axioms and concepts from experience with the world, he does not need to resort to experience to validate an economic hypothesis. Instead, deductive reasoning from sound basics will validate it.

The later Aristotelian, neo-Thomistic, and natural-law-oriented Rothbard refers to laws of reality that the mind apprehends by examining and adducing the facts of the real world. Conception is a way of comprehending real things. It follows that perception and experience are not the products of a synthetic a priori process but rather are apprehensions whose structured unity is due to the nature of reality itself. In opposition to Mises, Rothbard contends that the action axiom and its subsidiary axioms are derived from the experience of reality and are therefore radically empirical. These axioms are based on both external experience and universal inner experience.

Rothbard nevertheless endorses Mises's monumental, integrated, and systematic treatise, *Human Action*, as a complete and correct paradigm based on the nature of man and individual choice. Although Rothbard disagrees with Mises's epistemology, he does agree that Mises's praxeological economics appropriately begins with, and verbally deduces logical implications from, the fact that individuals act. Rothbard contends that it is time for Mises's paradigm to be embraced if we are to find our way out of the methodological and political problems of the modern world.

Recommended Reading

By Mises:

The Anti-Capitalist Mentality. Princeton: Van Nostrand, 1956.
Bureaucracy. New Haven: Yale University Press, 1944.
A Critique of Interventionism [1929]. Translated by Hans F. Sennholz. New Rochelle, N.Y.: Arlington House, 1977.
Epistemological Problems of Economics [1933]. Translated by George Reisman. Princeton: Van Nostrand, 1960.
The Free and Prosperous Commonwealth: An Exposition of the Ideas of Classical Liberalism [1927]. Translated by Ralph Raico. Princeton, N.J.: Van Nostrand, 1962. Later editions were published under the title Liberalism: In the Classical Tradition.
The Historical Setting of the Austrian School of Economics. New Rochelle, N.Y.: Arlington House, 1969.
Human Action: A Treatise on Economics. New Haven, Conn.: Yale University Press, 1949. This work is a revision, expansion, and translation of an earlier German-language book, Nationalökonomie: Theorie des Handelns und Wirtschaftens, Geneva, 1940.
Nation, State, and Economy [1919]. Translated by Leland B. Yeager. New York: New York University Press, 1983.
Omnipotent Government: The Rise of the Total State and Total War. New Haven, Conn.: Yale University Press, 1944.
Planned Chaos. Irvington-on-Hudson, N.Y.: Foundation for Economic Education, 1947.
Planning for Freedom, and Other Essays and Addresses. South Holland, Ill.: Libertarian Press, 1952.
Socialism: An Economic and Sociological Analysis [1922]. Translated by J. Kahane. London: Jonathan Cape, 1936.
Theory and History: An Interpretation of Social and Economic Evolution. New Haven, Conn.: Yale University Press, 1957.
The Theory of Money and Credit [1912]. Translated by H. E. Batson. London: Jonathan Cape, 1934.
The Ultimate Foundation of Economic Science: An Essay on Method. Princeton, N.J.: Van Nostrand, 1962.

On Mises:

Butler, Eamonn. Ludwig von Mises: Fountainhead of the Modern Microeconomic Revolution. Universe Books, 1988.
Ebeling, Richard M., ed. Human Action: A Fifty-year Tribute. Hillsdale, Mich.: Hillsdale City Press, 2000.
Eshelman, Larry J. "Ludwig von Mises on Principle." Review of Austrian Economics 6, no. 2 (1993): 3–41.
Garrison, Roger W. "In Defense of the Misesian Theory of Interest." Journal of Libertarian Studies 3, no. 2 (1990): 141–50.
Gonce, R. A. "Natural Law and Ludwig von Mises's Praxeology and Economic Science." Southern Economic Journal 39 (April 1973): 490–507.
Gordon, David. "The Philosophical Contributions of Ludwig von Mises." Review of Austrian Economics 7, no. 1 (1994): 95–106.
Herbener, Jeffrey M. "Ludwig von Mises and the Austrian School of Economics."

Review of Austrian Economics 5, no. 2 (1991).

———. *The Meaning of Ludwig von Mises: Contributions in Economics, Sociology, Epistemology, and Political Philosophy.* Kluwer Academic Publishers, 1992.

Kirzner, Israel M. *Ludwig von Mises.* Wilmington, Del.: ISI Books, 2001.

———. *Method, Process, and Austrian Economics: Essays in Honor of Ludwig von Mises.* Lanham, Md.: Lexington Books, 1982.

Kirzner, Israel M. "Reflections on the Misesian Legacy in Economics." *Review of Austrian Economics* 9, no. 2 (1996): 143–54.

Raico, Ralph. "Mises on Fascism, Democracy, and Other Questions." *Journal of Libertarian Studies* 12, no. 1 (Spring 1995): 1–27.

Rothbard, Murray N. "Laissez-Faire Radical: A Quest for the Historical Mises." *Journal of Libertarian Studies* 5, no. 3 (Summer 1981): 237–53.

———. "Ludwig Von Mises and Natural Law: A Comment on Professor Gonce." *Journal of Libertarian Studies* 4, no. 3 (1980): 289–97.

Salerno, Joseph T. "Ludwig von Mises as Social Rationalist." *Review of Austrian Economics* 4, no. 1 (Spring 1990): 26–54.

Tucker, Jeffrey A., and Llewellyn H. Rockwell Jr. "Cultural Thought of Ludwig von Mises." *Journal of Libertarian Studies* 10, no. 1 (Fall 1991): 284–320.

Yeager, Leland B. "Mises and Hayek Dehomogenized." *Review of Austrian Economics* 6, no. 2 (1993): 113–48.

3

Ayn Rand's Philosophy for Living on Earth

Edward W. Younkins

Achievement of your happiness is the only moral purpose of your life, and that happiness, not pain or mindless self-indulgence, is the proof of your moral integrity, since it is the proof and the result of your loyalty to the achievement of your values.

—Ayn Rand

Ayn Rand (1905-1982), the best-selling novelist and world-renowned philosopher, developed a unique philosophical system called Objectivism which has affected many lives over the last half century. This chapter represents an introduction to her systematic vision by presenting her essential ideas in a logical, accessible manner. This should contribute toward the appreciation of Rand's profoundly original philosophical system.

The specific purpose of this chapter is to introduce, logically rearrange, and clarify through rewording the ideas scattered throughout her books, essays, lectures, and novels, especially *Atlas Shrugged* (1957), her masterwork of logic that most completely expounds her exhaustive, fully integrated philosophy. Written from the viewpoint of a generalist in economics, philosophy, and the social sciences, this chapter is meant to provide a background for readers who wish to study specialized aspects of Rand's philosophy in greater detail.

Metaphysics is the branch of philosophy that studies the nature of the universe as a totality. Epistemology is concerned with the relationship between a man's mind (i.e., his consciousness) and reality (i.e., the nature of the universe) and with the operation of reason. In other words, epistemology investigates the fundamental nature of knowledge, including its sources and validation. One's theory of knowledge necessarily includes a theory of concepts and one's theory of concepts determines one's theory or concept of value (and ethics). The key to understanding ethics is in the concept of value and thus ultimately is located in epistemology and metaphysics. The purpose of this chapter is to delineate the inextricable and well-argued linkages between the various components of Ayn Rand's philosophy of Objectivism. Rand's philosophy is a systematic and integrated unity with every part depending upon every other part.

The Essence of Objectivism

Hierarchically, philosophy, including its metaphysical, epistemological, and ethical dimensions, precedes and determines politics, which, in turn, precedes and determines economics. Rand bases her metaphysics on the idea that reality is objective and absolute. Epistemologically, the Randian view is that man's mind is competent to achieve objectively valid knowledge of that which exists. Rand's moral theory of self-interest is derived from man's nature as a rational being and end in himself, recognizes man's right to think and act according to his freely chosen principles, and reflects a man's potential to be the best person he can be in the context of his facticity. This leads to the notion of the complete separation of political power and economic power—the proper government should have no economic favors to convey. The role of the government is, thus, to protect man's natural rights through the use of force, but only in retaliation and only against those who initiate its use. Capitalism, the resulting economic system, is based on the recognition of individual rights, including property rights, in which all property is privately owned. For Rand, capitalism, the system of laissez-faire, is the only moral system.

Aristotle: Ayn Rand's Acknowledged Teacher

Ayn Rand, whose philosophy is a form of Aristotelianism, had the highest admiration for Aristotle (384-322 B.C.). She intellectually stood on Aristotle's shoulders as she praised him above all other philosophers. Rand acknowledged Aristotle as a genius and as the only thinker throughout the ages to whom she owed a philosophical debt. According to Rand, Aristotle, the master of those who know, is responsible for every achievement in civilized society including science, technology, progress, freedom, romantic art, and the birth of America itself.

Aristotle espouses the existence of external objective reality. For Aristotle, the existence of the external world and of men's knowledge of it is self-evident. He contends that the basic reality upon which all else depends is the existence of individual entities. He insists upon an independent existing world of entities or beings and that what exists are individuals with nothing existing separately from them. For Aristotle, the ontologically ultimate is the individual.

The basic laws of being, or first principles of reality, in Aristotle's metaphysics, are the philosophical axioms or laws of noncontradiction, identity, and excluded middle. According to Aristotle, these presuppositions or assumptions govern, direct, or command scientific explanation.

For Aristotle, causality is a law inherent in being qua being. To be is to be something with a specific nature and to be something with a specific nature is to act according to that nature.

Aristotle heralds the role of reason in a proper human life. He examines the nature of man and his functions and sees that man survives through purposeful conduct which results from the active exercise of man's capacity for rational thought. The ability to reason separates man from all other living organisms and supplies him with his unique means of survival and flourishing. It is through purposive, rational conduct that a person can achieve happiness. For Aristotle, a being of conceptual consciousness must focus on reality and must discover the knowledge and actions required if he wants to fully develop as a human person.

Aristotle is a this-worldly metaphysician who avowedly rejects mysticism and skepticism in epistemology. His view is that human nature is specific and definite and that there is some essence apparent in each and every person and object.

An advocate of this worldly cognition, Aristotle's theory of concepts is reality oriented. It follows that Aristotle considers essences to be metaphysical and every entity to be comprised of form, the universalizing factor, and matter, the particularizing factor.

For Aristotle, essences or universals are phenomena intrinsic in reality and that exist in particulars. It follows that to comprehend essences or universals is at root a passive intuition or receptivity. Aristotle, the naturalistic realist, explains that knowledge begins and arises out of our sense experiences which are valid. It follows that a man can build on the evidence of the senses through reason, which includes logic and the formation of abstractions.

Rand finds fault in Aristotle for viewing essences as metaphysical rather than as epistemological, which is how she regards them. She opposes Aristotle's intuitionist view that essences are simply "intellectually seen." Rand contends that universals or concepts are the epistemological products of a classification process that represents particular types of entities.

The highest or most general good to which all individuals should aim is to live most fully a life that is proper to man. The proper function of every person is to live happily, successfully, and well. This is done through the active exercise of a man's distinctive capacity, rationality, as he engages in activities to the degree appropriate to the person in the context of his own particular identity as a human being.

Because man is naturally social, it is good for him to live in a society or polis (i.e., a city-state). Aristotle emphasizes the individuating characteristics of human beings when he proclaims that the goodness of the polis is inextricably related to those who make it up. For Aristotle, social life in a community is a necessary condition for a man's complete flourishing as a human being.

Aristotle explains that friendship, the mutual admiration between two human beings, is a necessary condition for the attainment of one's *eudaimonia*. Because man is a social being, it can be maintained that friendship has an egoistic foundation. It follows that authentic friendship is predicated upon one's sense of his own moral worth and on his love for and pride in himself. Moral admiration, both of oneself and of the other, is an essential component of Aristotelian friendship. Self-perfection means to fulfill the capacities that make a person fully human, including other-directed capacities such as friendship.

Noting that individuals form communities to secure life's necessities, Aristotle also emphasizes the importance of active citizen participation in government. Of course, he does view the proper end of government as the promotion of its citizens' happiness. It follows that the goodness of the polis is directly related to the total self-actualization of the individuals who comprise it.

Aristotle contends that the state exists for the good of the individual. He thus prefers the rule of law over the rule of any of the citizens. This is because men have private interests whereas laws do not. It follows that the "mixed regime" advocated by Aristotle is the beginning of the notion of constitutionalism, including the separation of powers, and checks and balances. He is the first thinker to divide rulership activities into executive, legislative, and judicial functions. Through his support for a mixed political system, Aristotle is able to avoid and reject both Platonic communism and radical democracy.

For Aristotle, an entity that fulfills its proper (i.e., essential) function is one that performs well or excellently. He explains that the nature of a thing is the measure or standard in terms of which we judge whether or not it is functioning appropriately or well. Things are good for Aristotle when they advance their specific or respective ends.

Aristotle bases the understandability of the good in the idea of what is good for the specific entity under consideration. For whatever has a natural function, the good is therefore thought to reside in the function. The natural function of a thing is determined by its natural end. With respect to living things, there are particular ways of being that constitute the perfection of the living thing's nature.

According to Aristotle, there is an end of all of the actions that we perform which we desire for itself. This is what is known as *eudaimonia*, flourishing, or happiness, which is desired for its own sake with all other things being desired on its account. Eudaimonia is a property of one's life when considered as a whole. Flourishing is the highest good of human endeavors and that toward which all actions aim. It is success as a human being. The best life is one of excellent human activity.

For Aristotle, the good is what is good for purposeful, goal-directed entities. He defines the good proper to human beings as the activities in which the life functions specific to human beings are most fully realized. For Aristotle, the good of each species is teleologically immanent to that species. A person's nature as a human being provides him with guidance with respect to how he should live his life. A fundamental fact of human nature is the existence of individual human beings, each with his own rational mind and free will. The use of one's volitional consciousness is a person's distinctive capacity and means of survival.

One's own life is the only life that a person has to live. It follows that, for Aristotle, the "good" is what is objectively good for a particular man. Aristotle's eudaimonia is formally egoistic in that a person's normative reason for choosing particular actions stems from the idea that he must pursue his own good or flourishing. Because self-interest is flourishing, the good in human conduct is connected to the self-interest of the acting person. Good means "good for" the individual moral agent. Egoism is an integral part of Aristotle's ethics.

In his ethical writings, Aristotle endorses egoism, rationality, and the value of life. He insists that the key idea in ethics is a human individual's own personal happiness and well-being. Each man is responsible for his own character. According to Aristotle, each person has a natural obligation to achieve, become, and make something of himself by pursuing his true ends and goals in life. Each person should be concerned with the "best that is within us" and with the most accomplished and self-sufficient success and excellence.

According to Aristotle, the "moral" refers to whatever is related to a person's character. He teaches that the value of virtuous activity resides in realizing a state of eudaimonic character. Such a state must be achieved by a man's own efforts. A person needs to pursue rational or intelligent efforts in obtaining goods and in otherwise taking control of his own life. Because a man might fail or be thwarted in his efforts, Aristotle explains that a person should be more concerned with his fitness to achieve success than with the existential attainment of the success itself.

Aristotle insists that ethical knowledge is possible and that it is grounded in human nature. Because human beings possess a nature that governs how they act, the perfection or fulfillment of their nature is their end. A human being is ordered to self-perfection and self-perfection is, in essence, human moral development. The goal of a person's life is to live rationally and to develop both the intellectual and moral virtues. There are attributes central to human nature the development of which leads to human flourishing and a good human life. According to Aristotle, the key characteristics of human nature can be discerned through empirical investigation.

Aristotle teaches that ethical theory is connected to the type of life that is most desirable or most worth living for each and every human being. It follows that human flourishing is always particularized and that there is an inextricable connection between virtue and self-interest. He explains that the virtuous man is constantly using practical wisdom in the pursuit of the good life. A man wants and needs to gain a knowledge of virtue in order to become virtuous, good, and happy. The distinction of a good person is to take pleasure in moral action. In other words, human flourishing occurs when a person is concurrently doing what he ought to do and doing what he wants to do. When such ways of being occur through free choice, they are deemed to be choiceworthy and the basis for ethics.

The purpose of ethical inquiry is a practical matter according to Aristotle. He explains that practical wisdom is not only concerned with universals (such as good or value), but also with particulars which become known through experience in the choices and activities of life. He states that it is important to have practical experience with particulars if one is to optimally benefit from philosophical inquiry into ethics. Aristotle thus emphasizes the power of judgment beyond the guidance of general theory. Experience helps to perfect a person's power of moral judgment. He notes that one's facticity, including his past choices, and the contingent situation are relevant considerations in determining a correct choice. Proper actions are in the particulars that differ considerably from case to case.

Aristotle does not regard ethics as an exact science. He says that matters of conduct are not found in an exact system, not only in dealing with specific cases of conduct, but also with respect to the general theory of ethics. He explains that a person must both investigate the nature of virtue and learn through experience to discern, consider for himself, and competently judge the particulars of the circumstances of each situation. Aristotle thus emphasizes both the difficulty of devising general principles of moral action and the importance of perception and judgment in practical decisions. One's practical wisdom is a kind of insight, perception, or sense of what to do.

Aristotle tells us that virtues, as constituents of happiness, are acquired through habituation. He also explains that virtue can be understood as a moral mean between two vices—one of excess and one of deficiency. Such a mean is not scientific or easy to calculate. Aristotle's moral virtues are desire-regulating character traits which can be found at a mean between extreme vices. For example, courage is the virtuous mean between rashness as a vice of excess and cowardice as a vice of deficiency.

With respect to ethical judgments, Aristotle expounds that a person should not expect more certainty in methods or results than the nature of the subject matter permits. It is obvious then that Aristotle does not regard ethics as an exact science. The Randian explanation of Aristotle's position on ethical exactness is that it is a consequence of the intrinsicist elements of his epistemology. Because Aristotle considers universals, concepts, or essences as metaphysical rather than as epistemological, it is difficult, if not impossible, for him to explain how one sees or intuits "good," "value," "ethical," and so on when he is confronted with various optional actions or objects. We will see how Rand has addressed this problem when we discuss her epistemology and ethics later in this chapter.

Immanuel Kant: Ayn Rand's Intellectual Enemy

Ayn Rand considers Immanuel Kant (1724-1804) and his philosophy to be evil and condemns what she perceives as the intended goal, methods, and conclusions of his philosophical arguments. She accuses Kant of hating life, man, and reason. Rand observes that, since Kant, the dominant trend in philosophy has been aimed at the destruction of the human mind and that a philosophy seeking to destroy man's mind is a philosophy of hatred for man, his life, and all human values. In Kant's teachings, Rand sees contempt and detestation of the strong, able, successful, virtuous, confident, and the happy. It follows that Rand's own philosophical system is an attempt to exalt happiness and to answer and oppose Kant's epistemology and ethical theory.

David Hume (1711-1776) had contended that neither inductive nor deductive reasoning could supply men with real, certain, and necessary knowledge. He asserted that he had never seen "causality" nor experienced "self" or "consciousness." According to Hume, men merely experienced a fleeting flow of sensations and feelings. He also observed that the apparent existence of something did not guarantee that it would be there an instant later. Hume thus surmised that consciousness was limited to the perceptual level of awareness.

Desiring to refute Hume's conclusion, Kant also searches for the perceptual manifestation of necessity. In order to avoid the conclusions reached by Hume, it is necessary for Kant to build a formidable philosophical structure.

Kant divides propositions into two types—analytic, which are true by definition, and synthetic, which assert empirical facts. He says that analytic statements are logically true but provide no information about reality and that synthetic statements provide information about reality but cannot be logically proven. Analytic truths can be validated through an analysis of the meanings of their component concepts and synthetic propositions cannot be validated through an analysis of the definitions of their constituent concepts. Analytic truths are necessary, logical, and tautological whereas synthetic truths are contingent, unprovable, and factual. According to Kant, one cannot irrefutably prove a synthetic proposition.

For Kant, analytical truths are logical and can be validated independent of experience. These propositions are a priori and nonempirical. On the other hand, he says that synthetic propositions or truths are empirical, a posteriori, and dependent upon experience in order to be validated. Kant contends that analytic propositions provide no information about reality and that synthetic ones are factual but are uncertain, improvable, and contingent.

According to Rand, there is no basis upon which to differentiate analytic propositions from synthetic ones. As we shall see later in this chapter, her theory of concepts undermines Kant's idea of an analytic-synthetic dichotomy. For Rand, concepts express classifications of observed existents according to their relationship to other observed entities. Rand explains that a concept refers to the actual existents which it integrates including all their characteristics currently known and those not yet known. She argues that concepts subsume all the attributes of the existents to which they refer and not simply the ones included in the definition. Her objective theory of concepts is the tool she uses to abrogate Kant's analytic-synthetic dichotomy.

Kant's analytic truths are in reality contingent upon what is included in the espoused "meaning" of a concept. The way Kant formulates his theory allows a person to validate a concept merely by including an attribute in the meaning of a concept. Choices are made regarding which characteristics are included in a definition and which are not. Depending upon whether or not a specific characteristic is included in the definition determines whether or not the characteristic is a necessary one or merely a contingent one!

In his attempt to refute Hume, Kant declares that there are synthetic a priori categories or concepts built into the human mind. Kant argues that concepts are certain inherent features of human consciousness. Man's basic concepts (e.g., time, space, entity, causality, etc.) are not derived from reality or experience, but instead stem from an automatic system of filters in his consciousness. These filters, which he calls categories and forms of perception, dictate their own structure on his perception and conception of the external world, thus making it impossible for him to perceive and conceive it in any other way than the one in which in fact he does perceive and conceive it. Empirical reality, according to Kant, conforms to the mind of man, which lays down a "grid," consisting of the categories and the intuitions of time and space, over "things in themselves." Because men have no choice in whether or not they apply this grid to experience, it follows that people cannot know the real world and can only have appearances as our minds have created them.

According to Kant, the a priori includes what is in the mind before one has any sense experiences plus whatever judgments the mind is capable of making which are not based on sense experience. The forms of space and time and the transcendental categories are innate in the mind and comprise its structure prior to a person's sense experience. He says that the common experience that everyone shares has the appearance and character it does because it has been given the makeup it has by the inherent structure of the human mind.

Kant attempts to demonstrate that the world that we experience is not the real world that does not include our species's concepts of space, time, entity, causality, and so on. He contends that the phenomenal world of appearances that we experience is metaphysically inferior to the noumenal world of true reality. The noumenal world is the world of things in themselves, higher truth, and real reality.

Kant explains that the phenomenal world is the world of earthly physical reality including man's senses, perceptions, reason, and science. This phenomenal world, as perceived by a man's mind, is a distortion or misrepresentation of the real world. Kant contends that the distorting mechanism is man's conceptual faculty itself. He argues that what the human mind perceives and conceives the world to be is not the world as it really is but rather as it appears to a specifically structured human reasoning faculty.

Kant laments the fact that a person can only perceive and comprehend things through his own consciousness. He also explains that men are limited to a consciousness of a particular nature that perceives and conceives through particular means. For Kant, man's knowledge lacks validity because his consciousness possesses identity. According to Kant, knowledge, to be valid, must not be processed in any way by consciousness. Kant's criterion for truth is to perceive "things in themselves," unprocessed by any consciousness. For Kant, only knowledge independent of perception is valid. Unfortunately, such knowledge is impossible!

He argues that human knowledge is subjective because it is not relevant to "things in themselves." Real truth is unknowable because to know it a person would have to relate to reality directly without depending upon his conceptual mechanism. For Kant, the real is the object "in itself" out of all relation to a subject. This means that the consciousness or awareness of things cannot be mediated by any process or faculty whose nature affects the appearance of the object because any process or faculty would distort one's perceptual awareness. According to Kant, everything is merely phenomenal that is relative and everything is relative that is an object with respect to a conscious subject. Kant is looking for knowledge that could be called absolute, unqualified, pure, or diaphanous.

Kant maintains that identity, which itself is the essence of existence, invalidates consciousness. Any knowledge attained by a process of consciousness is inescapably subjective and therefore cannot match the facts of reality because it is processed or altered knowledge. Because all consciousness is a relationship between a subject and an object, it follows that for a person to acquire a knowledge of what is real, he would have to go outside of his consciousness. To know what is true, a man would have to abandon his own nature, which is an absurd impossibility. In order to know true reality requires a consciousness not limited by any specific means of cognition. This is the criterion or goal of Kant's argument.

Ayn Rand sees the Kantian argument as an attack on all forms of consciousness. Because consciousness exists, it possesses particular means and forms of cognition and thus is invalidated by Kant as a faculty of cognition. It follows that because men depend upon the type of mental constitution they have, that man's mind is impotent, reality is unknowable, and knowledge is merely an illusion. According to Kant, if consciousness possesses its own identity, then it cannot grasp the identity of anything external to it. The Kantian argument thus divorces reason from reality. Reason, according to Kant, is limited, only deals with appearances, and is unable to perceive reality or "things as they are in themselves." Reason is powerless to deal with the fundamental metaphysical concerns of existence that properly reside in the noumenal world that is unknowable.

For Kant, the cognitive structure that all men have in common is what creates the phenomenal world. Man's innate mental structure is what gives rise to the empirical world. Kant explains that man's categories or concepts form a collective delusion from which no human being can escape. In essence, Kant switches the collective for the objective when he advances the idea of common mental categories collectively creating a phenomenal world. He also reassigns the validity of reason from its place in the objective world to the collective delusional world. Reality as perceived by man's mind is a distortion and man's mind is a distorting faculty.

Kant's concern is with judgments that can be known with certainty. He says that this disqualifies reason because of a priori limitations on what can be known via reason. Because the mind's categories are limited to appearance, knowledge of the real world is foreclosed. The inability to know reality leads to relativism and skepticism.

According to Kant, the deepest level of reality is inaccessible to human rationality. For him, rational certainty is impossible. He says that to "know" the other higher reality that is teleologically ordered and exempt from time, space, causality, etc., a man needs to turn to feeling, intuition, or faith that exist in the form of pure a priori judgments or intuitions. Kant's solution is to try to demonstrate that the "real" and the "ought" rests in something called pure reason that is metaphysically intrinsic to all persons. He says that the "real" and the "ought" are different from what we know through experience. Kant contends that intellectual intuition (i.e., pure reason) has the function of accessing these a priori ideas.

Kant assigns one's emotions the power to know the metaphysically superior "unknowable" noumenal world by indefinable means that he terms "pure reason." Pure reason resides in a special inexplicable or incomprehensible instinct for duty. Duty is a categorical impulse that one "just knows." Kant holds that an action is moral only if a person performs it out of a special sense of duty. Morality is therefore derived through feelings from the noumenal dimension of reality. Duty involves inspiration supplied by, or emanating from, noumenal reality itself. Given his reliance on the noumenal realm, Kant makes morality appear to be mystical.

According to Kant, a person must act from duty, which he views as an act of pure or abject selflessness. One's duty is thus to sacrifice himself to duty, which is a dictate of pure reason. Moral duties are categorical imperatives that hold for all rational beings with absolute certainty regardless of their desires, individual characteristics, and other contingent factors. Kant's fundamental principle of morality thus binds a person independently of any particular ends or preferences he may have. Kantian morality pertains to actions that apply categorically and that are good in themselves. Duty is the requirement to act out of respect for the moral law rather than from one's desires or inclinations.

Kant declares that his altruist morality is derived from pure reason. He says that only "knowledge" of the concept of duty from pure reason can succeed in deriving the moral law. Kant views morality as a set of rules embedded in pure reason. Pure reason or intellectual intuition is the means used to gain moral knowledge.

Kant maintains that a person should do what conforms to having a good will and that the ought is inherent in pure reason. For Kant the good will, the will acting from duty, is unconditionally good. He argues that the good will, separate from any consequences, is an end in itself.

According to Kant, morality has its basis in a law of the will. He says that an action is morally good if it flows from a good will. A will is unconditionally good when it acts purely and solely out of a sense of duty and for the sake of duty. A will thus acts for the sake of duty when it acts out of pure respect for moral law. A person's good will is primary and acting for the sake of duty is the ultimate good.

The ought proceeds from the a priori and is embedded in the structures of the mind. Kant explains that the function of one's will is to force obedience to the a priori. In effect, Kant's reliance on the a priori is an effort to circumvent the formulation of concepts from observation by regarding certain concepts (e.g., duty) as self-evident and not dependent on the causal context that exists in nature. Kant's profession of the moral a priori necessitates a pervasion of the human functions of cognition and evaluation.

Kant detaches morality from any concerns regarding man's existence. For Kant, morality has no association with the material world, reason, or science. He states that an action is moral only if a person has no desire to perform it, but performs it totally out of a sense of duty and derives no benefit of any kind from it. Kant makes moral duty an obligation completely independent of a person's desires and totally without any connection to factual considerations, including the facts of one's human nature.

Kant's moral philosophy deprives self-interest of any and all honor. The rejection of self-interest is also a rejection of all human values and goals because to pursue one's self-interest means to pursue values and goals. For Kant, morality must bind a person independently of any specific desires, ends, or inclinations he may have. Kant's idea of duty serves morality from both reason and values.

Kant says that an act is moral only if no benefit of any kind is derived from it. He excludes all personal desires and benefits from the realm of morality. To be moral, a man must perform his duty without reference to any personal goals, values, or effects on his own life and happiness. A benefit destroys the moral value of an action. Kantian moral theory can thus be viewed as act-centered and not as agent-centered.

What Kant has done is to allow man's reason to conquer the material (i.e., the phenomenal) world but eliminate reason from the choice of the goals or ends for which men's material achievements are to be employed. Kant assigns the unreal material world to science and reason but leaves morality to faith. Science and reason are limited and valid only as long as they are concerned with a fixed determined collective delusion. The higher reality, the noumenal world, dictates to man the rules of morality through a special manifestation, the categorical imperative, which involves a special sense of duty known through intuition or feeling.

Duty is the moral requirement to perform certain actions without regard to any personal values, goals, motives, intentions, or desires. These a man should sacrifice from duty as an end in itself. An action is moral only if a person has no desire to perform it but performs it out of a sense of duty and receives no benefit from it of any kind. Kant thus denies that anything done to secure one's own well-being and flourishing can have any moral significance. For Kant, morality does not and cannot involve the virtue of prudence (i.e., practical wisdom). He sees a distinct division between prudence and morality.

Kant holds that the pursuit of a person's own happiness or interest is of no moral worth whatsoever. He insists that we can never determine whether or not an action is good or right by considering its effect on one's happiness. Kant explains that happiness is contingent upon conditions and factors outside of a person's control and external to the human will. He contends that the ultimate purpose of human striving must reside in something that depends on the person alone and must be unconditionally good. It follows that the only unconditional and ultimate good is the good will.

According to Kant, a person is amoral when he acts to attain his values. For Kant, all ends (except for the specifically moral) are reducible to a person's own happiness, nonmoral, and incapable of producing any categorical imperatives. For Kant, what is necessary for a legitimate moral philosophy are obligations that are categorical (i.e., moral duties). The ethical is therefore what everyone ought to do.

Kant contends that moral worth is intrinsic to the act and thus valuable in itself apart from any particular valuer. For Kant, a man's natural end of happiness cannot be the foundation for moral motivation. Unlike Aristotle, Kant draws a sharp distinction between moral and nonmoral reasoning. Kant rejects any moral philosophy that holds a person's happiness as his ultimate end and maintains that the determination of the moral is made without reference to a man's desires and to the facts of his nature. For Kant, morality elevates man above the sensible world. He views prudence as nonmoral and self-interest as different from doing what is right to do.

Kant provides a test for determining the moral status of various actions. He says that a person who performs his moral duty in the teeth of his contrary inclinations exhibits moral worth. On the other hand, a person who helps other people and gains pleasure from such actions displays no moral worth. Similarly, if a person wants to be honest he deserves no moral credit. An individual who does not have a natural desire to help others or to be honest but nevertheless does so from duty does display moral worth.

According to Ayn Rand, Kant's objective is to save the morality of altruism, self-sacrifice, and self-abnegation. Kant's vision of morality consists of total, abject selflessness. Kantianism sharply opposes the pursuit of happiness to the practice of one's duty. Kant's morality of duty restricts the importance of an individual's experiences and thought and teaches that morality depends on adherence to a priori truths and on ignoring the real world. Rand thus sees Kantianism as a grand rationalization for his hatred of reason and reality and his view of the supremacy of the emotions.

Metaphysics

Metaphysics is the first philosophical branch of knowledge. At the metaphysical level, Rand's Objectivism begins with axioms—fundamental truths or irreducible primaries that are self-evident by means of direct perception, the basis for all further knowledge, and undeniable without self-contradiction. Axioms cannot be reduced to other facts or broken down into component parts. They require no proofs or explanations. Objectivism's three basic philosophical axioms are existence, consciousness, and identity—presuppositions of every concept and every statement.

Existence exists and encompasses everything including all states of consciousness. The world exists independently of the mind and is there to be discovered by the mind. In order to be conscious, we must be conscious of something. There can be no consciousness if nothing exists. Consciousness, the faculty of perceiving that which exists, is the ability to discover, rather than to create, objects. Consciousness, a relational concept, presupposes the existence of something external to consciousness, something to be aware of. Initially, we become aware of something outside of our consciousness and then we become aware of our consciousness by contemplating on the process through which we became aware.

The axiom of identity says that to be is to be "something" in particular. Identity means that a thing is "this" rather that "that." What exists are entities and entities have identity. The identity of an entity is the sum of its characteristics or attributes, including its potentialities for change. To have identity is to have specific characteristics and to act in specific ways. What an entity can do depends on what it is. A thing must be something and only what it is. In order for knowledge to exist, there must be something to know (existence), someone to know it (consciousness), and something to know about it (identity). That existence exists implies that entities of certain types exist and that a person is capable of perceiving that entities of various types exist. Existence is identity and consciousness is identification.

All actions are caused by entities. Rand connects causality to the law of identity and finds necessity in the nature of the entity involved in the causal process. She explains that the law of causality is the law of identity applied to action and that the nature of an action is caused and circumscribed by the natures of the entities that act—a thing cannot act in contradiction to its nature.

The concept of entity is presupposed by all subsequent human thinking since entities comprise the content of the world men perceive. Rand contends that the universe is not caused, but simply is, and that cause and effect is a universal law of reality. Knowledge of causality involves apprehending the relationship between the nature of an entity and its method of action.

Rand explains that the metaphysically given (i.e., any fact inherent in existence apart from the human action) is absolute and simply is. The metaphysically given includes scientific laws and events taking place outside of the control of men. The metaphysically given must be accepted and cannot be changed.

She explains, however, that man has the ability to adapt nature to meet his requirements. Man can creatively rearrange the combination of nature's elements by enacting the required cause, the one necessitated by the immutable laws of existence. The man-made includes any object, institution, procedure, or rule of conduct created by man. Man-made facts are products of choice and can be evaluated and judged and then accepted or rejected and changed when necessary. Rand explains that the existence of consciousness is axiomatic, that consciousness is an attribute of certain living organisms, that consciousness has causal efficacy, and that there is a fundamental harmony between mind and body. To deny consciousness is self-refuting. That consciousness can direct action is evident through extrospection (i.e., observation) and introspection. Consciousness is connected to the body of a living organism, is nondeterministic, and is under direct volitional control. Rand contends that there is only one reality (not two opposing ones), that consciousness is awareness (rather than creation), and that the products of consciousness are the caused results of interactions between conscious organisms and reality.

She concludes that all arguments offered for the idea of God contradict or violate the three basic axioms. For example, the first-cause argument makes God's consciousness metaphysically prior to existence. She explains that existence precedes consciousness and that God is said to have (or be) consciousness, a faculty of awareness, not of creation. Consciousness is limited and finite. It is a faculty with a nature which includes specific instrumentations that enable it to achieve awareness. The attributes of omnipotence, omniscience, and infinity all violate identity, and the notion that God knows and acts without means violates causality. To advance God as maker of the universe is to postulate a consciousness that could exist without anything to be conscious of. This, she says, is a contradiction in terms. Dismissing cosmology from the realm of philosophy, Rand simply says that "existence exists" and that all the rest is epistemology, the means, rules, and methods of human knowledge.

Epistemology

Epistemology refers to the nature and starting point of knowledge, with the nature and correct exercise of reason, with reason's connection to the senses and perception, with the possibility of other sources of knowledge, and with the nature and attainability of certainty. Rand explains that reason is man's cognitive faculty for organizing perceptual data in conceptual terms through the use of the principles of logic. Knowledge exists when a person approaches the facts of reality through either perceptual observation or conceptualization.

Epistemology exists because man is a limited fallible being who learns in disjointed incremental steps and who therefore requires a proper procedure to acquire the knowledge necessary to act, survive, and flourish. A man does not have innate knowledge or instincts that will automatically and unerringly promote his well-being. He does not inevitably know what will help or hinder his life. He therefore needs to know how to acquire reliable and objective knowledge of reality. A man has to gain such knowledge in order to live. A person can only know from within the context of a human way of knowing. Because human beings are neither omniscient nor infallible, all knowledge is contextual in nature.

Sense perception is man's primary and direct form of what exists (i.e., of entities, including their characteristics, relations, and actions). Senses provide man with the start of the cognitive process. The senses neither err nor deceive a man. The senses do not judge, identify, or interpret, but simply respond to stimuli and report or present a "something" to one's consciousness. The evidence provided by the senses is an absolute, but a man must learn to use his mind to properly understand it. The task of identification belongs to reason operating with concepts. Man's senses only inform him that something is, but what it is must be learned by the mind which must discover the nature, the causes, the full context of his sensory material, and so on. It is only at the conceptual level, with respect to the "what," that the possibility of error arises. On the conceptual level, awareness can lead to mistaken judgments about what we perceive. Conceptualization entails an interpretation that may differ from reality. However, man's reason can be used to correct wrong judgments and expand one's knowledge of the world.

A man's senses react to the full context of the facts. Sense perceptions are valid in that they are perceptions of entities which exist. Sensations are caused by objects in reality and by a person's organs of perception. It is the purpose of the mind to analyze the perceptual evidence and to identify the nature of what is and the causes in effect.

A difference in sensory form among various perceivers is merely a difference in the form of perceiving the same object in reality. As long as a person perceives the underlying objects and relationships in reality in some form, the rest is the mind's work, not the work of the senses.

Any perceptual mechanism is limited. It follows that the object as perceived is the result of an interaction between external entities and a person's limited perceptual apparatus. Forms of perceptions are circumscribed by a person's physical abilities to receive information interacting with external objects in connection with the laws of causality. In other words, perceptual awareness is the product of a causal interaction between physical entities and physical sense organs.

Perceptual awareness marks the beginning of human knowledge. In order to understand the world in conceptual form, man must integrate his percepts into concepts. A concept integrates and condenses a number of percepts into a single mental whole. Although based on sensory percepts, human knowledge, being conceptual in nature, can depart from reality. The mind is not infallible nor automatic and can distort and be mistaken. A man can only obtain knowledge if he adheres to certain methods of cognition. The validity of man's knowledge depends upon the validity of his concepts.

Whereas concepts are abstractions (i.e., universals), everything that man apprehends is specific and concrete. Concept formation is based on the recognition of similarity among the existents being conceptualized. Rand explains that an individual perceptually discriminates and distinguishes specific entities from their background and from one another. A person then groups objects according to their similarities, regarding each of them as a unit. He then integrates a grouping of units into a single mental entity called a concept. The ability to perceive entities or units is man's distinctive method of cognition and the gateway to the conceptual level of man's consciousness. According to Rand, a concept is a mental integration of two or more units which are isolated according to one or more characteristics and united by a specific definition. A definition is the condensation of a large body of observations.

Whereas a concept is assigned precise identity through the use of a definition, the integration (i.e., the concept) itself is kept in mind by referring to it by a perceptual concrete (i.e., a word). Words are concrete audiovisual representations of abstractions called concepts. Words transfer concepts into mental entities whenever definitions give them identity. Language makes this type of integration possible.

Concept formation is largely a mathematical process. There is a connection between measurement and conceptualization. Similarity, an implicit form of measurement, is the relationship between two or more existents which possess the same attributes but in different measures or degrees. The mental process of concept formation consists in retaining the characteristics but omitting their measurements. The relevant measurement of a particular attribute must exist in some quantity, but may exist in any quantity. The measurements exist, but they are not specified. A concept is a mental integration of units possessing the same differentiating characteristics with their particular measurements omitted.

Rand states that a conceptual common denominator is made up of the characteristic(s) reducible to a unit of measurement by which a person distinguishes two or more existents from other existents possessing the characteristic(s). In other words, the comprehension of similarity is necessary for conceptualization.

Perceptual data lead to first level concepts. In turn, higher-level concepts are formed as abstractions from abstractions (i.e., from abstractions and subclassifications of previously formed concepts). Concepts differ from each other not only with respect to their referents but also in their distances from the perceptual level. Knowledge is hierarchical with respect to the order of concept formation. It consists of a set of concepts and conclusions ranked in order of logical dependence upon one another.

The last step in concept formation is definition. A definition identifies a concept's units by particularizing their fundamental attributes. A definition identifies the nature of the units subsumed under a concept. A definition differentiates a given concept from all others and keeps its units distinguished in a person's mind from all other existents. The differentiation must be limited to the essential characteristics. Rand employs Aristotle's "rule of fundamentality" when she states that the essential characteristic is the one that is responsible for, and therefore can explain, the greatest number of the unit's other distinguishing characteristics.

She explains that concepts are instruments to save space and time and to attain unit-economy through the condensation of data. Concepts have a metaphysical basis since consciousness is the ability of comprehending that which exists. Concepts result from a particular type of relationship between consciousness and existence.

Definitions are statements of factual data as compressed by a human consciousness. Definitions, as factual statements, involve the condensation of a multitude of observations of similarity and difference relationships. They are also contextual since they depend, in part, on the definer's context of knowledge. A new or revised definition does not invalidate the objective context of the old definition. It simply encompasses the requirements of an expanding cognitive context—the sum of cognitive elements conditioning an item to knowledge. Full context is the sum of available knowledge.

The essential characteristics of a concept are epistemological rather than metaphysical. Rand explains that concepts are neither intrinsic abstract entities existing independently of a person's mind nor are they nominal products of a person's consciousness, unrelated to reality. Concepts are epistemologically objective in that they are produced by man's consciousness in accordance with the facts of reality. Concepts are mental integrations of factual data. They are the products of a cognitive method of classification whose processes must be performed by a human being, but whose content is determined by reality. For Rand, essences are epistemological rather than metaphysical.

Rand contends that, although concepts and definitions are in one's mind, they are not arbitrary because they reflect reality, which is objective. Both consciousness in metaphysics and concepts in epistemology are real and part of ordinary existence—the mind is part of reality. She views concepts as open-ended constructs which subsume all information about their referents, including the information not yet discerned. New facts and discoveries expand or extend a person's concepts, but they do not overthrow or invalidate them. Concepts must conform to the facts of reality.

In order to be objective in one's conceptual endeavors, a human being must fully adhere to reality by applying certain methodological rules based on facts and proper for man's form of cognition. For man, a being with rational consciousness, the appropriate method for conforming to objective reality is reason and logic. In order to survive, man needs knowledge, and reason is his tool of knowledge.

Rand observes that human knowledge is limited and that humans are beings of bounded knowledge. It is because of this constraint that it is imperative for a man to identify the cognitive context of his analysis and conclusions. She points out that contextualism does not mean relativism and that context is what makes a properly specified conclusion objective. Certainty is a contextual evaluation.

Where do emotions fit in the Randian world? According to Rand, an emotion is an automatic response to a situation based on a person's perception, identification, and evaluation of the situation. Emotions are states of consciousness with bodily accompaniments and intellectual causes. Different from sensations, emotions are caused by what a person thinks. Emotions are the result of a man's value premises which result from the thinking that one has done in response to situations he has met in life. After a person has made a range of value judgments, he makes them automatic. Present in one's unconscious, value judgments affect man's evaluative and affective experiences. Emotions are reactions to a person's perceptions and are the automatic results of a mind's previous conclusions. Emotions are not tools of thinking—they are not a substitute for reason. Truth cannot be attained through one's feelings. However, emotions do play a key role in one's life. They do provide the means for enjoying life. A person could not achieve happiness without them.

Rand contends that people are born both conceptually (i.e., cognitively) and emotionally tabula rasa. For her, emotions are dependent phenomena and are the automatic products of man's value judgments. Rand believes that reason must program emotions properly if a person is to achieve happiness. She sees man with no inborn instincts and views reason as a person's only guide to knowledge. According to Rand, people do not have inborn emotions, temperaments, desires, personality characteristics, or ingrained behavior of any kind. She says that men's brains are not hardwired and that all human behavior is learned behavior.

Most contemporary philosophers, biologists, and evolutionary psychologists reject Rand's tabula rasa view of human emotions, urges, desires, and interests.

They believe that many of a person's predispositions, desires, interests, etc., are natural and stem from biological or genetic characteristics held in common by all people, most people, a segment of the population, or that distinguish one man's individual personality. It follows that people have individual propensities and personalities and that men are genetically influenced in what they do. A person has specific predispositions and traits that delimit what he can do and offer guidance with respect as to what he should do.

Today, there is general agreement that men have instinctual drives that influence (but do not determine) their behavior. Many of these instincts are generally beneficial, guide a person, and encourage his flourishing and happiness. Because a man has free will, he can choose to follow his direction-giving instincts or attempt to change or override them. By employing reason, a person can validate his instincts and emotions or he can identify them as personally destructive and/or in conflict with his chosen goals and values. In other words, a person's predispositions can be a proper and valid motivation if acting in accordance with them furthers his life and happiness. Furthermore, a person does not always have to depend upon his will. His habitual and instinctual responses may oftentimes be appropriate and only occasionally may have to be overridden. Valuations can be automatic or can be based on value judgments. When necessary a person can correct and override his instinctual and emotional responses by acting on an intellectual or rational level. The key is awareness of situations in which rational deliberation is called for.

Ethics: Deriving the "Ought" from the "Is"

Objectivism's ethical system rests upon the claim to have derived the "ought" from the "is." The defense of this claim starts by inquiring about the facts of existence and man's nature that result in value—that which one acts to gain and/or keep. The concept of value presupposes an entity capable of acting to attain a goal in the face of an alternative. Where no alternative exists, no goals and therefore no values are possible. The one basic alternative in the world is existence vs. nonexistence. Since the existence of inanimate matter is unconditional, it is only a living organism that faces the constant alternative of life or death. Inanimate matter may change forms, but it cannot go out of existence. When a living organism dies, however, its basic physical elements remain, but its life ceases to exist. Life, the process of self-sustaining and self-generated action, makes the concept of "value" meaningful. An organism's life is its standard of value. Whatever furthers its life is good and that which threatens it is evil.

The nature of a living entity determines what it ought to do. All living entities, with the exception of man, are determined by their nature to undertake automatically the actions necessary to sustain their survival. Man, like an animal or a plant, must act in order to live and must gain the values that his life requires. Man's distinctive nature, however, is that he has no automatic means of survival. Man does not function by automatic sensory or chemical reactions.

Thinking, the process of abstraction and conceptualization, is necessary for man's survival. Thinking, man's basic virtue, is exercised by choice—man is a being of volitional consciousness. Reason, the faculty that perceives, identifies, and integrates the material provided by the senses, does not work automatically. Man is free to think or not to think. The tool of thought is logic—the act of non-contradictory identification.

According to Rand, man has no innate knowledge and, therefore, must determine through thought the goals, actions, and values upon which his life depends. He must discover what will further his own unique and precious individual human life and what will harm it. Refusal to recognize and act according to the facts of reality will result in his destruction. The Randian view is that the senses enable man to perceive reality, that knowledge can only be gained through the senses, and that the senses are able to provide objectively valid knowledge of reality.

For man to survive, he must discern the principles of action necessary to direct him in his relationships with other men and with nature. Man's need for these principles is his need for a code of morality. Men are essentially independent beings with free wills; therefore, it is up to each individual to choose his code of values using the standard that is required for the life of a human being. If life as a man is one's purpose, he has the right to live as a rational being. To live, man must think, act, and create the values his life requires.

Rand explains that moral values are not subjective constructs nor intrinsic features of morality, but rather are objective. The good is neither an attribute of things in themselves nor of a person's emotional state, but is an evaluation made of the facts of reality by man's consciousness according to a rational standard of value. When one attributes moral value to something, he must address the questions of "to whom" and "for what." If something is a value, it must have a positive relationship to the end of a particular individual's life. Value is a function of the interaction between what is deemed valuable and the person to whom it is valuable. Value is neither totally internal nor completely external but is a function of a specific connection between external objects and an individual's ends.

Rand states that values reflect facts as evaluated by persons with respect to the goal of living. Whether or not a given object is a value depends upon its relationship to the end of a person's life. Life's conditionality is the basis of moral value. The thing in question must have certain attributes in order to further an individual's life, and the individual must seek his life, for that object to be valuable. The objectivity of value derives from the fact that particular kinds of action tend to promote human life. A specific object's value is a function of the factual relation between the object and a particular person's life. The valid attribution of value reflects a factual relationship.

The requirements of a man's survival are determined by reality and the good is an aspect of reality that has a positive relationship to a man's life. An object's value thus depends on what the object is and on the way in which it affects a particular person. It follows that a variety of different things can be objectively valuable to different persons.

Rand's theory of objective value is both functional (i.e., directed toward certain ends) and naturalistic. It is naturalistic because values stem from certain facts about the nature of human life. A man's consciousness and elements of the external world must connect in order to judge particular things as valuable.

Of course, from another perspective, it is individuals who are objective (or are not objective) with respect to their judgments regarding value. A value's objectivity also reflects the reality that values are the conclusions of a person's volitional consciousness and that individuals can be mistaken in their judgments and choices. An authentic value must derive both from a life-affirming relationship to a human being and must exist in a correct connection to his consciousness.

For Rand, the designation, objective, refers to both the functioning of the concept-formation process and to the output of that process when it is properly performed. A man's consciousness can acquire objective knowledge of reality by employing the proper means of reason in accordance with the rules of logic. When a correct cognitive process has been followed it can be said that the output of that process is objective. In turn, when the mind conforms to mind-independent reality, the theory of conceptual functioning being followed can be termed objective.

Rand explains that all abstractions stem from facts including the abstraction "value." All ideas, including the idea of value, are features of reality as they pertain to individuals. Values are ontologically objective when their attainment requires adhesion to reality and are metaphysically objective when they are discovered via objective conceptual processes.

Rand asks what fact or facts of reality give rise to the concept of value. She reasons that there must be something in perceptual reality that results in the concept value. She argues that it is only from observing other living things (and one's self introspectively) in the pursuit of their own lives that a person can perceive the referents of the term value. For example, people act to attain various material and other goods and determine their choices by reference to various goals, ends, standards, or principles.

For Rand, the concept of value depends upon and is derived from the antecedent concept of life. It is life that entails the possibility of something being good or bad for it. The normative aspect of reality arises with the appearance of life.

The fundamental fact of reality that gives rise to the concept of value is that living beings have to attain certain ends in order to sustain their lives. The facts regarding what enhances or hinders life are objective, founded on the facts of reality, and grounded in cognition. This should not be surprising because people do think, argue, and act as if normative issues can be decided by considering the facts of a situation.

Rand explains that the key to understanding ethics is found in the concept of value—it is thus located in epistemology. Her revolutionary theory of concepts is what directly leads her to innovations in the fields of value theory and ethics and moral philosophy.

Rand's theories of concepts, values, and ethics accurately reflect a man's epistemic nature. Objectivism endorses a theory of objective value and an ethics that reflects the primacy of existence. Because Rand identifies and comprehends the epistemological nature of concepts and the nature of the concept of value itself, it is possible for us to understand them and to explain to others the logical steps that are included in their formulation.

Without self-value, no other values are possible. Self-value has to be earned by thinking. Morality, a practical, selfish necessity, requires the use of man's rational faculty and the freedom to act on his judgments. A code of values accepted by rational choice is a code of morality—choice is the foundation of virtue. Happiness is the state of consciousness that results from the achievement of one's values.

Because men are creatures who think and act according to principle, a doctrine of rights ensures that an individual's choice to live by those principles is not violated by other human beings. For Rand, all individuals possess the same rights to freely pursue their own goals. Since a free man chooses his own actions, he can be held responsible for them.

Ayn Rand's Value Theory and Ethics: A Closer Look

According to Rand, all concepts are derived from facts, including the concept "value." All concepts, including the concept of value, are aspects of reality in relationship to individual men. Values are epistemologically objective when they are discovered through objective conceptual processes and are metaphysically objective when their achievement requires conformity to reality.

Ayn Rand defines value as that which one acts to gain and/or keep. A value is an object of action. In this sense we can say that everyone pursues values. This includes any goal-directed behavior. The term, value, thus can refer in a general, neutral, or descriptive sense to what is observable. We see people going after things. Initially, we do not consider whether or not people are properly employing their free will when they pursue their values. As children, we first get the idea of value implicitly from observation and introspection. We then move from an initial descriptive idea of value toward a normative definition of value that includes the notion that a legitimate value serves one's life. Because reality is the source and standard of rational values, exposure to reality is the means by which we discover them.

The first generic and descriptive idea of value ties value to reality and is a precondition to an objective and normative perspective on value. The second, narrower way of looking at value adds the words "which furthers one's life" and the idea of the proper and rational use of a person's free will. The second definition or Objectivist concept of value is a derivative or inference from the first. The first view of value comes before the knowledge of life as the standard of value. The second view of value gives normative guidance and provides an objective standard to evaluate the use of one's free will.

Each derivative value exists in a value chain or network in which every value (except for the ultimate value) leads to other values and thus serves both as an end and as a means to other values. A biological ends-means process leads to the ultimate end of the chain, which, for a living entity, is its life. For a human individual, the end is survival and happiness, and the means are values and virtues that serve that end. Values and virtues are common to, and necessary for, the flourishing of every human person. However, each individual will require them to a different degree. Each man employs his individual judgments to determine the amount of time and effort that should go into the pursuit of various values and virtues. Finding the proper combination and proportion is the task for each person in view of his own talents, potentialities, and circumstances. Values and virtues are necessary for a flourishing life and are objectively discernable, but the exact weighting of them for a specific person is highly individualized.

In order for a chain of values to make sense, there must be some end in itself and ultimate value for which all other values are means. An end in itself is something that we pursue for its own sake rather than pursuing it for the sake of something else. An ultimate value is sought for its own sake and for the sake of which we pursue everything else. An infinite progression or chain of ends and means toward a nonexistent end is a metaphysical and epistemological impossibility. All must converge on an ultimate value.

There are some values that we pursue both for their own sake and for the sake of something further. Such a value is an end in itself but is not an ultimate value. A value in a chain or hierarchy can at once be a whole and at the same time a part. Life, one's ultimate value, is a process of action that has certain requirements such as productive work, friendship, love, art, and so on. A person's work life, love life, home life, social life, etc., are necessary components of the action of one's life. Each part or ingredient is a means to the end of life while, at the same time, being part of what living is. The process of life subsumes each of its components. It follows that all elements of one's life are both means and ends in themselves, but they are not the ultimate value. They are means to the whole of one's life. Every aspect of a person's life is an end in itself that also serves the further end of maintaining the overall process of which it is a component. One's life itself in total is the ultimate and regulatory value of all of a person's other values.

An ultimate value is necessary if a person is to make rational choices. One ultimate value is required for a person to decide how to act. Evaluation necessitates teleological measurement in order to make our potential values commensurable. An ultimate value is needed by which a person can decide to apportion his time and effort and to judge the relevant amounts and proportions of each. Teleological measurement is required in order to establish a graded or ordinal relationship of means to ends. A person must be able to make various values, in the form of means and ends, comparable in order to decide what to do in inevitable cases of conflicts. When different values come into conflict a person refers to a higher value in order to resolve the conflict.

An individual's task is to choose from among numerous values to find the most appropriate for himself. A person must make specific choices with respect to his career, his relationships, and so on. A hierarchy of values helps people make judgments regarding what to do or to pursue. To do this, an individual must assign a weight, either explicitly or implicitly, to his values. Values need to be weighted or ranked in terms of ordinal numbers. A man requires a prioritized enumeration of values. He must judge the ultimate contribution to the value of his life that exists at the apex of his hierarchy.

A man needs ideas regarding what to pursue in life and ideas with respect to the required means to get what he is seeking. Each person must form values, hierarchize them, and pursue them. A man must expose himself to many aspects of reality in order to discover the things that he loves (i.e., his values). After a man immerses himself in observational reality he must then choose to delimit them to those that most excite and interest him and ignite his soul. He needs to identify the crucial indispensable values to his life and distinguish them from lesser values and nonvalues. He requires an explicit value hierarchy and should organize his time, effort, and lifestyle around that hierarchy. A person's top values get a disproportionate amount of his attention, the next highest level of values gets the next call, and so on down his hierarchy. By eliminating nonvalues, filling his life with things that he loves, and doing those things in the order in which he loves them, a man is on track to accomplish what he wants to do with his finite life. Of course, he should select and pursue values that are rational and metaphysically appropriate for him. Whether or not the means chosen to achieve one's values will be sufficient is determined by objective reality.

A value is an object of goal-directed action. The fact that a person has values implies the existence of his goal-directed actions. Values are distinct from goals despite the fact that in general parlance goals and values are often used interchangeably. One's goals depend upon one's values, and for a rational person values depend upon the judgment of his mind. A man acts in order to achieve goals that result in his obtaining values. Actions are performed in response to one's values and are undertaken to achieve some goal or end.

To be a value means to be good for someone and for something. Life is one's fundamental value because life is conditional and requires a particular course of action to maintain it. Something can be good or bad only to a living organism, such as a human being, acting to survive. Man's life is the ultimate value and the standard of value for a human being.

A man must make value judgments in order to act. He must choose in the face of an alternative that having or not having the value makes some difference to him. The difference it makes is the alternative he faces. A value exists in a chain of values and must have some ending point. There must be some fundamental difference or fundamental alternative that marks the cessation of one's value chain. There must be some basic alternative that makes no additional difference or, stated differently, a fundamental difference that makes all the difference. It is his life, the process of self-sustaining action, that is the fundamental alternative at the end of a man's value chain. One's life is the alternative that underpins all of his evaluative judgments. It is his ultimate value and the proper end of all the valuer does. One's life is not pursued for the sake of anything beyond itself. It is gained and maintained through a constant process of self-sustaining action.

Ethics, a code of values to rationally guide man's choices and actions, is an objective, metaphysical necessity for a man's survival. A proper ethics gives practical guidance to help people think and direct their lives. Ethics aids a man in defining and attaining his values, goals, and happiness. A man needs ethics because he requires values to survive. The telos of ethics is a person's own survival and happiness. The realm of ethics includes those matters that are potentially under a man's control. A man's uncoerced volition is necessary to have an objective theory of morality. He can discover values only through a volitional process of reason.

Rand's ethics identifies the good and bad according to the rational standard of value of man's life qua man. Her Objectivist Ethics focuses on what is, in reality, good or best for each unique individual human being. Such an ethics is rational, objective, and personal. Accordingly, a man's goal should be to become the best possible person in the context of who and what he is and of what is possible for him.

Rand explains that objective and contextual knowledge, including ethical knowledge, can be obtained through rational means. A person requires conceptual knowledge in the form of abstractions to guide his actions. Moral concepts necessarily come into play when one acts. A man needs to acquire knowledge of external reality and self-knowledge in order to discover and choose his values, goals, and actions. He requires knowledge of what is possible and of the potential means to achieve that which is possible.

To acquire knowledge, a person needs to function at a certain level of abstraction. A man subsumes concretes under abstractions and his hierarchy of abstractions leads to general evaluative principles. A principle is a proposition that integrates facts, observations, experiences, and knowledge about subjects and cases. A man needs an adequate set of principles to provide basic guidance in living well. He must consciously identify the principles he wants to live by and must critically evaluate his values and principles.

Rational moral principles guide us toward values and are essential for achieving moral integrity, character, and happiness. Living by rational principles tends to make principled thought and actions habitual. When we habitually act on sound moral principles we develop virtues and incorporate our moral orientation into our character. Rand connects virtues to the objective requirements of man's survival and flourishing. Moral principles are needed because the standard of survival and flourishing is too abstract. To act in a concrete situation, a man needs to have some basic view of what he is acting for and how he should act. Because actions are subsumed under principles, it is imperative to adopt and automatize good principles. Acting on principles cultivates corresponding virtues which, in turn, leads to value attainment, flourishing, and happiness.

Focus involves a man's decision to activate his mind. A person can choose to make a self-starting decision to stay open to the positive aspects of reality that enable him to gain and keep life-promoting values. Of course, he will also want to be alert for negative aspects of reality that should be avoided. It takes effort to stay in focus by using your free will to mobilize your consciousness and mental resources. Although focus is not automatic and is demanding, it is rewarding, natural, and enjoyable. It takes effort, but does not involve pain or suffering. To be in focus does not involve continuous mental work. Focus, a quality of alertness, is a precondition of awareness of reality and of cognition. It is one's readiness to direct his attention. Focus is immediately available to each individual and has no correlation with his ability to conceptualize, to use logic, to be objective, and so on. Focus comes before any knowledge of methodology. Focus simply means that one is ready to think and to learn and to use the best approach known to him. Focus means readiness to proceed and to turn on the mental mechanism. It is volitional. It is like waking up and saying to yourself that you are alert and ready for whatever the world has in store for you. You are ready to call on whatever ability and power you have and are ready to spring into action. Although mental activity depends upon and presupposes focus, focus does not necessarily involve mental activity. Naturally, when a person is in focus, he will discover many reasons to use his cognitive abilities.

The choice to focus enters both in the formation of one's ideas, values, and principles, and in keeping his knowledge and values active in mind so that they can frame his actions. Free will is used in the choice to focus or not when determining how one will reach factual and value judgments. A person must be alert for opportunities to form one's ideas, values, and principles. When a man uses volition to focus and think before he decides to accept ideas, he is evoking a causal process. A man must also use his free will to be in focus for his thinking to guide his actions. Free will and focus are indispensable in both the critical thought process and in translating thinking into action.

A person uses his free will to determine his focus and how logical to be. Through the employment of his free will, a man forms and selects the principles that underlie his actions. Focusing one's mind, staying in focus, thinking, and critically assessing one's principles includes introspection to identify and assess the principles that one has automatized.

A man who thinks in principles makes himself aware of the best means of attaining his ends in the full context of his life. Moral principles are true in a delimited context. Recognizing the moral context of a situation precedes one's chosen actions in that situation. A man should not evade relevant knowledge nor drop context when he acts. Moral principles are absolute within the context in which they are defined and applied. Of course, some cases will fall outside the context in which they are defined and applicable. It is therefore essential for a person to validate his principles and to understand the contexts that give rise to these principles.

Thinking is needed in order to understand the facts of a situation and to apply appropriate principles to the circumstances. For example, honesty, as a principle, states that it is immoral to misrepresent the truth in a context in which a person's goal is to obtain values from others. It follows that in a different context in which a person is attempting to use deceit or force in order to gain values from an individual, it is appropriate for the wronged individual to select self-defense as his appropriate principle instead of honesty. The context is different from one calling for honesty on his part.

Honesty is an essential principle because the proper end of a man's actions is his own objective flourishing. The moral appropriateness of honesty is grounded in metaphysics. A person must focus on what reality requires if he is to attain his ends. A person should tell the relevant truth. What the relevant truth is depends on the type of relationship a person has with the individual with whom he is dealing.

In Rand's biocentric ethics, moral behavior is judged in relation to achieving specific ends with the final end being an individual's life or flourishing. The act of deciding necessitates the investigation of how an action pertains to what is best for one's own life. This is not done in a duty-based ethic that is limited to precepts and rules. In a duty-oriented ethical system, rules or duties are placed between a person and reality. In a biocentric ethics what is moral is the understood and the chosen rather than the imposed and the obeyed. Principles are valuable ethical concepts that do not require imperatives or obligations as their justification.

Altruist moralities hold that morality is painful and difficult and involves ideas such as self-abnegation and self-sacrifice. Contrariwise, an egoist morality, such as the one found in Objectivism, maintains that morality is natural, attractive, and enjoyable. Of course, there is work involved in staying in focus, acquiring knowledge, formulating moral principles, and applying them in the appropriate contexts. Morality is demanding but it is also indispensable and rewarding. Remember, the purpose of morality is to enjoy life, flourish, and be happy.

Values and Virtues

Rand explains that to live, men must hold three ruling values—reason, purpose, and self-esteem. These values imply all of the virtues required by a man's life. Rationality, the primary virtue, is the recognition of objective reality, commitment to its perception, and the acceptance of reason as a man's only judge of values and guide to knowledge and action. Independence, the acceptance of one's intellectual responsibility for one's own existence, requires that a man form his own judgments and that he support himself by the work of his own mind. Honesty, the selfish refusal to seek values by faking reality, recognizes that the unreal can have no value. Integrity, the refusal to permit a breach between thought and action, acknowledges the fact that man is an indivisible, integrated entity of mind and body. Justice, a form of faithfulness to reality, is the virtue of granting to each man that which he objectively deserves. Justice is the expression of man's rationality in his dealings with other men and involves seeking and granting the earned. A trader, a man of justice, earns what he receives and neither gives nor takes the undeserved. Just as he does not work except in exchange for something of economic value, he also does not give his love, friendship, or esteem except in trade for the pleasure he receives from the virtues of individuals he respects. Love, friendship, and esteem, as moral tributes, are caused and must be earned. Productiveness, the virtue of creating material values, is the art of translating one's thoughts and goals into reality. Pride, the total of the preceding virtues, can be thought of as moral ambitiousness.

Capitalism and Individual Rights

Rand's justification of capitalism is that it is a system based on the logically derived code of morality outlined above—a code of morality that recognizes man's metaphysical nature and the supremacy of reason, rationality, and individualism. The ruling principle of capitalism is justice. The overall social effect—the fact that individuals and groups who live under capitalism prosper—is simply a byproduct or secondary consequence. Political and economic systems and institutions which encourage and protect individual rights, freedom, and happiness are proper systems.

A right is a moral principle defining and sanctioning a man's freedom of action in a social context. According to Rand, rights are innate and can be logically derived from man's nature and needs. The state is not involved in the creation of rights and simply exists to protect an individual's natural rights. There are no group rights—only individual rights. Group rights are arbitrary and imply special interests.

Humans are material beings who require material goods to sustain their existence. If one's life is the standard, man has the right to live and pursue values as his survival requires. He has the right to work for and keep the fruits of his labor—the right of property. Without property rights, no other rights are possible. A man who has no right to the product of his efforts is not free to pursue his happiness and has no means to sustain his life.

A violation of a man's property rights is an expression of force against the man himself. The purpose of government is to protect man's rights (including property rights) and enforce contractual agreements—a breach of contract is an indirect use of force. The state's function is thus restricted to the retaliatory use of force.

Under Randian capitalism, which historically has never existed, there is a complete separation of state and economics. Men deal with each other voluntarily by individual choice and free trade to their mutual benefit. The profit motive is just and moral. Profit is made through moral virtue and measures the creation of wealth by the profit-earner. The market price is objectively determined in the free market and represents the lowest price a buyer can find and the highest price a seller can obtain. Freedom guarantees that both parties will benefit—no one is willing to enter into a one-sided bargain to his detriment. A person's wealth under capitalism depends on his productive achievements and the choice of others to recognize them. Rewards are tied to production, ability and merit. A producer can do with his wealth what he chooses. Charity is rational, objective, and genuine when, rather than being offered indiscriminately, it is offered only to those who deserve it. Generosity toward those who are innocent victims of injustice or who are fighting against adversity is proper. It is wrong to help persons with no virtue. By giving unconditionally you deceive the recipient into thinking that wealth and happiness are free. Charity must be voluntary. Forced redistribution will result in the curtailment of effort of the productive and a decrease in the amount of real wealth (i.e., real virtue) within society.

Esthetics

Rand's philosophy extends to esthetics, the philosophy of art. Her goal is to place esthetics on a logical foundation. For Rand, art is a concretization of metaphysics, with each work of art projecting the artist's view of the world and of man's possibilities in that world. Objectivism holds that art has a rational, practical, worldly purpose and fulfills a spiritual need that humans have. Objectivism's rational esthetics teaches that art is for man's sake. The purpose of art is to show that an idea can exist in reality. The artwork is thus a concrete embodiment of the artist's philosophy. Works of art concretize philosophical ideas.

Rand defines art as a selective re-creation of reality according to the artist's metaphysical value judgments. These metaphysical value judgments may be viewed as the bridge between metaphysics and ethics. An artist chooses those aspects of human nature he regards as indicative of human nature. The artist selects from the various available art forms (i.e., literature, painting, sculpture, music, drama, dance, and song) and picks a subject that is significant to him.

The content of the artwork is based on an artist's sense of life which is his emotional evaluation of the world. Rand explains that every individual has a subconscious view of the nature of the universe and of life. An artist creates from his sense of life, and the reader, viewer, or listener responds from his. A sense of life is subconsciously formed through the process of emotionally integrating innumerable emotions and value judgments over one's life. People respond to art in deeply personal terms.

Art brings abstractions down to a perceptual level and makes it possible to grasp complex abstractions in the form of a concrete. Dropping what he considers unimportant, the artist retains only what he judges to be significant. By means of the art product, abstractions acquire the directness of a perceivable concrete.

According to Rand, the reader, viewer, or listener reacts to a work of art on the basis of the level of agreement or disagreement of his sense of life with that of the creator. If the philosophical ideas embodied in the art are congruent with one's own ideas, he is likely to experience a sense of affirmation. Art that objectifies an individual's metaphysics tends to inspire that person and provide him with emotional fuel.

Rand distinguishes between the Romantic and Naturalistic schools of art. Whereas Romanticism recognizes that man possesses the faculty of volition, Naturalism is the esthetic expression of determinism. Romanticism exalts heroes and glorifies the best of man. Naturalism views man as weaker than nature and destined to be destroyed. Rand emphasizes and favors the superior value of Romantic art. Romantic art is fuel for man's soul. Such art expresses ethical themes since volition involves choice and the potential for moral conflict. Romantic art is concerned with the power of moral values in shaping character and deals with universal, timeless issues of man's existence.

Rand adopts the Aristotelian perspective that fiction is more important than history because fiction can portray men and events as they might be and ought to be rather than as they are or have been. In her esthetics, Rand's primary focus is on the art of literature. Her esthetic judgments are not as fully developed with respect to other art forms.

Conclusion

Despite inciting a number of vehement and critical commentaries, Rand's controversial, original, and systematic philosophical positions should be taken seriously and treated with respect. She persuasively expounds a fully integrated defense of capitalism and the component metaphysical, epistemological, psychological, ethical, social, political, cultural, and historical conditions necessary for its establishment and survival. Rand presents Objectivism as an integrated new system of thought with an organized, hierarchical structure. Whatever one's ultimate evaluation of her theories, Rand's unique vision should be considered worthy of comprehensive, scholarly examination.

Ayn Rand was a philosophical system-builder who consistently integrated the various aspects of her clearly written and compelling work. Rand's view of the world and of human possibility in the world is at the heart of her system. She sees a benevolent world that is open to man's achievement and success. Happiness and great accomplishment are possible in the world. To succeed man must comprehend the nature of the world and of man and must define, choose, and passionately pursue rational values. Moral greatness is possible for each of us if we rationally strive to live up to our potential, whatever that potential may be. A person who selects rational values and who chooses ends and means consonant with the nature of reality and with the integrity of his own consciousness exemplifies a moral ideal and can certainly be viewed as heroic. As a rational goal, Rand's ideal of moral greatness is available to every human being.

Recommended Reading

By Rand:

The Voice of Reason. Edited by Leonard Peikoff. New York: The New American Library, 1989.
Philosophy: Who Needs It. Edited by Leonard Peikoff. New York: Bobbs-Merrill, 1982.
The Romantic Manifesto. New York: The New American Library, 1971.
Capitalism: The Unknown Ideal. New York: The New American Library, 1967.
Introduction to Objectivist Epistemology. New York: The Objectivist, 1967.
The New Left. New York: Signet, 1963.

Journals of Ayn Rand. Edited by David Harriman. New York: Plume, 1997.
For the New Intellectual. New York: Random House, 1961.
Atlas Shrugged. New York: Random House, 1957.

On Rand:

Badhwar, Neera K. *Is Virtue Only a Means to Happiness? An Analysis of Virtue and Happiness in Ayn Rand's Writings.* Poughkeepsie, N.Y.: The Objectivist Center, 2001.
Baker, James T. *Ayn Rand.* Boston: Twayne, 1987.
Binswanger, Harry. *The Ayn Rand Lexicon: Objectivism from A to Z.* New York: New American Library, 1988.
Den Uyl, Douglas, and Douglas Rasmussen, eds. *The Philosophical Thought of Ayn Rand.* Chicago: University of Illinois Press, 1984.
Ellis, Albert. *Is Objectivism a Religion?* New York: Lyle Stuart, 1968.
Erickson, Peter. *The Stance of Atlas: An Examination of the Philosophy of Ayn Rand.* New York: Herakles Pub., 1997.
Gladstein, Mimi. *The Ayn Rand Companion.* Westport, Conn.: Greenwood, 1984.
———. *The New Ayn Rand Companion, Revised and Expanded Edition.* Westport, Conn.: Greenwood Publishing Group, 1999.
Gotthelf, Allan. *On Ayn Rand.* Belmont, Calif.: Wadsworth, 2000.
Greiner, Donna, and Theodore B. Kinni. *Ayn Rand and Business.* New York: W. W. Norton & Company, 2001.
Hamil, Virginia L. L. *In Defense of Ayn Rand.* Brookline, Mass: New Beacon, 1990.
Kelley, David. *The Contested Legacy of Ayn Rand.* Poughkeepsie, N.Y.: The Objectivist Center, 2000.
Long, Roderick T. *Reason and Value: Aristotle versus Rand.* Poughkeepsie, N.Y.: The Objectivist Center, 2000.
Machan, Tibor, R. *Ayn Rand.* New York: Peter Lang, 1999.
Merrill, Ronald E. *The Ideas of Ayn Rand.* Chicago: Open Court, 1991.
Nyquist, Greg S. *Ayn Rand Contra Human Nature.* iUniverse.com, 2001.
O'Neill, William F. *With Charity Toward None.* New York: Philosophical Library, 1991.
Peikoff, Leonard. *Objectivism: The Philosophy of Ayn Rand.* New York: Dutton, 1991.
Porter, Tom. *Ayn Rand's Theory of Knowledge.* Tom Porter, 1999.
Robbins, John W. *Answer to Ayn Rand.* Washington, D.C.: Mount Vernon Publishing, 1974.
———. *Without a Prayer: Ayn Rand and the Close of Her System.* Unicoi, Tenn.: Trinity Foundation, 1997.
Ryan, Scott. *Objectivism and the Corruption of Rationality: A Critique of Ayn Rand's Epistemology.* Lincoln, Neb.: Writers Club Press, 2003.
Sciabarra, Chris Matthew. *Ayn Rand: Her Life and Thought.* Poughkeepsie, N.Y.: The Objectivist Center, 1999.
———. *Ayn Rand: The Russian Radical.* University Park: Pennsylvania State University Press, 1995.
Seddon, Fred. *Ayn Rand, Objectivists, and the History of Philosophy.* Lanham, Md.: Rowman & Littlefield, 2003.
Yang, Michael B. *Reconsidering Ayn Rand.* Cincinnati: Enclair Publishing, 2000.

PART II

SCHOLARLY PERSPECTIVES

4

The Methodological Debate between Carl Menger and the German Historicists

Samuel Bostaph

Introduction

During the past thirty years methodology and methodological issues have become a significant preoccupation of prominent economists in almost every field of the discipline. Most attention seems to focus on the question of the "realism" of economic theory and/or the adequacy of its "foundations" or basic assumptions.

General questions pertaining to "realism" and complaints about the "unreality" of economic theory are not new ones. In the nineteenth century, the historical school accused the classical school of economics and then the Austrians of producing "unrealistic dogma" and "fantasies" divorced from empirical reality. In return, Carl Menger criticized the historicists for their incapacity to transcend that same empirical reality, that is, for their failure to deal with what he termed "economic reality." The resulting bitter and inconclusive dispute between the two factions became known to economists as the *Methodenstreit* ("Conflict of Methods").

One of its major consequences has been to nurture the apparently widespread belief that methodological conflicts are at best sterile and irresolvable and, at worst, positively counterproductive. Such a belief can hardly lead to a sanguine view of current discussions and arguments.

It is the main purpose of this chapter to present an analysis of the Methodenstreit that both explains its inconclusiveness and suggests how it and similar disputes may be more productively evaluated.[1] It is hoped that by so doing, the good name of methodology may be restored to some extent and current disputes placed in a more favorable light. The major argument of this paper is that opposed epistemological positions underlay the methodological and morphological

113

issues actually debated by parties to the Methodenstreit. Unfortunately, neither faction clearly and explicitly recognized that the source of their differences in methodological beliefs was epistemological. To this is attributed the inconclusiveness of the debate and the participants' preoccupation with more subsidiary matters. It is contended that the failure to identify the epistemological aspect of the conflict has led historians of economic thought to assessments that are inadequate as explanations of the quarrel's value, sources, and basic rationale.

The next section summarizes the historical aspects of the Methodenstreit, speculates on its genesis, and notes its historical results. The section on previous assessments classifies and summarizes previous assessments of the conflict. The section on epistemological differences between disputants offers a new and substantially original thesis concerning the questions really at issue between the Historical and the Austrian schools and the requirements for their solution, and the section on errors in previous assessment concludes with a brief evaluation of Menger's part in the debate.

History of the Dispute

The Methodenstreit took place in the form of an exchange of publications between Carl Menger (1840-1921) and Gustav von Schmoller (1838-1917). Menger, the founder and chief spokesman of the Austrian school of economic theorists, directed an attack in 1883 against the German Historical school, of which Schmoller was the leader and primary spokesman at the time. The attack occurred in an essay on the subject of the appropriate goals and methodology of the social sciences, titled *Untersuchungen über die Methode der Socialwissenschaften und der Politischen Ökonomie insbesondere* (Menger 1883). In that essay Menger not only presented his own views on the nature, problems, limits, and methodology appropriate to economics and other social sciences, but he incisively criticized those of the historical school.

The publication of Menger's essay was anything but gratefully received by the historicists. Gustav Schmoller reviewed the book in his journal and expressed strong opposition to key elements of Menger's position (Schmoller 1883). The rebuttal to this adverse review took the form of a series of sixteen letters to a friend, published under the title *Die Irrthümer des Historismus in der Deutschen Nationalökonomie* (Menger 1884). The letters were highly polemical in nature and consisted mainly of a restatement of Menger's position on each question in dispute, laced with a few choice invectives directed against Schmoller.[2]

Not surprisingly, Schmoller took enough offense from Menger's polemic that he closed the debate abruptly by not reviewing the book and returning the review copy of *Die Irrthümer* to Menger with an insulting cover letter that was subsequently printed in Schmoller's journal.

Despite the brevity of the debate itself, the specific publications through which it was conducted were representative of much more than merely a difference of opinion on methodological issues between the spokesmen of two rival schools. They represented a fundamental opposition between two basic methodological tendencies, the historical-empirical and the abstract-theoretical.

Menger's initial attack was directed not at Schmoller, but at the entire school of economists and historians of which Schmoller happened to be the leading contemporary representative. This school—the historical school—originated in Germany in the 1840s with Wilhelm Roscher and existed until well after the turn of the century. On the other hand, Menger's school—the Austrian school—began with his first publications in the 1870s and still exists in the form of fifth and sixth generations of scholars today (Dolan 1976).

If the historicists had not been so critical of the classical school and so intolerant of any methodologies that they interpreted to exemplify the "excesses" of the deductive method of that school, Menger might have had less reason to open the debate with an attack on the historical school itself. Additionally, animus between members of each school continued to exist after the formal end of the debate in 1884 and surfaced in the form of sporadic statements, book reviews, and so on, for at least two decades thereafter. Rather than just a conflict between two scholars, the Methodenstreit represented a general clash between the entire German Historical school and the Austrian school.

The genesis of the conflict is by no means as easy to document as its denoument. The publication of Menger's *Principles of Economics* in 1871 received little response outside Austria (Menger 1871). (It was not translated into English until seventy-nine years after its publication.) In Germany, the historical school was growing in influence and becoming increasingly critical of any faction which had any affinity to, or smacked of, theoretical analysis in the tradition of "Manchestertum." Despite the obvious differences in general methodology employed by Menger compared with that of the English Classical school, the stigma of an "abstract-deductive" system was enough to preclude his work from consideration by the "more advanced" or "modern" school—as the historicists (and especially Schmoller) viewed themselves.

This situation must have been an intolerable one for Menger, given the originality and ambitiousness of his own work. He had, of course, intended the *Principles* to be only the first, general part of a comprehensive treatise on economic theory. But as Hayek explains (1934, 405): "under these conditions it was only natural that Menger should consider it more important to defend the method he had adopted against the claims of the Historical School to possess the only appropriate instrument of research, than to continue the work on the *Grundsätze.*" Perhaps this can be more readily seen if the reception of Menger's *Principles* by the German journals of the time is reviewed.[3]

In the early 1870s only four professional journals devoted to economics were published in Germany: *Jahrbücher für Nationalökonomie und Statistik; Vierteljahrschrift für Volkswirtschaff und Kulturgeschichte; Zeitschrift für die gesammte Staatswissenschaft;* and *Jahrbuch für Gesetzgebung, Verwaltung und Volkswirtschaft,* known as *Schmollers Jahrbuch* and an organ for the historical school. Of these four, only the first three published reviews of the *Principles* (*Jahrbücher,* 342–45; *Vierteljahrschrift,* 194–205; *Zeitschrift,* 183–84). The review in the *Zeitschrift für die gesammte Staatswissenschaft* missed the central idea of the book while that in the *Vierteljahrschrift für Volkswirtschaft und Kulturgeschichte* did little better, agreeing with Menger's method but finding no innovation in his theory of value. The journal founded in 1863 by the historicist Bruno Hildebrand (and the best of the four), the *Jahrbücher für Nationalökonomie und Statistik* reviewed the *Principles* by deploring the writing of short textbooks on economics by young men, while *Schmollers Jahrbuch,* the principal historicist organ, did not review the book at all.

Menger must have regarded his work as a positive contribution and an addition to the research previously published in Germany. Had he not dedicated the book to Wilhelm Roscher "with respectful esteem" and concluded his preface with the following tribute? (Menger 1871, 49): "Let this work be regarded, therefore, as a friendly greeting from a collaborator in Austria, and as a faint echo of the scientific suggestions so abundantly lavished on us Austrians by Germany through the many outstanding scholars she has sent us and through her excellent publications."

One can imagine the frustrations of the young author (Menger was only thirty-one when he published the *Principles)* at the reception of his efforts. It would be entirely understandable for him to investigate the question of the sources of the poor reception of such an original work.

Not only that, but given his own strong convictions concerning the methodology proper to the derivation of general economic theory, he had ample incentive to publish his views in the form of an essay. He would have had even more reason to publish such a work when he concluded, as he did, that his *Principles* was poorly received because the historicists granted no legitimacy to his method while failing to recognize the limitations of their own. As Hayek remarks (1934, 405), "he might well have thought that it would be wasted effort to continue [his work on his treatise on economic theory] while the question of principle was not decided." Whatever his reasons, the *Untersuchungen* was published in 1883; and this time *Schmollers Jahrbuch* not only did not fail to print a review as it had failed to do of his *Principles,* but Schmoller himself wrote that review.

The actual issues considered by Schmoller and Menger in the course of the conflict between their schools included: (1) the criteria for designating economic history, economic theory, economic policy, public finance, and statistics as "branches" of economics; (2) the scope and goals of each "branch"; (3) the usefulness of theory in the explanation of empirical events; (4) collectivistic versus individualistic conceptions of economic phenomena; (5) the nature of institutions and their development; (6) the extent to which historical and statistical material—as opposed to the experience of everyday life—are germane to the abstractions of economic theory; (7) the related question of the relevance for economic theory of the complexity of man's psychological nature and the impact of his cultural setting on it; and (8) the "necessity," or causal status, of economic laws and the testing of such laws (and economic theory itself) with empirical data (Bostaph 1976).

The Methodenstreit was inconclusive at the time, and later assessments (to be reviewed in the next section of this chapter) by historians of economic thought have been generally negative. Because of his influence, Schmoller was able to exclude all adherents of the Austrian school and the "Austrian method" from academic posts in Germany (Mises 1969). Menger was mainly preoccupied for the remainder of his life with the questions raised in the dispute and with other methodological considerations. To this fact has been attributed his failure to complete the writing and publication of his own general economic treatise (Hayek 1934, 406, 415; 1968a, 460; 1968b, 125–26).

Previous Assessments

Assessments of the general historical and methodological value of the Methodenstreit published by historians of economic thought and others may be usefully divided into three categories: (1) those that argue that it was largely a waste of valuable time by the parties involved (Wicksell 1958; Gide and Rist 1948; Schumpeter 1954; Hutchison 1953, 1973; Seligman 1962; Lekachman 1959; Newman 1952; Landreth 1976; Ekeland and Hebert, 1975); (2) those that take no position on the value of the controversy itself, but merely attempt to outline it and comment on the issues and implications (Ingram 1967; Haney 1949; Rima 1978; Roll 1974; Oser and Blanchfield, 1975); and (3) those that indicate the controversy was an important and valuable one (Böhm-Bawerk 1890; Seager 1893; Hayek 1968b).

Reasons given for viewing the dispute as a "fruitless" waste of time are varied. Knut Wicksell sees the choice of method to be a pragmatic question not worth such a "literary feud" (Wicksell, 193). Charles Rist makes clear his own belief in a place for the historical method coequal with the abstract approach favored by the classical school (which he also identifies as Menger's method) (Gide and Rist, 400).

This status of the two methods is supported by Ben Seligman (Seligman, 274), "since there ought to be enough room for both approaches in a field that pretends to deal with human society in motion"; by Robert Lekachman (Lekachman, 249) because "some problems yield to one technique and other problems to its alternative"; and by Harry Landreth (Landreth, 275) because "a healthily developing discipline requires a variety of methodological approaches."[4] Joseph A. Schumpeter regards the clash as one that (Schumpeter, 814) "was about precedence and relative importance and might have been settled by allowing every type of work to find the place to which its weight entitled it."[5]

In a 1973 article, T. W. Hutchison identifies the differences in method advocated by the two schools as determined by the differences in the field of studies of interest to each. He argues that Menger's methodology is suited to the study of microeconomics, while that of the historicists is suited to the study of macroeconomics. Thus, the Methodenstreit was "a clash of interests regarding what was the most important and interesting subject to study."[6] He concludes that the two methods must be combined in order to find answers to the important economic questions in all fields. A more naive version of this conclusion is that of Philip Charles Newman (Newman, 195) that "the inductive method is an indispensable complement to the deductive."

Those writers who take no explicit position on either the historical or methodological value of the Methodenstreit generally present the same or similar assessments of its nature as do those who denigrate it. John Kells Ingram (Ingram, 235) concludes that the differences that existed between the two factions "[were] mainly differences of emphasis [of how important theory is and what are the practical economic sciences] due to radical temperamental differences." He argues that the dispute served to reveal similarities in the views of Schmoller and Menger in that each method had its place and each was essential to the development of economics. Lewis Haney argues that each method has its place and prescribes a need for both inductive and deductive methods, as does Ingrid Rima (Haney, 550; Rima, 177).

Characterizing the initiation of the Methodenstreit as "a means by which the new theory [marginal utility] sought to clear its own mind," Eric Roll argues that there were actually no substantial points of disagreement between the two factions and that they both eventually realized this, which led to the decline of the controversy. Specifically, Roll explains (Roll 1974, 307–10):

> The two methods which were contrasted were not mutually exclusive and had indeed been used together by the greatest of the classics. There is clearly room for serious disagreement about the choice of premises; but it is generally admitted that premises which stand at the beginning of the deductive process are themselves empirical in origin. Induction and deduction are interdependent.

The same general conclusion characterizes the views of Jacob Oser and William Blanchfield (Oser and Blanchfield, 204–11).

Three writers take the position that the Methodenstreit was worth the time and effort expended on it. H. R. Seager was a student at both Berlin and Vienna during the early 1890s and studied with both Schmoller and Menger. Although he takes no position on one side of the dispute or the other, he argues that it is certainly time (1893) to be deciding what methods are appropriate to conduct what studies. The conflict was thus "of a decided scientific value" because it cleared away many misapprehensions (Seager, 237). Eugen von Böhm-Bawerk argues for the parity of the two methods assigning each to its proper sphere of concern (Böhm-Bawerk, 256), although he reserves the category of theoretical problems for the Austrian approach (Böhm-Bawerk, 258).

Lastly, Friedrich A. von Hayek (Hayek 1934, 406) identifies Menger's emphasis on the "atomistic" method of analysis and his "extraordinary insight into the nature of social phenomena" as valuable results of the dispute.

In general, it can be seen that whatever their differences regarding the fruitfulness of the Methodenstreit, most of the major historians of economic thought who have examined the dispute are united in the belief that the methods advocated by the two schools are, if not complementary goods, at least coequal in their usefulness for research. According to this view, some economic problems are best investigated through the use of the "historical method," while others require the "abstract, deductive method." Some may even benefit from the use of both methods together. In cruder (and more simplistic) terms, both "induction" and "deduction" have their place. Acceptance of this position could (and, in some cases, did) then quite understandably lead to a negative value assessment of a controversy between factions who apparently failed to realize this simple truth, and who each fought unrelentingly for the exclusive adoption of that faction's own method in economic research.

In addition, because neither side in the dispute was converted to the other point of view and a great deal of lasting antagonism was generated between the two schools, the debate has been generally regarded as counterproductive on these grounds alone. Add to this a belief that the issues in dispute were minor or irrelevant and/or the positions of the adversaries highly similar, but obscured by rhetoric, and it is not difficult to accept the view, as many have, that the controversy was wasted energy—a pointless quarrel.

But, why would one of the most brilliant theoretical minds in the history of economics (Menger) waste his energies in a pointless quarrel? It is the purpose of the next section of this paper to demonstrate that such views result from a superficial evaluation of the conflict and an inadequate understanding of its sources and basic rationale.

Epistemological Differences between Disputants

Ludwig von Mises recently identified the Methodenstreit as an epistemological struggle generated by Menger's rejection of the epistemological foundations of historicist methodology; however, he concluded that the controversy (Mises, 27) "contributed but little to the clarification of the problems involved." Schumpeter had started in the same direction many years previously in his *Economic Doctrine and Method* when he noted that (Schumpeter 1924, 169) "epistemological differences, which in themselves have nothing to do with economic method, were dragged into the discussion; nevertheless, it brought about without a doubt a clarification of views."

Unfortunately, Mises did not state his reasons for his conclusion and Schumpeter grew to accept the viewpoint that the debate was about precedence and relative importance. This section will summarize a recent analysis by this author of the Methodenstreit that clearly identifies its nature as an epistemological struggle at root and infers the main epistemological issues and their positions on those issues from the specific writings of the disputants.[8] The key to the recognition of the epistemological nature of the quarrel is found in arguments concerning the last three of the eight major issues debated (summarized above at the end of the section on the history of the dispute).

In arguing issues (6) and (7), the historicists and Menger were actually arguing over the theory of concepts. The question that underlay issue (6) was: Are concepts merely labels attached to universal summarizations that are subject to alteration depending on how extensive the data is from which they are derived

(Schmoller), or are they abstract generalizations from only a few instances that have universal applicability (Menger)? That is, for issue (7), does the concept of a complex entity, such as man, have to refer to an enumeration of all his empirical characteristics and recognize all these when it is used in the construction of theory (Schmoller)? Or is there some central characteristic, such as "self-interest," which can be emphasized without robbing the derivation and use of the concept of all legitimacy (Menger)?

With respect to issue (8), another issue underlay the ostensive one: the issue of the nature of the law of causality and its application to economic laws and reasoning. Does an "empirical" law make the same statement of necessity as an "exact," or deductive law (Schmoller), or is there a difference in kind between them (Menger)? What, then, is the nature of causality?

The position that each faction took on these epistemological issues led them to their methodological positions and prevented methodological agreement between them. I shall argue that those epistemological differences underlay the methodological criticisms and dissatisfactions expressed by each party to the dispute; that is to say, conflict on the epistemological level surfaced as conflict on the methodological one.[9] Some supporting and conflicting material from other sources will be indicated where appropriate.

The German Historical school is conventionally divided into the "Older" and "Younger" Historical schools—Wilhelm Roscher, Bruno Hildebrand, and Karl Knies being identified as the Older school, and Gustav von Schmoller being the leader and spokesman for the Younger school. In spite of the fact that the Older and Younger Historical schools differed in many respects (the most significant being the absence of any belief in either organicism or "absolute" laws of economic development in Schmoller's writings), they were united in their primarily empiricist orientation. As empiricists, the similarity between them rested most firmly in their argument for the application of a descriptive "historical method" to the data of history in order to derive economic laws—whatever they may have argued concerning the scope or necessity of those laws. This does not mean that they made such an application, it means only that they argued in favor of such an approach.

Roscher asserted that he sought absolute laws of economic development in intertemporal and interspatial comparisons between societies, social processes, and social institutions. Rather than the study of individual economic behavior, Roscher advocated a "holistic" approach, an examination through historical comparative studies of *national* economic behavior. Hildebrand and Knies differed with Roscher concerning the "absolute" nature of any laws of development so obtained, but they did not reject his empiricist and holistic method. The laws of development that Roscher hoped to derive through historical comparative studies were to be different in nature from the economic laws that would characterize a given "stage" of a particular society. Such "short-run" laws would be relative in space and time and could not claim universality. For short-run purposes, the "physiological" processes of specific economies were to be described and "relative" economic laws formulated. This utilization of an empirically descriptive approach to derive laws differing in their degree of necessity implied epistemological inconsistency—an inconsistency that Schmoller later es-chewed.[10]

In his own version of the "historical method," Schmoller denied entirely the existence of nonempirical law in economics, that is, the existence of any "abso-lute" laws of development embodying a degree of necessity not found in "rela-tive" laws; however, Schmoller's writings contain the most significant clues to the historicist theory of concepts and the most explicit statements of their view of causal relations. A coherent, reasonably consistent epistemological frame-work can be constructed for the entire historical school on the basis of Schmoller's writings that explains and, in a sense, brings consistency to the writ-ings of his forebears to a degree that they failed to achieve. It also preserves their identification as empiricists.

The historicist position has been aptly labeled "methodological collectiv-ism" by Schumpeter because of its concentration on social institutions and proc-esses that are collectives of individuals or of their relations. Roscher and the Older historical school were more interested in the study of the entire social "or-ganism" and its evolution, while Schmoller studied institutions and their interre-lation, and social processes within the national economy. More specifically, Schmoller argued for the observation, description, classification, and formation of concepts of social institutions, their relations, and the relation of the state to the economy. He viewed his descriptive work as the necessary preparation for describing the "general essence" of economic phenomena, or general theory.

Schmoller, in searching for the "essence" of specific phenomena though, desired a description of all characteristics to the greatest extent possible. The more complete the description, the more accurate and representative he believed the concept of a phenomenon to be. "Essence" was to be obtained by a summa-rization over entities of all their characteristics, rather than an apprehension or perception of a central and defining characteristic. Schmoller can thus be most usefully identified as a "nominalist" in his theory of universals, although a less consistent and more investigative nominalist can scarcely be imagined.[11] Schmoller's "essences" are virtually encyclopedic, while most nominalists would find such completeness unnecessary.

Schmoller's notion of causality, like his notion of concepts, is a descriptive one; it is one of empirically observed and verified uniformity in sequence. To Schmoller, the essence of a concept is subject to modification as the number of existents to which it applies increases. Because a theory of concepts is an im-plicit assumption in any theory of causality, it follows that causal relations among existents must also appear contingent on the experiential context in which they occur to someone believing concepts are contingent—if he is consis-tent. By the examination of experience using the comparative method, Roscher had hoped to distill generalizations of uniformities of sequence in phenomena in the form of laws of development. But Roscher had expected these to be "abso-lute" laws, whereas the laws for which Schmoller searched were not viewed in that manner. Instead, he confined his attention to the discovery of "short-run" empirical economic law.

The notion of causality that best explains the "short-run" relative laws sought by the Older historical school and the empirical laws sought by Schmoller is that of David Hume. It is Hume who originally offered the explanation of the causal relation as merely uniformity in succession. In this theory events are perceived either together or in succession. All that is meant by causality is that events have been perceived in succession, not that any intrinsic or necessary connection uniting these events has been perceived. Human thought processes interpret this sequence into the relation of cause and effect. Thus, necessity is something that exists only in the mind, not in objects. It is such an "inner necessity" of thought to which Schmoller must have been referring when he argued that empirical laws obtained by the "historical method" embody the same degree of necessity as laws obtained by Carl Menger's "exact" or abstract deductive method.[12]

Just as the "essences" of Schmoller's concepts of things are subject to alteration as additional characteristics of the subject phenomena are observed through time or across cultures (and so his concepts are dependent on the context for their content), so perceived causal relations (that is, economic laws) are subject to change as further investigations of empirical phenomena reveal apparent influences other than those first identified. Because every empirical context differs in some respect(s), no concept or conceptual relation is ever truly universal. All are relative to the context from which they are derived.[13] Schmoller's view of causation is thus a strictly empirical one and is fully consistent with his theory of concepts.[14]

Unlike the historicists, who spoke of only a single method appropriate to economics, Carl Menger maintained that several methods are useful in economic research. The methods of economic history differ from those of economic theory, which differ from those of economic policy. This is so because the formal nature of the knowledge in each subdivision is different, as are the goals sought.

He argued that the goal of economic history is the description of the individual nature and individual connection of economic phenomena; however, in order to summarize and generalize over time, history must consider economic phenomena *collectively* (as opposed to the *singular* consideration of an individual). Economic theory, on the other hand, seeks to discover the *general* nature and *general* connections of economic phenomena. *Collective* and *general,* then, have entirely different meanings, and considerations of collective phenomena and general phenomena are each appropriate to different branches of economics.

He believed that in seeking the general nature and general connections of economic phenomena, economic theory may employ two different approaches— the "exact" and the "realistic-empirical." Both result in economic theory, but differ in the degree of "absoluteness" to be assigned to their results.

Regularities in the coexistence and succession of phenomena discovered by the "exact" approach admit no exceptions because of the process of cognition by which they are recognized. In order to derive "exact" laws, it is first necessary to establish what constitute typical phenomena. Thus, Menger's initial concern was the theory of concepts, or universal ideas. To Menger, the identification of an empirical form or type was the identification of an essential *defining quality* or "essence" *in* individual phenomena *that made possible their recognition* as representatives of that type. Menger's view of essence was thus different from Schmoller's.

In his solution of the problem of universals, Menger can usefully be identified as a "moderate realist" or "Aristotelian."[15] Menger sought the "simplest" elements of everything real, the essences, the nature *(das Wesen)* of the real. In his exact approach, he used a process of abstraction from the individual phenomena of the empirical world to discover their essences, to isolate them, and then to utilize the "simple elements" so obtained to deduce "how more complicated phenomena develop from the simplest, in part even unempirical elements of the real world."[16] This approach has been designated as "methodological individualism " by Schumpeter.

The objects of Menger's epistemological considerations—the objects of his thought—were the essential characteristics of the individuals and how those characteristics in the form of "simple elements" could be used to explain how more complicated phenomena arise from individual phenomena. It cannot, in justice, be called an a priori method because it begins with "simplest elements" *that are derived from empirical reality* by the mental process of concept- formation and are not simply assumed a priori. Menger sought not only the general knowledge exemplified in *types,* but also that exemplified in *typical relationships.* These typical relationships, or general connections between economic phenomena, could be discovered in an exact sense as exact laws. An exact, or causal law was an absolute statement of necessity to which, Menger pointed out, exceptions were inconceivable due to the "laws of thinking."

In the Aristotelian epistemology, all thinking takes place in accordance with these laws, which are known respectively as the "law of identity," the "law of contradiction," and the "law of excluded middle." But, these are not just laws of thinking, they are laws of things, they are statements that are attributed to the real because they are apprehended in the real. They are the apprehension of a necessity in the being of things and thus are metaphysical or ontological. In addition, the law of causality is derived from the law of identity. The causal connection exists and is to be detected between determinate things in existence that have a determinate nature. To apprehend a causal relation is to apprehend this connection *by means of* the determinate things in the connection whose action produces it. To act at all, determinate things must act in accordance with their nature and must produce effects necessarily in accordance with that nature.

In identifying the essence or "simple elements" of economic phenomena, Menger was identifying the nature according to which he believed those phenomena must act. He was making possible the identification of the causal laws that would connect some phenomena to others or would show how more complicated economic phenomena develop from the simplest. Menger's references to "abstract economic reality" as the domain of the "exact" approach were not a reference to some other dimension of reality, but to the necessity revealed in the connections of things and inherent in their nature.

In summary, because his view of reality was Aristotelian, he believed that entities in reality act according to their nature in "typical" relationships. Thus, a concept of an entity, if it embodies the essence of that entity as an instance of a type, will embody its nature. Reasoning which uses those conceptual "simple elements" will be reasoning that proceeds according to the premise that entities act according to their natures, and will construct (deduce) conceptual systems of causality corresponding to the causality of the empirical world. Thus, conceptual or "theoretical" causal laws are laws of the real. Menger concluded that the exact method derived "laws of phenomena which are not only absolute, but according to our laws of thinking simply cannot be thought of in any other way but as absolute."[17]

Typical relationships could also be discovered in a "realistic-empirical" sense as empirical laws, argued Menger. An empirical law is a summary of observed regularities in the coexistence and succession of actual phenomena. Exceptions to it are both conceivable and probable due to its nature qua empirical. Depending solely upon observation, only the actual regularities belonging to observed empirical forms can be identified. There is no assurance that these regularities are "absolute" or (to use the usual phrase implying causality) that they are "laws of nature," admitting no exception. They are merely what is observed. No question of intrinsic relations, and thus causality, is involved in the knowledge of the external regularities in the coexistence and succession of economic phenomena that such laws provide.

Empirical laws are truly "historical knowledge" of the real. They embody and summarize all the influences present in real economic phenomena, that is, they include the "totality and whole complexity" of empirically observed phenomena, not just their general nature or "essence." It follows that they are modified by temporal change and vary from culture to culture. To the extent that the historical school confined its research efforts to the use of some collectivistic form of the "realistic-empirical" method—as Menger believed their "historical method" to be—they would tend to find some confirmation of their expectations regarding the relativity of economic laws.

Menger entirely rejected any attempt to verify laws obtained using one orientation of research by the other orientation, viz., the attempt to modify "exact" laws by "realistic-empirical" research or to place "realistic-empirical" research (the results of the use of a "historical method") above exact research. He argued that this was similar to trying to test the principles of geometry by measuring real objects. For example, no amount of time-series data relating price and quantity could disprove the "exact" law of demand. Also, Menger believed that any attempt to derive the exact, or general, theory of economics from a study of the history of economies was either the result of a failure to recognize the fundamental differences between the discipline "economic theory" and the discipline "economic history" or, alternatively, between the exact method and the "realistic-empirical" method. In his own view, it was exact theory that *explained* history and economic development while the "realistic-empirical" approach passively summarized it. "Realistic-empirical" laws were not "laws" in the same sense that the general, or exact laws of economics were "laws."[18]

It is not difficult to understand the historicist rejection of the deductive universalistic theory implied by Menger's exact approach, given their strong empiricist orientation and fundamental rejection of any more abstraction from the whole empirical complexity of economic phenomena (as they occur in specific social contexts) than pragmatically necessary. Menger's use of the "simple element" of self-interest would be "unrealistic" from the viewpoint of someone who saw economic behavioral motives to be multitudinous in any empirical context and who saw all theory to be rooted in an empirical context. Likewise, Menger's monocausal approach would be considered wrongheaded to anyone who saw empirical phenomena to be the product of multitudinous influences in any empirical context and who saw all theory, all causal relations, to be rooted in an empirical context. The historicists rejected universality in economic theory because they believed that theory should be empirically descriptive of a given social context. As the social context changed, the theory must necessarily change.

On the other hand, Menger refused to grant full theoretical status to any theory generated by a historical method, because he held theories of concepts and causality that differed from those of the historical school. The essences of economic phenomena with which he was concerned were "atomistic" or "individualistic" rather than "collectivistic"; they were what made an individual concrete a member of a type and did not depend upon the social context for their content. In his opinion, the collective concepts of the historicists were not *types,* they were *assemblages* of individuals. They were not *general.* As a result, he had no use for a "holistic" and contextual approach. Menger refused to grant causal status to historicist empirical laws because he believed that it transcended experience to state that an empirically observed phenomenon followed another empirically observed phenomenon "absolutely." Only the exact approach with its "intrinsic" causality could transcend experience in this manner. He thus implicitly rejected the "nonintrinsic" theory of causality of the historical school.

The Methodenstreit can, in the light of the above, now be seen to have been rooted in opposed epistemological positions that by no stretch of the imagination could be termed complementary goods. Consequently, it is not surprising that Schmoller and Menger should fail to grant value to each other's views. Unfortunately, neither of them clearly realized the epistemological nature of the issues that separated them, or clearly identified the position of the other faction as determined by epistemological considerations. To this may be attributed the inconclusiveness of the debate and the preoccupation with the more subsidiary matters of economic methodology and morphology that has misled historians of economic thought.[19]

A clear recognition of their epistemological differences might have resulted in less wasted effort through a discussion of the issues underlying the apparent points in dispute. This is not to say that there is any surety that those issues would have been resolved, but at least the debate would have been confined to a relatively limited sphere of subjects rather than roaming the whole field of the social and natural sciences, as it unfortunately tended to do. Ultimately, such very basic epistemological differences are so incompatible that resolution of arguments concerning them by disputants not trained specifically in philosophy may be entirely too much to expect and may most usefully be left to philosophers. The greatest service to the disputants is then merely to identify the source of their dispute as epistemological and hope for the best. There is no reason to suppose that this service would be any less useful to disputants today than it would have been to the parties to the Methodenstreit.[20]

Errors in Previous Assessments

Previous assessments of the Methodenstreit can now be seen to contain a number of errors as a result of the failure to identify the argument as, at heart, epistemological. The argument that the two methods contrasted were not "mutually exclusive," that induction and deduction are interdependent, misses the point of the debate. The question of "induction versus deduction" was never really at issue between the parties involved. It may be admitted that in the usual construction of general theory, "inductive" and "deductive" procedures are used together; that is, premises are induced from empirical reality and then deductive arguments constructed from them. Whatever their views on this might have been, there was a significant difference in how each faction in the Methodenstreit viewed the *conception* of premises and the *derivation* of economic causal laws. Only Menger's "exact" method was uncompromising in its view of economic law as deductive in origin from "induced" premises. Historicism saw economic concepts and law as empirical summarization.

The view that both methods are "equally necessary" to the economics profession as a whole fails to state clearly for what they are necessary. Menger was certainly not so ambiguous. He argued that a "historical method" was not the way to construct economic theory if it was desired that theory be general. On the other hand, the exact method would not be applicable to the writing of history (although the results of it, in the form of general theory, would) in his view. To call the two methods coequal and to fail to state a basis of coequality is to leave the matter ambiguous. A similar criticism can be made of the assertion that some problems yield to one technique and some to another.

The conclusion that the differences between the position of the historicists and that of Menger were minor compared to the similarities seems wholly unsupported. The differences (in epistemological beliefs) were so great that the debate raged and, more than likely, was not resolved *because* the fundamental sources of the disagreement lay unidentified and (substantially) untreated by both factions. The epistemological points at issue are matters of crucial importance to anyone who attempts to be self-conscious about his own methodological choices. Expenditures of time on such considerations can hardly be viewed as wasteful because an inappropriate choice can (potentially) lead to a lifetime of wasted effort. In that sense, the debate was important and valuable. On the other hand, the failure to debate the "right" issues did lead to a relative waste of valuable time in an inconclusive and agonized exercise in mutual frustration. The degree of that waste is difficult to evaluate, given the importance of the topic.

With respect only to Menger's part in the debate, there is no difficulty whatsoever in recognizing that his substantial contributions as a methodologist exhibited the same power of mind and originality of thought as his contributions to economic theory proper. In addition to his other virtues, Carl Menger: (1) stated his epistemological assumptions and methodological prescriptions more precisely and at greater length than virtually any economic theorist either before or since his time (Mises was certainly a most welcome exception to this generalization); (2) intentionally sought to develop a methodologically self-conscious economic theory; and (3) began the tradition of methodological individualism that an increasing number of economists are coming to believe is *the* epistemologically legitimate and potentially most productive general methodological approach for economic theory.

For these reasons alone, there is ample cause to be glad that Menger was drawn into a Methodenstreit and did publish his methodological and epistemological views. It is only to be regretted that his research work on these topics in later life has not been published.

Notes

First published in *Atlantic Economic Journal* 6, no. 3 (September 1978): 3–16.

1. For a detailed discussion of the question of the origin of methodological disputes among economists (and, by implication, among all social scientists) and a presentation of what is needed to settle such disputes, see Bostaph, 1977.

2. Menger justified the relatively low scholarly level of his comments and the frequent use of ad hominem against Schmoller by arguing that when scholars, such as himself, are attacked by an "ignoramus" (Schmoller), they should use the opportunity to address his audience and peers—the lay public—on a level that they can understand. See Menger 1884, 2.

3. The following is based on material found in Howey.

4. It is difficult to be sure to what "method" Landreth refers. He cites a differentiation of theory from history, deduction from induction, and abstract model building from statistical data gathering without rigorously linking each to a faction in the Methodenstreit, or clearly indicating how each constitutes a methodology opposed to the other. This may account for his apparent failure to recognize the differences in Menger's methodology compared to that of Jevons and Walras, with whom Menger is uncritically lumped.

5. Schumpeter is only referring, insofar as the historicists are concerned, to the Younger Historical school. He does not consider the Older Historical school to actually be a "school" in the sense of "a definite sociological phenomenon." Cf. Schumpeter 1954, 808–9 in this regard.

6. Hutchison 1973, 34. Unfortunately, Hutchison interprets a comment made by Menger in 1894—to the effect that the difference between the two schools was founded on a different view of the objectives of research—to denote confirmation of his (Hutchison's) own conclusion. Menger probably meant that the historical method was useful for some purposes (history and empirical studies—given that they were conducted on the foundation of adequate general theory) while the "isolating" method was the means of constructing such theory. If Menger had meant that the historical method was at all useful for constructing general theory (macro or any other), he would have been repudiating a

decade of his own stated views.

7. Cf. Hayek 1973, 8–9.

8. Bostaph 1976. The multitude of sources used and their correct identification precludes specific reference to them here. Interested readers should refer to the dissertation itself for detailed specific references and justification for the interpretation of them presented in this current paper. Other aspects of the Methodenstreit not mentioned here due to space limitations are also treated in that work.

9. A discussion of the general relation between epistemology and methodology and the use of the knowledge of this relation in the examination of methodological conflict will be found in Bostaph 1977.

10. Detailed references and justification for the foregoing interpretation of the Older Historical school will be found in Bostaph 1976, Chapter 2.

11. Nominalism holds that concepts are names applied to existential phenomena after men arbitrarily pick certain characteristics of those phenomena to designate them in the future. Only the name is universal, not the phenomena. Designating Schmoller a nominalist reconciles his position on the theory of universals with that on the nature of causality—which seems thoroughly nominalist. For an argument that historicism actually embodies the "methodological essentialism" of Aristotle see Popper. Popper may be describing as "essentialist" the Hegelian elements in the approach of the Older historicists (Roscher, in particular) rather than characterizing the historical school as a whole. Unfortunately, he identifies no members of the historical school specifically.

12. Schmoller 1883, 280 (978). The transmission of Hume's epistemology to the historical school occurred, more than likely, through the medium of John Stuart Mill. Schumpeter argues (1954b, 540) that "Roscher . . . went out of his way to express agreement with J. S. Mill's methodology." Cf. Roscher, 105–6. Hume's influence on Mill is specifically mentioned in Windelband, 635; Jones, 164. Schmoller, also, speaks approvingly of Mill Schmoller 1883, 281 (97). Nevertheless, the identification in this paper of historicist epistemology as Humian rests on similarities in expressed views rather than on any historical "detective" work.

13. Schmoller's methodological views on the use of statistics substantiate these conclusions about his notion of causality. To Schmoller, the science of statistics is the proper tool to examine and identify the actual relations that are present in every experiential context. It yields causal explanations and makes possible the measurement of the degree of "influence" of "essential and contributing causes." Cf. (Schmoller, 1893, p. 37).

14. Detailed references and justification for the foregoing interpretation of Schmoller's position will be found in Bostaph 1976, chapters 4 and 5).

15. Moderate realism, or Aristotelianism, holds that concepts are formed by the mental intuition of the pure essences of existential phenomena from the phenomena themselves, in which the essences are somehow manifest. After concluding my own original research, it was with a great deal of pleasure that I found an identification of Menger's epistemology as Aristotelian in works by Emil Kauder. See Kauder 1958, 413–25; 1965, 97–100. Kauder identifies not only Menger, but also Böhm-Bawerk as Aristotelian and is quite specific in showing how this influence entered and influenced the development of early Austrian economics.

16. Menger 1883, 61. This applies only to Menger's "exact" approach. How this is related to the "realistic-empirical" approach by Menger is not explicitly treated but may be inferred. The "realistic-empirical" approach involves the observation of types as they exist in their "full empirical reality," says Menger (61). "Realistic-empirical" description of types implies abstraction of some sort because selection is implicit in any description, and selection is an abstracting process. But the search for essences for "simplest elements" is not necessitated by that method—only a cataloging of characteristics and rela-

tions. On the other hand, a knowledge of the essences is needed to identify the entities to be included in "realistic-empirical" description and the principle of the selection process. The characteristics of an empirical form of money cannot usefully be described without an identification of its "essence" or defining characteristic. Thus the concept "money," obtained by identifying the "essence" of its empirical form, gives a point of view that allows the organization of any description into a meaningful whole—whether the description is infinite in detail or brief. Many forms of money actually occur and have occurred, but all forms embody the essence "money" in this view.

17. Menger 1883, 61. Menger's idea of causality is also one of "mono-causality." Given an initial set of conditions, only one thing can occur in this view.

18. Detailed references and justification for the foregoing interpretation of Menger's position will be found in Bostaph 1976, chapters 3, 4, 5.

19. Cf. Schmoller 1883, 286 (982), 280 (978); Menger 1883, 108, 31. Of course, Menger stated in the preface to his *Untersuchungen* that methodology proper was not the subject of his work because the question of the nature of economics itself and its proper research goals had to be agreed upon first, before methodology could be argued. Then he proceeded to treat methodological questions as well as questions of both goals and the morphology of economics in his text. It does not seem unreasonable to have expected a more explicit treatment of the historicists' method from him in this regard—especially since he was so outspoken about the "erroneousness" of that method.

20. A beginning in this direction will be found in Bostaph 1976, chapter 6.

References

Böhm-Bawerk, Eugen von. "The Historical vs. the Deductive Method in Political Economy." *Annals of the American Academy of Political and Social Science* 1 (October 1890): 244–271.

Bostaph, Samuel. *Epistemological Foundations of Methodological Conflict in Economics: The Case of the Nineteenth-Century Methodenstreit.* Ph.D. Dissertation, July 1976, Southern Illinois University.

———. "On the Origin of Methodological Differences among Economists and the Resolution of Resulting Conflicts Over Method." Paper presented at the University of Delaware to 1977 Symposium on Methodology, sponsored by the Institute for Humane Studies.

Dolan, Edwin G., ed. *The Foundations of Modern Austrian Economics.* Kansas City: Sheed & Ward, 1976.

Ekeland, Robert B., Jr. and Robert F. Hebert. *A History of Economic Theory and Method.* New York: McGraw-Hill, 1975.

Gide, Charles and Charles Rist. *A History of Economic Doctrines*, 2nd English ed. Boston: D.C. Heath, 1948.

Haney, Lewis H. *History of Economic Thought*, 4th ed. New York: Macmillan, 1949.

Hayek, Friedrich A. von. "Carl Menger." *Economica.* (November 1934): 393–420.

———. "The Austrian School." *International Encyclopedia of the Social Sciences.* Stanford, Calif.: Elsevier, 1968a.

———. "Carl Menger." *International Encyclopedia of the Social Sciences.* Stanford, Calif.: Elsevier, 1968b: 124–25.

———. "The Place of Menger's Grundsatze in the History of Economic Thought." *Carl Menger and the Austrian School of Economics.* Edited by J. R. Hicks and W. Weber. London: Oxford University Press, 1973.

Howey, R. S. *The Rise of the Marginal Utility School: 1870-1889*. Lawrence: University of Kansas Press, 1960.

Hutchison, T. W. *A Review of Economic Doctrines: 1870-1929*. Oxford: Clarendon Press, 1953.

―――. "Some Themes from 'Investigations into Method.'" *Carl Menger and the Austrian School of Economics*. Edited by John R. Hicks and W. Weber. London: Oxford University Press, 1973, 15–31.

Ingram, John Kells. *A History of Political Econom*, new enl. ed., 1915; reprinted. New York: Augustus M. Kelley, 1967.

Jahrbucher für Nationalökonomie und Statistik 18 (1872).

Jones, W. T. *Kant to Wittgenstein and Sartre*, 2nd ed. New York: Harcourt, Brace and World, 1969.

Kauder, Emil. "Intellectual and Political Roots of the Older Austrian School." *Zeitschrift für Nationalökonomie* 17 (1958).

―――. *A History of Marginal Utility Theory*. Princeton, N.J.: Princeton University Press, 1965.

Landreth, Harry. *History of Economic Theory*. Boston: Houghton Mifflin, 1976.

Lekachman, Robert. *A History of Economic Ideas*. New York: McGraw-Hill, 1959.

Menger, Carl. *Grundsätze der Volkswirtschaftslehre*, 1871. Translated into English as *Principles of Economics*, edited by James F. Dingwell and Bert F. Hoselitz. Glencoe, Ill.: Free Press, 1950.

―――. *Untersuchungen über die Methode der Socialwissenschaften und der Politischen Ökonomie insbesondere*, 1883. Translated into English as *Problems of Economics and Sociology*, edited by Louis Schneider. Urbana: University of Illinois Press, 1963.

―――. *Die Irrthümer des Historismus in der Deutschen Nationalökonomie*. Vienna: Alfred Hölder, 1884. A paraphrased and abbreviated translation of most of the content of these letters can be found in Albion W. Small, *Origins of Sociology*, Chicago: University of Chicago Press, 1924.

Mises, Ludwig von. *The Historical Setting of the Austrian School of Economics*. New Rochelle, N.Y.: Arlington House, 1969.

Newman, Philip Charles. *The Development of Economic Thought*. New York: Prentice-Hall, 1952.

Oser, Jacob and William Blanchfield. *The Evolution of Economic Thought*, 3rd ed. New York: Harcourt Brace Jovanovich, 1975.

Popper, Karl. *The Poverty of Historicism*. London: Routledge and Kegan Paul, 1957.

Rima, Ingrid Hahne. *Development of Economic Analysis*, 3rd ed. Homewood, Ill.: Richard D. Irwin, 1978.

Roll, Eric. *A History of Economic Thought*, 4th ed. Homewood, Ill.: Richard D. Irwin, 1974.

Roscher, Wilhelm. *Principles of Political Economy*, 2 vols. Translated from the 13th (1877) German ed. Chicago: Callaghan and Co., 1882.

Schmoller, Gustav von. "Zur Methodologie der Staats-und Sozialwissenschaften." *Schmollers Jahrbuch für Gesetzgebung, Verwaltung und Volkswirtschaft* 7, 1883. The article was reprinted, with minor changes, as "Die Schriften von K. Menger und W. Dilthey zur Methodologie der Staats-und Sozialwissenschaften," in Gustav von Schmoller, *Zur Litteraturgeschichte der Staats-und Sozialwissenschaften*, Leipzig: Duncker and Humboldt, 1888; reprint ed., Bibliography and Reference Series, No. 169, New York: Burt Franklyn, 1968. Page numbers given in references to this article are from the 1968 ed.; however, corresponding page numbers of the 1883 version are given in parentheses for cross-comparison.

———. *Die Volkswirtschaft, die Volkswirtschafs lehre und ihre Methode*. Frankfurt: Vittorio Klosterman, 1949; reprint of the 1893 ed.

Schumpeter, Joseph A. *Economic Doctrine and Method*. Translated from the 1924 German language ed. New York: Oxford University Press, 1954a.

———. *History of Economic Analysis*. London: Allen and Unwin, 1954b.

Seager, H. R. "Economics at Berlin and Vienna." *Journal of Political Economy* 1 (1893): 236–62.

Seligman, Ben B. *Main Currents in Modern Economics*. New York: Free Press of Glencoe, 1962.

Vierteljahrschrift für Volkswirtschaft und Kulturgeschichte 35 (1871).

Wicksell, Knut. "The New Edition of Menger's *Grundsütze*." Knut Wicksell, *Selected Papers on Economic Theory*. Edited by Erik Lindahl. London: Geo. Allen and Unwin, 1958.

Windelband, Wilhelm. *A History of Philosophy*, rev. ed., 2 vols. New York: Macmillan, 1901.

Zeitschrift für die gesammte Staatswissenschaft 28 (1872).

5

Truth in Economic Subjectivism

Gloria L. Zúñiga

The Problem of Subjectivism

The notion of *subjectivism* has a significant place in the body of economic theory, most notably in the theory of subjective value.[1] There is, however, one concern that some philosophers have raised about truth in normative judgments that puts economic subjectivism seriously into question.[2] This concern can be articulated as the following question: Is there truth regarding economic value judgments? The answer to this question is pertinent not only for an improved understanding of economic value theory but also for such philosophical investigations as realism, epistemology, ontology, and ethics. Nonetheless, the answer is not readily available in the body of economic theory. The ensuing discussion will explore the issue of whether the truth of economic judgments can be settled objectively and, if so, how truth is made known.

What Is Subjective Economic Value?

Subjectivism is commonly predicated on normative expressions of beliefs, attitudes, and emotions by a judging subject. In economics, however, the meaning of subjectivism is more complex. When economists speak of the value of economic goods as subjective, they not only refer to a judgment by an economic agent but also to the status of the object to which the judgment is directed. There are, then, two senses of *subjective*:

1. The evaluation of an object perceived by an individual as having a causal connection with the satisfaction of an end.

2. The subject-dependent status of objects in their role as economic goods.

The first is an epistemic sense of *subjective* that provides an account of choice given the constraint of limited resources despite unlimited wants. The second is an ontological sense of *subjective* that describes the economic character of things as dependent on human acts of valuing.

Carl Menger advanced this account of the subjective theory of value in his *Principles of Economics,* first published in 1871. The significance of his contribution lies in the transcategorical description of social phenomena. While most accounts reduce value either to the mind or to some intrinsic property of things, Menger demonstrated that all social phenomena was composed of varying combinations of beliefs and entities, judgments and facts, mind and matter. In order to achieve such a transcategorical account of value, Menger first provided an epistemic account of economic valuation by grounding his analysis on the experience of the valuing individual. Second, he provided a description of exact laws of economic phenomena, thus advancing an ontology of economic objects. The achievement of such a theoretical account of value could not have been reached without the recognition that, barring exact laws, there could not be any science of economics, and that, without any sort of empirical realism, economics could not rightfully be called a *social* science. What will be useful, then, in the task of tackling the question of truth in economic valuation will be to explore how Menger employs the notion of subjectivism both epistemically and ontologically.[3]

Epistemic Sense of *Subjective*

When considering the epistemic sense of subjective economic value, we must keep in mind two features of the economic species of value. First, the economic judgments that individuals make indicate the extent to which they believe an object may satisfy their needs. According to Menger, an individual makes an economic judgment on the basis of the causal connection he perceives between a thing and the satisfaction of a mediate or immediate end. Accordingly, an individual's judgment directed at a thing has an interested nature since his evaluation of the thing involves an expectation of what the thing will fulfill for him.

Second, the judgment is called *economic* because it involves an evaluation directed at making a choice among known alternatives. Every choice involves important elements of scarcity, such as limited time, income, productive resources, physical and intellectual limitations, levels of satiety, and so on. Coping with scarcity is a fundamental feature of the human condition that involves the allocation of means to meet ends. Menger was the first to ground the analysis of economic value on the notion of scarcity.[4] If there is no perceived scarcity, the judgment is not an economic judgment.[5]

Since an economic judgment of value is subjective, its truth or falsity cannot be settled by an objective appeal to facts observed by a third party. This does not imply, however, that we may never be wrong in our economic judgments. Menger acknowledged error as the most fundamental epistemological problem.[6]

If we can err, there must be judgments that are false. Parenthetically, it is also worth mentioning that the discovery of error in our judgments suggests that the fulfillment of expectations corresponds to putative features of the object toward which our judgment is directed. It may be the case, then, that the truth of an economic judgment can be settled objectively by facts about the object that correspond to the individual's expectations. Clearly, no one but the acting subject could make this determination.

The problem with erroneous judgments, to return to the issue of error, is that we only discover our mistakes *ex post,* sometimes immediately after and sometimes long after a choice has been made. However, we must also consider the case that the agent remains forever fooled by an apparent fulfillment of his expectations. Suppose, for example, that Oedipus dies before finding out that Jocasta, the woman he loved and married, was his mother. In this case, Oedipus never learns of his error, so he dies convinced that his expectations of love have been fulfilled. Objectively speaking, however, there are facts in the world, such as the identity of Jocasta as his mother, that are not in agreement with his expectations.

The question that immediately comes to mind is this: If agents are not likely to find out whether their economic judgments are true, at least in time to make corrections, can any kind of individual economic planning ever be possible? This question addresses a central problem in economics regarding the dispersed nature of knowledge. The problem is not that knowledge is dispersed but, rather, that there might be systemic obstacles to acquiring knowledge of the facts relevant to the economic activity of individuals. Such systemic obstacles are always the result of the constraints imposed by economic systems that do not allow for unfettered exchange. Conversely, in free-market systems, prices serve as the medium of communication of facts relevant to economic activity. As Hayek writes, "In a system in which the knowledge of the relevant facts is dispersed among many people, prices can act to coordinate the separate actions of different people in the same way that subjective values help the individual to coordinate the parts of his plan."[7]

Yet, suppose that there is counterfeit money in an economy. Economic agents might be fooled by the token objects they believe to be genuine members of the type-category "money." One way to analyze this problem is to attribute the cause to subjectivism. In other words, the criticism would be that any token object is *arbitrarily* designated to be a member of a type-category such as "money" by simply being believed to be so. This criticism, however, is mistaken since it misconstrues the notion of subjectivism in economic judgments. A better way to view this problem is to consider that an error in a judgment directed at an object does not modify the object such that the object becomes what we believe it to be. As we shall see in the ensuing discussion of the ontological sense of subjective economic value, universal categories such as "money" are objectively describable by exact laws such that a counterfeit dollar bill is not a genuine instance of the category "money." What is important to this epistemic analysis is that instances of error in our knowledge of objects do not alter the objects by shaping them according to our mistaken beliefs any more than false tokens of a type-category alter the category itself. We have thus come to the threshold of the second sense of *subjective* in Menger's theoretical account of economic value.

The Ontological Sense of *Subjective*

Menger developed a complex ontology of social objects that have a unique nature. According to Menger, economic objects are not merely describable by their physical properties since, for example, money is not reducible to the paper, metal, plastic, or electronic components that comprise the various kinds of currency we acknowledge as money.[8] In fact, there is no single physical property that is common to all members of the class of objects we call money. But what makes a dollar bill money or, more generally, what makes any one thing an economic good, is a combination of two things: first, the views we hold about things as economic objects;[9] second, the exact laws governing the categories of economic objects. Each of these requires some careful elaboration.

Concerning our views about things, the economic character attributed to the thing to which the judgment is directed depends on the perceived significance of the thing in relation to an end. In Menger's analysis, we find a distinction between things and economic goods that shows us how a thing acquires an economic character and is thus perceived as an economic good.[10] Accordingly, there are certain conditions:

1. A judging subject must perceive a thing as scarce, in relation to his total supply of the thing.

2. Hence, the thing is evaluated in relation to an end known to the judging subject as more urgent than any other end. Otherwise, scarcity would not be an issue at all.

3. The thing thus acquires an importance to the judging subject in relation to his unmet need or want since the judging subject perceives a causal connection between the thing and the fulfillment of his need or want. It is with the association of the judging subject's expectations with the thing that the thing acquires its economic character, that is, it becomes an economic good.

4. Finally, we must not neglect the judging subject's belief that he has a feasible command of the thing sufficient to be able to direct it to the satisfaction of his need or want. If, for example, the subject merely wishes to own a castle but he knows that this wish is beyond his means, then the castle is a thing merely desired on occasion. Unless he evaluates the castle as a serious alternative in making a choice directed at fulfilling a need or want, the castle does not enter into any economic valuation and, thus, it does not acquire an economic character.[11]

What these conditions describe is the subject-dependent mode of existence of a thing as an economic good. Hence, the economic character of a good cannot be instantiated in a thing apart from a judging mind. Now, this analysis applies not just to material objects but also to intangible ends, such as acquiring an education, acting virtuously, making friends, and finding love. These intangible ends almost always have tangible objects as mediate ends.[12]

We act economically in our attempts to meet any of these ends, not just those of the mundane sort or, as commonly believed, those that involve money or are employed in production. An important implication of this analysis is that the province of economics is broader than typically believed. Subjects, for example, can acquire an economic property if we evaluate them in an interested way, such as wanting to meet them, to know them, to spend time with them, to make friends with them, or to marry them. Chicago economists Gary Becker and George Stigler have advanced interesting theories of love and marriage consistent with this economic framework.[13]

Since we have now completed the first task of identifying what makes subjects hold economic views concerning particular objects, we can move on to the second task of describing the categories to which economic objects belong. Menger advanced exact laws for classifying economic kinds such as money, value, price, capital, and exchange. Without doing a survey of all of the economic categories in Menger's analysis, we may get a glimpse of his ontological enterprise by presenting the method he used.

For Menger, economic kinds have an intrinsic intelligibility since human beings discover their essence in everyday social activities of an economic nature. In his theoretical framework, Menger was able to reconcile the subject-dependent status of economic phenomena with the objectivity of description concerning the nature of such phenomena. Since all economic phenomena is not of the same kind, it was important for Menger to advance a description of categories such as money, price, capital, and so on. Unfortunately, however, Menger's elaborate description of economic kinds is often cumbersome to read and lacking suitable names for the distinguishing features and conditions belonging to each category. The inadequate attention given to Menger's ontology of economic objects is due in no small measure to his difficult style of writing. Nevertheless, his description is significant because it offers the truth-making conditions for settling objectively whether the views individuals have about an instance of an economic kind indeed correspond to that kind.

For example, suppose that individuals in Peru buy dollar bills in the black market because they think that the dollar has greater stability than the sol, the Peruvian currency. Further, suppose that some of these dollar bills are counterfeit but the individuals view them as genuine money. Clearly, their views do not affect the nature of the objects they believe to be money. In other words, they have, in effect, purchased very expensive paper but not money. Although the acceptance of a currency as money is one of the conditions for the category "money" in Menger's ontological description, it is not the only condition. As the case of counterfeit money should make clear, individuals may be wrong in their recognition of genuine token instances of commonly accepted currency.[14] Custom and practice will create certain commonly held beliefs about the usefulness of type-categories, such as U. S. dollars, based on marketability. But tokens that look like instances of U. S. dollars are not always money. There are, Menger writes, legal orders that have an influence on the money-character of token instances of money. In our present nationalized money systems, it is only by means of the sanction of the state that any one token instance of money has "the attribute of being a universal substitute in exchange."[15] This is an important fact in the description of money that offers an objective means to determine real money from counterfeit money, independently of the views or beliefs of individuals in particular instances.

Truth in Economic Judgments

Having laid out the epistemic sense of *subjective* in economic judgments, and the ontological or subject-dependent status of economic goods, I will offer the following answer to the initial question in this paper, that is, Is there truth regarding economic judgments?

"The truth of a subject's judgment pertaining to the economic value of a good corresponds to facts in the world about the thing in its role as economic good and the agreement such facts have with the subject's expectation of such a thing." This statement presents, in a concise way, the ontological and epistemic senses of *subjective*. On the one hand, an economic object is a subjective entity since its mode of existence depends on it being perceived by a subject as *economic*. On the other hand, the judgment that the agent makes regarding the economic object is subjective but its truth or falsity can be settled objectively by the correspondence of the judgment with facts in the world.[16] My answer, I believe, follows easily from Menger's framework. The upshot of all of this is that Menger's contributions provide us with an ample crop of ideas from which we can draw a rich ontology of subject-dependent economic objects and an epistemology that is both realist and consistent with a correspondence theory of truth. Having answered the initial question posed at the beginning of this essay, let us briefly survey some philosophical consequences that may be drawn from our discussion of economic subjectivism.

Arbitrariness and Cognitive Relativism

It should be clear by now that the way in which the term *subjective* is employed in economics is not as a predicate of judgments that are produced by a particular state of mind, such as feelings or attitudes, which have little or nothing to do with facts, real objects, or states of affairs in the world. This kind of subjectivism is more akin to cognitive relativism: the view that the world has no objective properties but just different ways of interpreting it. By contrast, economic subjectivism is consistent with philosophical realism.

Furthermore, economic judgments are not arbitrary in the sense that an economic agent can arbitrarily designate any object to be whatever he believes it to be. Let us recall from the earlier discussion of exact laws that the economic categories to which genuine instances of these categories belong are not determinable by the wishing or believing of agents. According to economic theory, economic categories obey exact laws that are intrinsically intelligible.

The Problem of Error

The problem of error needs to be addressed once again. We may be wrong in our economic judgments because our knowledge of things in the world is not always in agreement with how things actually are. *A fortiori,* economic judgments depend on minds for their existence, but they do not depend on minds for their truth. Therefore, truth in economic judgments is not dependent on the subject's knowledge of the correspondence between his expectations and the facts about the object to which his judgment is directed. There are very few facts of which we may be indubitably certain.[17] The rest of the facts that are not fully given in knowledge are known to us only with varying degrees of certainty.

Moral Relativism

Perhaps the most troublesome criticism advanced against economic subjectivism is the charge that it is either consistent with, or an endorsement of, moral relativism. This criticism, however, conflates economic value with moral value, two wholly distinct species of value. Epistemically speaking, economic judgments are distinct from moral judgments in the sense that while the former is an interested judgment, the latter is not.

Although many, if not most, actions are economic actions, not all economic actions are morally relevant. There are certain actions that are *only* economically relevant. If, for example, I decide to purchase a hat and have to decide between a red one and a yellow one, this action has no moral relevance. There are also certain actions that are *only* morally relevant. An act of forgiveness has no economic relevance.[18] But if my decision is between buying a hat and donating money to the poor, then this action has two aspects. It has an economic aspect since I have limited resources and I can allocate these resources to only one of the two choices. It also has a moral aspect since being charitable is morally relevant. Frequently, in fact, we may find that judgments that are beneficial from an economic, self-interested perspective are also wrong from a moral perspective. Having a new hat would be economically beneficial for me since it would add a nice accessory to my wardrobe. However, from a moral perspective, it might be seen as a frivolous choice in light of my knowledge of someone's need for food. Since economic judgments involve a set of considerations that are orthogonal to those involved in moral judgments, there is no necessary relation between economic value and moral value.

The argument for truth in economic judgments, however, has a significant philosophical import to ethics. If economic judgments can correspond to facts and thus instantiate truth, then other normative judgments, such as moral judgments, can be similarly consistent with realism. For example, consider the following: The truth of a moral judgment may be instantiated in the correspondence of the moral agent's intuition of the action as a good action and the objective essence of the act as a morally good act. This can be construed as a defense of moral realism.

Ontologically speaking, the objective essence of a moral act can be either good or evil, right or wrong, depending on the context. It is the context of the moral act that will identify the moral category to which it belongs. Killing is wrong, but if I kill in self-defense, then the act might not belong to the moral category "killing." Instead, it may fall into another category such as "defending life," "protecting life," or some other designation. Clearly, these desultory remarks on moral value are inadequate to the complexity of this topic. Nonetheless, this brief analysis of the philosophical consequences of economic subjectivism has shed light on the possibility of importing economic realism into the sphere of ethics in the form of moral realism.

Notes

First published in *Journal of Markets and Morality* 1, no. 2 (1998): 158–68.

1. It was not until 1871, with the publication of the *Principles of Economics* by the Austrian economist Carl Menger, that the notion of subjective value replaced the ill-conceived labor theory of value. According to Menger, "Value is the importance that individual goods or quantities of goods attain for us because we are conscious of being dependent on command of them for the satisfaction of our needs." See Carl Menger, *Principles of Economics* (New York and London: New York University Press, 1976), 115.

2. See Tibor Machan, "Subjective Arbitrariness," *Vera Lex* 11 (1991): 44. Machan writes, "It [subjective value theory] does not help with the evident problem of our often being wrong about how we judge, or of regretting it and indeed acting in light of that fact alone—confessing to crimes or moral failings, etc."

3. I am indebted to John Searle for bringing his clear exposition of the epistemic and ontological senses of the term *subjective* to the fore of present-day philosophical analysis. For, otherwise, I might not have been able to recognize in Menger's work what Searle's clarification makes so perspicuous. For a detailed statement of his argument, see John Searle, *The Construction of Social Reality* (New York: The Free Press, 1995), 7–9.

4. Menger does not use the term *scarcity* in his analysis but the meaning is implicit in his use of the expression *insufficient quantity*. Carl Menger, *Principles of Economics*, trans. J. Dingwall (New York: New York University Press, 1976 [1871]).

5. Instead, it might be a judgment of taste, such as: "I value reading more than watching television." In this example, the term *value* does not refer to an economic judgment of value but designates the positioning of one thing over another in an abstract hierarchy of taste. In this case, the terms *prefer* or *like* could easily be substituted for the term *value* without changing the meaning of the statement.

6. Menger writes, "Men can be in error about the value of goods just as they can be in error with respect to all other objects of human knowledge." *Principles of Economics*, 120.

7. Friedrich von Hayek, "The Use of Knowledge in Society," in *Individualism and Economic Order* (London: Routledge & Kegan Paul Ltd., 1949), 85.

8. Jerry Fodor might disagree with this view. In his article, "The Special Sciences, or The Disunity of Science as a Working Hypothesis," *Synthese* 28 (1974): 97–115, he argues that the generality of the science of physics implies that any economic theory has a physical description that can be subsumed under the laws of physics. Therefore, bridge statements about economic laws can be made such that they express token event identi-

ties with their physical properties. John Searle, however, disagrees with Fodor because there is no one-to-one correspondence between mental and physical events. Searle argues that money is money because we believe it to be money and, as a result of such a self-referential feature of social phenomena, there are no necessary physical identities to which any such social phenomena can be reduced. Searle adds that there is a radical discontinuity between the social sciences and physics. Cf., John Searle, *Minds, Brains, and Science* (Cambridge, Mass.: Harvard University Press, 1984), 71–85.

9. Hayek makes this point in "The Facts of the Social Sciences," in *Individualism and Economic Order*, 59. He writes, "Money is money, a word is a word, a cosmetic is a cosmetic, if and because somebody thinks they are." Ibid., 60. John Searle has argued similarly in *Minds, Brains, and Science* and *The Construction of Social Reality* that money is what people think, use, and treat as money.

10. In *Principles of Economics*, Menger calls "free goods" what I have referred to as "things."

11. This exposition of conditions for a thing to acquire a goods-character is slightly different from that described by Menger but is consistent with his principles. See Menger, *Principles of Economics*, 52.

12. Consider, for example, that books are necessary, mediate objects toward pursuing an education. Or consider further that a particular person is necessarily involved in the development of friendship or love. Perhaps only some virtuous acts do not require mediate, material objects for their fulfillment.

13. Gary Becker, "A Theory of Marriage: Part I," and "A Theory of Marriage: Part II," in *The Essence of Becker*, ed. Ramon Felereo and Pablo S. Schwartz (Stanford: Hoover Institution Press, 1995), 273–309, 310–28; and *A Treatise on the Family* (Cambridge, Mass.: Harvard University Press, 1981). See also George Stigler, *The Theory of Price*, 4th ed. (New York: Macmillan Publishing Company, 1987), 246–47. For a critique of Becker's theory, see Christopher Westley, "Matrimony and Microeconomics: A Critique of Becker's Neoclassical Analysis of Marriage," *Journal of Markets & Morality* 1 (March 1998): 67–74.

14. Menger calls this acceptance of a type-category, such as the U. S. Dollar, the *general acknowledgment* of any one commodity. *Principles of Economics*, 261.

15. Ibid., 262.

16. This explanation is consistent with Searle's description of the epistemic and ontological senses of *subjective*. The important point is that a true judgment is objective insofar as it corresponds to objective facts. Searle, *The Construction of Social Reality*, 7–9.

17. Edmund Husserl speaks of these facts as "objectivity in itself." When such "objectivity in itself" is given in knowledge, such objectivity is possessed by the mind and becomes subjective. See Dallas Willard, "Knowledge," in *The Cambridge Companion to Husserl*, eds. Barry Smith and David Woodruff (Cambridge: Cambridge University Press, 1995), 161.

18. I am indebted to Barry Smith for this insight.

6

Ludwig von Mises and the
Paradigm for Our Age

Murray N. Rothbard

Unquestionably the most significant and challenging development in the historiography of science in the last decade is the theory of Thomas S. Kuhn. Without defending Kuhn's questionable subjectivist and relativistic philosophy, his contribution is a brilliant sociological insight into the ways in which scientific theories change and develop.[1] Essentially, Kuhn's theory is a critical challenge to what might be called the "Whig theory of the history of science." This "Whig" theory, which until Kuhn was the unchallenged orthodoxy in the field, sees the progress of science as a gradual, continuous, ever-upward process; year by year, decade by decade, century by century, the body of scientific knowledge gradually grows and accretes through the process of framing hypotheses, testing them empirically, and discarding the invalid and keeping the valid theories. Every age stands on the shoulders of and sees further and more clearly than every preceding age. In the Whig approach, furthermore, there is no substantive knowledge to be gained from reading, say, nineteenth-century physicists or seventeenth-century astronomers; we may be interested in reading Priestley or Newton or Maxwell to see how creative minds work or solve problems, or for insight into the history of the period; but we can never read them to learn something about science which we didn't know already. After all, their contributions are, almost by definition, incorporated into the latest textbooks or treatises in their disciplines.

Many of us, in our daily experience, know enough to be unhappy with this idealized version of the development of science. Without endorsing the validity of Immanuel Velikovsky's theory, for example, we have seen Velikovsky brusquely and angrily dismissed by the scientific community without waiting for the patient testing of the open-minded scientist that we have been led to believe is the essence of scientific inquiry.[2] And we have seen Rachel Carson's critique of pesticides generally scorned by scientists only to be adopted a decade later.

But it took Professor Kuhn to provide a comprehensive model of the adoption and maintenance of scientific belief. Basically, he states that scientists, in any given area, come to adopt a fundamental vision or matrix of an explanatory theory, a vision that Kuhn calls a "paradigm." And whatever the paradigm, whether it be the atomic theory or the phlogiston theory, once adopted the paradigm governs all the scientists in the field without being any longer checked or questioned—as the Whig model would have it. The fundamental paradigm, once established, is no longer tested or questioned, and all further research soon becomes minor applications of the paradigm, minor clearing up of loopholes or anomalies that still remain in the basic vision. For years, decades or longer, scientific research becomes narrow, specialized, always within the basic paradigmatic framework.

But then, gradually, more and more anomalies pile up; puzzles can no longer be solved by the paradigm. But the scientists do not give up the paradigm; quite the contrary, increasingly desperate attempts are made to modify the particulars of the basic theory so as to fit the unpleasant facts and to preserve the framework provided by the paradigm. Only when anomalies pile up to such an extent that the paradigm itself is brought into question do we have a "crisis situation" in science. And even here, the paradigm is never simply discarded until it can be replaced by a new, competing paradigm which appears to close the loopholes and liquidate the anomalies. When this occurs, there arrives a "scientific revolution," a chaotic period during which one paradigm is replaced by another and which never occurs smoothly as the Whig theory would suggest. And even here, the older scientists, mired in their intellectual vested interests, will often cling to the obsolete paradigm, with the new theory only being adopted by the younger and more flexible scientists. Thus, of the codiscoverers of oxygen in the late eighteenth century, Priestley and Lavoisier, Joseph Priestley never, till the day he died, conceded that he had in fact discovered oxygen; to the end he insisted that what he had discovered was merely "dephlogisticated air," thus remaining within the framework of the phlogiston theory.[3]

And so, armed with Kuhn's own paradigm of the history of scientific theories, which is now in the process of replacing the Whig framework, we see a very different picture of the process of science. Instead of a slow and gradual upward march into the light, testing and revising at each step of the way, we see a series of "revolutionary" leaps, as paradigms displace each other only after much time, travail, and resistance. Furthermore, without adopting Kuhn's own philosophical relativism, it becomes clear that, since intellectual vested interests play a more dominant role than continual open-minded testing, it may well happen that a successor paradigm is less correct than a predecessor. And if that is true, then we must always be open to the possibility that, indeed, we often know less about a given science now than we did decades or even centuries ago. Because paradigms become discarded and are never looked at again, the world may have forgotten scientific truth that was once known, as well as added to its stock of knowledge. Reading older scientists now opens up the distinct possibility that we may learn something that we haven't known—or have collectively forgotten—about the discipline. Professor de Grazia states that "much more is discovered and forgotten than is known," and much that has been forgotten may be more correct than theories that are now accepted as true.[4]

If the Kuhn thesis is correct about the physical sciences, where we can obtain empirical and laboratory tests of hypotheses fairly easily, how much more must it be true in philosophy and the social sciences, where no such laboratory tests are possible! For in the disciplines relating to human action, there are no clear and evident laboratory tests available; the truths must be arrived at by the processes of introspection, "common sense" knowledge, and deductive reasoning, and such processes, while arriving at solid truths, are not as starkly or compellingly evident as in the physical sciences. Hence, it is all the more easy for philosophers or social scientists to fall into tragically wrong and fallacious paradigms and thus to lead themselves down the garden path for decades, and even centuries. For once the sciences of human action adopt their fundamental paradigms, it becomes much easier than in the physical sciences to ignore the existence of anomalies, and therefore easier to retain erroneous doctrines for a very long time. There is a further well-known difficulty in philosophy and the social sciences which makes systematic error still more likely: the infusion of emotions, value judgments, and political ideologies into the scientific process. The angry treatment accorded to Jensen, Shockley, and the theorists of inequalities of racial intelligence by their fellow scientists, for example, is a case in point. For underlying the bulk of the scientific reception of Jensen and Shockley is the thought that even if their theories are true, they should not say so, at least for a century, because of the unfortunate political consequences that may be involved. While this sort of stultifying of the quest for scientific truth has happened at times in the physical sciences, it is fortunately far less prevalent there; and whatever the intellectual vested interests at stake, there was at least no ideological and political buttressing for the phlogiston theory or the valence theory in chemistry.

Until recent decades, philosophers and social scientists harbored a healthy recognition of vast differences between their disciplines and the natural sciences; in particular, the classics of philosophy, political theory, and economics were read not just for antiquarian interest but for the truths that might lie there. The student of philosophy read Aristotle, Aquinas, or Kant not as an antiquarian game but to learn about answers to philosophical questions. The student of political theory read Aristotle and Machiavelli in the same light. It was not assumed that, as in the physical sciences, all the contributions of past thinkers had been successfully incorporated into the latest edition of the currently popular textbook; and it was therefore not assumed that it was far more important to read the latest journal article in the field than to read the classical philosophers.

In recent decades, however, the disciplines of human action—philosophy and the social sciences—have been frantically attempting to ape the methodology of the physical sciences. There have been many grave flaws in this approach, which have increasingly divorced the social sciences from reality: the vain substitute of statistics for laboratory experimentation, the adoption of the positivistic hypothesis-testing model, the unfortunate conquest of all of the disciplines—even history, to some extent—by mathematics, are cases in point. But here the important point is that in the aping of the physical sciences, the social disciplines have become narrow specialties; as in the physical sciences, no one reads the classics in the field or indeed is familiar with the history of the discipline further back than this year's journal articles. No one writes systematic treatises anymore; systematic presentations are left for jejune textbooks, while the "real" scholars in the field spend their energy on technical minutiae for the professional journals.

We have seen that even the physical sciences have their problems from uncritical perpetuation of fundamental assumptions and paradigms; but in the social sciences and philosophy this aping of the methods of physical science has been disastrous. For while the social sciences were slow to change their fundamental assumptions in the past, they were eventually able to do so by pure reasoning and criticism of the basic paradigm. It took, for example, a long time for "marginal utility" economics to replace classical economics in the late nineteenth century, but it was finally done through such fundamental reasoning and questioning. But no systematic treatise—with one exception to be discussed below—has been written in economics, not a single one, since World War I. And if there are to be no systematic treatises, there can be no questioning of the fundamental assumptions; deprived of the laboratory testing that furnishes the ultimate checks on the theories of physical science and now also deprived of the systematic use of reason to challenge fundamental assumptions, it is almost impossible to see how contemporary philosophy and social science can ever change the fundamental paradigms in which they have been gripped for most of this century. Even if one were in total agreement with the fundamental drift of the social sciences in this century, the absence of fundamental questioning—the reduction of every discipline to narrow niggling in the journals—would be cause for grave doubts about the soundness of the social sciences.

But if one believes, as the present author does, that the fundamental paradigms of modern, twentieth-century philosophy and the social sciences have been grievously flawed and fallacious from the very beginning, including the aping of the physical sciences, then one is justified in a call for a radical and fundamental reconstruction of all these disciplines and the opening up of the current specialized bureaucracies in the social sciences to a total critique of their assumptions and procedures.

Of all the social sciences, economics has suffered the most from this degenerative process. For economics is erroneously considered the most "scientific" of the disciplines. Philosophers still read Plato or Kant for insights into truth; political theorists still read Aristotle and Machiavelli for the same reason. But no economist reads Adam Smith or James Mill for the same purpose any longer. History of economic thought, once required in most graduate departments, is now a rapidly dying discipline, reserved for antiquarians alone. Graduate students are locked into the most recent journal articles, the reading of economists published before the 1960s is considered a dilettantish waste of time, and any challenging of fundamental assumptions behind current theories is severely discouraged. If there is any mention of older economists at all, it is only in a few perfunctory brush strokes to limn the precursors of the current Great Men in the field. The result is not only that economics is locked into a tragically wrong path, but also that the truths furnished by the great economists of the past have been collectively forgotten by the profession, lost in a form of Orwellian "memory hole."

Of all the tragedies wrought by this collective amnesia in economics, the greatest loss to the world is the eclipse of the Austrian school. Founded in the 1870s and 1880s, and still barely alive, the Austrian school has had to suffer far more neglect than the other schools of economics for a variety of powerful reasons. First, of course, it was founded a century ago, which, in the current scientific age, is in itself suspicious. Second, the Austrian school has from the beginning been self-consciously philosophic rather than "scientistic." Far more concerned with methodology and epistemology than other modern economists, the Austrians arrived early at a principled opposition to the use of mathematics or of statistical "testing" in economic theory. By doing so, they set themselves in opposition to all the positivistic, natural-science-imitating trends of this century. It meant, furthermore, that Austrians continued to write fundamental treatises while other economists were setting their sights on narrow, mathematically oriented articles. And third, by stressing the individual and his choices, both methodologically and politically, Austrians were setting themselves against the holism and statism of this century as well.

These three radical divergences from current trends were enough to propel the Austrians into undeserved oblivion. But there was another important factor, which at first might seem banal: the language barrier. It is notorious in the scholarly world that, "language tests" to the contrary notwithstanding, no American or English economists can really read a foreign language. Hence, the acceptance of foreign-based economics must depend on the vagaries of translation. Of the great founders of the Austrian school, Carl Menger's work of the 1870s and 1880s remained untranslated into English until the 1950s; Menger's student Eugen von Böhm-Bawerk fared much better, but even his completed work was not translated until the late 1950s. Böhm-Bawerk's great student, Ludwig von Mises, the founder and head of the "neo-Austrian" school, has fared almost as badly as Menger. His classic *Theory of Money and Credit,* published in 1912, which applied Austrian Economics to the problems of money and banking, and which contained the seeds of a radically new (and still largely unknown) theory of business cycles, was highly influential on the continent of Europe, but remained untranslated until 1934. By that time, Mises's work was to be quickly buried in England and the United States by the fervor of the Keynesian Revolution, which was at the opposite pole from Mises's theory. Mises's book of 1928, *Geldwertstabilisierung und Konjunkturpolitik,* which predicted the Great Depression on the basis of his developed business cycle theory, remains untranslated to this day. Mises's monumental systematic treatise, *Nationalöko-*

nomie, integrating economic theory on the grounds of a sound basic epistemology, was also overlooked as a consequence of its being published in 1940, in a Europe preoccupied with war. Again its English translation as *Human Action* (1949) came at a time when economics had set its methodological and political face in a radically different direction, and therefore Mises's work, as in the case of other challenges to fundamental paradigms in science, was not refuted or criticized but simply ignored.

Thus, while Ludwig von Mises was acknowledged as one of Europe's most eminent economists in the 1920s and 1930s, the language barrier shut off any recognition of Mises in the Anglo-American world until the mid-1930s; then, just as his business cycle theory was beginning to achieve renown as an explanation for the Great Depression, Mises's overdue recognition was lost in the hoopla of the Keynesian Revolution. A refugee deprived of his academic and social base in Europe, Mises emigrated to the United States and was at the mercy of his newfound environment. For while, in the climate of the day, the leftist and socialist refugees from Europe were cultivated, feted, and given prestigious academic posts, a different fate was meted out to a man who embodied a methodological and political individualism that was anathema to American academia. Indeed, the fact that a man of Mises's eminence was not offered a single regular academic post and that he was never able to teach in a prestigious graduate department in this country is one of the most shameful blots on the none-too-illustrious history of American higher education. The fact that Mises himself was able to preserve his great energy, his remarkable productivity, and his unfailing gentleness and good humor in the face of this shabby treatment is simply one more tribute to the qualities of this remarkable man.

One may agree then that Ludwig von Mises's writings are the embodiment of a courageous and eminent man hewing to his discipline and to his vision, unheeding of shabby maltreatment. Apart from this, what substantive truths do they have to offer an American in 1971? Do they present truths not found elsewhere and therefore do they offer intrinsic interest beyond the historical record of a fascinating personal struggle? The answer—which obviously cannot be documented in the compass of this article—is simply and startlingly this: that Ludwig von Mises offers to us nothing less than the complete and developed correct paradigm of a science that has gone tragically astray over the last half-century. Mises's work presents us with the correct and radically divergent alternative to the flaws, errors, and fallacies which a growing number of students are sensing in present-day economic orthodoxy. Many students feel that there is something very wrong with contemporary economics, and often their criticisms are trenchant, but they are ignorant of any theoretical alternative. And, as Thomas Kuhn has shown, a paradigm, however faulty, will not be discarded until it can be replaced by a competing theory. Or, in the vernacular, "you can't beat something with nothing," and "nothing" is all that many present-day critics of economic science can offer. But the work of Ludwig von Mises furnishes that "something"; it furnishes an economics grounded not on the aping of physical science, but on the very nature of man and of individual choice. And it furnishes that economics in a systematic, integrated form that is admirably equipped to serve as a correct paradigmatic alternative to the veritable crisis situation—in theory and public policy—that modern economics has been bringing down upon us. It is not exaggeration to say that Ludwig von Mises is the Way Out of the methodological and political dilemmas that have been piling up in the modern world. But what is needed now is a host of "Austrians" who can spread the word of the existence of this neglected path.

Briefly, Mises's economic system—as set forth particularly in his *Human Action*—grounds economics squarely upon the axiom of action: on an analysis of the primordial truth that individual men exist and act, that is, make purposive choices among alternatives. Upon this simple and evident axiom of action, Ludwig von Mises deduces the entire systematic edifice of economic theory, an edifice that is as true as the basic axiom and the fundamental laws of logic. The entire theory is the working out of methodological individualism in economics, the nature and consequences of the choices and exchanges of individuals. Mises's uncompromising devotion to the free market, his opposition to every form of statism, stems from his analysis of the nature and consequences of individuals acting freely on the one hand, as against governmental coercive interference or planning on the other. For, basing himself on the action axiom, Mises is able to show the happy consequences of freedom and the free market in social efficiency, prosperity, and development, as against the disastrous consequences of government intervention in poverty, war, social chaos, and retrogression. This political consequence alone, of course, makes the methodology as well as the conclusions of Misesian economics anathema to modern social science.

As Mises puts it:

> Princes and democratic majorities are drunk with power. They must reluctantly admit that they are subject to the laws of nature. But they reject the very notion of economic law. Are they not the supreme legislators? . . . In fact, economic history is a long record of government policies that failed because they were designed with a bold disregard for the laws of economics.

> It is impossible to understand the history of economic thought if one does not pay attention to the fact that economics as such is a challenge to the conceit of those in power. An economist can never be a favorite of autocrats and demagogues. With them he is always the mischief-maker.

> In the face of all this frenzied agitation, it is expedient to establish the fact that the starting point of all praxeological and economic reasoning, the category of human action, is proof against any criticisms and objections. . . . From the unshakable foundation of the category of human action, praxeology and economists proceed step by step by means of discursive reasoning. Precisely defining assumptions and conditions, they construct a system of concepts and draw all the inferences implied by logically unassailable ratiocination.[5]

And again:

The laws of the universe about which physics, biology, and praxeology (essentially economics) provide knowledge are independent of the human will; they are primary ontological facts rigidly restricting man's power to act. . . . Only the insane venture to disregard physical and biological laws. But it is quite common to disdain economic laws. Rulers do not like to admit that their power is restricted by any laws other than those of physics and biology. They never ascribe their failures and frustrations to the violation of economic law.[6]

A notable feature of Mises's analysis of *interventionism*—of government intervention in the economy—is that it is fundamentally what could now be called "ecological"; for it shows that an act of intervention generates unintended consequences and difficulties, which then present the government with an alternative: either more intervention to "solve" these problems, or repeal of the whole interventionist structure. In short, Mises shows that the market economy is a finely constructed, interrelated web; and coercive intervention at various points of the structure will create unforeseen troubles elsewhere. The logic of intervention, then, is cumulative; and so a mixed economy is unstable—always tending either toward full-scale socialism or back to a free-market economy. The American farm-price support program, as well as the New York City rent-control program, are almost textbook cases of the consequences and pitfalls of intervention. Indeed, the American economy has virtually reached the point where the crippling taxation, the continuing inflation, the grave inefficiencies and breakdowns in such areas as urban life, transportation, education, telephone and postal service, the restrictions and shattering strikes of labor unions, the accelerating growth of welfare dependency, all have brought about the full-scale crisis of interventionism that Mises has long foreseen. The instability of the interventionist welfare-state system is now making fully clear the fundamental choice that confronts us between socialism on the one hand and capitalism on the other.

Perhaps the most important single contribution of Mises to the economics of intervention is also the one most grievously neglected in the present day: his analysis of money and business cycles. We are living in an age when even those economists supposedly most devoted to the free market are willing and eager to see the state monopolize and direct the issuance of money. Yet Mises has shown that:

1. there is never any social or economic benefit to be conferred by an increase in the supply of money;

2. the government's intervention into the monetary system is invariably inflationary;

3. therefore, government should be separated from the monetary system, just as the free market requires that government not intervene in any other sphere of the economy.

Here Mises emphasizes that there is only one way to ensure this freedom and separation: to have a money that is also a useful commodity, one whose production is like other commodities subject to the supply and demand forces of the market. In short, that commodity money—which in practice means the full gold standard—shall replace the fiat issue of paper money by the government and its controlled banking system.[7]

Mises's brilliant theory of the business cycle is the only such theory to be integrated with the economists' general analysis of the pricing system and of capital and interest. Mises shows that the business cycle phenomenon, the recurring alternations of boom and bust with which we have become all too familiar, cannot occur in a free and unhampered market. Neither is the business cycle a mysterious series of random events to be checked and counteracted by an ever-vigilant central government. On the contrary, the business cycle is generated by government: specifically, by bank credit expansion promoted and fueled by governmental expansion of bank reserves. The present-day "monetarists" have emphasized that this credit expansion process inflates the money supply and therefore the price level; but they have totally neglected the crucial Misesian insight that an even more damaging consequence is distortion of the whole system of prices and production. Specifically, expansion of bank money causes an artificial lowering of the rate of interest, and an artificial and uneconomic over-investment in capital goods: machinery, plant, industrial raw materials, construction projects. As long as the inflationary expansion of money and bank credit continues, the instability of this process is masked, and the economy can ride on the well-known euphoria of the boom; but when the bank credit expansion finally stops—and stop it must if we are to avoid a runaway inflation—then the day of reckoning will have arrived. For without the anodyne of continuing inflation of money, the distortions and misallocations of production, the overinvestment in uneconomic capital projects and the excessively high prices and wages in those capital goods industries become evident and obvious. It is then that the inevitable recession sets in, the recession being the reaction by which the market economy readjusts itself, liquidates unsound investments, and realigns prices and outputs of the economy so as to eliminate the unsound consequences of the boom. The recovery arrives when the readjustment has been completed.

It is clear that the policy prescriptions stemming from the Misesian theory of the business cycle are the diametric opposite of the post-Keynesian policies of modern orthodox economics. If there is an inflation, the Misesian prescription is, simply, for the government to stop inflating the money supply. When the inevitable recession occurs, in contrast to the modern view that the government should rush in to expand the money supply (the monetarists) or to engage in deficit spending (the Keynesians), the Austrians assert that the government should keep its hands off the economic system—should, in this case, allow the painful but necessary adjustment process of the recession to work itself out as quickly as possible. At best, generating another inflation to end the recession will simply set the stage for another, and deeper, recession, later on; at worst, the inflation will simply delay the adjustment process and thereby prolong the recession indefinitely, as happened tragically in the 1930s. Thus, while current orthodoxy maintains that the business cycle is caused by mysterious processes within the market economy and must be counteracted by an active government policy, the Mises theory shows that business cycles are generated by the inflationary policies of government and that, once underway, the best thing that government can do is to leave the economy alone. In short, the Austrian doctrine is the only consistent espousal of laissez-faire; for, in contrast to other "free-market" schools in economics, Mises and the Austrians would apply laissez-faire to the macro as well as the micro areas of the economy.

If interventionism is invariably calamitous and self-defeating, what of the third alternative: socialism? Here Ludwig von Mises is acknowledged to have made his best-known contribution to economic science: his demonstration, over fifty years ago, that socialist central planning was irrational, since socialism could not engage in that "economic calculation" of prices indispensable to any modern, industrialized economy. Only a true market, based on private ownership of the means of production and on the exchange of such property titles, can establish such genuine market prices, prices which serve to allocate productive resources—land, labor, and capital—to those areas which will most efficiently satisfy the demands of consumers. But Mises showed that even if the government were willing to forget consumer desires, it could not allocate efficiently for its own ends without a market economy to set prices and costs. Mises was hailed even by socialists for being the first to raise the whole problem of rational calculation of prices in a socialist economy; but socialists and other economists erroneously assumed that Oskar Lange and others had satisfactorily solved this calculation problem in their writings of the 1930s. Actually, Mises had anticipated the Lange "solutions" and had refuted them in his original article.[8]

It is highly ironic that, no sooner had the economics profession settled contentedly into the notion that Mises's charge had been refuted, when the Communist countries of Eastern Europe began to find, pragmatically and much against their will, that socialist planning was indeed unsatisfactory, especially as their economies were becoming industrialized. Beginning with Yugoslavia's breakaway from state planning in 1952, the countries of Eastern Europe have been heading with astonishing rapidity away from socialist planning and toward free markets, a price-system, profit-and-loss tests for enterprises, and so on. Yugoslavia has been particularly determined in its cumulative shift toward a free market and away even from state control of investments—the last government stronghold in a socialistic economy. It is unfortunate but not surprising that, neither in the East nor in the West, has Ludwig von Mises's name been brought up as the prophet of the collapse of central planning.[9]

If it is becoming increasingly evident that the socialist economies are collapsing in the East, and, on the other hand, that interventionism is falling apart in the West, then the outlook is becoming increasingly favorable for both East and West to turn before very long to the free market and the free society. For this courageous and devoted champion of liberty, there could be no more welcome prospect in his ninetieth year. But what should never be forgotten is that these events are a confirmation and a vindication of the stature of Ludwig von Mises, and of the importance of his contribution and his role. For Mises, almost single-handedly, has offered us the correct paradigm for economic theory, for social science, and for the economy itself, and it is high time that this paradigm be embraced, in all of its parts.

There is no more fitting conclusion to a tribute to Ludwig von Mises than the moving last sentences of his greatest achievement, *Human Action*:

> The body of economic knowledge is an essential element in the structure of human civilization; it is the foundation upon which modern industrialism and all the moral, intellectual, technological, and therapeutical achievements of the last centuries have been built. It rests with men whether they will make the proper use of the rich treasure with which this knowledge provides them or whether they will leave it unused. But if they fail to take the best advantage of it and disregard its teachings and warnings, they will not annul economics; they will stamp out society and the human race.[10]

Thanks in no small measure to the life and work of Ludwig von Mises, we can realistically hope and expect that mankind will choose the path of life, liberty, and progress and will at last turn decisively away from death and despotism.

Notes

First published in *The Logic of Action One: Method, Money, and the Austrian School*. Cheltenham, UK: Edward Elgar, 1997: 195–210.

1. Philosophically, Kuhn tends to deny the existence of objective truth and therefore denies the possibility of genuine scientific progress. Thomas S. Kuhn, *The Structure of Scientific Revolutions*, 2nd ed. (Chicago: University of Chicago Press, 1970).

2. On the sociology of the reception of Velikovsky in the scientific community, see Alfred de Grazia, "The Scientific Reception Systems," in *The Velikovsky Affair*, Alfred de Grazia, ed. (New Hyde Park, N.Y.: University Books, 1966), 171–231.

3. Kuhn, *The Structure of Scientific Revolutions*, 2nd ed. (Chicago: University of Chicago Press, 1970), 53–56.

4. De Grazia, "The Scientific Reception Systems," in *The Velikovsky Affair*, Alfred de Grazia, ed. (New Hyde Park, N.Y.: University Books, 1966), 197.

5. Ludwig von Mises, *Human Action* (New Haven, Conn.: Yale University Press, 1949), 67.

6. Ibid., 755–56. As Mises indicates, the revolt against economics as the harbinger of a free-market economy is as old as the classical economists whom Mises acknowledges as his forebears. It is no accident, for example, that George Fitzhugh, the foremost Southern apologist for slavery and one of America's first sociologists, brusquely attacked classical economics as "the science of free society," while upholding socialism as "the science of slavery." See George Fitzhugh, *Cannibals All!*. C. Vann Woodward, ed. (Cambridge, Mass.: Harvard University Press, 1960), xviii; and Joseph Dorfman, *The Economic Mind in American Civilization* (New York: Viking Press, 1964), vol. 2, 929. On the statist and anti-individualist bias embedded deep in the foundations of sociology, see Leon Bramson, *The Political Context of Sociology* (Princeton, N.J.: Princeton Uni-

versity Press, 1961), esp. 11–17.

7. Thus, see Ludwig von Mises, *The Theory of Money and Credit* (Irvington-on-Hudson, N.Y.: Foundation for Economic Education, 1971).

8. Mises's classic article was translated as "Economic Calculation in the Socialist Commonwealth," in *Collectivist Economic Planning*, F. A. Hayek, ed. (London: George Routledge and Sons, 1935), 87–130. Mises's and other articles by Lange and Hayek are reprinted in *Comparative Economic Systems*, Morris Bornstein, ed., rev. ed. (Homewood, Ill.: Richard D. Irwin, 1969). An excellent discussion and critique of the whole controversy may be found in Trygve J. B. Hoff, *Economic Calculation in the Socialist Society* (London: William Hodge, 1949).

9. On Yugoslavia, see Rudolf Bicanic, "Economics of Socialism in a Developed Country," in *Comparative Economic Systems*, M. Bornstein, ed., 222–35; on the other countries of Eastern Europe, see Michael Gamarnikow, *Economic Reforms in Eastern Europe* (Detroit, Mich.: Wayne State University Press, 1968).

10. Mises, *Human Action*, (New Haven, Conn.: Yale University Press, 1949), 881.

7

Ludwig von Mises and the Austrian School of Economics

Jeffrey M. Herbener

Everyone carries a part of society on his shoulders: no one is relieved of his share of responsibility by others. And no one can find a safe way for himself if society is sweeping towards destruction. Therefore everyone, in his own interests, must thrust himself vigorously into the intellectual battle. No one can stand aside with unconcern: the interests of everyone hang on the result. Whether he chooses or not, every man is drawn into the great historical struggle, the decisive battle into which our epoch has plunged us. (Mises 1988, 169)

This is the message of Ludwig von Mises. No one has ever fought the battle more courageously than Mises, nor had a more decisive long-run effect. Murray Rothbard is correct when he says, "if the world is ever to get out of its miasma of statism, or, indeed, if the economics profession is ever to return to a sound and correct development of economic analysis, both will have to abandon their contemporary bog and move to that high ground that Mises developed for us" (Rothbard 1983, 5).

Now, as the battle appears to be turning in favor of freedom, is an appropriate time to reconsider the role of economic theory in these worldwide changes. Specifically, it is time to consider the work of Mises and the Austrian school in the development and dissemination of the economic principles of social progress. Two steps are necessary to complete this task. The first is to demonstrate the preeminence of the Austrian school in developing the principles of free enterprise. The second is to demonstrate that Mises is the champion of this tradition in the twentieth century.

Method and the Austrian Tradition

Carl Menger founded the Austrian school during the marginalist revolution of the late nineteenth century in his attempt to correct the errors of the classical economists. As Menger said:

> Adam Smith and this school have neglected to reduce the complicated phenomena of human economy in general, and in particular of its social form, "national" economy" to the efforts of individual economies, as would be in accordance with the real state of affairs. They have neglected to teach us to understand them theoretically as the result of individual efforts. Their endeavors have been aimed, rather, and to be sure, subconsciously for the most part, at making us understand them theoretically from the point of view of the "national economy" fiction. On the other hand, the historical school of German economists follows this erroneous conception consciously. (Menger 1985, 195–96)

It is the adherence to these methodological precepts of individualism and essentialism that distinguish the Austrian school from all others. Although Mises significantly refined and improved his position, Menger laid the groundwork:

> This is the ground on which I stand. In what follows I have endeavored to reduce the complex phenomena of human economic activity to the simplest elements that can still be subjected to accurate observation, to apply to these elements the measure corresponding to their nature, and constantly adhering to this measure, to investigate the manner in which the more complex economic phenomena evolve from their elements according to definite principles. (Menger 1976, 47)

> It is now the task of the reader to judge to what results the method of investigation I have adopted has led, and whether I have been able to demonstrate successfully that the phenomena of economic life, like those of nature, are orderly strictly in accordance with definite laws. (Menger 1976, 48)

Via this method, Menger solved the paradox of value, derived the subjective theory of value, developed a unified theory of price, and reconstructed the origin of social institutions such as money, markets, property, and law. More than this, he began the process, culminating in the work of Mises, that has resulted in universally correct economic laws of social systems. As Menger stated:

> The aim of this orientation, which in the future we will call the *exact* one, an aim which research pursues in the same way in all realms of the world of phenomena, is the determination of strict laws of phenomena, of regularities in the succession of phenomena which do not present themselves to us as absolute, but which in respect to the approaches to cognition by which we attain to them simply bear within themselves the guarantee of absoluteness. (Menger 1985, 59)

In contrast, most other schools of economic thought deny, because of their methodological positions, the existence of universal laws of economics. Most prevalent are empirically based schools such as the German Historical school that Menger fought. Menger was quite clear on this:

> If, therefore, exact laws are at all attainable, it is clear that these cannot be obtained from the point of view of empirical realism, but only in this way, with theoretical research satisfying the presuppositions of the above rule of cognition.
>
> But the way by which theoretical research arrived at the above goal, a way essentially different from Bacon's empirical-realistic induction, is the following: it seeks to ascertain the *simplest elements* of everything real, elements which must be thought of as strictly typical just because they are the simplest.
>
> The specific goal of this orientation of theoretical research is the determination of regularities in the relationships of phenomena which are guaranteed to be absolute and as such to be complete.
>
> It examines, rather, how more complicated phenomena develop from the simplest, in part even unempirical elements of the real world in their (likewise unempirical) isolation from all other influences.
>
> Science starts out, however, with these assumptions, since it would never be able otherwise to reach the goal of exact research, the determination of strict laws. On the other hand, with the assumption of strictly typical elements, of their exact measure, and of their complete isolation from all other causative factors, it does to be sure, and indeed on the basis of the rules of cognition characterized by us above, arrive at Jaws of phenomena which are not only absolute, but according to our laws of thinking simply cannot be thought of in any other way but as absolute. (Menger 1985, 60–61)

Menger, like Mises, leaves no doubt regarding his view of the efficacy of empirically testing economic theory; providing a refutation of positivism and falsification in economics almost a century before Milton Friedman and F. A. Hayek espoused them.

> Among economists the opinion often prevails that the empirical laws, "because they are based on experience," offer better guarantees of truth than those results of exact research which are obtained, as is assumed, only deductively from a priori axioms.
>
> The error at the basis of this view is caused by the failure to recognize the nature of the exact orientation of theoretical research, of its relationship to the realistic, and by applying the points of view of the latter to the former.
>
> Nothing is so certain as that the results of the exact orientation of theoretical research appear insufficient and unempirical in the field of economy just as in all the other realms of the world of phenomena, when measured by the standard of realism. This is, however, self-evident, since the results of exact research, and indeed in all realms of the world of phenomena, are true only with certain presuppositions, with presuppositions which in reality do not always apply. Testing exact theory of economy by the full empirical method is simply a methodological absurdity, a failure to recognize the bases and presuppositions

of exact research. At the same time it is a failure to recognize the particular aims which the exact sciences serve. To want to test the pure theory of economy by experience in its full reality is a process analogous to that of the mathematician who wants to correct the principles of geometry by measuring real objects, without reflecting that the latter are indeed not identical with the magnitudes which pure geometry presumes or that every measurement of necessity implies elements of inexactitude. Realism in theoretical research is not something higher than exact orientation, but something different.

The results of realistic orientation stand in an essentially different relationship to the empirical method than those of exact research. The former are based, of course, on the observation of phenomena in their "empirical reality" and complexity, and of course the criterion of their truth is accordingly the empirical method. An empirical law lacks the guarantee of absolute validity a priori, i.e., simply according to its methodological presuppositions. It states certain regularities in the succession and coexistence of phenomena which are by no means necessarily absolute. But bearing this firmly in mind, we note that it must agree with full empirical reality, from the consideration of which it was obtained. To want to transfer this principle to the results of exact research is, however, an absurdity, a failure to recognize the important difference between exact and realistic research. To combat this is the chief task of the preceding investigations. (Menger 1985, 69–70)

While referring to the German Historical school, Menger also refuted the modern hermeneutic economists.

There is scarcely any need to remark that the nature and significance of the exact orientation of research is completely misunderstood in the modern literature on national economy. In German economics, at least in the historical school, the art of abstract thinking, no matter how greatly distinguished by depth and originality and no matter how broadly supported empirically—in brief, everything that in other theoretical sciences establishes the greatest fame of scholars—is still considered, along with the products of compilatory diligence, as something secondary, almost as a stigma. The power of truth, however, will finally also be tested for those who, sensing their inability to solve the highest problems of the social sciences, would like to raise their own inadequacy as a standard for the value of scientific work in general. (Menger 1985, 65)

Neither Hayek, who has come to accept the empirical method of Karl Popper, nor the modern hermeneuticians who advance the epistemology of subjective interpretation, have any grounding in Menger. Only Mises has accepted Menger's basic deductive procedure and forged ahead to refine it into praxeology. Mises is the true heir of the Austrian tradition and the person who has advanced the edifice of absolute economic laws in this century.

Hayek versus Menger

As Hayek progressively left his grounding in the praxeological method, he drifted further and further into error. This process has culminated in Hayek's latest work on socialism which he claims is based on Menger:

> But to me, at any rate, [*Investigation*'s] main interest to the economist in our days seems to lie in the extraordinary insight into the nature of social phenomena which is revealed incidentally in the discussion of problems mentioned to exemplify different methods of approach. . . . Discussions of somewhat obsolete views, as that of the organic or perhaps better physiological interpretation of social phenomena, gave him an opportunity for an elucidation of the origin and character of social institutions which might, with advantage, be read by present-day economists and sociologists. (Hayek 1976, 23)

> Menger was the only one of these to have come after Darwin, yet all attempted to provide a rational reconstruction, conjectural history, or evolutionary account of the emergence of cultural institutions. (Hayek 1988, 70)

> Adequate explanations of [the market, etc.] were disseminated . . . especially by the Austrian school following Menger, into what became known as the "subjective" or "marginal utility" revolution in economic theory. [The most elementary and important] was the discovery that economic events could not be explained by preceding events acting as determining causes that enabled these revolutionary thinkers to unify economic theory into a coherent system. (Hayek 1988, 97)

What Menger wrote about using organic analogies *in* the social sciences in no way justifies Hayek's claim. Menger stated clearly that the analysis of social development must be built from individual action and that reason is the guiding force in understanding social processes.

> In [the organic] category belong, above all, the attempts of those who think that they have solved the problem involved merely by designating as "organic" the developmental process we are discussing. The process by which social structures originate without action of the common will may well be called "organic," but it must not be believed that even the smallest part of the noteworthy problem of the social sciences that we alluded to above has been solved by this image or by any mystic allusions attached to it. (Menger 1985, 149)

Yet Hayek makes just such allusions when he claims that the spontaneous order of the market "forms itself" or:

> The answer to [how we came to acquire the economic order of the market] is built upon the old insight, well known to economics, that our values and institutions are determined not simply by preceding causes but as part of a process of unconscious self-organization of a structure or pattern. This is true not only of economics, but in a wide area, and is well known today in the biological sciences. (Hayek 1988, 9)

Menger sees two mistakes made in the analysis of social processes: the mystic one mentioned above and the view that society is a product of the "common will," that is, created by positive legislation.

> Just as meaningless is another attempt to solve the problem discussed here. I mean the theory, which has attained widespread currency, that recognizes in social institutions something *original,* that is, not something that has developed, but an *original* product of the life of the people. This theory (which, incidentally, is also applied by a few of its adherents, for whom a unified principle means more than historical truth or the logic of things, by way of a peculiar mysticism to social institutions created by positive laws) indeed avoids the error of those who reduce all institutions to acts of positive common will. Still, it obviously offers us no solution of the problem discussed here, but evades it. The origin of a phenomena is by no means explained by the assertion that it *was present from the very beginning* or that it *developed originally.* (Menger 1985, 149)

But Hayek is reduced to such a conclusion, "Although also acclaimed as a biologist, Aristotle lacked any perception of two crucial aspects of the formation of any complex structure, namely, evolution and the self-formation of order" (Hayek 1988, 45). Appeals to words like "evolution" or "self-formation" are not solutions to the problems of the origin and development of social institutions. Menger clearly looked to individual action as the foundation of the solution.

> Such a phenomenon must obviously have developed at some time from its simpler elements; a social phenomenon, at least in its most original form, must clearly have developed from individual factors. The view here referred to is merely an analogy between the development of social institutions and that of natural organisms, which is completely worthless for the purpose of solving our problem. It states, to be sure, that institutions are unintended creations of the human mind, but not *how* they came about. These attempts at interpretation are comparable to the procedure of a natural scientist who thinks he is solving the problem of the origin of natural organisms by alluding to their "originality," "natural growth," or their "primeval nature." (Menger 1985, 149)

In contrast, Hayek approvingly quotes Popper, who stated, "Cultural evolution continues genetic evolution by other means" (Hayek 1988, 16). He continues:

> For example, by the time culture began to displace some innate modes of behavior, genetic evolution had probably also already endowed human individuals with a great variety of characteristics which were better adjusted to the many different environmental niches into which men had penetrated than those of any nondomesticated animal. . . . Among the most important of these innate characteristics which helped to displace other instincts was a great capacity for learning from one's fellows, especially by imitation. (Hayek 1988, 18)

Menger pointed out the poverty of this line of argument:

The previous attempts to interpret the *changes* of social phenomena as "organic processes" are no less inadmissible than the above theories which aim to solve "organically" the problem of the *origin* of unintentionally created social structures. There is hardly need to remark that the changes of social phenomena cannot be interpreted in a social-pragmatic way, insofar as they are not the intended result of the agreement of members of society or of positive legislation, but are the unintended product of social development. But it is just as obvious that not even the slightest insight into the nature and the laws of the movement of social phenomena can be gained either by the mere allusion to the "organic" or the "primeval" character of the processes under discussion, nor even by mere analogies between these and the transformations to be observed in natural organisms. The worthlessness of the above orientation of research is so clear that we do not care to add anything to what we have already said. (Menger 1985, 150)

Hayek bases his analysis on exactly these allusions and analogies:

Despite such differences, all evolution, cultural as well as biological, is a process of continuous adaptation to unforeseeable events, to contingent circumstances which could not have been forecast. (Hayek 1988, 25)

Economics has from its origins been concerned with how an extended order of human interaction comes into existence through a process of variation, winnowing, and sifting far surpassing our vision or our capacity to design. . . . We are led—for example by the pricing system in market exchange—to do things by circumstances of which we are largely unaware and which produce results that we do not intend. (Hayek 1988, 14)

Menger rejected these mystic forces and Hayek's characterization of individuals as mindless, passive, and ignorant:

If this significant problem of the social sciences is truly to be solved, this cannot be done by way of superficial and, for the most part, inadmissible analogies. It can be done, in any case, only by way of direct consideration of social phenomena, not "organically," "anatomically," or "physiologically," but only in a *specifically sociological* way. The road to this, however, is *theoretical* social research, the nature and main orientations of which (the exact and the empirical-realistic) we have characterized above. (Menger 1985, 150)

Hayek relies upon evolution to explain language, law, morals, markets, and money (Hayek 1988, 24); in contrast Menger claims that these institutions can be understood as built upon individual action.

[These are] the unintended result of innumerable efforts of economic subjects pursuing *individual* interests. The theoretical understanding of them, the theoretical understanding of their nature and their movement can thus be attained in an exact measure only in the same way as the understanding of the above mentioned social structures. That is, it can be attained by reducing them to their elements, to the *individual* factors of their causation, and by investigating the laws by which the complicated phenomena of human economy under discussion here are built up from these elements. This, however, as scarcely needs saying, is that method which we have characterized above as the one adequate for the exact orientation of theoretical research in the realm of social phenomena in general. The methods for the exact understanding of the origin of the "organically" created social structures and those for the solution of the main problems of exact economics are by nature identical. (Menger 1985, 158–59)

Hayek versus Mises

Menger began to build the principles of economics from what he saw as the essence of these individual factors—the human need to satisfy material ends. From this idea of subjective value, he proceeded to derive principles of action of an isolated individual, then the more complex principles; two-person exchange (based upon mutual benefit), the social division of labor, and finally, a consistent, unified theory of price (see Menger 1976). These principles were the basis of his advocacy of laissez-faire (see Rothbard 1991).

Eugen von Böhm-Bawerk, accepting Menger's methodological position, constructed the theories of advanced social production, and capital and interest, and demolished the underpinnings of Marxian economics (Böhm-Bawerk 1959).

Refining and building upon this work, Mises constructed a very different picture of society's origin and development from that of Hayek (Salerno 1991). His answer to a Hayekian view of society is:

> To those pretending that man would be happier if he were to renounce the use of reason and try to let himself be guided by intuition and instincts only, no other answer can be given than an analysis of the achievements of human society. In describing the genesis and working of social cooperation, economics provides all the information required for an ultimate decision between reason and unreason. If man reconsiders freeing himself from the supremacy of reason, he must know what he will have to forsake. (Mises 1966, 91)

Mises saw society as a strategy of acting individuals in their struggle against scarcity; purposefulness is the essence of the market, not spontaneity.

> Seen from the point of view of the individual, society is the great means for the attainment of all his ends. (Mises 1966, 165)

> Society is concerted action, cooperation. Society is the outcome of conscious and purposeful behavior. This does not mean that individuals have concluded contracts by virtue of which they have founded human society. The actions which have brought about social cooperation and daily bring it about anew do not aim at anything else than cooperation and coadjuvancy with others for the

attainment of definite singular ends. The total complex of the mutual relations created by such concerted actions is called society. (Mises 1966, 143)

For Mises the division of labor (which is predicated on the inherent differences in individuals and natural resources) is the essence of society and the linchpin of all aspects of civilization.

Society is division of labor and combination of labor. (Mises 1966, 143)

The fundamental social phenomenon is the division of labor and its counterpart human cooperation. (Mises 1966, 157)

The fundamental facts that brought about cooperation, society, and civilization and transformed the animal man into a human being are the facts that work performed under the division of labor is more productive than isolated work and that man's reason is capable of recognizing this truth. But for these facts men would have forever remained deadly foes of one another, irreconcilable rivals in their endeavors to secure a portion of the scarce supply of means of sustenance provided by nature. (Mises 1966, 144)

The law of association makes us comprehend the tendencies which resulted in the progressive intensification of human cooperation. We conceive what incentive induced people not to consider themselves simply as rivals in a struggle for the appropriation of the limited supply of means of subsistence made available by nature. We realize what has impelled them and permanently impels them to consort with one another for the sake of cooperation. Every step forward on the way to a more developed mode of the division of labor serves the interests of all participants. In order to comprehend why man did not remain solitary, searching like the animals for food and shelter for himself only and at most also for his consort and his helpless infants, we do not need to have recourse to a miraculous interference of the Deity or to the empty hypostasis of an innate urge toward association. Neither are we forced to assume that the isolated individuals or primitive hordes one day pledged themselves by a contract to establish social bonds. The factor that brought about primitive society and daily works toward its progressive intensification is human action that is animated by the insight into the higher productivity of labor achieved under the division of labor. (Mises 1966, 160)

The degree to which individuals extend and intensify the division of labor depends on their understanding and acceptance of it. In contrast to Hayek, who says, "The curious task of economics is to demonstrate to men how little they really know about what they imagine they can design" (Hayek 1988, 76), Mises attached an important role to teaching people economic principles and persuading them to pursue their "rightly understood interests."

The principle of the division of labor is one of the great basic principles of cosmic becoming and evolutionary change. The biologists were right in borrowing the concept of the division of labor from social philosophy and in adapting it to their field of investigation. . . . But one must never forget that the characteristic feature of human society is purposeful cooperation; society is an outcome of human action, i.e., of a conscious aiming at the attainment of ends. No such element is present, as far as we can ascertain, in the processes which have resulted in the emergence of the structure-function systems of plant and animal bodies and in the operation of the societies of ants, bees, and hornets. Human society is an intellectual and spiritual phenomenon. It is the outcome of a purposeful utilization of a universal law determining cosmic becoming, viz., the higher productivity of the division of labor. As with every instance of action, the recognition of the laws of nature is put into the service of man's efforts to improve his conditions. (Mises 1966, 145)

The body of economic knowledge is an essential element in the structure of human civilization; it is the foundation upon which modern industrialism and all the moral, intellectual, technological, and therapeutical achievements of the last centuries have been built. It rests with men whether they will make the proper use of the rich treasure with which this knowledge provides them or whether they will leave it unused. But if they fail to take the best advantage of it and disregard its teachings and warnings, they will not annul economics; they will stamp out society and the human race. (Mises 1966, 885)

The prerequisite for advanced social production is calculation that allows purposeful action within the framework of the division of labor. Calculation requires money prices and thus, money and free exchange, which require private property.

Economic calculation is the fundamental issue in the comprehension of all problems commonly called economic. (Mises 1966, 199)

Monetary calculation is the guiding star of action under the social system of division of labor. It is the compass of the man embarking upon production.

The system of economic calculation in monetary terms is conditioned by certain social institutions. It can operate only in an institutional setting of the division of labor and private ownership of the means of production in which goods and services of all orders are bought and sold against a generally used medium of exchange, that is, money.

Monetary calculation is the main vehicle of planning and acting in the social setting of a society of free enterprise directed and controlled by the market and its prices.
    Our civilization is inseparably linked with our methods of economic calculation. It would perish if we were to abandon this most precious intellectual tool of action. (Mises 1966, 229–30)

From this analysis Mises made his criticism of socialism, that it cannot calculate and thus, it is not an economic system at all. The attempt to implement socialism must lead to poverty, death, and retrogression of civilization. Mises said, "In abolishing economic calculation the general adoption of socialism would result in complete chaos and the disintegration of social cooperation under the division of labor" (Mises 1966, 861). While Mises saw calculation as *the* problem of socialism, Hayek views it as a knowledge problem:

> To the naive mind that can conceive of order only as the product of deliberate arrangement, it may seem absurd that in complex conditions order, and adaptation to the unknown, can be achieved more effectively by decentralizing decisions, and that a division of authority will actually extend the possibility of overall order. Yet that decentralization actually leads to more information being taken into account. This is the main reason for rejecting the requirements of constructivist rationalism. (Hayek 1988, 76–77)

Mises demonstrated that even with *perfect* information, the central planners in socialism cannot rationally calculate how to combine resources to render efficient production (Ebeling 1991). They can only grope in the dark; as Mises put it, socialism is "planned chaos," an irrational endeavor that must leach off and mimic capitalism to provide even a subsistence standard of living to its citizens.

> The paradox of "planning" is that it cannot plan, because of the absence of economic calculation. What is called a planned economy is no economy at all. It is just a system of groping about in the dark. There is no question of a rational choice of means for the best possible attainment of the ultimate ends sought. What is called conscious planning is precisely the elimination of conscious purposive action. (Mises 1966, 700-701)

> If no other objections could be raised to the socialist plans than that socialism will lower the standard of living of all or at least of the immense majority, it would be impossible for praxeology to pronounce a final judgment. Men would have to decide the issue between capitalism and socialism on the ground of judgments of value and of judgments of relevance. . . . However, the true state of affairs is entirely different. Man is not in a position to choose between these two systems. Human cooperation under the system of the social division of labor is possible only in the market economy. Socialism is not a realizable system of society's economic organization because it lacks any method of economic calculation. (Mises 1966, 679)

Mises and the Austrian Tradition

These principles, representing the pinnacle of free-market economic theory, cannot be found in any other modern school of economic thought. By failing to correctly understand the process of the social creation of wealth these other schools have not played a significant, independent role in the current advancement of freedom. Advocates of the free market within other schools have relied upon the basic Austrian arguments or have been relatively ineffective, since their economic theories are more easily rebuffed.

What effective defense of the free market has been made by econometrics? By its nature all such work tells us only of what has happened and not what can happen—it cannot result in universal laws applicable to any conceivable historical episode. As such it is easily ignored by those who wish to conduct social experiments for the future. Furthermore, econometrics is coming under increasing criticism as a method capable of rendering useful knowledge at all (see Hoppe 1988).

This criticism extends with equal force to modern neoclassical theory, since it is built upon positivism (Friedman 1974). Milton Friedman tells us that all proper economic theory must be testable and subject to falsification; that economic propositions, like those in physics, are hypothetical, tentative, and forever subject to testing and potential rejection. Yet what basic principles of economics have neoclassical economists rejected for failing tests of statistical significance? The laws of supply and demand? The principle of diminishing marginal utility? The concept of opportunity cost? The idea that exchange leads to mutual benefit? Such basic principles are either nontestable, and thus, not positivist economic theories at all, or routinely rejected in econometric tests. Yet all economic defenses of the free market are built from basic principles. Friedman and other neoclassical economists say that economic theory must be empirical but they do economic theory deductively, although not as well as Mises.

Neoclassical economics has failed to provide any role in defense of the free market to the extent that it stands outside the Austrian tradition. It contains no free-market principles that are both unique and true. It should be kept in mind that after Mises's devastating article on the inability of socialism to calculate, socialists tried to refute him by using mathematical economics and econometrics to show that, in theory at least, the problem could be solved by a system of equations *if* the economy is perfectly competitive (Ebeling 1991). Their failure has not prevented others from employing the preeminent neoclassical theory as an argument *against* the free market. It is a common barb that the free market would be a superior economic system *if* it were perfectly competitive. And since it obviously is not perfectly competitive, then government control is essential.

To the contrary, Mises has shown that the argument for free markets does not depend on *any* type of competition, perfect or otherwise. In contrast, Hayek claims:

> One revealing mark of how poorly the ordering principle of the market is understood is the common notion that "cooperation is better than competition." Cooperation, like solidarity, presupposes a large measure of agreement on ends as well as on methods employed in their pursuit. It makes sense in a small group whose members share particular habits, knowledge, and beliefs about possibilities. It makes hardly any sense when the problem is to adapt to unknown circumstances; yet it is this adaptation to the unknown on which the coordination of efforts in the extended order rests. Competition is a procedure of discovery, a procedure involved in all evolution, that led man unwittingly to respond to novel situations; and through further competition, not through agreement, we gradually increase our efficiency.

To operate beneficially, competition requires that those involved observe rules rather than resort to physical force. Rules alone can unite an extended order. Neither all ends pursued, nor all means used, are known or need to be known to anybody, in order for them to be taken account of within a spontaneous order. Such an order forms of itself. (Hayek 1988, 19–20)

Biological and cultural evolution share other features too. For example, they both rely on the same principle of selection: survival or reproductive advantage. Variation, adaptation, and competition are essentially the same kind of process, however different their particular mechanisms, particularly those pertaining to propagation. Not only does all evolution rest on competition; continuing competition is necessary even to preserve existing achievements. (Hayek, 1988, 26)

Mises has shown that the social division of labor is not an arena of competition but cooperation, a complex network of voluntary interaction that is absolutely necessary for the continuing life and prosperity of the world's population. If people fail to understand this and act against their "rightly understood interests" then prosperity and civilization will end.

What makes friendly relations between human beings possible is the higher productivity of the division of labor. It removes the natural conflict of interests. For where there is division of labor, there is no longer question of the distribution of a supply not capable of enlargement. Thanks to the higher productivity of labor performed under the division of tasks, the supply of goods multiplies. A preeminent common interest, the preservation and further intensification of social cooperation becomes paramount and obliterates all essential collisions. Catallactic competition is substituted for biological competition. It makes for harmony of the interests of all members of society. The very condition from which the irreconcilable conflicts of biological competition arise—viz., the fact that all people by and large strive after the same things—is transformed into a factor making for harmony of interests. Because many people or even all people want bread, clothes, shoes, and cars, large-scale production of these goods becomes feasible and reduces the costs of production to such an extent that they are accessible at low prices. The fact that my fellow man wants to acquire shoes as I do does not make it harder for me to get shoes, but easier. What enhances the price of shoes is the fact that nature does not provide a more ample supply of leather and other raw material required, and that one must submit to the disutility of labor in order to transform these raw materials into shoes. The catallactic competition of those who, like me, are eager to have shoes makes shoes cheaper, not more expensive.

This is the meaning of the theorem of the harmony of the rightly understood interests of all members of the market society. (Mises 1966, 673–74)

Most free-market economists have failed to absorb Mises's analysis of capitalism and socialism and thus hold to some form of a mixed economy. As Mises has shown, this view is untenable.

The market economy must be strictly differentiated from the second thinkable—although not realizable—system of social cooperation under the division of labor: the system of social or governmental ownership of the means of production. This second system is commonly called socialism, communism, planned economy, or state capitalism. The market economy or capitalism, as it is usually called, and the socialist economy preclude one another. There is no mixture of the two systems possible or thinkable; there is no such thing as a mixed economy, a system that would be in part capitalistic and in part socialist. Production is directed by the market or by the decrees of a production tsar or a committee of production tsars.

If within a society based on private ownership by the means of production some of these means are publicly owned and operated—that is, owned and operated by the government or one of its agencies—this does not make for a mixed system which would combine socialism and capitalism. . . . These publicly owned and operated enterprises are subject to the sovereignty of the market. They must fit themselves, as buyers of raw materials, equipment, and labor, and as sellers of goods and services, into the scheme of the market economy. They are subject to the laws of the market and thereby depend on the consumers who may or may not patronize them. They must strive for profits or, at least, to avoid losses. The government may cover losses of its plants or shops by drawing on public funds. But this neither eliminates nor mitigates the supremacy of the market; it merely shifts it to another sector.

Nothing that is in any way connected with the operation of a market is in the praxeological or economic sense to be called socialism. The notion of socialism as conceived and defined by all socialists implies the absence of a market for factors of production and of prices of such factors. The "socialization" of individual plants, shops, and farms—that is, their transfer from private into public ownership—is a method of bringing about socialism by successive measures. It is a step on the way toward socialism, but not in itself socialism. (Mises 1966, 258—59)

This step-by-step process, in reverse, is the council given to the countries of Eastern and Central Europe by today's self-proclaimed, free-market economists. After moving toward capitalism, they are to stop at some optimum amount of government intervention. But Mises showed long ago that interventionism is an unstable middle ground between capitalism and socialism that must continue in motion toward one another.

The system of interventionism or of the hampered market economy differs from the German pattern of socialism by the very fact that it is still a market economy. The authority interferes with the operation of the market economy but does not want to eliminate the market altogether. It wants production and consumption to develop along lines different from those prescribed by an unhampered market, and it wants to achieve its aim by injecting into the working of the market orders, commands, and prohibitions for whose enforcement the police power and its apparatus of violent compulsion and coercion stand ready. But these are *isolated* acts of an integrated system which determines all prices, wages, and interest rates and thus places full control of production and consumption into the hands of the authorities.

The system of the hampered market economy or interventionism aims at preserving the dualism of the distinct spheres of government activities on the one hand and economic freedom under the market system on the other hand. What characterizes it as such is the fact that the government does not limit its activities to the preservation of private ownership of the means of production and its protection against violent or fraudulent encroachments. The government interferes with the operation of business by means of orders and prohibitions. (Mises 1966, 718)

The interventionist doctrinaires repeat again and again that they do not plan the abolition of private ownership of the means of production, of entrepreneurial activities, and, or market exchange. . . . It is necessary, they say, that the state interfere with the market phenomena whenever and wherever the "free play of the economic forces" results in conditions that appear as "socially" undesirable. In making this assertion they take it for granted that it is the government that is called upon to determine in every single case whether or not a definite economic fact is to be considered as reprehensible for the "social" point of view and consequently whether or not the state of the market requires a special act of government interference.

All these champions of interventionism fail to realize that their program thus implies the establishment of full government supremacy in all economic matters and ultimately brings about a state of affairs that does not differ from what is called the German or the Hindenburg pattern of socialism. If it is in the jurisdiction of the government to decide whether or not definite conditions of the economy justify its intervention, no sphere of operation is left to the market. Then it is no longer the consumers who ultimately determine what should be produced, in what quantity, of what quality, by whom, where, and how—but it is the government. For as soon as the outcome brought about by the operation of the unhampered market differs from what the authorities consider "socially" desirable, the government interferes. That means the market is free as long as it does precisely what the government wants it to do. . . . Thus the doctrine and the practice of interventionism ultimately tend to abandon what originally distinguished them from outright socialism and to adopt entirely the principles of totalitarian all-round planning. (Mises 1966, 723–24)

In Mises's view what we are witnessing today is not the collapse of socialism, since socialism cannot be realized in full, but the collapse of a form of interventionism. He predicted this in 1949: "The interventionist interlude must come to an end because interventionism cannot lead to a permanent system of social organization" (Mises 1966, 858). This must happen because interventionism restricts the goods available to consumers; and fails to bring about the end aimed at, leading to a situation worse than the preintervention once it has exhausted the "surplus" it seeks to confiscate (Mises 1966, 858). The outcome of changes in Europe depend upon understanding and accepting these Misesian ideas.

Optimists hope that at least those nations which have in the past developed the capitalist market economy and its civilization will cling to this system in the future too. There are certainly as many signs to confirm as to disprove such an expectation. It is vain to speculate about the outcome of the great ideological conflict between the principles of private ownership and public ownership, of individualism and totalitarianism, of freedom and authoritarian regimentation. All that we can know beforehand about the result of this struggle can be condensed in the following three statements:

(1) We have no knowledge whatever about the existence and operation of agencies which would bestow final victory in this clash on those ideologies whose application will secure the preservation and further intensification of societal bonds and the improvement of mankind's material well-being. Nothing suggests the belief that progress toward more satisfactory conditions is inevitable or a relapse into very unsatisfactory conditions impossible.

(2) Men must choose between the market economy and socialism. They cannot evade deciding between these alternatives by adopting a "middle-of-the-road" position, whatever name they may give to it.

(3) In abolishing economic calculation the general adoption of socialism would result in complete chaos and the disintegration of social cooperation under the division of labor. (Mises 1966, 861)

We are all participating in this great ideological struggle and thus economic education holds paramount importance.

Economics must not be relegated to classrooms and statistical offices and must not be left to esoteric circles. It is the philosophy of human life and action and concerns everybody and everything. It is the pith of civilization and of man's human existence.

There is no means by which anyone can evade his personal responsibility. Whoever neglects to examine to the best of his abilities all the problems involved voluntary surrenders his birthright to a self-appointed elite of supermen. In such vital matters blind reliance upon "experts" and uncritical acceptance of popular catchwords and prejudices is tantamount to the abandonment of self-determination and to yielding to other people's domination. As conditions are today, nothing can be more important to every intelligent man than economics. His own fate and that of his progeny at stake. (Mises 1966, 878)

Conclusion

The Austrian tradition is identified by and built upon praxeology—the application of deductive reasoning, to the irrefutable fact of human action. This method is the red thread that runs from Menger to Böhm-Bawerk to Mises to Murray Rothbard and the modern practitioners of Austrian economics. Working within this tradition, economists have produced a great edifice of irrefutable, universally applicable economic theory. They have shown how the free market advances mankind in its struggle against scarcity and why socialism cannot do so. They have taught us that we must choose one of these two social arrangements, since no system exists between them. We must make our selection and advance, by education and persuasion, either capitalism or socialism. Let us choose wisely.

Notes

First published in the *Review of Austrian Economics* 5, no. 2 (1991): 32–50.

References

Böhm-Bawerk, Eugen. *Capital and Interest.* Spring Mills, Penn.: Libertarian Press, 1959.

Ebeling, Richard. "Economic Calculation Under Socialism: Ludwig von Mises and His Predecessors." *The Meaning of Ludwig von Mises*, edited by Jeffrey Herbener. Boston: Kluwer Academic Publishers, 1991.

Friedman, Milton. "The Methodology of Positive Economics." *Essays in Positive Economics.* Chicago: University of Chicago Press, 1974, 3–43.

Hayek, F. A. "Introduction." *Principles of Economics*, edited by Carl Menger. New York: New York University Press, 1976, 11–36.

———. *The Fatal Conceit: The Errors of Socialism.* Chicago: University of Chicago Press, 1988.

Hoppe, Hans-Hermann. *Praxeology and Economic Science.* Auburn, Ala.: The Ludwig von Mises Institute, 1988.

Menger, Carl. *Principles of Economics.* New York: New York University Press, 1976.

———. *Investigations into the Method of the Social Sciences with Special Reference to Economics.* New York: New York University Press, 1985.

Mises, Ludwig von. *Human Action: A Treatise on Economics*, 3rd rev. ed. Chicago: Henry Regnery, 1966.

———. Quoted by Margit von Mises in "A Call to Activism." *The Free Market Reader.* Auburn, Ala.: The Ludwig von Mises Institute, 1988.

Rothbard, Murray. *The Essential Ludwig von Mises.* Auburn, Ala.: The Ludwig von Mises Institute, 1983.

———. "Mises and the Role of Economist in Public Policy." *The Meaning of Ludwig von Mises,* edited by Jeffrey Herbener. Boston: Kluwer Academic Publishers, 1991, 193–208.

Salerno, Joseph. "Ludwig von Mises as Social Rationalist." *The Meaning of Ludwig von Mises,* edited by Jeffrey Herbener. Boston: Kluwer Academic Publishers, 1991, 215–44.

8

Rand on Obligation and Value

Douglas B. Rasmussen

In 1990, I presented a paper before the Ayn Rand Society of the American Philosophical Association (Eastern Division) entitled "Rand on Obligation and Value," wherein I discussed the relationship between Rand's theory of obligation and her theory of value.[1] I asked: What is the relationship between her account of how one determines what one ought to do and her account of what is of ultimate value? I did not offer a definitive answer to the question, but I sought to initiate a deeper examination of Rand's position.

Because Objectivist philosophers—including Leonard Peikoff (1991, 244–45, 248), Allan Gotthelf (2000, 84), and Tara Smith (2000, 94, 104–11)—continue to insist that ethics depends upon a "pre-moral" choice to live, they continue to champion a view that I have always found problematic. Given that the issues remain current, I present here, in print, for the first time, my examination of the issues at hand—in the hopes of furthering a dialogue.

Rand's Theory of Obligation

Let us consider the following statements by Rand regarding the source of obligation:

> My morality, the morality of reason, is contained in a single axiom: existence exists—and in a single choice: to live. The rest proceeds from these. (Rand 1961, 128)

> Life or death is man's only fundamental alternative. To live is his basic act of choice. If he chooses to live, a rational ethics will tell him what principles of action are required to implement his choice. If he does not choose to live, nature will take its course.

Reality confronts man with a great many "musts," but all of them are conditional; the formula for realistic necessity is: "You must, if—" and "if" stands for man's choice: "—if you want to achieve a certain goal." You must eat, if you want to survive. You must work, if you want to eat. You must think—if you want to work. You must look to reality, if you want to think—if you want to know what to do—if you want to know what goals to choose—if you want to know how to achieve them. ("Causality versus Duty" (1970) in Rand 1982, 118–19)

It would appear from these statements, especially the one from her essay, "Causality versus Duty," that Rand is rejecting the idea that one can have any moral obligations apart from one's choice to attain a goal. Indeed, later in the same essay she describes the man who follows her ethics as "[a]ccepting no mystic 'duties' or unchosen obligations[.] [H]e is the man who honors scrupulously the obligations which *he* chooses" (121). All moral necessity would seem then to be of the hypothetical variety for Rand. It follows from one's choice to live.

Rand also endorses the idea that it is the goal of an action that determines the proper means. She has, to say the least, no use for deontologism.[2] She rejects in totality the idea that moral obligation could stem from duty alone, apart from a consideration of a person's goals, motives, desires, interests, and needs.

In order to make the choices required to achieve his goals, a man needs the constant, automatized awareness of the principle which the anticoncept "duty" has all but obliterated in his mind: the principle of causality—specifically, of Aristotelian *final causation* (which, in fact, applies only to a conscious being), that is, the process by which an end determines the means, that is, the process of choosing a goal and taking the actions necessary to achieve it.

In a rational ethics, it is causality—not duty—that serves as the guiding principle in considering, evaluating, and choosing one's actions, particularly those necessary to achieve a long-range goal. In choosing a goal, he considers the means required to achieve it, he weighs the value of the goal against the difficulties of the means and against the full, hierarchical context of all his other values and goals (119). The notion of duty is intrinsically anticausal. In its origin, a duty defies the principle of efficient causation—since it is causeless (or supernatural); in its effects, it defies the principle of final causation—since it is performed regardless of the consequences (121).

Thus, Rand's theory of obligation seems consequentialistic.[3] What determines whether an action ought to be taken depends on whether it will attain the goal chosen by the person. There can be no such thing as doing something from a motive of duty, viz., simply because one ought to.

Of the many issues raised by Rand's comments regarding the nature of obligation, the one that seems to be of primary importance is the claim that moral obligation is hypothetical in character. This leads to a most unusual situation for Rand's ethics—namely, that one can, so to speak, choose to opt out of the "moral game." If all moral obligations are hypothetical in character, that is, if a person if he is told, "You are guilty of a contradiction," *if* the possibility of "oughts" or "shoulds" for that person is dependent on his first choosing to live? he actually can choose *not* to live, and if no obligation can exist without the choice to live, then being told that he is inconsistent would make no difference his conduct. What would be the point of making such logical evaluations if his person is not also subject to moral evaluations? How could the logical evaluation of inconsistency get a person to change his beliefs or conduct, unless *ought* not to commit contradictions?[5] To the person who chooses *not* to live, and who, thus, has no obligations, the logical evaluations—"inconsistent" and "invalid"—do not obligate him to alter his choice. He has neither reason nor motivation.

From the perspective of morality, it seems that, despite Branden's claims, the choice to live is ultimately optional or arbitrary. There is no reason why one should choose to live or choose not to live. And if this is true, then Rand's derivation of an "ought" from an "is" seems of limited value: if I choose to live, then I ought to do such and such, but since there can be no obligation without this choice, there is nothing, either logically or morally, that obligates me to choose to live and thus no reason to be moral. Possibly, there was something to Hazel E. Barnes (1967) including a chapter on "Objectivist Ethics" in her book, *An Existentialist Ethics*. Morality seems to be based on an irrational or a rational commitment—the very thing Rand vehemently rejects.

Yet, it might be said that this conclusion is too quickly made. If it is true that logically one cannot value anything without valuing that which makes such valuation possible, and if life is the very thing that makes valuation possible, then the value of "life" is implicit in any choice or valuation a person makes, and thus in making *any* choice, one chooses to live. Even the person who chooses not to live thereby values and chooses life implicitly. Thus, it may be said that virtually everyone alive chooses to live. Only those who literally can make no choices would be outside the moral arena. But this, of course, is not unusual. Morality is generally understood as only applying to chosen actions. Thus, though Rand's "oughts" are only hypothetical imperatives, they apply to virtually everyone. Since the choice to live is so implicit or deep, it is not as easy to opt out of ethics as it first appeared.

This reply is not, however, sufficient. It only pushes the issue back another step, because it should now be asked: What does it mean to say that life as a value is *implicit* in any choice a person makes?[6] The point here is that "implicit" has to refer to more than a logical condition for something to be a value. The argumentative punch of the claim that the value of life is "implicit" in any choice has to be able to produce more than a charge of inconsistency against the person who fails to value that which makes any valuation possible. As I've already observed, if obligations are possible only on the condition of the choice to live, it is not at all clear how being guilty of a contradiction will make any difference to the belief or conduct of one who chooses not to live.

Further, just what does it mean to say that in making any choice, a person chooses to live? If the person who chooses not to live insists that he is not

the determination of what we ought or ought not do is only poss
chosen to live, then the decision to either live or not to live woul
ble of moral evaluation by Rand's ethics. No reasons or recomme
be given as to why one ought to choose to live or choose not to liv
live or choosing not to live would seem to be an ultimate humar
beyond the scope of ethics. Morally speaking, the choice not to
just as good (or bad) as the choice to live. Or, so it seems.

Nathaniel Branden in his essay, "The Moral Revolution in *At*
states that "[t]he man who does not wish to hold life as his goal ₐ
free not to hold it; but he cannot claim the sanction of reason: hᵢ
that his *choice* is as valid as any other. It is not 'arbitrary,' it is
whether or not man accepts his nature as a living being—just as
trary' or 'optional' whether or not he accepts reality" (in Brandeᵢ
1962, 27; emphasis added). Yet, as far as morality is concerne
choice not to live not as valid as any other? Why is it not arbitrₐ
whether a man accepts his nature as a living being or not? Why cₐ
tion of life as one's goal claim the sanction of reason? Is Braₙ
somehow that one ought to choose to live? What does Branden m
tion of reason," by "valid"?

Branden notes that Rand, by identifying the context in whic
existentially, demonstrates how an "ought" can be derived from a
plains that for a person *not* to hold man's life as one's standard fᵢ
ment is to be guilty of a *logical contradiction*. It is only to a liᵥᵢ
things can be good or evil; life is the basic value that makes all otʰ
sible; the value of life is not justified by a value beyond itself; to
justification—to ask: Why *should* man choose to live?—is to haᵥ
meaning, context and source of one's concepts. "Should" is a coₙ
have no intelligible meaning, if divorced from the concept *and valᵢ
27).

The argument seems to be that if one tries to value somethiₙ
accepting the basic value of life, which for a human being is man'ₛ
man, one is guilty of an inconsistency. If life is the basic value t
other values possible, including even one's valuing not to live, ᵢ
who prefers not to live is implicitly accepting the value of life. Thᵢ
who chooses not to live cannot claim the sanction of reason. He is
contradiction,[4] and since his activity of choosing not to live invoₗ
diction, logically his choice is not "valid."

While we may have questions about whether life is the basᵢ
makes all other values possible—and indeed about what this cl
amounts to when it comes to human beings—let us grant it, for tʰ
issue here. Rather, the issue concerns the primacy of choice in Raₙ
all judgments regarding what a person ought or ought not do are oₙ
that person first chooses to live, and if we are dealing with sᵢ
chooses not to live, then what force does the logical evaluation of ᵢ
involving an inconsistency have? In other words, what difference ᵢ

choosing life, how are we to say that his actions are for the sake of more than he claims for them? We might say that logically this person's choice has certain presuppositions and these must be part of his choice, but again how does that show that he ought to regard his action as being for the sake of something more? The ends of a person's actions seem to be entirely determined by what he says they are for, so the existentialist flavor of Rand's theory of obligation remains.

Rand's Theory of Value

I believe that something has gone wrong here, and I believe it is the assumption that there can be no obligation without the choice to live. Further, I believe that what Rand is claiming in "Causality versus Duty" is subject to a different interpretation than what has so far been presented, and I will get to that eventually. Yet, I think the best way to proceed now is to come at the question of what grounds obligation from another direction. So, let us consider these questions: Is life a value because we choose it, or do we choose life because it is a value? Is choice the cause of life being a value, or is life the value that is ultimately the cause of choice? The basis for answers to these questions appear to be found in the following well-known statement by Rand: "An *ultimate* value is that final goal or end to which all lesser goals are the means—and it sets the standard by which all lesser goals are *evaluated*. An organism's life is its *standard of value*: that which furthers its life is the *good*, that which threatens it is the *evil*."

Without an ultimate goal or end, there can be no lesser goals or means: a series of means going off into an infinite progression toward a nonexistent end is a metaphysical and epistemological impossibility. It is only an ultimate goal, an *end in itself*, that makes the existence of values possible. Metaphysically, life is the only phenomenon that is an end in itself: a value gained and kept by a constant process of action. Epistemologically, the concept of "value" is genetically dependent upon and derived from the antecedent concept of "life." To speak of "value" as apart from "life" is worse than a contradiction in terms. "It is only the concept of 'Life' that makes the concept of 'Value' possible."

In answer to those philosophers who claim that no relation can be established between ultimate ends or values and the facts of reality, let me stress that the fact that living entities exist and function necessitates the existence of values and of an ultimate value which for any given living entity is its own life. Thus the validation of value judgments is to be achieved by reference to the facts of reality. The fact that a living entity *is*, determines what it *ought* to do. So much for the relation between "is" and "ought." ("The Objectivist Ethics" (1961) in Rand 1964, 17)

Clearly, Rand is claiming that in reality there is something that is by its very nature an end in itself, an ultimate value, and this is life. It is the only phenomenon that is an end in itself or ultimate value. Life is the end or value that makes all other ends or values possible. It is the ultimate goal of a living thing's actions. Further, since "life" does not exist in the abstract, this means that for any living entity, its life is the ultimate end or value for its actions. Nowhere in this passage does Rand claim that the existence of life as the ultimate end, goal, or value is dependent on choice. Life is not a value because we choose it, but rather because of what it is—"(m)etaphysically, *life* is . . . an end in itself: a value gained and kept by a constant process of action" (17).

This claim requires, of course, much explanation, and this brief chapter is not the place for it. However, it is important for our purposes to consider if this claim conflicts with Branden's observation that "(i)n no sense does Ayn Rand regard any particular value as a metaphysical given, as preexisting in man or in the universe" (Branden and Branden 1962, 28). The crucial words in Branden's observation are, of course, "particular value." Life is the ultimate end or value, but this does not require that life be a particular end or value. Rather, it is an inclusive end or value. Life is an activity that is constituted by actions that are both productive of and expressive of it. Life is not some dominant end, separate and apart from the activities that make it up.[7] Nor is life, to use a term many readers of Rand are familiar with, an "intrinsic" value. It is something that is attained by the actions of a living thing, but life is not some thing that exists apart from this action. Branden's observation, then, does not seem to conflict with the claim that metaphysically, life is an end in itself.

As is well known, Rand holds that it is the specific nature or identity of a living being that determines which ends or values are proper for it. That which is required for man's survival qua man is the standard of value for a human being. It is this standard that determines what is good or bad for a human being.

That which his survival requires is set by his nature and is not open to his choice. What *is* open to his choice is only whether he will discover it or not, whether he will choose right goals and values or not (Rand 1964, 22).

The proper values or ends for a human being are not open to choice, according to Rand. Choice itself does not determine the end and standard by which choices are judged. Rather, choices are judged in terms of the end and standard of man's life. Choice is not the cause of the ultimate value of life, but life as the ultimate end is the cause—in the sense of creating the need for—the activity that is choice. It is by choosing, which for Rand ultimately refers to attaining and maintaining a conceptual focus regarding the world, that the life which is proper to a man is attained.

Nothing is given to man on earth except a potential and the material on which to actualize it. The potential is a superlative machine: his consciousness; but it is a machine without a spark plug, the self-starter and the driver; *he* has to discover how to use it and *he* has to keep it in constant action. Everything he needs or desires has to be learned, discovered, and produced by *him*—by his own choice, by his own effort, by his own mind (22).

A human consciousness is a potentiality that can only be actualized through an individual's own choice, and though it is through choice that human life and values come to actually exist, choice nonetheless has a function or end in terms of which it can be judged. Thus, when Rand states that man has to be man by choice and that he has to hold his life as a value by choice (23), she is speaking of choice—the exercise of mind—as necessary to actualize a potential. She is not saying that choice creates the potential or sets its own end.

Choice is crucial in attaining the ultimate value or end of a man's life qua man, but choice is not necessary for man's life to be the end or goal of human life. Choice does not determine the ultimate end of choice. This is the result of man's nature as a living being. The goal and standard of human life is man's survival qua man. This is, to put it plainly and controversially, man's natural end.[8] This is the Aristotelian flavor of Rand's ethics.

Yet, if this is so, then we need to reexamine the situation we faced earlier— namely, is it true that no moral evaluation can be made of the choice not to live? The answer now is "no." Since the goal and standard of human choice is man's life, moral evaluation of this choice, and any choice, is possible. We can even say that a person ought to choose to live.[9] There is no need of some value beyond life for this evaluation to be made. Rather, living as a human being— man's life—is the goal and standard set by our nature. If we return to the argument advanced by Branden against the person who chooses not to live, it can now be seen that being guilty of a contradiction does have force for this person. Even though this person chooses not to live, his activity of choosing has an end regardless of whether he intends it or not.[10] Man's life qua man is the ultimate end or goal of human action. This means that, for this person, living his life according to the principles his nature requires—for example, not committing contradictions—is good for him. There is nothing else in terms of which a reason can be given for why something ought or ought not to be done.[11] The obligation not to commit contradictions comes from a consideration of what is good for this person.[12] It is not from his choice or from a consideration of the "demands" of logic.

Reconsidering "Causality versus Duty"

Branden speaks of the choice not to live. I do also, but in the passage quoted from "Causality versus Duty" Rand speaks of someone either choosing to live or not choosing to live. Strictly speaking, not choosing is not a choice. This is an important difference. Not choosing involves no course of action being taken. This is sheer passivity. There is nothing to evaluate. Choosing not to X, even not to choose, is capable of evaluation. A course of action has been taken. It is not clear that Rand means what she literally says—that is, that she means "not choosing to live" as opposed to "choosing not to live." If she does, then there would be no reason to specify the choice in terms of life, for it would be choosing as opposed to not choosing that would make the principles of a rational ethics applicable, not the object of this choice. Yet, given (1) the fundamental value that life represents, (2) Rand's understanding of choice as the exercise of one's conceptual capacity, and (3) Rand's claim that it is only through the exercise of one's conceptual capacity that a person can live as a human being, it might be that she sees no difference between choosing and choosing to live. I am not sure what she means.

It should also be noted that the assumption that created the existentialist flavor of Rand's theory of obligation is the claim that judgments about what someone ought or ought not do are only possible if a person chooses to live. In other words, choosing to live is a necessary condition for the existence of obligation. Let us call this claim "CNO." Is this claim, CNO, actually being made in the passages quoted? Rand states that (A) if one chooses to live, then a rational ethics will tell one what principles of action to follow (viz., a rational ethics will be one's standard of moral evaluation). Further, she states that (B) if one does not choose to live, then nature will take its course. She does not, however, state that (C) if one does not choose to live, then a rational ethics will not tell one the principles of action to follow. Neither does she say that (D) if one chooses not to live, then a rational ethics will not tell one the principles of action to follow. Further, (C) is not implied by either (A) or (B), or even (A) and (B). The same is true for (D). Yet, in order for CNO to be made, Rand has to be claiming either (C) or (D). From what I can tell, she claims neither. Thus, maybe her theory of obligation is consistent with what seems to be the central feature of her theory of value—that is, the belief that man's life is the goal and standard for human choice.

Finally, it must be remembered that Rand is attacking Kant's duty ethics in this essay, and she is emphasizing how morality has to be related to the needs, interests, and goals of an individual.[13] I do not think, however, she needs to be interpreted as advocating that we can only know that we should practice the virtues required by a rational ethics after considering the consequences of a specific action. Nor am I sure that her moral principles—specifically the virtues that man's survival qua man require—are merely rules that a consideration of consequences has dictated. In other words, I am skeptical whether consequentialism best captures Rand's theory of obligation. It seems to me that virtue and value are too intimately related in Rand for her view of obligation to be seen as consequentialistic, but this must be an issue for another day.

Some Concluding Thoughts

In 1990, Allan Gotthelf responded directly to my initial challenge in his reply before the Ayn Rand Society of the American Philosophical Association. Though Gotthelf does not now accept all the formulations of his unpublished reply, he raises a few important issues that have been acknowledged in print with his approval.[14] Indeed, he continues to adhere to the view that "[m]orality rests on a fundamental, premoral choice" (Gotthelf 2000, 84). Strictly speaking, however, as Sciabarra (1995, 241) observes, for Gotthelf, "life is not a value because we choose it, nor do we choose life because it is a value. For Gotthelf, as for Rand, there are no human values apart from human choice." Sciabarra quotes Gotthelf:

The whole point of Ayn Rand's derivation of "ought" from "is," as it applies to humans, is that *if* you choose to exist, *then* you can consistently pursue that choice, and any other particular choice, only by holding life as your ultimate value—because life, by its nature, requires a specific course of action; only that fact about life gives point to any act of evaluation, any reason to choose—any basis for a *concept of value*. But that fact about life has no implication for action to beings who choose not to exist. The choice to live and the nature of life *together* ground the status of one's life as one's actual, and only rational, ultimate value. (Gotthelf in Sciabarra 1995, 241)

Sciabarra points out that both Leonard Peikoff and Harry Binswanger agree with Gotthelf that "the choice to live is indeed a metaethical commitment. It is a choice that both precedes and underlies the need for morality" (241).

I have called this view "existentialistic," but perhaps it is more precise to call this the "voluntarist" interpretation of Rand's theory of obligation. Something is obligatory only if we choose it. Does this position make sense? Is it the best way to understand what Rand is contending?

While it is true that nothing can be actually good for human beings apart from their having chosen it, it does not follow from this that our choosing alone makes something good for us. And it certainly seems doubtful that Rand (as well as most proponents of the voluntarist view) would ever want to hold that choosing is sufficient to make something good for human beings. Yet, if this is so, then we can legitimately speak of what would be actually good for human beings if they were to choose it. Further, we can contrast this with what would *not* be actually good for human beings if they were to choose it. Having made such a differentiation, however, we come to the fundamental question: Does that which would be actually good for human beings, if they were to choose it, have any claim on our choosing? Does it provide us with a reason for choosing? Does it have any directive power?

The voluntarists contend that apart from the choice to live, there is no implication for our conduct from any fact of nature. There is no fact of nature that by itself has any directive power for human choice. Yet, if this is so, the very legitimacy of speaking of what would be actually good for human beings if they were to choose it is placed in doubt. If such putative facts have no directive power for human choice, if they provide no reason for our choosing, then there is no point in speaking of them as "good for." Indeed, to say that X-ing would be actually good for human beings if they were to choose it is to say that X-ing is *worthy of choice*, and noting that X-ing is choiceworthy is just to say that we *ought* to choose it—everything else being equal. If choosing to live is logically prior to something being choiceworthy, then we cannot legitimately speak of what would be actually good for human beings if they were to choose it.

In addition, if that which would actually be good for human beings if they were to choose it carries no directive power by itself for human choice, then why is it needed for guidance, as the voluntarists suggest, once we make the choice to live? What does it provide? The supposed answer is, of course, that given the premoral choice to live, the nature of human life determines the means for attaining that end. Our choice sets the end, and the nature of life provides the means. In other words, we are to follow the voluntarist hypothetical imperative: If life is our goal, then we ought to adopt the means for its attainment.

But why should the nature of life be deemed capable of guiding our selection of means if no fact of nature can by itself provide such guidance? If something is only choiceworthy because it is chosen, then why does the fact that certain modes of conduct are necessary for human existence provide a reason for adopting such conduct? Why ought we choose the means to our ends? Why ought we follow the voluntarist hypothetical imperative?

If it is replied that our failing to choose the appropriate means entails our not achieving our end, then we return to the initial problem of this chapter: Why is achieving our end, living the life that is proper to man, choiceworthy? Why ought we to choose to live? The voluntarists can provide no answer—for this is ex hypothesi a premoral choice. But if this is so, it follows that they can provide no reason *why* we ought to choose the means to our end either.

Indeed, it is not even clear what it is to say that living is "our end" or "our choice" if the choice worthiness of life only results from our choice. Choosing to live cannot, for Rand, be simply a random act—something that just happens to come down in favor of life. Choosing must be done for a reason, and thus when one chooses to live, it is because one values life. But where does that value come from? What makes life something choiceworthy if it is not life itself? Without life being something that is choiceworthy, something that we ought to choose, there is really no meaning to the "choice to live."

Despite all the paraphrasing of selected statements from Rand, the fundamental problem with the voluntarist view does not go away. If the choice to live is a metaethical commitment that precedes and underlies the need for morality, then there is still no reason why one ought to choose to live and thus no reason to be moral. Nothing can be said to a person regarding why he or she ought to choose to live. A person cannot be told that it is wiser, better, more sensible, or more logical to choose to live. It is a choice that is outside of reason.

Furthermore, there is ambiguity in the voluntarist claim that there are no human values without choice. Does this mean merely that human choice is necessary for the achievement of human values, or does this also mean that nothing is in fact valuable for human beings unless they are first committed to living? The first is obvious and true, the latter is neither. There are many things that are good for human beings to choose regardless of whether they choose to live or not.

Finally, there may be a confusion of concept with reality here. It is certainly the case that one cannot have the concept of value without there being some human cognitive agency. Yet, this does not show that there are no realities that are valuable for human beings apart from the exercise of what Rand calls "volitional consciousness."[15] Human choice is necessary for the achievement of man's survival qua man, but it is not necessary for it to be the case that such a way of living is our ultimate good and thus something we ought to choose. We do not require any "premoral" choice.

Notes

First published in *The Journal of Ayn Rand Studies* 4, no. 1 (Fall 2002): 69–86.

1. The current chapter is a revised and extended version of my original address presented on 28 December 1990 at a meeting of the Ayn Rand Society of the American Philosophical Association (Eastern Division), Boston, Massachusetts. For their assistance and suggestions for revision, thanks are owed to Robert L. Campbell, Douglas J. Den Uyl ,and Chris Matthew Sciabarra.

2. A deontological theory is any theory in normative ethics that holds "duty" and "right" to be basic and defines the morally good in terms of them. Such theories attempt to determine obligations apart from a consideration of what promotes or expresses the human good. For Kantians, this is accomplished primarily by a universalizability test.

3. A consequentialistic theory is any theory in normative ethics that attempts to determine obligations *merely* by whether an action or rule produces the greatest, net expected "good" (or least "bad") consequences.

4. Despite appearances, this is not primarily an argument against suicide. See note 9 below. Further, I will leave for some other occasion a discussion of whether this inconsistency is of a formal or of a performative nature.

5. A contradictory belief is something that must be false, but it is not literally meaningless.

6. For a helpful discussion of the various meanings of "implicit" in Rand, see Campbell 2002.

7. Both a dominant ultimate end (or value) and an inclusive ultimate end (or value) are never sought for the sake of anything else; but the former reduces the value of everything else to that of a mere means, while the latter comprises activities that express the ultimate value in various forms. To better appreciate this distinction, focus on the difference between two relations of subordination to some end: the difference between (a) activities that are purely means or instruments to that end, and (b) activities that are ingredients in or constituents of that end.

For example, consider the relationship of obtaining golf clubs to playing golf, and the relationship of putting to playing golf. While both are "for the sake of" playing golf, the former is only a necessary preliminary, but putting is one of the activities that make golfing what it is. Further, the actions taken to obtain golf clubs produce an outcome separate from the activity—namely, the possession of golf clubs that can be used—while putting has no end or result apart from itself. Its value is not that of a mere means. Its value lies in its being an expression or realization of the activity of which it is a constituent. As J. L. Ackrill (1980, 19) notes: "One does not putt in order to play golf. . . . Putting *is* playing golf (though not all that playing golf is)."

If life is understood as an inclusive ultimate end, then it is an activity whose constituents express the value that is life. Their value is not determined because they are simply means. Furthermore, understanding life as an inclusive ultimate end (or value) has important implications for how one understands the ultimate moral value, "man's survival qua man." One might say, for instance, that such activities as friendship, knowledge, or virtue are valuable not simply because they produce a life that is appropriate to man, but also because they actually express what it is to live in such a manner. Causality is still the principle of determining one's obligations, but it would in this instance be *for-*

mal, not simply, efficient causality.

8. In *The Philosophic Thought of Ayn Rand*, Douglas Den Uyl and I argue that Rand accepts a biologically based natural teleology. See Den Uyl and Rasmussen 1984, especially chapter 4, "Life, Teleology, and Eudaimonia in the Ethics of Ayn Rand." In *Liberty and Nature*, we note that moral obligations for an ethics based on natural teleology are not hypothetical in the sense that they depend on merely what one wants or chooses. Rather, moral obligations are conditional on attaining one's human good, which is one's natural end. See Rasmussen and Den Uyl 1991.

9. Of course, there can be times in which choosing to die is better, because there might be no chance to live a life proper to a human being. In such a situation, choosing to die would, as odd as it might seem, actually be acting in accordance with the ultimate value of life and would be morally appropriate.

10. Once we awaken from our Cartesian slumbers, we can locate human choice in the middle ground between compulsion and radical freedom. On the one hand, human choice is not reducible to some causal string—the mere result of antecedent genetic or sociocultural factors. Human beings *are* moral agents, and choosing is the central, necessary element in the achievement of the life that is proper to man. It is the key to making the human good both actual and personal. On the other hand, human choice is not radically free. It does not create its context and is not some primitive, inexplicable, unconditioned act. It does not create ex nihilo either the need for choice or the way of living that constitutes what it is to *be* a good human being.

Accordingly, human beings can choose not to hold man's survival qua man as their moral standard, but they cannot choose not to be human or not to have the overall potentiality *for* such a manner of living. Nor can they choose to make the human good anything other than the actualization of this overall potentiality. That is something real, and it is that for the sake of which human choice is exercised. Living the life that is proper to man is the ultimate telos of human choice whether or not human beings recognize it or choose it.

11. If Rand rejects a deontological approach to moral obligation, then our obligations must, for her, be conditional on something. For Rand, our obligations are conditional either on a premoral choice to live or on the human good. If it is the former, then there is no reason why one ought to make this basic choice. Furthermore, there is no reason for accepting any moral obligations that depend on it. If it is the latter, then the ultimate reason why one ought to do anything is, as many a mother has said, "because it is good for you." Or, as Aquinas said in formulating the *first principle* of practical reasoning: "Good is to be done and pursued, and evil is to be avoided" (*Summa Theologiae* I–II, q. 94, a. 2).

12. Roderick Long has noted that there are three types of imperatives: "Problematic hypothetical imperative: *If* you seek this end, then you must take the following steps. Assertoric hypothetical imperative: *Since* you seek this end, then you must take the following steps. Categorical imperative: *Regardless* of what ends you seek, you must take the following steps" (Long 2000, 61 n. 65). Long identifies Rand's official position with the problematic imperative, but also notes that there are times Rand talks as if she follows Aristotle and uses the assertoric imperative. Regarding Rand's use of a problematic imperative, Long remarks that "it is difficult to avoid the implication . . . that the choice to live is arbitrary, a groundless, subjective, existentialistic commitment for or against which rationality has nothing to say" (34).

13. Rand's idea is now often expressed in an agent-relative theory of the human good. The human good, G, for a person, P, is agent-relative if and only if its distinctive presence in world W_1 is a basis for P ranking W_1 over W_2, even though G may not be a

basis for *any other* person's ranking W$_1$ over W$_2$. In other words, there is no such thing as the human good—*period*. The human good is always and necessarily the human good *for* some person or other. See Rasmussen 1999, for a discussion of this distinction and many other related issues. See also Den Uyl 1991.

14. With regard to Gotthelf's point that he no longer accepts all of his own formulations in reply to my original paper, see Sciabarra 1995, 419 n. 31.

15. There may be an important connection between what Rand calls "the choice to think" and "the choice to live," and it may be useful to resolving these difficulties in Rand's thought. Yet, this issue goes beyond our current scope; my stated aim is to simply begin a discussion.

References

Ackrill, J. L. "Aristotle on Eudaimonia." Pp. 15–33 in *Essays on Aristotle's Ethics*, edited by Amelie O. Rorty. Berkeley: University of California Press, 1980.

Barnes, Hazel E. *An Existentialist Ethics*. New York: Alfred A. Knopf, 1967.

Branden, Nathaniel and Barbara Branden. *Who Is Ayn Rand?* New York: Paperback Library, 1962.

Campbell, Robert L. "Goals, Values, and the Implicit: Explorations in Psychological Ontology." Pp. 289–327 in *Journal of Ayn Rand Studies* 3, no. 2 (Spring 2002).

Den Uyl, Douglas J. *The Virtue of Prudence*. New York: Peter Lang, 1991.

Den Uyl, Douglas J. and Douglas B. Rasmussen, eds. *The Philosophic Thought of Ayn Rand*. Urbana: University of Illinois Press, 1984.

Gotthelf, Allan. "The Choice To Value: Comments on Douglas Rasmussen's 'Rand on Obligation and Value.'" Ayn Rand Society address, Boston (28 December 1990).

———. *On Ayn Rand*. Wadsworth Philosophers Series. Belmont, Calif.: Wadsworth/Thomson Learning, 2000.

Long, Roderick T. *Reason and Value: Aristotle Versus Rand*. Objectivist Studies Monograph, no. 3. Poughkeepsie, N.Y.: The Objectivist Center, 2000.

Peikoff, Leonard. *Objectivism: The Philosophy of Ayn Rand*. New York: Dutton, 1991.

Rand, Ayn. *For the New Intellectual: The Philosophy of Ayn Rand*. New York: New American Library, 1961.

———. *The Virtue of Selfishness: A New Concept of Egoism*. New York: New American Library, 1964.

———. *Philosophy: Who Needs It*. Indianapolis/New York: The Bobbs-Merrill Company, 1982.

Rasmussen, Douglas B. "Human Flourishing and the Appeal to Human Nature." *Social Philosophy & Policy* 16, no. 1 (Winter 1999): 1–43.

Rasmussen, Douglas B. and Douglas J. Den Uyl. *Liberty and Nature: An Aristotelian Defense of Liberal Order*. LaSalle, Ill.: Open Court, 1991.

Sciabarra, Chris Matthew. *Ayn Rand: The Russian Radical*. University Park: Pennsylvania State University Press, 1995.

Smith, Tara. *Viable Values: A Study of the Root and Reward of Morality*. Lanham, Md.: Rowman & Littlefield, 2000.

9

The Growing Industry in Ayn Rand Scholarship

Chris Matthew Sciabarra

Since the 1982 death of novelist and philosopher Ayn Rand, there has been ever-growing interest in her thought. In the immediate aftermath of her death, Douglas Den Uyl and Douglas Rasmussen's edited collection, *The Philosophic Thought of Ayn Rand*, and the first edition of Mimi Reisel Gladstein's *Ayn Rand Companion* were published. This was followed in the late 1980s by the appearance of a memoir from Rand's closest associate, psychologist Nathaniel Branden, and a best-selling biography by Barbara Branden, *The Passion of Ayn Rand*. That biography was later adapted as a Showtime movie, starring the Emmy-award winning Helen Mirren as the Russian-born Rand. Rand's life was also the subject of a 1997 Academy Award-nominated documentary, *Ayn Rand: A Sense of Life*, directed by Michael Paxton and narrated by actress Sharon Gless. Randmania reached a cultural apex of sorts with the release, in 1999, of a United States commemorative postage stamp in her honor.

With her influence extending even to a Federal Reserve Chair, Alan Greenspan, who was a high profile member of her inner circle in the 1950s and 1960s, Rand citations have multiplied exponentially. Popular references to Rand can be found in the music of the rock band Rush (and in scholarship on progressive rock and the counterculture; see my "Rand, Rush, and Rock" and "Rand, Rock, and Radicalism"), in the comics of Frank Miller and *Spider-Man* cocreator Steve Ditko, in television series, such as *The Gilmore Girls, Queer as Folk, Judging Amy*, and *One Tree Hill*, and even in cartoons—from *South Park* to *The Simpsons*. Indeed, philosopher William Irwin and writer J. R. Lombardo, in an examination of textual allusion, tell us of Rand's appearance in *The Simpsons and Philosophy*:

> In "A Streetcar Named Maggie," Maggie is placed in the "Ayn Rand School for

Tots" where the proprietor, Ms. Sinclair, reads *The Fountainhead Diet*. To understand why pacifiers are taken away from Maggie and the other children one has to catch the allusion to the radical libertarian philosophy of Ayn Rand. Recognizing and understanding this allusion yields much more pleasure than would a straightforward explanation that Maggie has been placed in a day-care facility in which tots are trained to fend for themselves, not to depend on others, not even to depend on their pacifiers. (2001, 85)

Together with this heightened cultural awareness of Rand's life and thought, academic work has proceeded apace with some fanfare. Both *The Chronicle of Higher Education* and *Lingua Franca* featured major stories on new books and research projects involving philosophy, political theory, literary criticism, and feminism, highlighting how Rand had "finally caught the attention of scholars" (Sharlet 1999, A17). These articles note the increase in scholarly sessions devoted to Rand's work in organizational meetings of the Modern Language Association and the American Philosophical Association, Eastern Division, which includes an affiliated Ayn Rand Society.

My own *Ayn Rand: The Russian Radical*, published in 1995, was central to the *Chronicle* and *Lingua Franca* studies—as was my 1999 anthology, *Feminist Interpretations of Ayn Rand*, coedited with Mimi Reisel Gladstein. The former book rooted Rand's intellectual development in Silver Age Russian thought and reconstructed her Objectivist philosophy as a radical dialectical project. The latter book is part of the Penn State Press "Re-reading the Canon" series, edited by Nancy Tuana, in which nearly two dozen volumes center on questions of gender and sexuality in the works of thinkers as diverse as Plato, Aristotle, Hegel, Marx, Arendt, Sartre, Levinas, and Foucault. The Rand anthology includes original and reprinted contributions from writers across the globe, including Susan Brownmiller, Camille Paglia, Karen Michalson, and Melissa Jane Hardie.

Another measure of Rand's growing scholarly presence is the appearance of entries on her in textbooks—in philosophy, political science, and economics— and in reference works, such as Routledge's *Encyclopedia of Philosophy* and *Encyclopedia of Ethics*, Scribner's *American Writers*, Gale's *American Philosophers, 1950–2000* (a volume of the *Dictionary of Literary Biography*), and Lexington's *History of American Thought*. A Rand primer, by philosopher Allan Gotthelf, in the Wadsworth Philosophy Series, a volume by philosopher Douglas Den Uyl on *The Fountainhead* and another by Mimi Reisel Gladstein on *Atlas Shrugged*, in Twayne's Masterwork Series, Cliffs Notes monographs on *Anthem*, *The Fountainhead*, and *Atlas Shrugged* by philosopher Andrew Bernstein, and philosopher Fred Seddon's critical study, *Ayn Rand, Objectivists, and the History of Philosophy*, are further evidence of increased attention to Rand by professional scholars.[1] (It should be noted too that one can find an increasing number of master's and doctoral dissertations devoted to Rand's thought.[2]) Forthcoming literary collections include *Essays on Ayn Rand's "We the Living"* (edited by Robert Mayhew, who is also working on a book entitled *Ayn Rand*

and *'Song of Russia': Communism and Anti-Communism in 1940s Hollywood*)
and *The Literary Art of Ayn Rand* (edited by William Thomas and David Kelley). Forthcoming philosophical works include Thomas and Kelley's *The Logical Structure of Objectivism* and a book on induction and integration written by
Leonard Peikoff, entitled *The One in the Many: How to Create It and Why*.

One final measure of expanding Rand scholarship is the commencement in
the fall of 1999 of *The Journal of Ayn Rand Studies*, cofounded by R. W. Brad-
ford, literature professor Stephen Cox, and me. The journal is a nonpartisan
semiannual interdisciplinary double-blind peer reviewed scholarly periodical
dedicated to an examination of Rand's work and legacy. In its contents, one will
find essays by Objectivist philosophers and those sympathetic to Rand, as well
as critics of Objectivism, including Marxist aesthetician and literary theorist
Gene Bell-Villada, Marxist philosopher Bill Martin, and the Lacanian philosopher Slavoj Zizek. (Zizek, in fact, discusses Rand in his book *The Abyss of
Freedom*, 85–86; his essay, which serves as an introduction to Schelling's unfin-
ished *Ages of the World*, sees in Howard Roark of *The Fountainhead* a character
who inspires authenticity and benevolence.)

Clearly, the ever-expanding scope of Rand studies suggests that philosophers of various stripes have begun a long overdue reassessment of her thought.
This reassessment must proceed with a few caveats, however.

Rand was the charismatic leader of a kind of people's movement in philosophy. Her novels grew in popularity not because the literati praised them, but
because people—especially young people—were inspired by her tributes to individualism. *The Fountainhead* and *Atlas Shrugged* became underground classics by word of mouth—even as critics on the left recoiled in horror over her
moral defense of capitalism, while critics on the right detested her atheism and
her defense of reproductive freedom. With the establishment of the Nathaniel
Branden Institute in the late 1950s, Rand's philosophy was spread by live and
audio lectures. Rand was very much a public philosopher, appearing before
large crowds at Columbia, Princeton, Harvard, Yale, New York University, and
other colleges. Though she accepted an honorary degree, Doctor of Humane
Letters, at Lewis and Clark College in Portland, Oregon, in 1963, she and many
of her immediate followers reveled in their outsider status. While much of the
intellectual establishment dismissed her as a "pop philosopher," Rand's public
appeal grew. When her movement was sundered in 1968 by her break from Nathaniel Branden—rooted in the collapse of their personal relationship—many
saw the "excommunications" that followed as proof positive of the cult-like
character of Rand's Objectivism.

These purges continued even after Rand's death, leading to highly volatile
debates within Objectivism over what David Kelley has called "the contested
legacy of Ayn Rand." The "orthodox" branch of Objectivism, headed by Rand's
legal heir, Leonard Peikoff, views Objectivism as a "closed system." This approach is embodied in the Ayn Rand Institute (ARI), founded in 1985. ARI and
its affiliated scholars view Objectivism as the word of Ayn Rand—and *only* the
word of Ayn Rand. Indeed, Peikoff has stressed that not even his own work

qualifies as "Objectivism," for "'Objectivism' is the name of Ayn Rand's philosophy as presented in the material she herself wrote or endorsed" (Piekoff 1991, xv).

Since Rand's death, the estate of Ayn Rand has continued to issue a number of edited collections of Rand's writings. These books have—to varying degrees—aided scholars in their attempts to trace the development of Rand's thought. Among the posthumous collections are: *The Early Ayn Rand* (Rand's unpublished fiction); *The Voice of Reason* (reprints from Rand's periodicals, plus a brief memoir by Peikoff); *The Ayn Rand Column* (mostly from the *Los Angeles Times*); *Ayn Rand's Marginalia* (comments on the works of such writers as C. S. Lewis, Wilhelm Windelband, and F. A. Hayek); *Letters of Ayn Rand* (correspondence from 1926 to 1981); *Journals of Ayn Rand* (intellectual notes from 1927 to 1977), *Russian Writings on Hollywood* (translations of two booklets written by a teenaged Rand about the American film industry); *Objectively Speaking: A Collection of Ayn Rand Interviews* (includes Rand's first print interview from the *Oakland Tribune*, and transcripts from her "Ayn Rand on Campus" radio interviews, and audio and video interviews by Mike Wallace, Louis Ruykeyser, Johnny Carson, and others); *The Art of Fiction* and *The Art of Nonfiction*—both of which serve as guides on exposition for writers and readers, and which include many observations on the subconscious and tacit dimensions of creativity. The estate is also working closely with the institute in the preparation of an archival research library.

The central problem with the collections of previously unpublished material, however, is that it is virtually impossible to check the accuracy or quality of the editing. In some instances, because so much of Objectivist philosophy was long consigned to an oral tradition, the editors have had to edit down many hours of taped lectures into cohesive books. The editing is sometimes partisan in nature: those individuals who are persona non grata with the institute are subtly erased from historical memory. In other instances, certain passages in Rand's journals, for example, have been altered in a way that does damage to the historical record.[3] Tibor Machan observes that the hagiographic treatment of Rand by some of her orthodox followers is not unlike that shown to other charismatic philosophical figures—for example, Marx, Nietzsche, Freud, Wittgenstein, Popper, and Sartre—who were surrounded by "admirers and *epigone[s]*" (Machan 1999, xi). It is, therefore, questionable if the estate will ever open its archives to bona fide independent scholars or those affiliated with organizations deemed unacceptable.[4]

One such organization is The Objectivist Center (TOC)—originally the Institute for Objectivist Studies—founded in 1990 by philosopher David Kelley. TOC is much more ecumenical in spirit. Kelley himself views Objectivism in terms of its core ideas in each of the major branches of philosophy. But, for Kelley, Objectivism is an "open system." My own view, which shares Kelley's open-ended commitment, is that Objectivism—like other systems of thought—is evolving over time through a critical hermeneutic where people working in very different traditions engage one another in serious scholarly dialogue, propelling the discussion toward all sorts of provocative unintended intellectual consequences that vary in their implications and applications.

Among the most important recent volumes that have emerged from such scholarly engagement are works by Tibor Machan, Louis Torres and Michelle Marder Kamhi, Tara Smith, Neera K. Badhwar, and Roderick T. Long. In the remainder of this review essay, I will examine each of these works briefly.

Tibor R. Machan's *Ayn Rand* is part of the Peter Lang series, Master Works in the Western Tradition. It is in the spirit of the OUP Past Masters series and is an important step toward viewing Rand in terms of the larger community of Western philosophy. For Machan, Rand is a neo-Aristotelian whose system is founded on a minimalist metaphysics. Focusing on Rand's view of axiomatic concepts, Machan answers O'Neill's and Dancy's criticisms of the principle of noncontradiction. These axioms—of existence, identity, consciousness, and so forth—are not the basis of any rationalistic system. Rand endorses an ontological view of logic as laws not only of thought, but of existence itself. Her epistemology, however, is not of the classical (lower-case "o") objectivist sort; it views knowledge as a relational product of the mind's engagement with an objective reality, and it proposes a theory of definition and certainty that is fully contextual.

Machan traces the implications of Rand's naturalistic ethics and libertarian politics in a fruitful comparison with Marx's conception. He is deeply critical of the Hobbesian notion of the person; his own view of individualism, like that of Rand, is of an enriched classical sort. Machan argues, however, that Rand provided only "the broad outlines and some of the details of a complete philosophy which, however, is open-ended and allows for, indeed invites, continued development" (134). On this basis, he challenges Objectivists to extend Rand's insights in a discussion of induction, free will, evolution, aesthetics, moral obligation, and the family.

It might be said that Louis Torres and Michelle Marder Kamhi take up one of Machan's challenges since they devote a whole book to a development of Rand's aesthetics. *What Art Is: The Esthetic Theory of Ayn Rand* is easily the most important comprehensive study of Rand's philosophy of art ever published. Focusing on Rand's understanding of the cognitive function of art and its importance in human life, the authors provide scientific corroboration of many of her aesthetic insights and apply those insights to a full-fledged critique of modernist and postmodernist art. The authors clearly distinguish Rand's philosophy of art from her Romantic literary notions, and argue that, at its foundation, Rand's understanding of the creative process is "comparable to Aristotle's understanding of artistic *mimesis* ('imitation')" (28). Like Machan, Torres and Kamhi are fully committed to a respectful, critical engagement with Objectivism; they are not afraid to point out those areas where they believe Rand errs or to compare her theories to others in the history of their discipline. Along the way, they raise controversial points about such topics as architecture and photography, which have generated much discussion in the literature.[5]

Tara Smith's *Viable Values* is a reconstruction and defense of Rand's ethics. She carefully distinguishes between Rand's notion of ethics and competing "intrinsic" and "subjective" conceptions. For Smith, an objective conception of the good is one that is inherently relational; it relates to the moral agent's life, which is the "root and reward of morality." Arguing that "morality and rationality *are* tightly linked" (40), Smith takes on intuitionist, contractarian, and rationalist alternatives. Whereas Rand was not nearly as rigorous in her critique of philosophic adversaries, Smith exhibits detailed knowledge of her foes. She develops a case for eudaimonia, or flourishing, that is, in essence, a call for a principled egoism.

The debate between those who view Rand's egoism as "survivalist," as rooted in the life-and-death struggle of the organism, versus those who view it as "flourishing," in which the standard of morality is not *mere* life, but *human* life, with all the constituents this entails, is one that has preoccupied Rand scholars for many years. (Indeed, it is regrettable that Smith does not connect her own eudaimonistic view of Rand's ethics to those, like Den Uyl and Rasmussen, who argued the case more than fifteen years earlier in *The Philosophic Thought of Ayn Rand*.) Neera K. Badhwar's *Is Virtue Only a Means to Happiness?*, a monograph in The Objectivist Center's Objectivist Studies series, centers on this debate, and features commentaries by Jay Friedenberg, Lester H. Hunt, and David Kelley, as well as a reply by the author.

Objectivist Studies publishes works that advance the theoretical development or critical study of the philosophy. Whereas the first two volumes were singular presentations of David Kelley's "Evidence and Justification" (a reprint from *Reason Papers*) and Ken Livingston on the psychology of abstraction, the Badhwar and Long monographs are rife with just the kind of philosophical give-and-take that is essential to the scholarly dissemination of Objectivism.

Badhwar asks: "is virtue only a *means* to happiness, or also *constitutive* of it? If it is only a means, then happiness can be defined independently of virtue. If it is partly constitutive of happiness, then happiness must be defined partly in terms of virtue" (5–6). Badhwar argues that Rand sometimes equivocates on her use of the words "life" and "happiness" in her ethical writings—leading to confusion on this very question. Despite Rand's apparent "survivalist" view, in which happiness is "external to virtue" (9), Badhwar maintains that Rand's actual position is consistent with the "flourishing" argument.

Badhwar presents what she believes is "a more adequate conception of virtue" (12), one that pays attention to the "constitutive role of emotion in value" (14) and that bridges the gap between instrumental and substantive rationality. Taking issue with Rand's "hierarchical account of the emotions as programmed by an untouched intellect," Badhwar draws upon Aristotle's work to bolster the Objectivist view of the integrated person, whose "intellect and emotion grow and mature interdependently, each influencing the other" (23). This view, says Badhwar, is more prevalent in Rand's fiction than in her nonfiction essays.

Each of Badhwar's commentators offers an interesting retort. Friedenberg draws from evolutionary theory. Hunt, who takes issue with the fiction-nonfiction bifurcation of Rand's corpus, presents evidence that Rand's view of emotion may be asymmetric—in deference to thought—but it is definitely not unidirectional (58). Kelley, who has argued for a survivalist interpretation, presents Rand's "ethics as a kind of human ethology; her concept of 'man's life qua man' is really an ethological concept of man's mode of life. As such, it incorporates both survival and flourishing" (63).

Badhwar's rejoinder, however, disputes any strict diremption between value and virtue. Rand once stated that "*[v]alue* is that which one acts to gain and/or keep—*virtue* is the act by which one gains and/or keeps it" (*Virtue of Selfishness*, 25). Rand identified the cardinal values as reason, purposefulness, and self-esteem, and the cardinal virtues as rationality, productivity, and pride—but Badhwar doesn't "really see how the virtue of rationality can be a means to the faculty of thought, since the virtue of rationality presupposes the faculty, and one doesn't lose the faculty by lacking this virtue" (85). For Badhwar, there is an internal relationship of reciprocity here: "valuing reason entails being rational (and being rational entails valuing reason)" (86).

Given that so much of this discussion turns on the nature of internal and external relations, and their crucial importance to the debate over Rand's dialectical orientation, the writers in this superb monograph could have benefited from a more explicit consideration of these underlying methodological issues.

The dialectical subtext is not obscured by Roderick T. Long, in his *Reason and Value: Aristotle versus Rand*, which features commentaries by Fred D. Miller Jr. and Eyal Mozes, as well as a reply by the author. This Objectivist Studies monograph is as impressive as the Badhwar entry in the series. For Long, the dialectical orientation lies at the heart of Aristotle's approach (56 n. 4), but it is also "the key to much of Rand's persuasive power," insofar as she "expos[es] and eliminat[es] contradictions among the moral *endoxa*, and then incorporat[es] the surviving *endoxa* into a unified explanatory system" (55). But Long criticizes Rand for "her own version of foundationalist empiricism" (101) and her curious embrace of conflicting viewpoints; he ascribes to her a Platonist view of theoretical rationality and a Humean view of practical rationality. Like Badhwar, Long believes that Rand's approach is more Aristotelian (constitutive) in her fiction, and more Hobbesian (instrumentalist) in her nonfiction (34). The answer, for Long, lies in a fuller embrace of the Aristotelian moment in Rand's corpus.

Fred D. Miller Jr. finds Long's interpretation "surprising" (65), given Rand's long association with neo-Aristotelian philosophy. Rand herself credited Aristotle as her philosophic forebear; whatever her flirtations with Friedrich Nietzsche, who exerted a great influence over the Russian Silver Age of Rand's youth, it was to Aristotle that she expressed her "only philosophical debt" (*Atlas Shrugged*, "About the Author"). Miller is particularly distressed at Long's omission of Rand's epistemological contextualism (69). Eyal Mozes, who argues for the survivalist interpretation, tries to point toward a reconciliation of Long's Aristotelian "flourishing" approach with survivalism.

Long's reply to Miller and Mozes raises certain questions for Rand's contextualism; he wonders whether Rand "makes *truth* context-relative" or whether "it only makes *justification* context-relative" (107). Regardless of his specific criticisms, however, Long believes that "Rand's overall outlook is . . . remarkably on target. The reliability of her philosophical instincts on a vast range of issues—metaphysical, epistemological, psychological, ethical, political, sociological, and aesthetic—is impressive" (116). Even if he is critical of her various "attempts to articulate reasons to support those instincts," he recognizes that Rand has consummate "skill in presenting [her] ideas in such a powerfully attractive and inspiring way" (117).

What is important about all of these efforts is this: Rand may not have spoken the vernacular of contemporary analytic or continental philosophy. She did not write for academic journals and was an intellectual outsider. But for those scholars who remain impressed by her "powerfully attractive and inspiring" project—even for those scholars who criticize it—there is a great need to relate Rand's philosophic practice to contemporary categories in philosophy. The translation exercise is useful because it helps us to situate her in the contemporary continuum even as it helps us to see where she defies categorization. As is the case with many radical thinkers, Rand asked us to go to the root; that scholars are finally delving into her philosophic roots is a telling sign. We are at the beginning of a major scholarly engagement that will benefit sympathetic and critical readers alike.

Notes

An earlier version of this article was published as "Recent Work: Ayn Rand," in *Philosophical Books* 44, no. 1 (January 2003): 42–52.

1. There are also quite a few accessible works written by nonprofessional philosophers. See Ronald Merrill's *Ideas of Ayn Rand*, which focuses on the broad essentials of Rand's system of thought; Craig Biddle's *Loving Life*, which focuses on Rand's ethics; Alexandra York's *From The Fountainhead to the Future and Other Essays on Art and Excellence*, which deals with Objectivist aesthetics and romanticism; Tom Porter's *Ayn Rand's Theory of Knowledge*, which offers a commentary on Rand's *Introduction to Objectivist Epistemology*; Peter Erickson's *The Stance of Atlas*, which features critical discussion in dialogue form; and Greg S. Nyquist's *Ayn Rand Contra Human Nature*, which indicts Rand's argumentative strategies. Published commentaries by writers of a more religious bent include John Robbins's *Without a Prayer: Ayn Rand and the Close of Her System*, Michael B. Yang's *Reconsidering Ayn Rand*, and Scott Ryan's *Objectivism and the Corruption of Rationality: A Critique of Ayn Rand's Epistemology*, which critiques Rand from a perspective informed primarily by the work of Brand Blanshard and Josiah Royce. For a discussion of the relevance of Rand's ideas for business, management, and leadership, see Donna Greiner and Theodore B. Kinni's *Ayn Rand and Business*. For a discussion of Rand's Objectivist movement, starkly alternative readings are offered by Jeff Walker (*The Ayn Rand Cult*) and philosopher David Kelley (*The Contested Legacy of Ayn Rand*). A more personal view of Rand can be found in the Mary Ann and Charles Sures' memoir, *Facets of Ayn Rand*.

2. One notable published title is Gregory M. Browne's *Necessary Factual Truth*, which is an expansion of his philosophy dissertation. Browne discusses central themes in

Leonard Peikoff's "Analytic-Synthetic Dichotomy," which can be found in the expanded edition of Rand's *Introduction to Objectivist Epistemology*.

3. On these points, see my "Bowdlerizing Ayn Rand," "A Renaissance in Rand Scholarship," "Objectivism and Academe: The Progress, The Politics, The Promise," and "In Search of the Rand Transcript."

4. Some materials not held by the institute are publicly available to scholars, regardless of affiliation, in the Madison Building of the Library of Congress, which houses twenty-eight containers of the manuscripts for Rand's novels. Shoshana Milgram has done pioneering work in her examination of various drafts of *The Fountainhead* (see "Artist at Work").

5. See *Aesthetics Symposium* for a comprehensive discussion of the Torres and Kamhi book.

References

Works by Ayn Rand

Atlas Shrugged. New American Library, 1957.
The Virtue of Selfishness: A New Concept of Egoism. New American Library, 1964.
The Early Ayn Rand, edited and annotated by Leonard Peikoff. New American Library, 1984.
The Voice of Reason: Essays in Objectivist Thought, edited, with additional essays, by Leonard Peikoff. New American Library, 1989.
Introduction to Objectivist Epistemology, 2nd ed. expanded. New American Library, 1990.
Letters of Ayn Rand, edited by Michael S. Berliner, with an introduction by Leonard Peikoff. Dutton, 1995.
Ayn Rand's Marginalia: Her Critical Comments on the Writings of Over 20 Authors, edited by Robert Mayhew. Second Renaissance Books, 1995.
Journals of Ayn Rand, edited by David Harriman, with a foreword by Leonard Peikoff. Dutton, 1997.
Russian Writings on Hollywood, edited by Michael S. Berliner. Ayn Rand Institute Press, 1999.
The Art of Fiction: A Guide for Writers and Readers, edited by Tore Boeckmann, with an introduction by Leonard Peikoff. Plume, 2000.
The Art of Nonfiction: A Guide for Writers and Readers, edited by Robert Mayhew, with an introduction by Peter Schwartz. Plume, 2001.
Objectively Speaking: A Collection of Ayn Rand Interviews, edited by Marlene Trollope and Peter Schwartz. Ayn Rand Bookstore, 2003.

Works on Ayn Rand

Introductions

Bernstein, Andrew. *Cliffs Notes: Rand's Anthem; Rand's The Fountainhead; Rand's Atlas Shrugged*. IDG Books Worldwide, 2000.
Gotthelf, Allan. *On Ayn Rand*. Wadsworth/Thomson Learning, 2000.
Merrill, Ronald. *The Ideas of Ayn Rand*. Open Court, 1991.

Peikoff, Leonard. *Objectivism: The Philosophy of Ayn Rand.* Dutton, 1991.
Sciabarra, Chris Matthew. *Ayn Rand: Her Life and Thought.* Atlas Society, 1999.

Life and Work

Branden, Barbara. *The Passion of Ayn Rand.* Doubleday, 1986.
Branden, Nathaniel. *Judgment Day: My Years with Ayn Rand.* Hougton Mifflin Com-
    pany, 1989; rev. ed.: *My Years with Ayn Rand.* Jossey-Bass Publishers, 1999.
Gladstein, Mimi Reisel. *The Ayn Rand Companion.* Greenwood Press, 1984.
———. *The New Ayn Rand Companion, Revised and Expanded Edition.* Greenwood
    Press, 1999.
Sciabarra, Chris Matthew. "Investigation: The Search for Ayn Rand's Russian Roots,"
    Liberty 13, no. 10 (October 1999), pp. 47–50. Reprinted as "In Search of the Rand
    Transcript" at www.nyu.edu/projects/sciabarra/essays/randt1.htm.
———. "The Rand Transcript," *The Journal of Ayn Rand Studies* 1, no. 1 (Fall 1999),
    pp. 1–26. Also at www.nyu.edu/projects/sciabarra/essays/randt2.htm.
Sures, Mary Ann and Charles Sures. *Facets of Ayn Rand.* Ayn Rand Institute Press, 2001.
Walker, Jeff. *The Ayn Rand Cult.* Open Court, 1999.

Studies

Journal of Ayn Rand Studies (1999–). Though this is a print journal, abstracts, contribu-
    tor biographies, style guidelines, etc., can be found at www.aynrandstudies.com.
Badhwar, Neera K. *Is Virtue Only a Means To Happiness?* Objectivist Studies 4. The
    Objectivist Center, 2001. Commentaries by Jay Friedenberg, Lester H. Hunt, David
    Kelley, and a reply by the author.
Biddle, Craig. *Loving Life: The Morality of Self-Interest and the Facts that Support It.*
    Glen Allen Press, 2002.
Browne, Gregory M., *Necessary Factual Truth.* University Press of America, 2001.
Den Uyl, Douglas J. *The Fountainhead: An American Novel.* Twayne Publishers, 1999.
Erickson, Peter. *The Stance of Atlas: An Examination of the Philosophy of Ayn Rand.*
    Herakles Press, 1997.
Gladstein, Mimi Reisel. *Atlas Shrugged: Manifesto of the Mind.* Twayne Publishers,
    2000.
Greiner, Donna and Theodore B. Kinni. *Ayn Rand and Business.* Texere, 2001.
Kelley, David. *The Contested Legacy of Ayn Rand: Truth and Toleration in Objectivism,*
    2nd ed. The Objectivist Center / Transaction Publishers, 2000.
———. *Evidence and Justification.* Objectivist Studies 1. Institute for Objectivist Stud-
    ies, 1998.
Livingston, Kenneth. *Rationality and The Psychology of Abstraction.* Objectivist Studies
    2. Institute for Objectivist Studies, 1998.
Long, Roderick T. *Reason and Value: Aristotle versus Rand.* Objectivist Studies 3. The
    Objectivist Center, 2000. Commentaries by Fred D. Miller, Jr., Eyal Mozes, and a
    reply by the author.
Machan, Tibor R. *Ayn Rand.* Peter Lang, 1999.
Mayhew, Robert, ed. *Essays on Ayn Rand's "We the Living."* Rowman & Littlefield,
    2004.
Nyquist, Greg S. *Ayn Rand Contra Human Nature.* Writers Club Press, 2001.
Porter, Tom. *Ayn Rand's Theory of Knowledge: A Commentary.* Tom Porter, 1999.
Robbins, John W. *Without a Prayer: Ayn Rand and the Close of Her System.* The Trinity

Foundation, 1997.

Ryan, Scott. *Objectivism and the Corruption of Rationality: A Critique of Ayn Rand's Epistemology*. Writers Club Press, 2003.

Sciabarra, Chris Matthew. *Ayn Rand, Homosexuality, and Human Liberation*. Leap Publishing, 2003.

———. *Ayn Rand: The Russian Radical*. Pennsylvania State University Press, 1995.

Seddon, Fred. *Ayn Rand, Objectivists, and the History of Philosophy*. University Press of America, 2003.

Smith, Tara. *Viable Values: A Study of Life as the Root and Reward of Morality*. Rowman and Littlefield, 2000.

Torres, Louis and Michelle Marder Kamhi. *What Art Is: The Esthetic Theory of Ayn Rand*. Open Court, 2000. Also see www.aristos.org/editors/booksumm.htm.

Yang, Michael B. *Reconsidering Ayn Rand*. Winepress Publishing, 2000.

Collections of Essays

Aesthetics Symposium. A discussion of Ayn Rand's philosophy of art inspired by Torres and Kamhi's *What Art Is*, with contributions from Lester Hunt, Jeff Riggenbach, Gene H. Bell-Villada, Roger E. Bissell, John Hospers, David Kelley, John Enright, Barry Vacker, Michael Newberry, and Randall R. Dipert in *Journal of Ayn Rand Studies* 2, no. 2 (Spring 2001), 251–394.

Den Uyl, Douglas J. and Douglas Rasmussen, eds. *The Philosophic Thought of Ayn Rand*. University of Illinois Press, 1984.

Gladstein, Mimi Reisel and Chris Matthew Sciabarra, eds. *Feminist Interpretations of Ayn Rand*. Pennsylvania State University Press, 1999.

York, Alexandra. *From the Fountainhead to the Future and Other Essays on Art and Excellence*. Silver Rose Press, 2000.

Selected Essays and Chapters

Irwin, William and J. R. Lombardo. "The Simpsons and Allusion: 'Worst Essay Ever.'" *The Simpsons and Philosophy: The D'oh! of Homer*, Popular Culture and Philosophy, edited by William Irwin, Mark T. Conard, and Aeon J. Skoble. Open Court, 2001, pp. 81–92.

McLemee, Scott. "The Heirs of Ayn Rand: Has Objectivism Gone Subjective?" *Lingua Franca* 9, no. 6 (September 1999), pp. 45–55.

Milgram, Shoshana. "Artist at Work: Ayn Rand's Drafts for *The Fountainhead*, Part 1." *Intellectual Activist* 15, no. 8 (August 2001), pp. 9–20.

———. "Artist at Work: Ayn Rand's Drafts for *The Fountainhead*, Conclusion." *Intellectual Activist* 15, no. 9 (September 2001), pp. 23–31.

Sciabarra, Chris Matthew. "Ayn Rand in the Scholarly Literature II: Rand, Rush, and Rock." *Journal of Ayn Rand Studies* 4, no. 1 (Fall 2002), pp. 161–85.

———. "Bowdlerizing Ayn Rand," *Liberty* 11, no. 1 (September 1998). Also at www.nyu.edu/projects/sciabarra/essays/liberty.htm.

———. "Objectivism and Academe: The Progress, The Politics, The Promise." Enlightenment On-Line Conference (15 February 2001; 23 March 2001) at enlightenment.supersaturated.com/essays/text/chrissciabarra/openingaddress.html.

———. "Rand, Rock, and Radicalism." *Journal of Ayn Rand Studies* 5, no. 1 (Fall 2003), pp. 229–41. See also articles in this issue on Rand and progressive rock.

————. "A Renaissance in Rand Scholarship." *Reason Papers*, no. 23 (Fall 1998), pp. 132–59. Also at www.nyu.edu/projects/sciabarra/essays/rprev.htm.

Sharlet, Jeff. "Ayn Rand Has Finally Caught the Attention of Scholars." *Chronicle of Higher Education* 45, no. 31 (April 9, 1999), pp. A17–A18.

Walsh, George. "Ayn Rand and the Metaphysics of Kant." *Journal of Ayn Rand Studies* 2, no. 1 (Fall 2000), pp. 69–103.

Zizek, Slavoj. *The Abyss of Freedom / Ages of the World*. University of Michigan Press, 1997.

Films

Ayn Rand: A Sense of Life, directed by Michael Paxton. Narrated by Sharon Gless. (AG Media Corporation, Ltd. and Copasetic, Inc., 1997).

The Passion of Ayn Rand, directed by Christopher Menaul. Starring Helen Mirren, Eric Stoltz, Julie Delpy, and Peter Fonda. (Producers Entertainment Group and Showtime Networks, Inc., 1999).

10

Aristotle, Menger, Mises: An Essay in the Metaphysics of Economics

Barry Smith

Preamble

There are, familiarly, a range of distinct and competing accounts of the methodological underpinnings of Menger's work. These include Leibnizian, Kantian, Millian, and even Popperian readings; but they include also readings of an Aristotelian sort, and I have myself made a number of contributions in clarification and defense of the latter.[1] Not only, I have argued, does the historical situation in which Menger found himself point to the inevitability of the Aristotelian reading;[2] this reading fits also very naturally to the text of Menger's works.[3]

The diversity of interpretations is not, however, entirely surprising. It is on the one hand a consequence of the fact that Menger breaks new ground in economic theory in part by fashioning new linguistic instruments not yet readily capable of unambiguous interpretation. It reflects further a lack of knowledge on the part of historians of economic thought of the most recent scholarship on nineteenth and twentieth century Austrian philosophy and on the role of Aristotelianism therein.[4] Still more importantly, perhaps, it reflects the fact that Aristotelian ways of thinking were for so long alien to the modern philosophical and scientific mind. For non-Aristotelian readings were advanced above all by those who would be charitable to Menger by stripping his ideas of what was held to be an unfashionable residue of metaphysics.[5]

There is one further reason for the diversity of interpretation, however, which reflects a recurring problem faced by those of us who work in the history of ideas in general and in the history of Austrian ideas in particular. This is the problem of how much credence one ought to award to self-interpretations when seeking an assessment of the nature and significance of a given thinker's achievements. For self-interpretations are very often flawed as a result of the fact that their authors naturally give prominence to the detailed *differences* between their own ideas and the ideas of those around them; they pay attention, in other words, to what is original, quirky, or odd. That which they take for granted, and which they have imbibed from their surrounding culture, is hereby no less naturally, and inevitably ignored. Now as anyone who has worked through the writings of Menger's Austrian philosophical contemporaries very soon becomes aware, the tacit intellectual background of educated Austrians in Menger's day and beyond was Aristotelian through and through to such an extent that Menger himself might have felt the need to draw attention to this background only when attempting to explain his ideas to those, such as Walras or his own son Karl Jr., who did not share it. Menger is otherwise relatively silent as far as methodological self-interpretation is concerned, at least in the sense that he does not ally himself explicitly for example with the Aristotelian camp.[6] Problems arise, however, when we consider the writings of those of Menger's Austrian contemporaries and successors including Mises and Hayek, as well as Karl Jr., who have sought self-interpretations of Menger at one remove. Such Austrian Austrians are, I want to suggest, least likely to enjoy a conscious awareness of the essence of Austrian economic thinking. Their interpretations of Menger will tend to pick out what is quirky, or especially modern, in Menger at the expense of the shared, and therefore for practical purposes invisible, background that holds his work together. And this background is, as cannot be too often stressed, Aristotelian even if only in the watered-down sense that is still to be more precisely specified. Indeed the Aristotelian background permeated Austrian thought to such an extent that even the newly burgeoning empiricism of the Austrian positivist movement was crucially colored by it.[7]

The Basic Doctrine

Those who have seen fit to advance an Aristotelian reading have of course themselves often left much to be desired in the way of precision and detail. Here, therefore, I shall do my best to set out the precise form of the Aristotelian doctrine that is relevant to the thinking of Menger and his Austrian contemporaries. I shall then go on to demonstrate how the Menger-Mises relation and the general issue of apriorism in economics might profitably be reexamined in its light.

I shall confine myself hereby to general philosophy: the ways in which Aristotle's ethics and politics filtered through into the thinking of the Austrians will not be of concern.[8] As will become clear, it is a highly refined and purified and indeed simplified version of Aristotle's general philosophy that is at issue when we are dealing with nineteenth- and early twentieth-century Austrian thought. It is an Aristotelianism shorn of all reference to, say, a passive or active intellect or to queer mechanisms for coming to know the world via a "making actual" within the soul of essences existing only "potentially" within things.

Only as a result of more recent work on Austrian and German philosophy in general, and on the Brentano school and on the early phenomenologists in particular, has clarity as concerns the nature of Austrian Aristotelianism become possible. And this allows also a move beyond such earlier defenses of an Aristotelian interpretation of Menger's work, as were advanced for example by Kauder and Hutchinson, which based themselves on little more than superficial analogies.

What then is the basic doctrine of Austrian Aristotelianism that is shared, above all, by Menger, Brentano, and their immediate followers? If, at the risk of a certain degree of painful obviousness, we attempt an assay of the common axis running through a number of otherwise disparate modes of thinking, then the basic doctrine might be said to embrace the following theses:

1. *The world exists independently of our thinking and reasoning activities.* This world embraces both material and mental aspects (and perhaps other sui generis dimensions, for example of law and culture). And while we might shape the world and contribute to it through our thoughts and actions, detached and objective theorizing about the world in all its aspects is nonetheless possible.

2. *There are in the world certain simple "essences" or "natures" or "elements," as well as laws, structures, or connections governing these, all of which are strictly universal.* Strictly universal, both in that they do not change historically and in the sense that they are capable of being instantiated, in principle (which is to say: if the appropriate conditions are satisfied), at all times and in all cultures. The fact that the simple essences and essential structures do not themselves change or develop implies in addition that historical change is a matter, not of changes in the basic building blocks of reality, but of changes in the patterns of their exemplification and in the ways in which they come together to form more complex wholes.

Propositions expressing universal connections amongst essences are called by Menger 'exact laws.' Such laws may be either static or dynamic, they may concern either the coexistence or the succession of instances of the corresponding simple essences or natures. It is exact laws, as Menger sees it, which constitute a scientific theory in the strict sense. The general laws of essence of which such a theory would consist are subject to no exceptions. In this respect they are comparable, say, to the laws of geometry or mechanics, and contrasted with mere statements of fact and with inductive hypotheses. The aim of the "exact orientation of research" is, as Menger puts it, "the determination of strict laws of the phenomena, of regularities in the succession of phenomena which not only present themselves as exceptionless, but which, when we take account of the ways in which we have come to know them, in fact bear within themselves the guarantee of their own exceptionlessness" (1883, 38; Eng., 59, translation corrected).

3. *Our experience of this world involves in every case both an individual and a general aspect.* As in Aristotle himself, so also in Menger and in the work of other Aristotelians such as Brentano and Reinach, a radical empiricism hereby goes hand in hand with essentialism. The general aspect of experience is

conceived by the Aristotelian as something entirely ordinary and matter-of-fact. Thus it is not the work of any separate or special faculty of "intuition" but is rather involved of necessity in every act of perceiving and thinking a fact which makes itself felt in the ubiquitous employment of general terms in all natural languages. Thus the general aspect of experience is as direct and straightforward as is our capacity to distinguish reds from greens, circles from squares, or warnings from congratulations.

For Menger, as for Aristotle, what is general does not exist in isolation from what is individual. Menger is, like other Aristotelians, an immanent realist.[9] He is interested in the essences and laws manifested in *this* world, not in any separate realm of incorporeal Ideal Forms such as is embraced by philosophers of a Platonistic sort. As Brentano formulates the matter in his study of Aristotle's psychology: "The scientist wants to get to know the crystals and plants and other bodies that he finds here on earth; if therefore he were to grasp the concepts of tetrahedra and octahedra, of trees and grasses, which belong to another world, then he would clearly in no way achieve his goal" (1867, 135; Eng., 88).

Things are no different even in the case of mathematical knowledge:

> The individual straight line which is in the senses, and the being of this line which the intellect grasps, are essentially identical. One is therefore not allowed to suppose that the intellect should grasp something more immaterial than sense, that it should take into itself something incorporeal or at least something non-sensory. No: the very same thing which is in the intellect is also in the senses, but related to other things in different ways. (op. cit.)

As Menger puts it: "The goal of research in the field of theoretical economics can only be the determination of the general essence and the general connection of economic *phenomena*" (Menger 1883, 7, n. 4; Eng., 37).

The theoretical scientist, then, has to learn to recognize the general recurring structures in the flux of reality. And theoretical understanding of a concrete phenomenon cannot be achieved via any mere inductive enumeration of cases. It is attained, rather, only by apprehending the phenomenon in question as a special case of a certain regularity (conformity to law) in the succession, or in the coexistence of phenomena. In other words, we become aware of the basis of the existence and the peculiarity of the essence of a concrete phenomenon by learning to recognize in it merely the exemplification of a conformity-to-law of phenomena in general (Menger 1883, 17; Eng., 44f.).

4. *The general aspect of experience need be in no sense infallible (it reflects no special source of special knowledge), and may indeed be subject to just the same sorts of errors as is our knowledge of what is individual.* Indeed, great difficulties may be set in the way of our attaining knowledge of essential structures of certain sorts, and of our transforming such knowledge into the organized form of a strict theory. Above all we may (as Hume showed) mistakenly suppose that we have grasped a law or structure for psychological reasons of habit. Our knowledge of structures or laws can nevertheless be exact. For the quality of exactness or strict universality is skew to that of infallibility. *Episteme* may be

ruled out in certain circumstances, but true *doxa* (which is to say, "orthodoxy") may be nonetheless available.

5. *We can know, albeit under the conditions set out in 4, what the world is like, at least in its broad outlines, both via common sense and via scientific method.* Thus Aristotelianism embraces not only commonsense realism but also scientific realism, though Aristotle himself ran these two positions together in ways no longer possible today.[10] The commonsense realism of Menger (as of all Austrian economists) is seen in his treatment of *agents, actions, beliefs, desires,* etc. In regard to these sorts of entities there is no opposition between reality as it appears to common sense and reality as revealed to scientific theory. Menger's (or the Austrian economists') scientific realism, on the other hand, is revealed in the treatment of phenomena such as spontaneous orders and invisible hand processes, where common sense diverges from the fine structures disclosed by theory.[11]

Taken together with 3, this aspect of the Aristotelian doctrine implies that we can know what the world is like both in its individual and in its general aspect, and our knowledge will likely manifest a progressive improvement, both in depth of penetration and in adequacy to the structures penetrated. Indeed Menger points at the very beginning of the *Principles* to a correlation between the higher culture of a people and the extent to which 'human beings penetrate more deeply into the true essence of things and of their own nature (1871, 4; Eng., 53).

6. *We can know what this world is like, at least in principle, from the detached perspective of an ideal scientific observer.* Thus in the social sciences in particular there is no suggestion that only those who are in some sense part of a given culture or form of life can grasp this culture or form of life theoretically. The general structures of reality are not merely capable of being exemplified, in principle, in different times and cultures; like the basic laws of geometry or logic they also enjoy an intrinsic intelligibility which makes them capable of being grasped, again in principle and with differing degrees of difficulty, by knowing subjects of widely differing sorts and from widely differing backgrounds. Indeed, because the essences and essential structures are intelligible, the corresponding laws are capable of being grasped by the scientific theorist in principle on the basis of a single instance.[12]

7. *The simple essences or natures pertaining to the various different segments or levels of reality constitute an alphabet of structural parts.* These can be combined together in different ways, both statically and dynamically (according to coexistence and according to order of succession). Theoretical research, for Menger, "seeks to ascertain the simplest elements of everything real, elements which must be thought of as strictly typical just because they are the simplest" (1883, 41; Eng., 60). The theorist must therefore learn to penetrate through the dross of ephemeral detail. He must seek to determine the elements "without considering whether they are present in reality as independent phenomena; indeed, even without considering whether they can at all be presented in their full purity. In this manner theoretical research arrives at qualitatively strictly typical forms

of the phenomena" (loc. cit.).

Scientific theory results, then, at least in part, when means are found for mapping or picturing the composition of such simple and prototypical constituents into larger wholes. Thus the theoretical science of psychology, for Brentano, "seeks to display all the ultimate psychic components from whose combination one with another the totality of psychic phenomena would result, just as the totality of words is yielded by the letters of the alphabet" (quoted in Brentano 1982, x–xi). Such "combination" or "composition" is not simply a matter of heaping or gluing together. It is a matter of certain entities or features or properties of entities arising in reflection of the existence of special sorts of combinations of other sorts of entities. Thus for example a *good* exists as such only if the following prerequisites are simultaneously present:

1. A need on the part of some human being.

2. Properties of the object in question which render it capable of being brought into a causal connection with the satisfaction of this need.

3. Knowledge of this causal connection on the part of the person involved.

4. Command of the thing sufficient to direct it to the satisfaction of the need.[13]

If a good exists, then as a matter of *de re* necessity, entities of these other sorts exist also. I shall return in the sequel to the treatment of such simple structures of *de re* necessitation. It is these structures, I want to claim, which lie at the core not only of Menger's work but of the entire tradition of Austrian Economics.

Aristotelianism vs. Accidentalist Atomism

Many of the above theses are of course thin beer and might seem trivially acceptable. Taken together, however, they do have a certain metaphysical cutting power. It is thesis 5, above all, which establishes the line between the Aristotelian doctrine and that of Kant (for whom there looms behind the world we know an inaccessible world of "things in themselves"). Theses 1 and 5 mark off Austrian Aristotelianism from all idealist doctrines of the sort which embrace the view that the world of experience or of scientific inquiry is somehow created or constituted by the individual subject or by the linguistic community or scientific theory, or what one will. Theses 2 and 6 distinguish the doctrine from all sorts of historicism, as also from hermeneuticist relativism and other modern fancies. And theses 2 and 5 tell us that, for the Aristotelian, scientific or theoretical knowledge is possible even of the structures or essences of the social world, a view shared in common by both Menger and Brentano, and denied (in different ways) by historicists and relativists of differing hues.

Most importantly, however, the doctrine is distinguished via theses 3 and 5 from the positivistic, empiricistic methodology which has been dominant in philosophical circles for the bulk of the present century and which enjoys a position as the unquestioned background of almost all theorizing among scientists themselves. Positivism has its roots in atomism, the view that all that exists is atoms associated together in accidental and unintelligible ways and that all intelligible structures and all necessities are merely the result of thought-constructions introduced by man. The origins of the struggle between atomists and Aristotelians in ancient Greek thought are well summarized by Meikle:

> On the one hand there were Democritus and Epicurus, who thought of reality as atomistic small-bits that combine and repel in the void, and who had a hard job accounting for the persisting natures of things, species, and genera on that basis. On the other hand there was Aristotle, who realised that no account of such things could be possible without admitting a category of form (or essence), because what a thing is, and what things of its kind are, cannot possibly be explained in terms of their constituent matter (atoms), since that changes while the entity retains its nature and identity over time. (1985, 9)

Where the atomist sees only one sort of structure in re, the structure of accidental association, the Aristotelian sees in addition intelligible or law-governed structures that he can understand. Where the atomist sees only one sort of change, accidental change (for example of the sort which occurs when a horse is run over by a truck), the Aristotelian sees in addition intelligible or law-governed changes, as, for example, when a foal grows up into a horse. Just as for the Aristotelian the intelligibility of structure can imply that there are certain sorts of structure which are intelligibly impossible, for example a society made up of inanimate objects, so for the Aristotelian there are intelligibly impossible *changes*, for example of a horse into a truck, or of a stone into a color. The presence of intelligible changes implies, moreover, that there is no "problem of induction" for a thinker of the Aristotelian sort. When we understand a phenomenon as the instance of a given species, then this understanding relates also to the characteristic patterns of growth and evolution of the phenomenon and to its characteristic modes of interaction with other phenomena.

The Special Doctrine
(Forms of Aristotelianism in the Social Sciences)

We have not yet gone far enough, however, in picking out the essence of the doctrine of Austrian Aristotelianism. For Aristotelianism played a crucial role also in the philosophy of German social thinkers such as Marx,[14] and many other German political economists and legal theorists of the nineteenth and even of the twentieth centuries could have accepted at least the bulk of what has been presented above.[15] The opposition between German and Austrian modes of thinking should not, in this respect, be exaggerated. Thus Brentano, normally and correctly regarded as the Austrian philosopher (and as the philosophical representative of Austrian Aristotelianism) par excellence, was in fact born in Germany.

Moreover, his Aristotelianism was decisively influenced by the thinking of the great German metaphysician F. A. Trendelenburg. Equally, however, it would be wrong to ignore the crucial differences, above all as between Marx's methodology on the one hand and the basic doctrine of Austrian Aristotelianism on the other. Thus Menger's doctrine of the strict universality of laws is denied by Marx, for whom laws are in every case specific to "a given social organism."[16] Moreover, while Marx and Menger share an Aristotelian antipathy to atomism, the holism or collectivism propounded by Marx is in this respect radically more extreme than anything that could have been countenanced by Menger.

Hegel, too, is correctly described as an Aristotelian in many aspects of his thinking. His case is somewhat different from that of Marx, however, since it seems that he denied thesis 1. More precisely, Hegel failed to draw the clear line between act and object of cognition which 1 requires, and he refused to acknowledge any sort of independence of the latter from the former. As he himself writes (in dealing with Aristotle): "Thought thinks itself by participation in that which is thought, but thought becomes thought by contact and apprehension, so that *thought and the object of thought are the same.*"[17] Or as Allen Wood expresses it: "Marx parts company with Hegel precisely because Hegel makes the dialectical nature of thought the basis for the dialectical structure of reality, where Marx holds that just the reverse is the case" (1981, 215).

To specify, therefore, the exact nature of the Austrian Aristotelian view, it will be useful to add to our basic doctrine a number of additional theses specific to the domain of social science which are formulated in such a way as to bring out as clearly as possible the opposition between the Austrian view and views shared by the principal German social theorists who had been influenced by Aristotelian ideas:

8. *The theory of value is to be built up exclusively on "subjective" foundations, which is to say exclusively on the basis of the corresponding mental acts and states of human subjects.* Thus value for Menger, in stark contrast to Marx, is to be accounted for exclusively in terms of the satisfaction of human needs and wants. Economic value, in particular, is seen as being derivative of the valuing acts of ultimate consumers, and Menger's thinking might most adequately be encapsulated as the attempt to defend the possibility of an economics which would be at one and the same time both theoretical and subjectivist in the given sense. Among the different representatives of the philosophical school of value theory in Austria (Brentano, Meinong, Ehrenfels, etc.) subjectivism as here defined takes different forms.[18] All of them share with Menger however the view that value exists only in the nexus of human valuing acts.

9. *There are no "social wholes" or "social organisms."* Austrian Aristotelians hereby, leaving aside the rather special case of Wieser, embrace a doctrine of *ontological* individualism, which implies also a concomitant *methodological* individualism, according to which all talk of nations, classes, firms, etc., is to be treated by the social theorist as an in principle eliminable shorthand for talk of individuals. That it is not entirely inappropriate to conceive individualism in either sense as "Aristotelian" is seen for example in Aristotle's own treatment of

knowledge and science in terms of the mental acts, states, and powers or capacities of individual human subjects.[19]

Economics is methodologically individualist when its laws are seen as being made true in their entirety by patterns of mental acts and actions of individual subjects, so that all economic phenomena are capable of being understood by the theorist as the results or outcomes of combinations and interactions of the thoughts and actions of individuals. Such combinations and interactions are not mere "sums." Thus neither ontological nor methodological individualism need imply any sort of atomistic reductionism: the individual of which the social theorist treats is, as a result of different sorts of interaction with other individuals, a highly complex entity. He might more properly be conceived as something like a node in the various spontaneous orders in which he is involved. This is a familiar idea which extends back at least as far as Aristotle.[20] As the Hungarian philosopher Aurel Kolnai puts it in his defense of "conservative libertarianism" published in 1981:

> society is not only composed of various parts, it is composed of various parts in a multiplicity of ways; and consequently its component parts cannot but *overlap*. In other words, it consists ultimately of individuals, but only in the sense that it divides into a multiplicity of individuals across several social subdivisions, such that it comprehends the same individual over and over again in line with his various social affiliations. (319)

Every individual therefore "embodies a multiplicity of social aspects or categories," and these play a crucial role in determining which sorts of essential structures the individual might exemplify.

10. *There are no (graspable) laws of historical development.* Where Marx, in true Aristotelian spirit, sought to establish the "laws of the phenomena," he awarded principal importance to the task of establishing *laws of development*, which is to say, laws governing the transition from one "form" or "stage" of society to another. He "treats the social movement as a process of natural history governed by laws,"[21] and he sees the social theorist as having the capacity to grasp such laws and therefore also in principle to sanction large-scale interferences in the social "organism." Marx himself thereby accepted both methodological and ontological collectivism; he saw social science as issuing in highly macroscopic laws, for example to the effect that history must pass through certain well-defined "stages." The Aristotelianism of the Austrians is in this respect more modest: it sees the exact method as being restricted to certain simple essences and essential connections only, in ways which set severe limits on the capacity of theoretical social science to make predictions. The methodological individualism of the Austrians has indeed been criticized by Marxists as a branch of atomism, though such criticisms assume too readily that methodological individualism trades in "sums."

What, now, of the German Historical economists? As already noted, Aristotelian doctrines played a role also in German economic science, not least as a result of the influence of Hegel. Thus for example Roscher not only accepted many of the tenets of the basic Aristotelian doctrine listed above, he also developed, as Streissler has shown, a subjective theory of value along lines very similar to those later taken up by Menger.[22] Such subjectivism was accepted also by Knies. Moreover, Knies and Schmoller agreed with the Austrians in denying the existence of laws of historical development. In all of these respects, therefore, the gulf between Menger and the German historicists is much less than has normally been suggested. The German historicists are still crucially distinguished from the Austrians, however, in remaining wedded to a purely inductivistic methodology, regarding history as providing a basis of fact from out of which laws of economic science could be extracted. For an Aristotelian such as Menger, in contrast (cf. thesis 3 above), enumerative induction can never yield that sort of knowledge of exact law which constitutes a scientific theory.

Apriorism

Austrian Aristotelianism as formulated above is first and foremost a doctrine of ontology: it tells us what the world is like and what its objects, states, and processes are like, including those capacities, states, and processes we call knowledge and science. More generally, it tells us what sorts of relations obtain between the various different segments of reality. The question of apriorism, on the other hand, which is skew to all such ontological concerns even to concerns pertaining to the ontology of knowledge relates exclusively to the sort of account one gives of the conditions under which knowledge is *acquired.*

Defenders of apriorism share the assumption that we are capable of acquiring knowledge of a special sort, called "a priori knowledge," via noninductive means. They differ, however, in their accounts of where such knowledge comes from. Two broad families of apriorist views have to be distinguished in this regard.

On the one hand are what we might call *impositionist views,* which hold that a priori knowledge is possible as a result of the fact that the content of such knowledge reflects merely certain forms or structures that have been imposed or inscribed upon the world by the knowing subject. Knowledge, on such views, is never directly of reality itself; rather, it reflects the "logical structures of the mind," and penetrates to reality only as formed, shaped, or modeled by a mind or theory.

On the other hand are *reflectionist views,* which hold that we can have a priori knowledge of what exists, independently of all impositions or inscriptions of the mind, as a result of the fact that certain structures in the world enjoy some degree of intelligibility in their own right. The knowing subject and the objects of knowledge are for the reflectionist in some sense and to some degree *pre-tuned* to each other. Direct a priori knowledge of reality itself is therefore possible, at least at some level of generality knowledge of the sort that is involved for example when we recognize the validity of a proof in logic or geometry (where it is difficult to defend the view that the character of validity would be somehow imposed upon the objects in question by the epistemic subject).

This brings us to the principal argument of the reflectionist against all versions of impositionism, which we might call the argument from arbitrariness. Let us suppose, for the moment, that the impositionist is correct in his view that the a priori quality of laws or propositions is entirely a matter of impositions. Imagine, now, that the totality of all laws or propositions is laid out before us. Is it to be completely arbitrary which of these laws or propositions are to enjoy the "imposed" quality of aprioricity? A positive answer to this question is belied by the extent to which there is wide agreement across times and cultures as to which the candidate a priori laws or propositions are. A negative answer, on the other hand, implies that there is some special quality on the side of certain laws or propositions themselves, in virtue of which precisely those laws or propositions do indeed serve as the targets of imposition. Clearly, however, this special quality must itself be prior to any sort of mental imposition which might come to be effected, which means that the original impositionist assumption, to the effect that the a priori quality of laws or propositions is entirely a matter of imposition, turns out to be self-refuting.

The impositionist view finds its classical expression in the work of Kant (whose ideas may be safe against the argument just presented), and special versions of impositionism are to be found also in Hume (in his treatment of causality), in Mach (in his theory of thought economy), and in the work of the logical positivists. The reflectionist view, on the other hand, finds its classical expression in Aristotle; it was developed further by successive waves of scholastics extending far into the modern era, and brought to perfection by Brentano and his successors, above all by Adolf Reinach and other realist phenomenologists in the early years of this century, the latter building on ideas set out by Husserl in his *Logical Investigations*.

Against the Kantian Confusion

There are obvious affinities between the reflectionist view and the doctrine of Austrian Aristotelianism outlined above. Reflectionism can be made compatible also however with other, variant doctrines. Thus the theories of *Verstehen* propounded by Dilthey (traces of which are perhaps to be found also in Mises) can be said to result when the reflectionist doctrine is combined with a cancellation (for the social sciences) of thesis 6, which asserts the possibility of detached scientific theory.

For Menger, we have argued, at least some of the propositions of economics are a priori in the sense that the corresponding structures enjoy an intrinsic simplicity and intelligibility which makes them capable of being grasped by the economic theorist in principle in a single instance. Note again, however, that the fact that such structures are intelligible need not by any means imply that our knowledge of them is in any sense infallible or incorrigible, nor that it need in every case be easy to obtain or to order into the form of a rigorous theory. In-

deed much confusion in the literature on Austrian methodology has arisen because the alien moment of incorrigibility, together with connotations of special
mental processes of "insight" or "intuition," have come to be attached to the
aprioristic thesis in a way which has made the latter seem eccentric and unscien-
tific.

Still greater confusion has arisen, however, as a result of the no-less-
pervasive assumption that all talk of the a priori must of necessity imply an impositionist or Kantian framework. For the apriorism lying in the background of
Menger's thinking is quite clearly reflectionist. Menger believes that there are a
priori categories ("essences" or "natures") in reality and that a priori propositions reflect structures or connections among such essences existing autonomously in the sense that they are not the result of any shaping or forming of reality on the part of the experiencing subject. The impositionist apriorist, in
contrast, insists that a priori categories must be creatures of the mind. He, therefore, may hold that the issue as to which sorts of economic structures exist is a
matter for more or less arbitrary legislation by the economic theorist, or a matter
of the "conceptual spectacles" of the economic agent. No grain of such ideas is
to be found in Menger.

Menger is working, rather, against the background of an assumption to the
effect that the universals of economic reality are not created or imposed in any
sense, but are discovered through our theoretical efforts. Economists do not
study concepts or other creatures of the mind. Rather, they study the qualitative
essences or natures of and the relations between such categories as value, rent,
profit, the division of labor, money: "Theoretical economics has the task of investigating the *general essence* and the *general connection* of economic phenomena, not of analyzing economic *concepts* and of drawing the conclusions
resulting from this analysis. The phenomena, or certain aspects of them, and not
their linguistic image, the concepts, are the object of theoretical research in the
field of economy" (Menger 1883, 6, n. 4; Eng., 37).

Menger, we might say in this light, seeks to develop a categorial ontology
of economic reality in just the Aristotelian sense, and in just the sense, too, in
which Brentano sought a categorial ontology of psychological reality. He seeks
to establish how the various different sorts of building blocks of economic reality can be combined together in different sorts of simple structured wholes, and
to establish through the application of what he himself called a genetico-
compositive method how such wholes may originate and how they may develop
and become transformed over time into other kinds of wholes.

There is, however, one reason why an impositionist or Kantian reading of
Menger's views has seemed so tempting to so many. This turns on the fact that
Menger lays stress both on the subjectivism and on the methodological individualism of economics. Indeed, the status and possibility of economics as a
theoretical science can be said to rest, in his eyes, precisely on the acceptance of
the two theses of subjectivism and methodological individualism. For subjectivism implies that an economy is not an autonomous formation with unintelligible
properties of its own. Rather one can *understand* the workings of an economy by

coming to an understanding of how the value of goods at earlier stages in the process of production is derived from the value to actual consumers of the products of the later stages. Moreover, one can see why this same understanding must apply ceteris paribus to every economy in whatever time or place. Methodological individualism implies that the whole of economics can in principle admit of an understanding of this sort, that there are no economic structures that cannot be grasped at least in principle in the thought-experiments of the economist. The latter must, as it were, put himself into the shoes of the individual subjects whose processes of thought and action come together to exemplify the structures of which he treats.

None of the above, however, implies that the economist's understanding might flow from the fact that the propositions of economics reflect structures that have been imposed upon the world in Kantian fashion by either the economic theorist or the economic agent. That is, the intelligibility of basic economic structures does not imply ontological dependence of such structures on the mind along the lines suggested by the impositionist. Rather, Menger's view implies precisely that economic reality is such as to manifest certain simple intelligible structures in and of itself. Economic reality is built up in intelligible ways out of structures involving human thought and action. It is for this reason that we are able, by appropriate efforts, to read off these structures in and of themselves.

Such structures, because they are so simple, are (to different degrees) intelligible. But for the same reason they are also universal, in the sense that because they are indispensable to every economic action as such, or to every instance of exchange, barter, rent, profit, etc. they are manifested (in principle) in every economy. They are at least in principle intelligible to everyone who has dealings with the objects concerned (i.e., to every economic agent, to every observer of the behavior of markets). Yet this does not imply that it is in every case a simple matter to discover what such structures are and nor, a fortiori, does it imply that it is a simple matter to formulate workable theories about them.

Austrian Economics is entirely comparable in this respect to the more recent "universals of language" research program in linguistics. Here, too, the assumption is made that there are structures in (linguistic) reality which are universal to all languages. Such structures are at least tacitly familiar to everyone who has dealings with the objects concerned (i.e., to every speaker of a language). Yet this does not by any means imply that it is a simple matter to discover what such structures are and to formulate workable theories about them. Nor, either, does it imply that the issue as to which sorts of linguistic structures are universal is a matter of the "logical structure of the human mind" or of the "conceptual spectacles" of the language-using subject. Nor does it imply that this issue is merely a matter for arbitrary legislation by the linguistic theorist. Universals of language are not created by the linguist. They are discovered through painstaking theoretical efforts.

Apriorism in economics, now, does not mean any more than in the case of linguistic universals that economic theory must be free of empirical components.

Indeed, it is a difficult matter to sort out precisely what the appropriate role for empirical investigations in economics (and in related disciplines) ought to be. This itself is not something that can be decided a priori. What is certain for apriorists of whatever hue, however, is that quantitative investigations in economics can be carried out coherently only on the basis of at least some prior understanding of the natures of the entities to be measured and compared. For otherwise the economist is not merely measuring in the dark; he is also without any means of tying down the results of his quantitative theorizing to economic reality itself. Preempirical (qualitative) categorizations of this reality must necessarily exist before empirical (quantitative) economics can begin. The only issue is the extent to which such categorizations are conscious and explicit.

The ontological grammar of economic reality that is sketched by Menger can be seen in this light as providing a preempirical qualitative framework in whose terms specific empirical hypotheses can be formulated and specific mathematical models be given concrete interpretation. Such a foundation cannot itself be derived, on pain of circularity, either from empirical investigations of the more usual sort or from mathematical analyses. It must rather be derived at least in part, or so the apriorist argues, from that familiarity with particular economic phenomena which we are all of us able to acquire as economic agents.

Mises, Kant, and Positivism

That the author of *Human Action* sees his methodology primarily in terms recalling Kantian doctrines is seen, for example, in passages such as: "The a priori sciences logic, mathematics, and praxeology aim at a knowledge unconditionally valid for all beings endowed with the logical structure of the human mind" (Mises 1966, 57).

We know now that there is an Aristotelian alternative to the Kantian form of apriorism. This alternative seems not to have been explicitly recognized as such by Mises; but this is hardly surprising, given that, for reasons pointed out above, the special nature of Austrian Aristotelian apriorism was appreciated by very few at the time when Mises was working out the philosophical foundations of his praxeology.[23]

Common to all aprioristic doctrines is a view to the effect that there are laws or propositions which are on the one hand universal and necessary and on the other hand intelligible (capable of being grasped by noninductive means). Kantian impositionism is the view that such a priori laws or propositions reflect categorial impositions of the mind. As a result of the influence of Frege and Wittgenstein, now, especially as filtered down through the logical positivism (logical atomism) of the Vienna circle, recent Kantian varieties of apriorism have tended to take an extreme form which sees such categorial impositions as effected always via logic or language. More specifically, a priori propositions are seen as being characterized by the fact that they can in every case be exposed via a process of stripping out defined terms and replacing them with *definiens* consisting of more primitive expressions as mere tautologies or analytic truths, entirely empty of content and consistent with any and every factual state of the world. "All bachelors are married" is revealed as analytic in this way by being converted into "All unmarried men are unmarried," which is an instance of the logical truth: "All A's which are B are B."

Mises qua methodologist was very clearly tempted by the idea that the laws of praxeology should be analytic in this sense. The theoretical part of economics would then be a purely formal or analytic discipline whose principles would flow from the logical analysis of certain concepts. Consider, first of all, Mises's assertion to the effect that the propositions of praxeology:

> are not derived from experience. They are, like those of logic and mathematics, a priori. They are not subject to verification or falsification on the ground of experience and facts. They are both logically and temporally antecedent to any comprehension of historical facts. They are a necessary requirement of any intellectual grasp of historical events. Without them we should not be able to see in the course of events anything else than kaleidoscopic change and chaotic muddle. (1966, 32)

Here the (Kant and Wittgenstein-inspired) positivist conception of analyticity is only latently at work. Almost all of the above would, if suitably interpreted, be perfectly consistent with a view of praxeology as an a priori discipline of economics conceived in reflectionist Aristotelian fashion. When we read on, however, then we discover that Mises does in fact run together what is a priori with what is analytic. Praxeology, we are told, is like logic and mathematics in the sense that its content is a matter of empty tautologies: "Aprioristic reasoning is purely conceptual and deductive. It cannot produce anything else but tautologies and analytic judgments." Thus for example: "In the concept of money all the theorems of monetary theory are already implied" (1966, p. 38).

Thus while impositionism is not explicitly defended by Mises qua methodologist, he does insist on the analytic character of all a priori propositions. The methodology which results is thereby rendered inconsistent with a reflectionist apriorism, since it implies that a priori propositions are empty of content, and clearly propositions that are empty of content are unable to picture anything (intelligible) on the side of the objects of the corresponding theory.

If, however, we wish to hold on to the view that all the propositions of praxeology are analytic in this sense, then we shall have to insist that the whole of praxeology can be erected on the basis of premises involving, at most, one single primitive nonlogical concept.[24] For suppose that there were two such concepts, neither definable in terms of the other. Consider, now, the propositions expressing the nontrivial relations between these concepts. These cannot, ex hypothesi, be analytic, for there are now no defined nonlogical terms which could be eliminated in such a way as to reveal the corresponding statements as truths of logic, and no truth of logic contains a plurality of nonlogical terms in other than trivial ways. But nor, from the Misesian point of view, can they be merely factual (synthetic a posteriori). On the positivist reading of the aprioristic doctrine, however, no third alternative is available, which implies that the original assumption that there are two (or more) such concepts must be rejected.[25] This helps to make intelligible the repeated insistence of Mises and his followers (and critics) that there is but one single nonlogical concept (or "category" or "essence") of the praxeological discipline, the concept *human action*, from which all propositions of the discipline would somehow be derived:

> The scope of praxeology is the explication of the category of human action. All that is needed for the deduction of all praxeological theorems is knowledge of the essence of human action. . . . The only way to a cognition of these theorems is logical analysis of our inherent knowledge of the category of action. . . . Like logic and mathematics, praxeological knowledge is in us; it does not come from without. (1966, 64)[26]

Mises the Aristotelian

When once we examine Mises's *practice*, however, then a quite different picture emerges, and we discover that Mises, too, was not at his best in his methodological self-interpretations. For we are forced to recognize that there is a veritable plenitude of nonlogical primitive concepts at the root of praxeology. Indeed, Mises's descriptions of this plenitude in his actual practice in economics, and also in occasional passages in his methodological writings,[27] can be seen to represent what is almost certainly the most sustained realization of the Aristotelian idea in the literature of economic theory.

Action, we are told by Mises, involves *apprehension of causal relations and of regularities in the phenomena*. It presupposes *being in a position to influence causal relations*. It presupposes *felt uneasiness*. It involves the *exercise of reason*. It is a *striving to substitute a more satisfactory for a less satisfactory state of affairs*.

Acting man *transfers the valuation of ends he aims at to the means he anticipates utilizing*. Action *takes time*, which, like other *scarce factors*, must be *economized*. Action presupposes *choosing between various opportunities offered for choice*.

Action involves *the expectation that purposeful behavior has the power to remove or at least alleviate uneasiness*. It presupposes the *uncertainty of the future*. It involves *meanings which the acting parties attribute to the situation*. A thing becomes a *means* only when reason *plans to employ it for the attainment of some end and action really employs it for this purpose*.

Certainly some of the concepts involved in the above may reasonably be counted as logical concepts; others may no less reasonably be conceived as being introduced by definitions formulated in terms of other, more primitive concepts. Consider, however, the concepts *causation, relative satisfactoriness, reason, uneasiness, valuation, anticipation, means, ends, utilization, time, scarcity, opportunity, choice, uncertainty, expectation*, etc. The idea that one could simultaneously and without circularity reduce every one of the concepts in this family to the single concept of action, that they could all be defined by purely logical means in terms of this one single concept, is decisively to be rejected.[28]

How much better would it be to accept that we are dealing here with a family of a priori categories and categorial structures which would be, in the jargon, not analytic but synthetic. The laws governing such structures can almost all of them be very easily expressed in the form of what linguists like to call "implicative universals," which is to say principles to the effect that, if instances of some given species or category K_1 exist, then as a matter of necessity these and those other categories $K_2,...,K_n$ must be instantiated also. Instances of the necessitating category K_1 are then said to be one-sidedly dependent upon instances of the necessitated categories $K_2,...,K_n$. The formal ontological theory of such dependence relations has been worked out in some detail.[29] It can be illustrated in Menger's already mentioned account of the essence of goods at the beginning of the *Principles*: "If instances of the species *good* exist, then there exist also instances of the species *need, human being, causal connection, knowledge, command*, etc." And it is to be found at work also in the context of Misesian praxeology, for example in laws such as: "If instances of the species *action* exist, then there exist also instances of the species *choice, apprehension of causal regularities, felt uneasiness*, etc." If instances of the species *choice of ends* exist, then so also do instances of the species *apprehension of causal regularities*, etc.

We might represent the a priori relations between such species (relations of *de re* necessitation) in diagrammatic form as follows, employing links connecting broken to solid walls of adjacent frames to represent relations of one-sided dependence between the entities concerned:

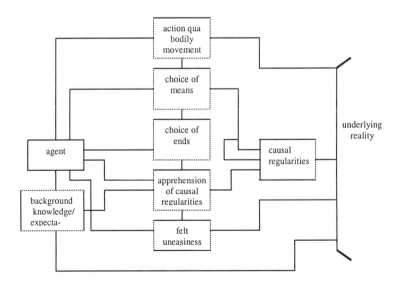

A diagram of this sort is, we might say, a picture of an a priori structure in the sphere of human action. Similar diagrams can be produced also following indications set out by Reinach in his monograph on speech act theory of 1913 for the a priori necessitation structures exemplified by speech acts of the various different types,[30] and I have sought elsewhere to show how they can be extended also to the structures of entrepreneurial perception analysed by Israel Kirzner, for example in his 1979.[31]

If Austrian Economics Did Not Exist, Would It Be Necessary to Invent It?

Austrian Economics, we have said, is both theoretical and subjectivist. Neoclassical economics, in contrast, is neither the one nor the other. For it rests on the positivist thesis that economic reality lacks intrinsic intelligibility tout court, so that no nontrivial part of economic theory could be a priori in any of the senses distinguished above. The propositions of economics are mere inductive hypotheses, and the method of economics consists in the building of testable models, selection among which is effected, at least in principle, on the basis of relative predictive strength. Because realism (in the reflectionist sense) falls out of account as a criterion of selection, such models are repeatedly threatened with becoming shorn of their relation to those basic everyday categories in which the science of economics has its roots. Austrian Economics, in contrast, is marked by a willingness to sacrifice both the goal of predictive power and the mathematical tools associated therewith precisely in order to come to an understanding of these basic categories themselves.

The contrast here has seemed to many to justify the striking of pugilistic attitudes. From the Aristotelian apriorist perspective, however, it might begin to appear as if the principles underlying both sorts of economic methodology might possess some grain of truth. For Austrian Economics might then be conceived not as an alternative to the economics of model-building and prediction but as a preliminary activity of establishing this missing connection to ground-level economic realities. Austrian Economics might, in other words, be conceived as a safe harbor for a practice which at present takes place among neoclassicists only surreptitiously and unsystematically, a practice sometimes referred to under the rubric of "taking subjectivism seriously." This practice might also be conceived as the attempt to exert control in the direction of greater commonsensical realism over the model-building tendencies of mathematical economists. The exercise of such control might lead from this admittedly somewhat idealized perspective to the construction of different kinds of models. But then also it may even be that empirical and mathematical economics will in certain circumstances lead to results which constrain a revision of Austrian Economics itself. A view of this sort can be found in germ already in the work of Wieser.[32] He, too, saw economic theory as beginning with the description based in part on introspection, as he saw it of the simplest structures of economic reality, a description which may then be supplemented and to some extent corrected by empirical research into the various ways in which these simple structures may come to be affected contingently, for example, in different social and historical contexts.

For the moment, though, I am suggesting merely that we consider a thought-experiment, or pipe-dream, to the effect that Austrian Economics might be seen as providing a certain sort of foundation for empirical-mathematical economics in something like the way in which geometry provides a foundation for the discipline of physics. We have said that from the Aristotelian perspective a proposition's being a priori signifies that it (or the structure which makes it true) enjoys some degree of intelligibility. What it does not signify is that our knowledge of such a proposition must be in any sense incorrigible or infallible. Indeed, the idea that empirical discoveries might lead in principle to a correction of the a priori foundation of the economic discipline opens up the exciting prospect of something like a *non-Euclidean* Austrian Economics, perhaps even to a family of such non-Euclidean disciplines, each of which could claim some degree of a priori support. I must confess at once, however, that I have no notion as to how such disciplines might look.

Notes

First published in *History of Political Economy*, Annual Supplement to Vol. 22 (1990): 263–88.

1. See the items listed in the bibliography below, especially my 1986 and 1989, and compare also Fabian and Simons 1986.

2. Here we can distinguish as sources of Menger's Aristotelianism first of all the *Popularphilosophie* which was imposed on educational institutions throughout the Habsburg Empire and which incorporated, besides elements derived from the thinking of Leibniz and Wolff, also watered-down versions of Aristotelian and scholastic doctrines. Secondly, there is the nineteenth-century German and Austrian textbook tradition in the social sciences. Here Aristotelian elements played a crucial role not only in the textbook literature of economics (and not least in the work of Mischler, under whom Menger had studied), but also in textbooks of history, legal theory, and for example in the writings on political householding of the cameralists (discussed by Silverman in his 1989). On Mischler, see Streissler 1989.

3. Valuable source material in this respect has been assembled in Milford 1988, who however draws different conclusions from the cited texts, above all because he is concentrating on the implications of Menger's work for economic *methodology*. Here, in contrast, I am concerned with more basic matters of general philosophy.

4. The most relevant material is summarized in Grassl and Smith, eds., 1986. See also the papers collected in Nyíri, ed. 1986.

5. Such misplaced charity is illustrated for example in the decision of Menger's translators to translate the technical (and in Menger's usage Aristotelian) term "*Wesen*," normally and correctly translated as "essence," with the more colloquial "nature." (The translations given here have been adjusted accordingly.)

For an illuminating discussion of an interestingly parallel case of misplaced charity in interpretation, see Meikle 1985 (esp. 8ff.), which rightly lays stress on the Aristotelianism at the core of Marx's thinking. Meikle's work is one among many indications of the extent to which, among philosophers at least, Aristotelian ideas are beginning once more to be taken seriously.

6. The *Investigations* are, as Alter rightly stresses (1989, pp. 12f.), a critique of the methodological views of the German historicists. They are not the positive statement of Menger's own thinking in this respect announced in 1883, p. 43n (Eng. p. 62).

7. This thesis is defended at length in my 1987. I believe that the remarks in the text have important consequences also for the correct interpretation of Hayek's thinking. Thus John Gray's contention that Hayek's "central theory" is fundamentally Kantian in nature, a thesis based in part on Hayek's own retrospective self-interpretation, is otherwise supported by very little evidence in either the spirit or the letter of Hayek's writings. It is essentially one single passage from Hayek's *The Sensory Order*, which is held by Gray to mark the Kantian strain in Hayek's thought: "The fact that the world which we know seems wholly an orderly world may thus be merely a result of the method by which we perceive it" (Hayek 1952, 8.39, cf. Gray, 12).

When taken in its context, this passage is part of the physiological argument of *The Sensory Order*—an argument in the spirit of Mach—to the effect that it is the physical similarity of stimuli and their relative frequency of occurrence which gives rise to the order of our sensations. Like other relevant writings of Hayek, such as his "Rules, Perception and Intelligibility" of 1962, it presents a picture of a philosopher allied with Mach and the early precursors of what later came to be called "Gestalt psychology,": a picture which is supported also by a historical examination of the influences on Hayek's thought at the time when the first version of *The Sensory Order* was being written. For both Hayek and Mach, now, there is no distinction between the phenomenal and noumenal world. Indeed there is no transcendentalism of any sort in either thinker. Yet Kantianism, as one normally conceives it, is characterized precisely by the presence of such a transcendental dimension.

8. See the relevant section of Alter (1990), and also the material collected in Grassl and Smith (eds.) for a treatment of this issue in relation to Menger. For the views of the Brentanists on ethics and the theory of value see Kraus 1937.

9. See the discussion of universals in re in Johansson 1989, e.g. 11, 147, and also Maki 1989.

10. On the opposition between commonsense and scientific realism from the point of view of contemporary philosophy see Devitt 1984. Compare also the illuminating discussion of "level ontologies" in Johansson 1989, 26ff.

11. Cf. Maki 1989.

12. Cf. Menger 1883, 40 (Eng., 60) on the "rule of cognition" for the investigation of theoretical truth:

There is one rule of cognition for the investigation of theoretical truths which is not only, as far as this is possible, verified by experience, but is verified in indubitable fashion by our very laws of thinking. . . . This is the thesis that *whatever was observed in even only one case must always come to appearance again under exactly the same factual conditions.* . . . This rule holds not only of the *essence* of phenomena, but also of their *measure* (translation amended).

13. Cf. Menger 1871 3 [Eng., 52 (section 1, "On the Essence of Goods")].

14. Cf. Gould 1978, Wood 1981, Sowell 1985, and above all Meikle 1985. In the light of 6 above it is worth pointing out that Marx embraces also the assumption that science is able to penetrate through the ideological obfuscations by which the common-

sensical mind is (as he conceives things) of necessity affected.

15. The survival of Aristotelian ideas in contemporary German legal theory is illustrated for example by Karl Larenz's standard textbook of legal methodology (1983), for example, in his discussion of the "legal structural types" which the legal theorist "discovers in reality" (338).

16. Cf. Meikle 1985, 6, n. 4.

17. *Lectures on the History of Philosophy*, trans. by E. Haldane and F. Simson, London, 1894, vol. 2, 147, emphasis mine.

18. See, on this, my 1986a and also the papers collected in Grassl and Smith, eds., 1986.

19. On methodological individualism in Aristotle see also Kraus 1905.

20. See Menger's discussion of the view attributed to Aristotle to the effect that the state is a phenomenon co-original with the existence of man, in his 1883, 267–70 (Eng., 220–22).

21. Passage cited by Marx himself in the afterword to the second German edition of vol. 1 of *Capital* and adopted as a motto to Meikle 1985.

22. See esp. Streissler 1989.

23. Again, the work of the phenomenologist Adolf Reinach is especially important in this regard. For Reinach, who achieved for legal science what Menger and his school have achieved in the field of economics, was especially aware of the non-Kantian nature of his aprioristic views. See also ch. 2 of Max Scheler's *Formalism in Ethics and Non-Formal Ethics of Value*, a work in part inspired by the reflectionist theory of the a priori defended by Reinach.

24. We shall need, too, some criterion as to what is to count as a nonlogical concept. Consider, for example, the concept *part of*. This is a formal concept, in the sense that it can be applied, in principle, to all matters without restriction. But it is not treated as a logical concept in the standard textbooks, nor can it be defined in terms of the logical concepts which are standardly recognized as such. Indeed it seems that the concept *part of* is a nonlogical primitive concept. Consider, now, the proposition: If A is part of B, and B is part of C, then A is part of C. Which asserts that the corresponding relation is transitive. This proposition is not analytic, for there is no law of logic to which it would correspond as a substitution instance. Hence it must be synthetic. But it is surely also a priori, and indeed a priori in the (reflectionist) sense that it pictures the (intelligible) way in which part-whole relations are nested together in the world, independent of our thoughts and actions.

25. I have developed this argument at greater length in my 1986.

26. See also Rothbard 1957.

27. Consider for example the paragraph beginning, "The most general . . ." in his 1981.

28. Hans-Hermann Hoppe's 1988, to which I hope to return elsewhere, is an interesting defense of a purportedly Kantian reading of Mises which seeks to break through the opposition between impositionism and reflectionism set out above.

29. See Smith, ed., 1982, Simons 1987, Part 3, and Johansson 1989, ch. 9.

30. Compare the papers collected in Mulligan, ed., 1987.

31. See my 1986. Marx, too, utilized necessitation structures of exactly this sort, for example in his analysis of human work in chapter 5 of book 1 of *Capital*. See, on this, my 1988.

32. See for example, Wieser 1927, 5ff. The idea may be less at home in Menger's own thinking. For Menger the idea of testing the exact theory of economy by the full empirical method is simply a methodological absurdity, a failure to recognize the basis of

presuppositions of exact research (1883, 54; Eng., 69).

Examining Menger's account of the ways in which exact types are painstakingly extracted from the realm of economic phenomena by the economic theorist suggests however that he, too, might have assented to something like the retroactive control that is here described. See, on this whole issue, Menger's promissory note on p. 43 (Eng., 62) of the *Investigations*.

References

Alter, M. What Do We Know About Menger? *Working Paper* 71, Duke University Program in Political Economy, 1989.

Alter, M. *Carl Menger and the Origins of Austrian Economics*. Boulder, Colo.: Westview Press, 1990.

Brentano, F. *Die Psychologie des Aristoteles insbesondere seine Lehre vom nous poietikos*, Mainz: Kirchberg, 1867. Repr. Darmstadt: Wissenschaftliche Buchgesellschaft, 1967 Eng. trans. by R. George, *The Psychology of Aristotle*. Berkeley: University of California Press, 1977.

Brentano, F. *Deskriptive Psychologie*. Edited by R. M. Chisholm and W. Baumgartner. Hamburg: Meiner, 1982.

Devitt, M. *Realism and Truth*. Oxford: Blackwell, 1984.

Fabian, R. and P. M. Simons. "The Second Austrian School of Value Theory." Pp. 37–101 in *Austrian Economics: Historical and Philosophical Background*, edited by W. Grassl and B. Smith. London: Croom Helm, 1986.

Gould, Carol C. *Marx's Social Ontology: Individuality and Community in Marx's Theory of Social Reality*. Cambridge, Mass.: MIT Press, 1978.

Grassl, W. and B. Smith, eds. *Austrian Economics: Historical and Philosophical Background*. London: Croom Helm, 1986.

Gray, John. *Hayek on Liberty*, 2nd ed. Oxford: Blackwell, 1986.

Hayek, F. A. von. *The Sensory Order: An Inquiry into the Foundations of Theoretical Psychology*. London: Routledge and Kegan Paul, 1952.

Hayek, F. A. von. "Rules, Perception and Intelligibility." *Proceedings of the British Academy* (1962) 48. Repr. in Hayek's *Studies in Philosophy, Politics, and Economics*. London: Routledge and Kegan Paul, 1967, 43–65.

Hegel, G. W. F. *Lectures on the History of Philosophy*. Translated by E. Haldane and F. Simson. London: , 1894.

Hoppe, H. H. *Praxeology and Economic Science*. Auburn, Ala.: The Ludwig von Mises Institute, 1988.

Husserl, E. *Logische Untersuchungen*, 1900-01. Critical ed., Dordrecht: Nijhoff, 1975, 1984 (A = first edition). Eng. trans. of second ed. by J. N. Findlay as *Logical Investigations*. London: Routledge and Kegan Paul, 1970.

Johansson, I. *Ontological Investigations: An Inquiry into the Categories of Nature, Man, and Society*. London: Routledge, 1989.

Kirzner, I. *Perception, Opportunit,y and Profit: Studies in the Theory of Entrepreneurship*. Chicago: University of Chicago Press, 1979.

Kolnai, A. "Identity and Division as a Fundamental Theme of Politics." Pp. 317–46 in *Structure and Gestalt: Philosophy and Literature in Austria-Hungary and Her Successor States,* edited by B. Smith. Amsterdam: John Benjamin, 1981.

Kraus, O. "Die aristotelische Werttheorie in ihren Beziehungen zu den modernen Psychologenschule." *Zeitschrift für die gesamte Staatswissenschaft* 61 (1905), 573–92.

Kraus, O. *Die Werttheorien: Geschichte und Kritik.* Brünn: Rohrer, 1937.

Larenz, K. *Methodenlehre der Rechtswissenschaft* 5th ed. Berlin: Springer, 1983.

Maki, U. The Best Way Forward: Scientific Realism. *Duke University Working Papers in Economics,* 1989.

Meikle, S. *Essentialism in the Thought of Karl Marx.* London: Duckworth, 1985.

Menger, Carl. *Grundsätze der Volkswirtschaftslehre.* Vienna: Braumüller, 1871. Trans. by J. Dingwall and B. F. Hoselitz as *Principles of Economics.* New York: New York University Press, 1981.

Menger, Carl. *Untersuchungen über die Methode der Socialwissenschaften, und der Politischen Oekonomie insbesondere.* Leipzig: Duncker & Humblot, 1883 Trans. by Francis J. Nock as *Investigations into the Method of the Social Sciences with Special Reference to Economics.* New York: New York University Press, 1985.

Milford, K. "Menger's Solution of the Problem of Induction: On the History of Methodological Thought in Economics." Department of Economics, University of Vienna. *Working Paper* 8806, 1988.

Mischler, P. *Grundsätze der National-Oekonomie.* Vienna: Friedrich Manz, 1857.

Mises, L. von. *Human Action.* 3rd rev. ed., Chicago: Henry Regnery Company, 1966.

Mises, L. von. *Epistemological Problems of Economics.* New York: New York University Press, 1981.

Mulligan, K., ed. *Speech Act and Sachverhalt: Reinach and the Foundations of Realist Phenomenology.* Dordrecht: Martinus Nijhoff, 1987.

Nyíri, J. C., ed. *From Bolzano to Wittgenstein: The Tradition of Austrian Philosophy.* Vienna: Hölder-Pichler-Tempsky, 1986.

Reinach, A. "Kants Auffassung des Humeschen Problems." *Zeitschrift für Philosophie und philosophische Kritik* 141 (1911), 176–209. Repr. in Reinach 1988. Eng. trans. by J. N. Mohanty in *Southwestern Journal of Philosophy* 7 (1976), 161–88.

Reinach, A. "Die apriorischen Grundlagen des bürgerlichen Rechts." *Jahrbuch fur Philosophie und phänomenologische Forschung* 1 (1913), 685–847. Repr. in Reinach 1988. Eng. trans. in *Aletheia* 3 (1983) 1–142.

Reinach, A. *Sämtliche Werke.* Edited by K. Schuhmann and B. Smith. Munich: Philosophia, 1989.

Rothbard, Murray N. "In Defense of 'Extreme Apriorism.'" *Southern Economic Journal* 23, (1957), 315–20.

Scheler, Max. *Formalism in Ethics and Non-Formal Ethics of Value.* Trans. by M. S. Frings and R. L. Funk. Evanston, Ill.: Northwestern University Press, 1973.

Schönfeld-Illy, L. 1924 *Grenznutzen und Wirtschaftsrechnung.* Vienna, repr. Munich: Philosophia, 1983.

Silverman, P. Antecedents in the Works of Sonnenfels and Kudler. *Duke University Working Papers in Economics,* 1989.

Simons, P. M. *Parts: A Study in Ontology.* Oxford: Clarendon Press, 1987.

Smith, B. "Introduction to Adolf Reinach, 'On the Theory of the Negative Judgment.'" In B. Smith, ed., 289–313, 1982.

Smith, B. "Austrian Economics and Austrian Philosophy." In W. Grassl and B. Smith, eds., 1–36, 1986.

Smith, B. "The Theory of Value of Christian von Ehrenfels." Pp. 85–111 in *Christian von Ehrenfels: Leben und Werk,* edited by R. Fabian. Amsterdam: Rodopi, 1986a.

Smith, B. "Austrian Origins of Logical Positivism." Pp. 34–66 in *Logical Positivism in Perspective,* edited by B. Gower. London: Croom Helm, 1987.

Smith, B. "Practices of Art." Pp. 172–209 in *Practical Knowledge: Outlines of a Theory of Traditions and Skills*, edited by J. C. Nyíri and B. Smith. London: Croom Helm, 1988.

Smith, B. "On the Austrianness of Austrian Economics." *Critical Review* 3 (forthcoming).

Smith, B., ed. *Parts and Moments: Studies in Logic and Formal Ontology.* Munich: Philosophia, 1982.

Sowell, T. *Marxism: Philosophy and Economics.* London: Unwin Paperbacks, 1985.

Streissler, E. The Influence of German Economics on the Work of Menger and Marshall. *Duke University Working Papers in Economics* 72, 1989.

Wieser, F. von. *Social Economics*, trans. by A. Ford Hinrichs. New York: Adelphi, 1927.

Wood, A. *Karl Marx.* London: Routledge and Kegan Paul, 1981.

11

The Libertarian Minimal State?
A Critique of the Views of
Nozick, Levin, and Rand

Walter Block

The concept of limited government libertarianism has been subjected to withering criticism in intellectual circles. Those who favor socialism, communism, central planning, and other governmental interventions into the economy see quite clearly that full free enterprise is not compatible with their own political economic philosophy. In contrast, there have been far fewer critiques of this system from the libertarian anarchist perspective. The present paper attempts to right this gigantic imbalance in a small way by calling into question the views of three advocates of free markets and limited government.

These three—Robert Nozick, Michael Levin, and Ayn Rand—are united in their view that laissez-faire capitalism is the only just economic system, that all men should obey the libertarian axiom of nonaggression against nonaggressors, a system based on self-ownership and private property, and that the sole legitimate function of government is to protect persons and property against force or the threat of force; and that to attain this end the only proper role for government is to maintain armies to ensure that foreigners do not overwhelm us, police to keep local villains from violating our rights, and courts to determine innocence and guilt.

Nozick

The most famous defense of such limited government libertarianism is Nozick (1974). This author argues that even if we begin with free market anarchism[1] we will still arrive at the position of limited government,[2] without violating a single solitary principle of the former. In other words, free-market anarchism is a dis-equilibrium state, and only limited government libertarianism attains the exalted status of sustainability.

How is this miracle accomplished? Simple. Assume that there is a dominant private defense agency, and also a group of similar but smaller competing business firms. What guarantee does the leading corporation have that these smaller private-market court, police, and army companies will follow legitimate procedures? It has none. Under anarchy, they are free to do as they please. Therefore, in order to safeguard its own citizens, the leading firm in this industry will have to seize a monopoly of law, defense, and protection of private property away from these potentially tyrannical smaller commercial endeavors. Having done this, however, the dominant firm is honor bound to give something back in return. And this is to extend to them, and to their customers, the same protection it affords to its own clientele: the enshrinement of the libertarian nonaggression axiom, and the protection of persons and legitimately owned property.

This thesis has been subjected to exhaustive criticism.[3] For one thing, there can be no such thing as "government" in Nozick's starting off position. There can only be free-market defense agencies in this libertarian Garden of Eden, all of them philosophically equal, at least in the starting position. Remember, Nozick is attempting to *derive* limited government libertarianism from anarchism; he cannot start out with this institution already in the picture. Of course, there can be a "dominant" defense firm, in the sense that one of the members of this industry is larger than the others, has more wealth, more customers, etc. However, this large business concern has no legal inner track as compared to the others. That is, it has no more right to impose its views of what constitutes proper procedure on its smaller competitors than they have to gang up on it, and impose their perspective on the dominant firm. Just because there is a danger that the small companies may one day utilize improper procedures in ferreting out justice does not give a warrant to the larger one to initiate violence against them. The procedural processes of the large firm are as liable to oversight as are those of the smaller competitors.

If Nozick's contention held true, then we would be justified in engaging in the preventive detention of all black, male teenagers, since they typically commit a disproportionately high percentage of all crimes (Levin 1997). Certainly, the initiation of violence that the dominant firm will commit on the smaller ones is incompatible with Nozick's supposed derivation of limited government from anarchism without violating the nonaggression axiom. Thus, he cannot maintain his thesis that free-market anarchism is a nonsustainable institution.

Levin

Levin (1982) also offers a justification of limited government libertarianism. But if Nozick's is widely known and celebrated, the exact opposite holds true in this case. In his little gem of an article, unjustifiably ignored in the anarcho-libertarian literature, Levin offers a unique defense, based on Hobbesian considerations. It is easily as sophisticated as Nozick's, and thus deserving of at least as much credit, even though it is flawed.

Levin's thesis is that it pays to cede our swords to an emperor sworn to protect persons and property and otherwise uphold the libertarian axiom in a way that it does not pay us to give him our plows. In one fell swoop, this philosopher accomplishes two tasks: he shows that limited government libertarianism is justified, but that the welfare state (for example, all plows owned or controlled by the government) is not.

Why is it that rational men would undertake the first act, but not the second? It is *not*, as might be expected, that the sovereign is a better fighter than he is a collectivized farmer. On the contrary, Levin specifically disavows this interpretation. Rather, the reason for this divergence is that, in giving up one's sword, a man signals to others his peaceful intentions. Thus, it is not merely a matter of helping the sovereign to uphold law and order. Were it so, then peace-keeping and growing food would be on a par. In contrast, there is no such signaling device that ensues when men give up their plows to their sovereign. This act, in and of itself, cannot grow wheat, as giving up implements of war can actually, in effect, "grow" peace. If anything, Levin is certainly enough of a free enterpriser, to stipulate that when we all put the sovereign in charge of plowing, we will have *less* wheat. Levin (1982, 341, 344) is worth quoting at length:

> The sovereign's fundamental right is to secure us all against attack—primarily each other's attacks—and we give him our swords for this security. . . . If we make the first bargain, Jones[4] will have the liberty to use our swords to do what we once did with them; if we make the second bargain, Jones will have the liberty to use our plows to do what we once did with them. But there is a big difference between the two bargains. As soon as you and I give our swords to Jones, and assuming our confidence in Jones is well placed, neither of us *needs* his sword any longer. You cannot attack me nor I you, so I no longer need my sword to protect myself and neither do you need your sword. The act of contractual surrender has eliminated the need which in the past we used our swords to meet—namely, fending off attack. *This* is what we expected to happen when we surrendered our swords, and why we surrendered them. It is not that we expect Jones actually to do, authorize, or coordinate all our old fighting for us; rather, since Jones has monopolized the means of fighting, we expect fighting to stop. It is this latter expectation that underlies the security we look forward to in civil society. Jones has the liberty to use our swords, but the whole idea is that now this liberty need never be exercised.
>
> By contrast, giving Jones our plows will have no like effect. The need to gather food—the need which up to now we have severally used our plows to meet—will persist after the surrender. The total amount of harvesting that must be done if you and I are to eat—to be secure against hunger—will remain the same even if we surrender our plows to Jones in exchange for his promise to use our plows to feed us. Someone is going to have to do the harvesting, whether each of us individually or our sovereign Jones. Jones's ability to protect us from hunger is enhanced only a very little by his simply having our

plows, and cannot compare to his ability to ease our fear of attack that is created by his simply having our swords. The point of surrendering one's sword
does not, therefore, apply to surrendering one's plow, or indeed to any other
liberty but those whose surrender eliminates their need.[5]

Ingenious as is this argument, there are several flaws in it. First, starting
with some minor ones, while Levin posits that his argument applies mainly or
"primarily" to attacks on us from each other, there is no warrant for such a conclusion. On the contrary, his argument applies *solely* to internal safety, and not
at all to the attack on us from foreigners stemming from abroad. In order to defend the realm against outsiders, it will not do, merely, for the sovereign to have
all of our swords. He has only two arms, despite his vast pretensions; at most he
can use two swords. He needs us if the foreign enemies are to be held at bay, in
much the same manner as he needs us to plant and harvest our crops.

This, of course, is only a minor problem, perhaps almost even unworthy of
mention, except for the fact that bringing in the international perspective allows
us to launch a reductio ad adsurdum against Levin. To wit, his argument, even if
correct, proves far too much. For what is true in the domestic arena is the case,
also, internationally, perhaps even more so. If we fear domestic attacks, how
much more are we afraid of the foreign variety? At least some others in the same
country as us are in part our friends, neighbors, and family members. The same
cannot of course be said for foreigners who wish to violate our rights. At worst
they are evil per se, they are untrustworthy, we never met a foreigner we liked,
they are interested in only "one thing," our total annihilation, etc. So, if Levin
sees reason for giving our swords to Jones, the local sovereign, how ever much
more powerful would our motivation be for giving them up to a world dictator
on these grounds? For then we would not only have domestic tranquility, we
would also have world peace. Since the latter encompasses the former, it must
be preferable.

But it is the rare limited government libertarian who will with equanimity
so blithely accept the prospect of world government. He knows full well that to
do so would unleash forces beyond our control. If there were a Hobbesian-type
world sovereign he might well determine that the relatively wealthy United
States should give up many of its "plows" to the countries in the Third or so
called "developing" world.[6] If this were run, somehow, on a democratic basis,
he knows we would be overwhelmed by votes from China and India, countries
not particularly well known for their adherence to free enterprise.

And yet, the argument is logically compelling. If anarchy between men in a
Hobbesian state of nature is problematic, then so is the present state of anarchy
that exists between the various nations of the globe. If Levin is correct in the
domestic context, his argument cannot possibly be rejected at the world level.
Let us search, then, for other flaws, lest we be compelled to favor, of all things,
world government.[7]

This brings us to the second fallacy in the Levin model, that which it holds
in common with all other theoretically constructed societies:[8] it fails to deal with

the fact that there never was, historically, any agreement or social contract, or compact between anyone. Let us stipulate for the moment that Levin is correct in the difference he notes between swords and plows. He still cannot reach his conclusion that any real world government is warranted. Just because rational men *would* theoretically give up their right to self-defense to the sovereign doesn't mean that any of them actually *did*. But unless the *latter* is true, the sovereign has no right to demand anything (e.g., taxes, loyalty, obedience) from the free men inhabiting the territory he claims as his own. That is, he has no right as a *libertarian*—and we are here concerned with limited government libertarianism,[9] not with any other kind of state apparatus. It matters not one bit that Levin has pointed out a reasonable distinction between plows and swords. Unless and until the citizenry actually *agree* to cede their power to a sovereign, his power is illegitimate. And yet, if we have learned anything from Spooner (1966), it is patently *false* that any such contract, constitution, agreement, whatever, has ever been signed. At most, the merest handful of people affixed their signatures to the Declaration of Independence, but why this should be thought to be binding on hundreds of millions of nonsignatories must remain one of the great mysteries of legal philosophy. In contrast, Levin (1982, 340) slips too quickly from the theoretical to the actual, "since all the covenantors have agreed to create a sovereign." They have never agreed to do any such thing.

The third fallacy is, if anything, even more problematic. The core of the Levin argument is that merely by giving up our swords, we pretty much guarantee domestic tranquility, not because the sovereign will keep the peace (no one man could possibly undertake such a task), but because the main cause of strife is the fear that if I disarm, you will take advantage of me, and vice versa, so that if we both disarm, why, then, all will be sweetness and light.

Put in this way, it is easy to see the difficulty. While Levin has no doubt put his finger on *one* antecedent of strife, fear of aggression, this is hardly the sole causal agent. Others that various commentators have mentioned include high time-preference rates (Banfield 1977), age, race (Levin 1997), poverty, and large variations in wealth (envy).[10] As well, there are sociobiological explanations for why people engage in criminal activity.[11] The point is that giving up our swords to an emperor who himself will do nothing to stop crime, will not protect us, given these many other causes of crime. Even a complete eradication of the fear of invasion will not be sufficient to reduce aggression to zero levels. Further, even after we all give up our weapons, we can still fight each other with fists, feet, teeth, head butts, etc. With no swords, by definition we need not fear that they shall be employed against us. But what about these bodily weapons? The weaklings amongst us will hardly feel safe. According to the Levin argument, they will be tempted to launch attacks upon the rest of us—and we, fearing them, will tend to think in terms of first strikes. This path leads back to the Hobbesian jungle, not to safety courtesy of the sovereign.

Let us state this somewhat differently: Government is only inefficient if it *does* something. This much we can concede to Levin. If, strictly speaking, government *does* nothing at all, then we are forced to "concede" that it is not such a bad thing; actually, not a bad thing at *all*. In Levin's model, government doesn't really *do* anything.[12] Rather, everyone gives the emperor their sword, and he just sort of sits on them. One might say that the sovereign is innocently providing "sitting" services,[13] but even this would not be strictly true. For in the Levin-Hobbes scenario, he is *forcing* people who have not committed any crime to give up their weapons, and this is surely incompatible with libertarianism. Such a government would not be *needed*, in any case, for the people could with as much effect throw their swords into the ocean. It cannot be objected in his defense that the sovereign provides the "service" of forcing people to give up their weapons—one, because this is a rights violation, and two, because, according to the theory, they *agree* on their own volition to do this in any case. The sovereign in this model serves as, in effect, a deus ex machina: he is not really needed, he can be dispensed with. No wonder he is pretty inoffensive. Say what you will about the anarcho-libertarian position, it doesn't really object to nonexisting governments, only to existing ones.

Perhaps we are misconstruing Levin. Maybe the sovereign, in his system, is really actively engaging in the internal protection of his citizenry. If so, private defense agencies are necessarily more effective than governmental ones.[14] The latter come to the fray with three strikes against them. First, government, by definition, consists of a monopoly of force within a given geographical area. But this is per se invasive. If the given government is "legitimate," under the libertarian legal code, it has no warrant to prevent competition with it by yet another "legitimate" government. If it allows this, it ceases to be a government at all, and instead enters the lists of private defense agencies, for that is all that a market firm that provides protection *is*: a "government-like"[15] entity that does not prevent competition, even within "its" geographical area. Second, a private defense agency does not force anyone to subscribe to its services in the first place, nor, as in the case of the Levin sovereign, to give up swords that were not used for invasive purposes. And third, there is the well-known greater efficiency of private over public institutions, based upon the weeding out process of profit and loss provided by the market, vis-à-vis the lack of same in the statist sector.

Having taken a critical look at Levin's core defense of limited government, let us analyze several other of his views on this subject. To begin with, Levin (1982, 339) "assume(s) that 'right' and 'wrong' are *ill-defined* in the state of nature, acquiring application only upon creation of 'civil society' by an original agreement."[16] But this wins the argument for limited government libertarianism vis-à-vis anarcho-capitalism merely by *assumption*. One could, with even more reason, simply invert this: maintain that right and wrong are ill defined under *government*. Indeed, a strong case can be made for this contention when we consider all the philosophical problems created for the libertarian by the state: should he use the public streets, school, libraries, roads?; should he avail himself of the "benefits" of rent control,[17] or other regulations, when it is in his interest to do so? By comingling monies through its tax subsidy system, the state, moreover, makes it well-nigh impossible to attain full justice through privatization and return of stolen tax revenues.

How, in any case, can it be denied that, absent any "agreement" establishing an emperor, it is wrong to initiate violence against nonaggressors or their legitimately held property? Certainly, no such position is compatible with libertarianism. But Levin is attempting to derive a *limited* or libertarian government. It ill behooves him to start out with premises that directly contradict this philosophy.

Levin, following Hobbes, posits a decidedly nonlibertarian ruler:

> Citizens will normally be free to raise their children, contract, and, so to speak, use their plows as they see fit, but only because the sovereign lets them. . . . He may without injustice seize your plow should he deem it "expedient." Nor does he lose this right if he errs about what is necessary for peace; if we reserved the liberty to contest his *judgment*, we would remain in the state of nature. (340–41)

This is *limited* government? It would appear from these words that we have the choice only between free-market anarchism and totalitarianism. Now this, to be sure, is one of the arguments of the anarcho-capitalists.[18] But to see it embraced, at the outset, by a critic of this philosophy is at least somewhat surprising.

Lastly, Levin argues: "The probability of a rogue sovereign is small, in turn, because it is in the sovereign's perceived interest to act as the contractors hope he will" (353). On the face of it, this is a curious viewpoint indeed. Certainly, it flies in the face of the overwhelming preponderance of the evidence.[19] Rogue sovereigns (Clinton? Hitler? Stalin? Lenin? Mao? Roosevelt? Kennedy? Pol Pot? Idi Amin? Trudeau? Castro? the Shah? Saddam Hussein? Milošević? Bush? Johnson? Nixon?) seem almost the rule, not the exception.[20] Hoppe (1995; 2001) has done yeoman work in showing Levin's claim to be *more* true for monarchies than democracies. That is, hereditary kings with, in effect, a private property interest in "their" countries have a greater incentive to rule in a long-run manner, so that they may be able to leave this property to their heirs. In contrast, presidents and prime ministers are in office for only a fixed term; they cannot bequeath control to their children.[21] Hence, they are likely to act in a short-term high time-preference manner; that is, take what they can immediately in a quick bout of pillage, for "in the long run we are all dead." But even Hoppe would not go so far out on a limb as to claim we can have any confidence in the benevolence of dictators, at least as compared to competing-market defense agencies. He defends monarchy vis-à-vis democracy, but not in comparison to anarcho-libertarianism.

Rand

By far the most famous advocate of this system of free-enterprise limited government was Ayn Rand (1964; 1967). In her view, "The source of the government's authority is 'the consent of the governed.' This means that the government is not the *ruler*, but the servant or *agent* of the citizens; it means that government as such has no rights except the rights *delegated* to it by the citizens for a specific purpose" (Rand 1964, 149).

There are difficulties here. For one thing, there simply is no evidence that any such delegation ever took place, not anywhere, and certainly not in the United States (Spooner 1966; Sechrest 2000). Yes, a group of men signed a few pieces of paper, but why they thought it would or should be binding on their progeny is an unwarranted extension of their act. As Sechrest (2000, 171–72) states:

> Spooner's point is really a rather simple one. Let's assume that the men who, in the late eighteenth century, formally consented to be bound by the Constitution did so willingly. How can the social contract into which those men entered automatically be binding upon later generations? The phrase, "We, the people of the United States," can only mean those individuals alive at the time. And the sentiment that the authors hoped to "secure the blessings of liberty" for their posterity as well as for themselves "neither expresses nor implies that they had any intention or desire, nor that they imagined they had any right or power, to bind their 'posterity' to live under it" (Spooner [1870] 1972, 2). Spooner likens this sentiment to a man building a home and hoping that its use by his descendants will enrich their lives. Despite wishing that they will benefit from it, that man knows he has neither the right nor the power to force any of his descendants to live in the home.
>
> As Spooner himself knew, some will claim in response that successive generations are indeed bound by the original political agreement, although implicitly rather than explicitly, because: 1) the nation is in some sense a single entity much like a corporation; 2) citizens vote in elections; or 3) citizens pay taxes. As for the first, the Constitution "does not speak of 'the people' as a corporation, but as individuals. A corporation does not describe itself as 'we,' nor as 'people,' nor as 'ourselves'" (3).
>
> The use of the ballot box also fails to prove that the citizens of a nation voluntarily support the government. If our elected representatives are merely acting to protect our rights, and thus are functioning not as our rulers but as our *agents*, why is voting done in secret? In a true principal-agent relationship, the agent is openly hired by the principal and strictly constrained in his actions to the powers delegated to him by the principal. Moreover, the principal is responsible for what his agent does on his behalf. With secret balloting, relationships are hidden, constraints are diluted, and no one accepts responsibility for the results (7–8). And some individuals may employ the ballot box in a defensive fashion. To protect themselves against those less honorable than themselves, that is, against those who will not hesitate to seek political advantages at the expense of others, some persons may decide to vote. But that is not evidence of their general support for the existing government. Similarly, the fact that most people pay their taxes is no proof that those taxes are paid voluntarily (6–13). As long as taxes are compulsory, it is impossible to know who would have paid in the absence of the compulsion.

For another thing, by buying into this "consent of the governed" philosophy, Rand clearly indicates her acquiescence in the following scenario: at once upon a time, before the establishment of a government, there was anarchy. Then, men, realizing the inadequacy of such a state of affairs, decided to end it, and create a government instead. The problem with this is that by her own admission, anarchy is a sort of political and ethical chaos. Anything goes. There are no—there can be no—legitimate rules without a government. The state is the fountainhead, so to speak, of all law. But if this is the case, then it cannot ever be determined that in such a situation the government was set up *properly*. Indeed, it cannot even be that the concept of propriety or legitimacy has any meaning in such a context. If government is the rule-making authority, the guarantor of legitimacy, and nothing proper can be done in its absence, this must perforce include its very initial setting up. Creating a government where none stood before would thus be akin to "lifting oneself up by one's bootstraps." It simply cannot be done.[22]

In the following passage, Rand (1964, 153) gives what she considers the coup de grace to the system of anarcho-capitalism:

Suppose Mr. Smith, a customer of Government A, suspects that his next-door neighbor, Mr. Jones, a customer of Government B, has robbed him; a squad of Police A proceeds to Mr. Jones's house and is met at the door by a squad of Police B, who declare that they do not accept the validity of Mr. Smith's complaint and do not recognize the authority of Government A. What happens then? You take it from there.

The problem with this challenge is that it has been answered eloquently and fully by several libertarian anarchists.[23] Theirs[24] is the view that laissez-faire capitalism is the only just economic system, that all men should obey the libertarian axiom of nonaggression against nonaggressors, and that it is a requirement of justice that *all* government functions—including those of protecting persons and property against invasion—be privatized.

Far from the "you take it from there" posited by Rand, these authors have specified in vivid and even excruciating detail the precise functioning of a private industry dedicated to defense of person and property. Rand offers a scenario where Smith, the client of police firm A finds himself in an altercation with Jones, the client of police firm B. Each calls his own police force to his aid, and as a consequence A and B confront each other; unreasoning and irrational physical violence would appear to be the only possible result.

But this is a straw man. First of all, it is exceedingly unlikely that any police force wishing to pass the market test would "send a squad" of officers to a non-customer's house, merely on the say-so of one of its clients. If it did, it would soon enough garner the reputation of an out-of-control gang, or a bunch of thugs, not a legitimate business firm attempting to attract and satisfy customers.[25] No, if it is worth its salt, no police firm would undertake any such action. Instead, it would first direct Smith to a court, in an attempt to gain a judicial finding in support of his contention against Jones.

Of course, this only puts off the inevitable confrontation that Rand seems so eager to lay at the door of anarcho-capitalism. For suppose that Smith and Jones refuse to take their cases to any one court, but insist on patronizing their own, A and B, respectively. To make matters worse, courts A and B disagree in their assessments, each finding in favor of their own clients. At this point, Rand throws up her hands in dismay, at the prospect of peaceful dispute resolution and settlement. But this is precisely where the anarcho-capitalists begin. They note that there are two possibilities: First, A and B will have already anticipated such a scenario and taken steps to resolve it beforehand, by agreeing, in advance, to be bound by the decision on this matter by a third court, C, to be chosen by prior mutual consent between A and B. In other words, what started out as a dispute between Smith and Jones, but has now become an altercation between police and then courts A and B, will finally and peacefully be resolved by the private "supreme court" C. Alternatively, even if A and B have somehow not anticipated such an eventuality, when now faced with it, they will agree to have it arbitrated by a third party, C. In this case, there will not be any more chaos than with a government system such as that employed by the United States. Indeed, there will be less, since C (and A and B as well for that matter) are chosen by a market process where a great weight is placed on consumer sovereignty. In contrast, Supreme Court and all other judges in the United States are picked (indirectly) by a political process, which is vastly inferior.

Or, second, they will not agree. If both refuse to mediate their dispute, their only recourse is to fight, precisely the alternative predicted by Rand. But the story does not end here. For suppose there are these two types of courts: those that will mediate when they find themselves on opposite sides of a decision from another court (call them the "legitimate" courts), and those that will not (call them the "illegitimate" courts). The latter, it is clear, will have to fight in every case. The former, only when faced with one of the latter. The point is, there will be a competitive advantage enjoyed by the legitimate courts vis-à-vis their illicit counterparts. Fighting is expensive. A firm that regularly engages in such activities will suffer additional costs for ammunition, tanks, airplanes, to say nothing of combat pay for its employees. Bandit courts will have to fight all of the time, legitimate ones only some of the time. There will be a tendency, therefore, for the legitimate firms to outcompete the bandits. But such a state of affairs is easy to anticipate. This furnishes yet an additional reason for expecting illegitimate courts to be very much the exception to the rule. For if even would-be or potential illegitimate courts realize they are likely to be consigned to the dustbin of economics, they will be less likely to start on this path than otherwise in the first place.

Rand's argument against laissez-faire capitalist anarchism is also vulnerable to the same internationalization of the argument employed against Levin. That is, if there is an onerous difficulty as Rand maintains when private courts A and B disagree with one another, the same applies when two countries find themselves on opposite sides of an issue. If a government is required to mediate the conflict between Smith and Jones, or A and B, then the same applies to a dispute between two countries. The point is, if Rand wishes to remain true to her domestic perspective on an international level, then she must embrace some version of the United Nations as a world government. It cannot be denied that the two people, Smith and Jones, and the two courts, A and B, stand in precisely the same relationship with one another as any two nations in the world. If governmental oversight is required and justified in the former case, then so must it be in the latter. But in the international context, this can only be a World Government, an institution that Rand would hardly have favored.

Conclusion

We have seen that the arguments of Nozick, Levin and Rand in behalf of free-enterprise, limited government cannot be sustained. Therefore, we are at least provisionally entitled to conclude that the anarcho-capitalist vision is the viable one.

Acknowledgments

The author wishes to thank an anonymous referee of the *Journal of Ayn Rand Studies* for helpful suggestions, and also Loyola University reference librarian Trish Del Nero for work over and above the call of duty.

Notes

First published in *Journal of Ayn Rand Studies* (Fall 2002): 141–60.

1. Rothbard 1965; 1970; 1973; 1978; 1982; Hoppe 1989; 1992; 1993a; 1993b. See also Anderson and Hill 1979; Benson 1986; 1988; 1989a; 1989b; 1990; 1991; 1992; 1993; 1998; Cuzán 1979; De Jasay 1985; Dauterive, Barnett, and White 1985; Friedman 1979; 1989; Martin 1970; Morriss 1998; Peden 1977; Sechrest 1999; 2000; Skoble 1995; Stringham 1998–1999; Tannehill 1984; Tinsley 1998–1999; Woolridge 1970; and Barnett 1998. Barnett (1998, n. 1, supra) uses the word "polycentric" to describe his position, completely eschewing "anarchy." (I am grateful to an anonymous referee for reminding me of this, and for making several other suggestions that have greatly improved the paper.) Nevertheless, it is my view that this author's views are sufficiently similar to these others who characterize themselves as anarchistic so as to justify including him in with them.

2. Nozick also maintains that we will not move from a limited government to a welfare state, but this is a contention that does not concern us at present, since we are here focusing attention only on the debate between anarcho-libertarians and limited government libertarians.

3. See Barnett 1977; Childs 1977; Evers 1977; Rothbard 1977; Sanders 1977.

4. Levin's name for the Hobbesian dictator.

5. Says Levin (1982, 348): "If I feel safer, you will feel safer from a preemptive at-

tack by me, and I will actually *be* safer (from a preemptive attack by you) because I *feel* safer."

6. A more accurate name for them would be retrogressing countries. On this see Gwartney, Lawson, and Block 1996.

7. Our leader, in this case, would not be named "Jones," but rather Boutros Boutros Ghali, U Thant, Kofi Annan, or some such.

8. See Rawls 1971 in this context.

9. Apart from distinguishing this phrase from anarcho-libertarianism, it is a redundancy, in that only the libertarian philosophy is compatible with limited government.

10. See on this Bauer 1982; Schoeck 1966.

11. Axelrod 1984; Axelrod and Hamilton 1981; Barkow, Cosmides, and Tooby 1992; Daly and Wilson 1988; Dawkins 1995; Dawkins 1976/1989; Frank 1988; Pinker 1997; Ridley 1986; Trivers 1985; Wilson 1975; Wright 1994.

12. Am I misinterpreting Levin? After all, he states: "If you and I give our swords to Jones, we will be greatly deterred from fighting by our awareness of Jones's preparedness to use his relatively great power against transgressors of the peace" (1982, 346). My claim is that this short statement is out of step with the general thrust of his remarks; that the essence of his case is that we give up our swords—and, by that fact alone, shall we be safe. I do not deny that he also at times speaks as if the sovereign will have to do a bit more to safeguard us, and thus is ambivalent on this point, but I take his concept of the do-nothing sovereign as the core of his position and the activist one as adventitious.

13. This would be about as limited as a government could be.

14. Levin (1982, 350) well appreciates the "inevitable failure of command economies." However, he applies this only to plows, not to swords. Why not to both? Levin is "assuming that anyone who knows as much as Rawls's contractors know [sic] enough not to be a socialist" (350 n. 19). Levin knows this too, but, again, only for plows, not for swords.

15. For essays that fail to maintain a properly sharp distinction between governmental and nongovernmental institutions, see Lee 1999; Holcombe 1994; Boudrouex and Holcombe 1989. For rejoinders, see Block (forthcoming A; forthcoming B).

16. This is in sharp contrast to the view Levin (1982, 338) correctly ascribes to Nozick: "Nozick assumes that we have certain rights that neither the state nor anyone else may violate." And again: "Hobbes's sovereign *creates* 'mine and thine,' while Nozick's individuals have property rights even in the state of nature" (343).

17. Tucker (1986) took Nozick to task for suing his landlord under this enactment.

18. Even Mises (1966), no anarchist he, argues strongly that the state must fully embrace free enterprise or slide down into socialism; that is, that all compromises between these two extremes are unstable.

19. See Rummell 1992; 1994; 1997; Conquest 1986; 1990; Courtois et al. 1999.

20. See Denson 2001 for an analysis of the *least* offensive of the U.S. presidents.

21. This applies even to political "dynasties" such as the Kennedys, Bushes, etc.

22. "Lifting oneself up by one's bootstraps" violates mere physical law. It implies no logical contradiction to suppose that it could be done; it is only incompatible with the findings of physics. In contrast, for a minarchist, or archist of any type, creating a government de novo is no less than a logical contradiction. For it implies extending legitimacy to some act (the establishment of a state, in this case) that was undertaken in its absence, that is, under anarchy, and this would be a logical anathema for the statist.

23. See note 1, supra. See especially Sechrest 1999, which focuses most specifically on Rand 1964; 1967.

24. The position taken by Sechrest (1999; 2000) strongly parallels my own analysis

of Rand 1964; 1967. See also Sechrest's detractors, Thomas 1999; Franck 2000; Enright 2000 and Ust 2000. From my perspective, Sechrest has much the better of this debate.

25. The scenario depicted by Rand sounds far more like something the government would do; for example, Ruby Ridge or Waco and the Branch Davidians.

References

Anderson, Terry and P. J. Hill. "An American Experiment in Anarcho-Capitalism: The *Not* So Wild, Wild West." *Journal of Libertarian Studies* 3, no. 1 (1979): 9–29.

Axelrod, R. *The Evolution of Cooperation.* New York: Basic Books, 1984.

Axelrod R., and W. D. Hamilton. "The Evolution of Cooperation." *Science* 211 (1981): 1390.

Banfield, Edward C. "Present-orientedness and Crime." *Assessing the Criminal: Restitution, Retribution and the Legal Process*, edited by Randy E. Barnett and John Hagel III. Cambridge, Mass.: Ballinger, 1977.

Barkow, J. H., L. Cosmides and J. Tooby eds. *The Adapted Mind: Evolutionary Psychology and The Generation of Culture.* New York: Oxford University Press, 1992.

Barnett, Randy E. "Whither Anarchy?: Has Robert Nozick Justified the State?" *Journal of Libertarian Studies* 1, no. 1 (Winter 1977): 15–22.

———. *The Structure of Liberty: Justice and the Rule of Law.* Oxford: Clarendon Press, 1998.

Bauer, Peter T. Ecclesiastical economics is envy exalted. *This World* 1 (Winter/Spring 1982): 56–69.

Benson, Bruce L. "The Lost Victim and Other Failures of The Public Law Experiment." *Harvard Journal of Law and Public Policy* 9 (1986): 399–427.

———. "Legal Evolution in Primitive Societies." *Journal of Institutional and Theoretical Economics* 144 (1988): 772–88.

———. "Enforcement of Private Property Rights in Primitive Societies: Law Without Government." *Journal of Libertarian Studies* 9, no. 1 (Winter 1989a): 1–26.

———. "The Spontaneous Evolution of Commercial Law." *Southern Economic Journal* 55 (1989b): 644–61.

———. *The Enterprise of Law: Justice without the State.* San Francisco: Pacific Research Institute for Public Policy, 1990.

———. "An Evolutionary Contractarian View of Primitive Law: The Institutions and Incentives Arising under Customary Indian Law." *Review of Austrian Economics* 5, no. 1 (1991): 41–65.

———. "Customary Law as a Social Contract: International Commercial Law." *Constitutional Political Economy* 2 (1992): 1–27.

———. "The Impetus For Recognizing Private Property and Adopting Ethical Behavior in a Market Economy: Natural Law, Government Law, or Evolving Self-Interest." *Review of Austrian Economics* 6, no. 2 (1993): 43–80.

———. *To Serve and Protect: Privatization and Community in Criminal Justice.* New York: New York University Press, 1998.

Block, Walter. "All Government Is Excessive: A Rejoinder To 'In Defense of Excessive Government,'" by Dwight Lee. *Journal of Libertarian Studies* 16, no. 3 (2002): 35–82.

———. "National Defense and the Theory of Externalities, Public Goods, and Clubs." *The Myth of National Defense*, edited by Hans Hermann-Hoppe. Auburn, Ala: The

Ludwig von Mises Institute, 2003: 301–4.

Boudreaux, Donald J. and Randall G. Holcombe." Government By Contract." *Public Finance Quarterly* 17, no. 3 (June 1989): 264–80.

Childs, Roy A., Jr. "The Invisible Hand Strikes Back." *Journal of Libertarian Studies* 1, no. 1 (Winter 1977): 23–34.

Conquest, Robert. *The Harvest of Sorrow.* New York: Oxford University Press, 1986.

———. *The Great Terror.* Edmonton, Alberta: Edmonton University Press, 1990.

Courtois, Stéphane, Nicolas Werth, Jean-Louis Panne, Andrzej Paczkowski, Karel Bartosek and Jean Louis Margolin. *The Black Book of Communism: Crimes, Terror, Repression.* Translated from the French by Jonathan Murphy and Mark Kramer. Cambridge, Mass.: Harvard University Press, 1999.

Cuzán, Alfred G. "Do We Ever Really Get Out of Anarchy?" *Journal of Libertarian Studies* 3, no. 2 (Summer 1979): 151–58.

Daly, M., and M. Wilson. *Homicide.* Hawthorne, N.Y.: Aldine de Gruyter, 1988.

Dauterive, Jerry W., William Barnett and Everett White. "A Taxonomy of Government Intervention." *Journal of the Southwestern Society of Economists* 12, no. 1 (1985): 127–30.

Dawkins, Richard. [1976]. *The Selfish Gene.* New York: Oxford University Press, 1989.

———. *River out of Eden: A Darwinian View of Life.* New York: Basic Books, 1995.

De Jasay, Anthony. *The State.* Oxford: Basil Blackwell, 1985.

Denson, John, ed. *Reassessing the Presidency: The Rise of the Executive State and the Decline of Freedom.* Auburn, Ala.: The Mises Institute, 2001.

Enright, Marsha. "Reply to Sechrest: On the Origins of Government." *Journal of Ayn Rand Studies* 2, no. 1 (Fall 2000): 137–39.

Evers, Williamson M. "Toward a Reformulation of the Law of Contracts." *Journal of Libertarian Studies* 1, no. 1 (Winter 1977): 3–14.

Franck, Murray. "Reply to Sechrest: Private Contract, Market Neutrality and 'The Morality of Taxation.'" *Journal of Ayn Rand Studies* 2, no. 1 (Fall 2000): 141–59.

Frank, R. H. *Passion within Reason: The Strategic Role of the Emotions.* New York: Norton, 1988.

Friedman, David. "Private Creation and Enforcement of Law: A Historical Case." *Journal of Legal Studies* 8 (1979): 399–415.

———. *The Machinery of Freedom: Guide to a Radical Capitalism.* 2nd edition. La Salle, Ill.: Open Court, 1989.

Gwartney, James, Robert Lawson, and Walter Block. *Economic Freedom of the World, 1975-1995.* Vancouver, B.C.: The Fraser Institute, 1996.

Holcombe, Randall G. *The Economic Foundations of Government.* New York: New York University Press, 1994.

Hoppe, Hans-Hermann. *A Theory of Socialism and Capitalism: Economics, Politics and Ethics.* Boston: Dordrecht, 1989.

———. "The Economics and Sociology of Taxation." In *Taxation: An Austrian View,* edited by L. Rockwell. Boston: Dordrecht, 1992.

———. "Fallacies of the Public Goods Theory and the Production of Security." In *The Economics and Ethics of Private Property: Studies in Political Economy and Philosophy.* Boston: Kluwer, 1993a.

———. *The Economics and Ethics of Private Property: Studies in Political Economy and Philosophy.* Boston: Kluwer, 1993b.

———. "The Political Economy of Monarch and Democracy, and the Idea of a Natural Order. *Journal of Libertarian Studies* 11, no. 2 (Summer 1995): 94–121.

———. *Democracy, the God that Failed: The Economics and Politics of Monarchy,*

Democracy, and Natural Order. New Brunswick, N.J.: Transaction Publishers, 2001.

Lee, Dwight R. "In Defense of Excessive Government." *Southern Economic Journal* 65, no. 4 (April 1999): 675–90.

Levin, Michael. "A Hobbesian Minimal State." *Philosophy and Public Affairs* 11, no. 4 (Fall 1982): 338–53.

———. *Why Race Matters.* Westport, Conn.: Praeger, 1997.

Martin, James J. *Men Against the State: The Expositors of Individualist Anarchism in America, 1827-1908.* Colorado Springs: Ralph Myles Publisher, 1970.

Mises, Ludwig von. *Human Action.* Chicago: Regnery, 1966.

Morriss, Andrew P. "Miners, Vigilantes, and Cattlemen: Overcoming Free Rider Problems in the Private Provision of Law." *Land and Water Law Review* 33, no. 2 (1998): 581–696.

Nozick, Robert. *Anarchy, State and Utopia.* New York: Basic Books, 1974.

Peden, Joseph R. "Property Rights in Celtic Irish Law." *Journal of Libertarian Studies* 1, no. 2 (Spring 1977): 81–96.

Pinker, Steven. *How the Mind Works.* New York: Norton, 1997.

Rand, Ayn. *The Virtue of Selfishness: A New Concept of Egoism.* New York: Signet Books, 1964.

———. *Capitalism: The Unknown Ideal.* New York: Signet Books, 1967.

Rawls, John. *A Theory of Justice.* Cambridge, Mass.: Harvard University Press, 1971.

Ridley, Mark. *The Problems of Evolution.* New York: Oxford University Press, 1986.

Rothbard, Murray N. "The Anatomy of the State." *Rampart Journal* (Summer 1965): 1–24.

———. *Power and Market: Government and the Economy.* Menlo Park, Calif.: Institute for Humane Studies, 1970.

———. *For A New Liberty.* New York: Macmillan, 1973.

———. "Robert Nozick and the Immaculate Conception of the State." *Journal of Libertarian Studies* 1, no. 1 (Winter 1977): 45–58.

———. "Society Without a State." In *Anarchism,* edited by J. Roland Pennock and John W. Chapman. New York: New York University Press, 1978, 191–207.

———. *The Ethics of Liberty.* Atlantic Highlands, N.J.: Humanities Press, 1982.

Rummel, R. J. *Democide: Nazi Genocide and Mass Murder.* New Brunswick, N.J.: Transaction Publishers, 1992.

———. *Death by Government.* New Brunswick, N.J.: Transaction, 1994.

———. *Statistics on Democide.* Center on National Security and Law, University of Virginia, 1997.

Sanders, John T. "The Free Market Model versus Government: A Reply to Nozick." *Journal of Libertarian Studies* 1, no. 1 (Winter 1977): 35–44.

Sechrest, Larry J. "Rand, Anarchy, and Taxes." *Journal of Ayn Rand Studies* 1, no. 1 (Fall 1999): 87–105.

———. "Rejoinder to Enright, Franck, Thomas and Ust: Taxation and Government Are Still Problematic." *Journal of Ayn Rand Studies* 2, no. 1 (Fall 2000): 163–87.

Schoeck, Helmut. *Envy: A Theory of Social Behavior.* New York: Harcourt Brace and World, 1966.

Skoble, Aeon J. "The Anarchism Controversy." In *Liberty for the 21st Century: Essays in Contemporary Libertarian Thought,* edited by Tibor Machan and Douglas Rasmussen. Lanham, Md.: Rowman & Littlefield, 1995, 77–96.

Spooner, Lysander. [1870] *No Treason.* Larkspur, Colo.: Ralph Myles, 1966.

Stringham, Edward. "Justice Without Government." *Journal of Libertarian Studies* 14, no. 1 (Winter 1998-1999): 53–77.

Tannehill, Morris and Linda Tannehill. *The Market for Liberty*. New York: Laissez-Faire Books, 1984.

Thomas, William. "Academic Interpretations of Ayn Rand." *Navigator* 2, no. 14 (November 1999): 10–15.

Tinsley, Patrick. "With Liberty and Justice For All: A Case For Private Police." *Journal of Libertarian Studies* 14, no. 1 (Winter 1998-1999): 95–100.

Trivers, R. *Social Evolution*. Reading, Mass.: Benjamin/Cummings, 1985.

Tucker, William. "Anarchy, State, and Rent Control." *New Republic* 195 (22 December 1986): 20–21.

Ust, Daniel. "A Minor Flaw." *Journal of Ayn Rand Studies* 2, no. 1 (Fall 2000): 161–62.

Wilson, E. O. *Sociobiology*. Cambridge, Mass.: Harvard University Press, 1975.

Woolridge, William C. *Uncle Sam the Monopoly Man*. New Rochelle, N.Y.: Arlington House, 1970.

Wright, R. *The Moral Animal*. New York: Pantheon, 1994.

12

Austrian Subjectivism vs. Objectivism

Richard C. B. Johnsson

Carl Menger is the founder of what has become known as the Austrian School of Economics. Many modern adherents of that School believe that one prominent feature of the "Austrian" body of thought is its subjective value theory. Ludwig von Mises summarized this view in *Human Action* (the Scholar's edition), as he stated that:

> [T]he ultimate ends of human action are not open to examination from any absolute standard. Ultimate ends are ultimately given, they are purely subjective, they differ with various people and with the same people at various moments in their lives. . . . Any examination of ultimate ends turns out to be purely subjective and therefore arbitrary. (95–96)

This statement tells us that the ultimate standard for judging value as well as values themselves are completely arbitrary and subjective. In contrast to this view, according to the objective value theory of Objectivism, the ultimate standard of value is life itself and values are objective, that is, based on facts of reality. From this we can conclude that more than a semantic change of the word *subjective* into, for example, *personal* (as Friedrich Wieser had suggested, and that Eugen von Böhm-Bawerk rejected in his *Capital and Interest*, vol. 2, book 3, ch 1, 125) is required to reconcile the two value theories. But interestingly, both bodies of thought reach the same conclusion about how to organize society; that of laissez-faire capitalism. How is it possible that such contradictory premises can lead to the same conclusion? This is clearly a case for checking the premises.

Starting with Menger, the alleged founder of the subjective value theory, and Böhm-Bawerk, the grand old master of Austrian value theory, I will review the earlier ideas on Austrian subjectivity and contrast it with the ideas of Ayn Rand's Objectivism. In this first part, I will first focus on possible differences when it comes to the ultimate standard of value. Next, the value theories of Menger and Böhm-Bawerk are studied to find out where the alleged subjectivity entered the picture. Finally, a possible direction towards the reconciliation of these two great bodies of thought is outlined. In a subsequent part, I will discuss the proposed solution in relation to Objectivism in general, to the theory of marginal utility and to some other aspects of economics. In doing all of this, I believe Menger's book will not be regarded as any less important—au contraire. For if Menger's *Principles of Economics* really contains ideas that can contribute to the reconciliation of these two great bodies of thought, the future of freedom and laissez-faire surely does not look any darker, and because of this, the book must be regarded as even more important.

The Ultimate Standard of Value

According to Objectivism, life is the ultimate standard of value (see Rand's essay *The Objectivist Ethics* for more on this). Now, what did the early Austrians say on this?

Starting with Menger, his words, "Aristotle (*Politics* i. 4. 1253b, 23–25) calls the means of life and well-being of men 'goods'" (286), reveal that he had the very same source to his ideas on value as did Rand. Aristotle's influence is also implied when Menger writes that "the attempt to provide for the satisfaction of our needs is synonymous with the attempt to provide for our lives and well-being. It is the most important of all human endeavors, since it is the prerequisite and foundation of all others" (77). From this, the step to saying that life is the ultimate standard of value, hardly could be considered far. Thus, we can conclude that Menger held basically the same idea, at least implicitly, as did Rand. Now, what did Böhm-Bawerk have to say about this—after all, he wrote an essay called *The Ultimate Standard of Value*. In that essay, there is a heading called "The Single Ultimate Standard of Value Is 'Human Well-Being'" (*Shorter Classics of Böhm-Bawerk*, 369), that shows that he recognized that the ultimate standard is life itself. Thus, Böhm-Bawerk seems to share the same idea as Menger and Rand. Finally, what did Mises have to say about this? The final words of the conclusions to his *Socialism*, reads (515):

> Whether Society is good or bad may be a matter of individual judgment; but whoever prefers life to death, happiness to suffering, well-being to misery, must accept society. And whoever desires that society should exist and develop must also accept, without limitation or reserve, private ownership in the means of production. (515)

Here, there is an implicit link between value and life itself. But at the same time we have the words from *Human Action* cited above, that must be regarded as remarkable and that leave us in doubt. Now that we have established that the early Austrian explicitly or implicitly agreed on the same standard of life as Rand, and that we cannot rule out the possibility that Mises and his followers might do the same, we can move on to examine the theories of value that these persons confessed to. At the center of this examination lies the question of the alleged subjective value theory of the Austrian School of Economics and its relation to the objective value theory of Rand.

The Early Austrians on Subjectivity

To examine if the Austrian school always has asserted that values are entirely subjective, like Mises does in the quotation above, let us have a look at the theory of value as proposed by Menger, as well as the theory of value of Böhm-Bawerk. But observe that I will only discuss those parts that have a bearing on the subject in question this chapter and is not aiming at being a review.

Early on in *Principles of Economics*, Menger identifies what a good is:

> If a thing is to become a good, or in other words, if it is to acquire goods-character, all four of the following prerequisites must be simultaneously present:
>
> A human need
>
> Such properties as render the thing capable of being brought into causal connection with the satisfaction of the need
>
> Human knowledge of this causal connection
>
> Command of the thing sufficient to direct it to the satisfaction of the need
>
> Only when all four of these prerequisites are present simultaneously can a thing become a good. (8)

For a thing to become a good in the first place, a valuer with sufficient knowledge is required. Hence goods are man-made.[1] Already at this stage, we can observe a difference between Menger and Böhm-Bawerk. The latter starts his chapter on value by making a distinction between goods of intrinsic value, that possess value for their own sake, and goods of extrinsic value, that possess value only as a means to an end lying outside themselves. Böhm-Bawerk clearly states that value can exist totally apart of any valuer (*Capital and Interest*, vol. 2, book 3, ch. 1, 121). He is in opposition on this matter against Menger, Rand, and Aristotle. Let us therefore continue with Menger.

Remember that Menger calls the means of life and well-being of men "goods," as did Aristotle, and Menger also showed us how things become goods, capable of serving as means of life. The quantities of goods that an individual must have to satisfy his needs, Menger calls his requirements. These requirements may be either less than or greater than (or equal to) the quantity of the good that is available. Examples of the first kind are air and sunlight, that is, where the needs for the goods are fully assured and it is impossible to exhaust when fulfilling the needs. Menger calls these noneconomic goods. Economic goods, on the other hand, are most goods around us, from apples to ships. If a unit of an economic good ceases to be a good, it leads to an unsatisfied need. Therefore, the individual wants to (i) maintain it at his disposal, (ii) conserve its properties, (iii) make choices between different uses of it, and (iv) obtain the greatest possible result with a given quantity (or a given result with the smallest possible quantity). These four objectives of the individual are the meaning of economizing. Hence, economic goods require economizing.

The difference between an economic and a noneconomic good lies in the relation between the requirements and the available quantity. It is not an internal property of the good itself. A noneconomic good can thus become an economic good, and vice versa, if the context changes. This last is a crucial point and I quote Menger on it: "Experience, moreover, teaches us that goods of the same kind do not show economic character in some places but are economic goods in other places, and that goods of the same kind and in the same place attain and lose their economic character with changing circumstances" (102).

Thus, a specific good can be either an economic good or a noneconomic good depending on the context. Variations in our requirements and/or the available quantity may occur over space as well as time.

The next chapter in Menger's book is devoted to his famous theory of value, later to be called the theory of marginal utility. Early on he notes that for economic goods, the satisfaction of a human need depends on the availability of each concrete, practically significant good. If an economizing individual becomes aware of this, the good will attain a significance called *value*. "Value is therefore nothing inherent in goods, no property of them, but merely the importance that we first attribute to the satisfaction of our needs, that is, to our lives and well-being, and in consequence carry over to economic goods as the exclusive causes of the satisfaction of our needs," Menger writes and continues, "From this, it is clear why only economic goods have value to us, while goods subject to the quantitative relationship responsible for non-economic character cannot attain value at all" (116). Furthermore, "Non-economic goods . . . not only do not have exchange value, as has previously been supposed in the literature of our subject, but no value at all, and hence no use value" (118).[2] Thus, Menger clearly states that goods that do not require economizing have no value whatsoever.[3]

Now Menger is close to presenting his theory in full, but before he does that he makes some important notes on the issue of objectivity. He writes, "The value of goods is . . . nothing arbitrary, but always the necessary consequence of human knowledge that the maintenance of life, of well-being, or of some ever so insignificant part of them, depends upon control of a good or quantity of goods," and he continues, "Regarding this knowledge, however, men can be in error about the value of goods just as they can be in error with respect to all other objects of human knowledge" (120). On the next page, he writes, "Hence, value does not exist outside the consciousness of men. It is, therefore, also quite erroneous to call a good that has value to economizing individuals a 'value,' or for economists to speak of 'values' as of independent real things, and to objectify value in this way. For entities that exist objectively are always only particular things or quantities of things, and their value is something fundamentally different from the things themselves; it is a judgment made by economizing individuals about the importance their command of the things has for the maintenance of their lives and well-being. Objectification of the value of goods, which is entirely *subjective* in nature, has nevertheless contributed very greatly to confusion about the basic principles of our science" (121. Emphasis in original.).

However, this is not the same idea as Böhm-Bawerk propounds. Having emphasized that the goods of intrinsic value are not having economic value, Böhm-Bawerk concentrates on the goods of extrinsic value. Value in its subjective sense "denotes the significance which a good . . . possesses for the well-being of a certain subject" (vol. 2, book 3, ch. 1, 121). He continues by writing that "The other kind of value is objective. It signifies our estimate of the capacity of a good to bring about some definite extrinsic objective result" (122). As an example of objective value he speaks of the relative fuel value of wood and coal, the physical characteristics of these different materials. (He goes on by declaring that goods, however, also have an objective exchange value. Thus, goods have subjective value to an individual but when taken to the market they gain an objective value. "Objective exchange value is one of the important results which it behooves economics to explain; subjective values belong to the means or tools by which economics is to achieve some of its explanations." [p.123])

As with the fundamental difference between Menger and Böhm-Bawerk when it comes to the latter's acceptance of goods of intrinsic value, I believe there is a fundamental difference hidden also in the view of the subjectivity and the objectivity of value. While Menger implies that there is no such thing as an objective value inherent in a good, Böhm-Bawerk means that there is. Moreover, and as a consequence of this, Böhm-Bawerk thinks that the next stage is that the individuals, that is, the subjects, value these goods differently, apart from their objective values (used in his sense). They are totally subjective. Menger on the other hand, uses the same term, but is not implying the same thing as Böhm-Bawerk does. But what does his use of the word imply then?

The Contextual Individual Objective Values

The idea that Menger must have had in mind when developing theory of marginal utility was *not* that values are subjective, not even in the sense of being personal. In understanding what idea Menger must have had in mind, I believe the path towards the reconciliation of his value theory with Objectivism lies open. I believe that all that is required to solve the "problem" of the Austrian "subjectivism" vs. Objectivism, is to note that all values depend of the context. Menger did emphasize this. *Values depend on the context.* Without this idea, Menger would not have been able to solve the old "value paradox" of the classical economists (i.e., why diamonds are more valuable than water). It is this basic idea that allowed Menger to develop his idea of goods having different value depending on the available quantity.

Let us see where this takes us by running through Menger's theory presented so far, and keeping this in mind all the time. First of all, the ultimate standard of value is life. But whose life? The life of the individual. For even if the individual has to figure out what kind of "Life" he as man qua man must live, applying "Life" in this abstract and impersonal meaning to his own concrete life means that it is his life that is the ultimate standard of value. *The ultimate standard of value is the life of the individual valuer.* (This is of course fully consistent with Rand's philosophy, for clearly, Rand did not suggest that someone else's life be the standard of value for an individual.)

The second important thing that Menger points out is that all the world around us consists of things, and some of these things could be turned into goods. A crucial prerequisite for this is the knowledge of the individual. But even if a thing is a good to the individual, it still need not have a value to the individual. For if a good is available in a quantity greater than our requirements, that is, our needs in the specific context, a loss of one unit of the good does not affect the life of the valuer. Thus, it cannot possess a value. And as all goods of that kind are the same, they cannot, each and every one of them viewed separately, have a value. *Hence, for a thing to possess value, we first recognize that the thing is a good that can serve our ends, then we proceed to check the availability and compare it to our requirements, and finally, if the requirements are greater than the availability, we determine if it is valuable to us.* This implies that there is no such thing as an objective value inherent in a good.

Instead, he writes that "entities that exist objectively are always only particular things or quantities of things, and their value is something fundamentally different from the things themselves; it is a judgment made by economizing individuals about the importance their command of the things has for the maintenance of their lives and well-being" (from the quote above). What this in turn implies is that a thing cannot possess value out of the concrete context. It cannot possess some sort of universal value, the same in all possible contexts (if not only by extreme coincidence). The value is totally separate from the good itself. However, Menger clearly states that values are judgments made by individuals.

These two points in the last two paragraphs together imply: (i) a thing possessing a value without a valuer would imply an intrinsic value and (ii) a thing valuable to a valuer without a concrete context implies a universal value, constant over all contexts. The first is an impossible contradiction and the second—"we would search in vain in the realm of experience for an example" of it, to paraphrase Menger. Hence, values can exist only within the concrete context of an individual valuer's life.

So far we have seen that both a valuer and a context is a necessary (but not sufficient) prerequisite for a value to exist. This helps us to understand the way in which the idea of objective values can be integrated into the ideas of the Austrian school of economics. It does so by implying, among other things, that:

- a good has the *same* objective value to two individuals in the *same* context
- a good has *different* objective value to an individual in *different* contexts
- a good has the *same* objective value to an individuals in the *same* context

As an example of the first case, consider the situation where Menger and I are sitting on the North Pole, with only one piece of wood available. Since the specific piece of wood, within the context, could mean the difference between life and death to each of us, it is plausible to say that it possesses the same objective value to each of us. An example of the second case is that the piece of wood certainly would not be as valuable to Menger in a virgin forest as it was in the former context (or if, on the Pole, half an hour later help arrives, with lots of firewood. Time is an important element here.). But if somehow, Menger suddenly found himself back on the North Pole, back in the first context, the piece of wood would have the same value again. That is an example of the third case. The first case, most objectivists would agree on directly. The second case the Austrians would agree on directly. The third is perhaps less controversial. But would both Austrians and objectivists agree on all three cases? Maybe not at this point, but let me explain how subjectivism fits into the picture.

Observe that there is nothing arbitrary or subjective in the three cases above. Subjectivism would enter into the picture if, in the first case, Menger did not realize the value of the piece of wood and, to my great anger, threw it to a seal. The point is that the objective value of the good is not printed on it. We have to figure it out. We have to make it a good by being able to put it in causal connection to the heat it can give us and to the fact that heat is very valuable in the context of the North Pole. However, normally the context is far more complex and it is harder to find the objective value of a good, in the particular context of the moment. If I manage to figure it out, it is still objective though (and not subjective). If I do not, the departure from the objective value is a case of subjectivism. There might in complex contexts of everyday life be a fair amount of subjectivism present in value judgments of individuals. It might be the case that we very seldom find the objective values of goods in the specific contexts. But that is really beside the point. Man is not omniscient. To further our lives we have to try to find the objective values. That is nothing different from saying that we have to try to figure out what is the best thing to do in every moment of our lives. The point is that there are objective values, and that we all have to try to find them since our lives and well-being depend on it. In doing this, the subjective dimension might play an important or even dominant role, and it will be more important the more complex the situation is, and the less able people are to figure things out.

There is another point in support of what I mean. When an individual passes a value judgment, it is from the point of view of what is his idea of the objective value in the context. The context involves his lifetime story, and, thus, the objective value for him might be different from the objective value of another individual. The differences in their lifetime stories might be so large that the objective valuations might differ, simply because the full context is so different. This would sound good to an Austrian, but perhaps less good to some objectivists. I think an example will clarify the point.

Imagine an auction where different individuals are allowed to bid on a table. They are all in the same place at the same time. They might appear to be in the same context, but are they really? Any differences in the bids of the persons would normally be attributed to differences in their subjective valuations. Economists in general, and modern Austrians in particular, would be happy with that. Some objectivists would probably say that the table has a metaphysical objective value and that differences are a case of irrational subjectivism. But are they really entirely subjective? The question could be answered by thinking of the three cases I just presented above. Suppose two persons were bidding for the table, me, a relatively poor Ph.D. student from poor Sweden, and a wealthy Bill Gates. In the context of my life, given my income and all other needs I have to satisfy, it would not be good for my life in total if I placed a bid on the table of $10,000. That would ruin me, even if I managed to come up with the money. Given that, if I actually did place the bid, that would be a case of subjectivism. I would have placed a bid as though I were rather wealthy, which I am not. Similarly, if Bill Gates had placed a bid on the table of $10,000, that would not have been a thing that ruined him. It could, given his wealth and income and all his other needs that he has to satisfy, be a perfectly reasonable thing to do. It could possibly be furthering his life. But if Bill Gates placed a bid on the table of $10,000,000, one could ask if that was a wise thing to do, since that is a lot of money for a table and probably nobody else would be close to matching that bid. From this example we can conclude that the differences in the bids on the same table between different individuals in the same place at the same time, can have *both objective and subjective* reasons. The individuals are not fully in the same context, even if simple inspection might suggest they are.

Noting that valuations are contextual implies that they often are very individual. But they could nevertheless be objective. And if the individual within a given context fails in finding the objective value, the difference is called subjective. This idea, I believe, puts the Austrian School of Economics on par with Objectivism. The only thing "subjectivist" Austrians have to realize is that things in given contexts have an objective value and to replace the word "subjective" by, for example, "contextual individual objective." The only things some objectivists have to change in their minds is to realize the obvious fact that individuals might have different valuations of the same thing, depending on the concrete context of each individual's life, and that things need not possess universal value.

In the next part, I will discuss the concept of *contextual individual objective values* (CIOV) in relation to Objectivism in general, to the theory of marginal utility, and to some other aspects of economics.

In the first part on the topic, I showed that at least the early economists of the Austrian School of Economics based values on the same ultimate standard as Objectivism, that is, life itself. I then proceeded to explain how the so-called subjective value theory of the Austrians could be reconciled with the objective value theory of Objectivism. This was made with the help of what I called *contextual individual objective values* (CIOV). According to CIOV, values depend on contexts. And contexts are closely connected to the individual valuer, whose life is the ultimate standard of those values.

CIOV vs. Objectivism

As I have already noted, I believe the concept of CIOV is fully consistent with the ideas of Ayn Rand. This involves the idea that the ultimate standard of value is the life of the valuer, the idea that values are contextual, the idea that the context is central to all value judgments, and the idea that goods have no intrinsic value. Furthermore, I think it reinforces the fact that because man is not omniscient, his life depends on trying to study the facts and do the best he can to evaluate them. (This also has bearing on the impossibility of central planning. This is because, with CIOV, the objective values a central planner has to try to find now are extended to possibly every living person. This could help explain why the collectivist governments have gotten rid of so many persons—it simply facilitates planning! The more homogenous the persons are, the easier the planning is.)

But what about the idea that two individuals can reach different objective values of the same good? Well, if we start by recognizing that one and the same person can reach different valuations of the same good in different contexts, I think the rest follows. Otherwise, that would be a rejection of the theory of marginal utility, a thing Rand did not propound as far as I know. Instead, this reinforces the importance of clearly defining the context when one discusses different topics and passes value judgments. Moreover, it does not exclude the case where two individuals reach the same objective valuation, despite their obvious differences in income, etc. For even if one individual, for example, has a different income from the other, they could nevertheless reach the same valuation. Furthermore, two persons can reach different conclusions even in a rather clearly defined context, without subjectivism being present. The differences in the contexts that stem from the special contexts of the individuals simply mean that the premises of the syllogism are different. And this does not exclude the possibility that one is right in saying to somebody that what they do is objectively not a good thing to do, it just suggests that one has to be a bit more careful in doing this to allow for possible objective differences in the persons' lives.

With CIOV, I believe the importance and significance of each and every individual in the theory of value is manifested. There can be no value without a valuer, and the valuer is always an individual, and the standard of value applied to the concrete context of the valuer is the individual valuer's own life. This clearly is fully consistent with the ideas of individuality of Objectivism and the ideas present in the principles of natural rights.

CIOV vs. the Theory of Marginal Utility

I have mentioned the theory of marginal utility a number of times so far. I have not told the reader exactly what it says yet (most readers probably know it already). In 1871, Leon Walras, Stanley Jevons, and Carl Menger independently published ideas leading to the theory of marginal utility.[4] The theory was a revolution, since for the first time, the so-called value paradox of the classical economists could be solved. The value paradox consists of the fact that things that are not very useful for the life of human beings, like diamonds, normally could be more valuable than things that are essential to the preservation of life itself, like water. The theory of marginal utility tells us that this is no paradox, and this can be explained by the famous example made by Eugen von Böhm-Bawerk (*Capital and Interest*, vol. 2, book 3, ch. 3, 143–45). A short version of it is that we imagine a pioneer farmer who has just harvested five sacks of grain. The first sack keeps him alive, the second healthy, the third is used to feed the poultry, the fourth to distill brandy, and the fifth to feed the parrots. Now, to use Böhm-Bawerk's own words, "What is the significance for his well-being of one sack of grain?" The answer is that any sack of grain is valued as the last, or marginal, sack. This follows, since if our pioneer would lose the sack that is supposed to preserve his life, he would simply eat out of the fifth sack. It is feeding the parrots he would choose to forego if he lost a sack, not dying. From this the law of diminishing marginal utility follows, summarized as, "The law of diminishing marginal utility states that the utility or, equivalently, the importance or personal value that an individual attaches to a unit of any good diminishes as the quantity of the good in his possession increases" (see George Reisman's *Capitalism*, 49).

Hence, the law of diminishing marginal utility provides a perfectly natural explanation to the alleged value paradox. The water, that is necessary for life preservation, is less valuable than diamonds, that are certainly not needed for the mere preservation of life, simply because if someone lost a cup of water, it could easily be replaced, while the same does not hold for diamonds. This law has to be applied to a specific context of the valuing individual. It is also perfectly natural if, in an extreme situation of a desert, an individual would value a cup of water higher than all the diamonds in the world, if obtaining the cup of water is the difference between life and death. Thus, Walras, Jevons, and Menger provided a solution to the value paradox.

Now, is this theory consistent with CIOV? Yes, I believe so. The only thing that has to be realized is that the context of the pioneer farmer changes as he gains or loses one sack of grain. In the context of only having one sack, the value of the sack is the same as his life, and in the context of having five sacks, the value is the same as the last sack he uses to feed the parrots. As a proof of the idea that it is the context that determines the value, I believe it is extremely important to realize that it is the idea of differences in values between contexts that has to have been the idea that helped Menger to develop the theory of marginal utility, and not that values differ between individuals per se. The latter is just an effect of the former (regardless of the fact that the existence of a valuer is a prerequisite of the value at all). Menger simply could not have developed the idea on the basis of values differing between individuals per se.

Böhm-Bawerk provides us with what probably is the most developed version of the theory of marginal utility. This includes the analysis of capital goods, that is, goods that are used in production of other goods. Although his view of value is not fully consistent with CIOV, the essence of his theory is not affected. One only has to keep in mind that he uses subjective and objective in a different way. One famous result of this is the fact that prices are determined by the marginal utility, but that this very often turns out to coincide with the case that prices are determined by cost of production. But the cost of production is in turn determined by the marginal utility of the factors of production. A crucial part of the explanation lies in that the many producers see the many uses of a factor of production, and value them according to their marginal use. But how can many producers reach the same conclusion about the marginal use and value of the factor of production if values are subjective? CIOV helps explain that they are objective, but the value of the factor of production depends on the context of the marginal use of it. So, also this part of his exposition of the theory of marginal utility fits in fine with CIOV. And this implies that Böhm-Bawerk really was on the same track as Menger. Moreover, we also see that the words by Mises quoted above—"they differ with various people and with the same people at various moments in their lives"—is consistent with the idea that values differ between contexts and hence between individuals. Thus, CIOV and the theory of marginal utility provide support for each other. They are fully consistent and one only has to make some semantic changes in the latter.

In connection to this I'd also like to comment on the following words by Mises in *Human Action*:

> Praxeology and history do not pretend to know anything about the intentions of an absolute and objective mind, about an objective meaning inherent in the course of events and of historical evolution, and about the plans which God or Nature or Weltgeist or Manifest Destiny is trying to realize in directing the universe and human affairs. They have nothing in common with what is called philosophy of history. They do not, like the works of Hegel, Comte, Marx, and a host of other writers, claim to reveal information about the true, objective, and absolute meaning of life and history. (28)

These lines reveal that Mises thought that objectivity has something to do with mysticism or paternalism, as opposed to reality, implying that Hegel, Comte, and Marx were objective. I believe this is implied also when he somewhat earlier in the book declared that:

> The ultimate goal of human action is always the satisfaction of the acting man's desire. There is no standard of greater or lesser satisfaction other than individual judgments of value, different for various people and for the same people at various times. What makes a man feel uneasy and less uneasy is established by him from the standard of his own will and judgment, from his personal and subjective valuation. Nobody is in a position to decree what should make a fellow man happier. (14)

No wonder Mises escaped to subjectivism if he thought objectivity leads to socialism! He must have believed he had no other place to go. But what is it Mises really objects to? Is it really objectivity? No, I believe it is the idea that economic goods have universal values, that is, the same value over all contexts, as for example in Marx's labor value theory. And then he continues by saying that they instead depend on the individual valuer. But since he supports the theory of marginal utility, he must really have supported that values depend on context, and only as a consequence of that, on the individual valuer. Hence, we see that the views of Mises are not really that far from CIOV or Objectivism.

There are at least two other aspects of economics that are related to values that Menger's theory does not answer that I would like to make some short comments on.

Are Economic Goods Always Valuable?

Remember Menger sorted out noneconomic goods from the economizing activity of individuals. Noneconomic goods were those that were available in quantities greater than our requirements. Instead individuals were economizing over goods that were available in less quantity than our requirements. If an economic good ever became superabundant, that is, the requirements became less than the availability, it turned into a noneconomic good, and vice versa. Menger tells us that non-economic goods cannot possess value. Does that mean that economic goods always possess value? Consider the following example: I have a limitless need for fast transportation. I need and desire a Porsche. I have a limitless need for food and drinks. I need and desire a soda. In both of these cases the availability clearly is less than our requirements, that is, the quantities of goods that an individual must have to satisfy his needs. These are classified as economic goods according to Menger. But do they necessarily possess value? This is a question Menger does not deal with, at least as far as I am aware. The theory of marginal utility does not provide an answer to this.

However, I think CIOV can provide a plausible answer to this: *an economic good does not by necessity possess a value*. This can be grasped by considering that a good can only possess a value to a valuer, in the context the individual is in at the moment of the valuation. When I say that a Porsche is valuable, and even more valuable than a soda, I am simply referring to the fact that a Porsche could be immensely valuable to me, if I ever were in the position to afford it. The statement refers to another context than the actual context of my life (as a Ph.D. student). Once this is grasped, it comes as no surprise that I end up spending one dollar for a soda and zero for a Porsche, since in the context of my life, the soda is worth one dollar and the Porsche not a thing. This helps explain why I do not put a value on all the wonderful and life-affirming things that are around. The Porsche may have a huge potential value, as opposed to the modest actual value of the soda. This is implied by the example of the table auction discussed in the first part. As we economize between economic goods, some just become out of the question.

The statement that the Porsche is more valuable than a soda is fully in line with the fact that our needs and desires for wealth are limitless, only bounded by our imagination, but that our possibilities of satisfying them are limited. Most of our needs lie dormant until they come within the reach of ours. Ours what? Our capacity to gain access to the goods in question. In a modern monetary economy, our capacity to gain access to the goods in question is manifested as a budget restriction. Menger notes this when he writes about the relation between our requirements vs. the availability of goods. Thus, we have a limitless need for wealth but are restricted by our budgets. With the help of CIOV we actually can explain how scarce economic goods can have no value to us. In a given context of an individual valuer, a good may be needed and desired, and at the same time scarce, but nevertheless possess no objective value to the individual. But as the context of an individual valuer is the only valid context, does this hold universally, economy-wide? No, because then I believe Say's law sets in, that is, the idea of the classical economists that the production creates demand. If we are able to produce something as useful as a Porsche and actually already have produced it, then the demand would adjust to allow for this useful thing. In an exchange economy, the exchange rates between goods would adjust and in a monetary economy, the prices of goods would adjust so that the Porsche is affordable within the total circulation. Thus, the implication only holds with regard to the individual valuer, and not economy-wide. The implication of CIOV that economic goods need not possess value is new as far as I know. Perhaps the reader knows better. A further implication is that valueless things can include all of Menger's following categories: nonuseful things, useful things, noneconomic goods and economic goods. That is, every conceivable kind of thing in the material world!

This is easier to understand as one recollects that any particular object can move between the categories, but it is only as economic goods that they *can* possess a value.

Stated Value Ex Ante vs. CIOV

The second major example I can come up with that Menger's theory does not answer is the following. Let us say I want to buy a new laptop. I say to my fiancée that I now can afford it since I have saved the money I think it will cost me. Assume this amount is $1,000. Then I head for the mall, and I find that I only have to pay $700. What is the objective value of the laptop? Well, it could easily be argued that it would be foolish of me to pay $1,000 for it, that is, that would be a case of subjectivism. I will surely not pay more than the $700. I argue that according to the idea of CIOV, the objective value is $700. My ex ante valuation of $1,000 was in a context other than the actual context of the purchase. The difference between my ex ante valuation of $1,000 and the $700 I paid was due to my misreading of reality (the context). Later I gained further knowledge about the facts of reality and learned that I could actually get it for $700 and that this saved me some money for the satisfaction of some other need of mine.

The difference between what I say I am willing to pay and what I actually pay is called the consumer surplus in mainstream economics. This is something that is supposed to be maximized. If that is so, in the example of the laptop, that means that what is supposed to be maximized actually is the difference that occurred due to my misreading of the real world context. What is maximized is ignorance. How strange can things be in mainstream economics?

I think most businessmen and marketing professionals would see the obvious difference between asking people what they want to pay for a thing, and what they find people actually pay. Recognition of this is actually a thing that sorts out good businessmen from bad. But observe, when businessmen try to figure out what people want, they do not try to figure out what people's subjective valuations are. That would be like rolling the dice, a thing a successful businessman would not let his success depend upon. And they do not try to find a thing of universal value, a thing that is as valuable in all possible contexts, because they know such a thing does not really exist. Instead, they try to figure out the needs and desires of people in the contexts of their lives. They try to find the objective value in a specific context, assured that if they find it, others will too, and they will become rich. That is the main objective of consumer segmentation, etc. in marketing. But in the global mass markets of capitalism, one might also earn a fortune by selling goods to people who share subjective values, even things that could not be justified on rational grounds, provided there are a sufficient amount of people and purchasing power for it. Furthermore, in reality, where there often is no point in putting more effort into finding the exact objective value, the fine-tuning around an objective value takes the form of tastes. If I buy a white or a black car might be of minor importance objectively, unless I'm an undertaker, and my choice may fit into an overall pattern that is my taste of color. Hence, subjectivity might play an important role as well.

The idea of ex ante valuations vs. CIOV has the rather strong implication: *the rejection of the theoretical difference between use value and exchange value.* Remember that Böhm-Bawerk wrote that "Objective exchange value (i.e., Menger's exchange value) is one of the important results which it behooves economics to explain; subjective values (i.e., Menger's use values) belong to the means or tools by which economics is to achieve some of its explanations." Could CIOV be the explanation with use value being the ex ante estimate of the value and the exchange value the actual objective value within the context of the purchase?

The discussion in this section is to be seen as some first thoughts around the concept of CIOV. It provides some loose ends to study further. However, it implies some possibly fresh ideas, that is, that (i) economic goods do not by necessity possess value and (ii) that there is no distinction between objective use value and objective exchange value. Any differences are due to subjectivity in the form of real life uncertainties and lack of time, that is, to the fact that Man is not omniscient.

Final Comments

Does the concept of contextual individual objective values pave way for subjectivism by proposing that people can say that their valuation is valid to them, to their life? It is possible. It is a risk. But that only tells us to be even more careful in defining matters. The true subjectivism around us is certainly common and has a strong hold on many sciences. I hope the reconciliation of the wonderful ideas of both the Austrian School of Economics and the Objectivism of Ayn Rand as presented here will strengthen the case for objective, meaningful values in life. I hope this chapter has shown that the ideas on value of Ayn Rand are in no essential way different than the ideas on value that Carl Menger, Eugen von Böhm-Bawerk, and even Ludwig von Mises held. And I hope the two great bodies of thought thereby can unite in the struggle for freedom and laissez-faire.

Notes

First published in *The Free Radical* (March-April [2003]): 26–29; (May-June [2003]): 24–26.

1. In the words of economist George Reisman, "Iron, which has been present in the earth since the formation of the planet and throughout the entire presence of man on earth, did not become a good until well after the Stone Age had ended. Petroleum, which has been present in the ground for millions of years, did not become a good until the middle of the nineteenth century, when uses for it were discovered. Aluminum, radium, and uranium also became goods only within the last century or century and a half." See his article, *Environmentalism Refuted,* readable at www.capitalism.net.

2. Menger differentiates between use and exchange value.

3. However, both economic and noneconomic goods possess utility, but, as just said, only the latter can possess value. Utility is the capability of a thing to serve for the satisfaction of human needs, and hence (provided the utility is recognized) it is a general prerequisite of goods-character. (p. 119)

4. Menger's exposition was in his *Principles of Economics*. The term was coined by Wieser (1884), in German, that is, *Grenznutzen*. See Friedrich von Wieser (1884), *Uber den Ursprung und die Hauptgesetze des wirtschaftlichen Wertes*.

References

Aristotle, n.d. *Topics*. W. A Pickard-Cambridge translation. Online at www.non-contradiction.com.

———. n.d. *Politica*. Rackham translation. Online at www.non-contradiction.com.

———. n.d. *Politics*. Jowett translation. Online at www.con-contradiction.com.

Böhm-Bawerk, Eugen von. *Capital and Interest*. 3 volumes: I. History and Critique of Interest Theories; II. Positive Theory of Capital; III. Further Essays on Capital and Interest. Translated by Hans F. Sennholz. South Holland, Ill.: Libertarian Press, [1884] 1959.

Menger, Carl. *Principles of Economics*. Translated by James Dingwall and Bert F. Hoselitz. Grove City, Pann.: Libertarian Press, [1871] 1994.

Mises, Ludwig von. *Human Action: A Treatise on Economics*. Scholars Edition. Auburn, Ala.: Ludwig von Mises Institute, [1949] 1998. Online at www.mises.org/humanaction.asp.

———. *Socialism*. Translated by J. Kahane. London: Jonathan Cope, [1922] 1936.

Rand, Ayn. The Objectivist Ethics." Pp. 13–35 in *The Virtue of Selfishness: A New Concept of Egoism*. New York: New American Library, 1964, 13–35.

Reisman, George. *Capitalism: A Treatise on Economics*. Ottawa, Ill.: Jameson Books, 1996.

———. "Environmentalism Refuted." *Mises Institute Daily Article*, April 20, 2001. Found online at www.mises.org/fullstory.asp?control=661.

13

Reappraising Austrian Economics' Basic Tenets in the Light of Aristotelian Ideas

Ricardo F. Crespo

Introduction

This chapter sustains that a reappraising of Austrian Economics in the light of Aristotelian ideas is not only possible but also fruitful. Firstly, I draw a sketch of the essentials of Austrian Economics. Next, I argue about the necessity for a thorough analysis of the notion of freedom, and I analyze Mises's conception of it. Next, I expose Aristotle's social, epistemological, and economic thought related to Austrian main traits. An account of how the exercise of Aristotelian virtues may be synergic with economic coordination and a sketch of the consequences of the proposal on the teaching of economics are then provided. Finally, the conclusion shortly sums up the content and relevance of Aristotle's contribution.

Reappraising Austrian Economics' Basic Tenets in the Light Of Aristotelian Ideas

A great deal has been written, studied and argued about the influences of Aristotle's philosophy on Menger's thought. The Aristotelian treatment of topics such as essences, value, need and goods, ideas on society, and so on, sufficiently justifies those theses. This chapter will precisely focus on Aristotle's role concerning Austrian Economics, however, in a different way from the ones that followed before. Although Aristotle was not a professional economist, he stated seminal concepts of economics. The chapter will show that these concepts were developed in an "Austrian spirit." Although social sciences had not yet emerged in Aristotle's time, he also proposed and developed an epistemological framework apt to them. The chapter will argue that that framework, called "practical science," perfectly fits in with the epistemological requirements of Austrian Economics. Moreover, those Aristotelian developments will prove to shed light on possible ways of solving some current Austrian debates.

I organized this chapter in the following way: Firstly, a brief sketch of the essentials of Austrian Economics must be drawn. Secondly, a relevant—though often forgotten—notion underlying the core of Austrian Economics will be stressed and briefly developed, that is, human freedom. Then, Mises's notion of freedom will be analyzed as both an example of the content of Austrian debates and as an introduction to the need for a perspective like the Aristotelian. Next, Aristotle's social, epistemological, and economic thought will be exposed in order to show how it corresponds with Austrian main traits. An account of how the exercise of Aristotelian virtues may be synergic with economic coordination and a sketch of the consequences of the proposal on the teaching of economics are then provided. Finally, the conclusion will emphasize the relevance and content of the contribution of Aristotle.

The Essentials of Austrianness

After the foundational works, from the 1970s to our time Austrian Economics has spread and made an effort at systematization. Prof. Israel Kirzner has had a relevant role in that task. He stated basic definitions in his article, "On the Method of Austrian Economics" (1976), published in a "defining work" as *The Foundations of Modern Austrian Economics*.[1] Explicitly drawing on Menger, Hayek, and Lachmann's contributions, he noted that the Austrian tradition had assigned "two tasks for economics explanations" and he distinguished "two basic Austrian tenets." In this article he not only defined main traits of Austrian Economics, but he also determined the future research program of Austrian Economics. The conclusive "prophetic" affirmation of Kirzner embraces everything:

> We have identified two requirements of economic explanations that Austrian economists consider important. We have also identified two basic tenets that seem fundamental to Austrian methodology. It turns out, however, that while one of these basic tenets, that of human purposefulness, is sufficient to sustain one of these requirements (that of making the world intelligible in terms of human action), the second, which asserts the unpredictability of human knowledge, is inconsistent with the requirement that economic explanations trace the unintended consequences of human action. It seems therefore that the future progress of the Austrian school in applying its basic methodological tenets requires some decision about the extent to which the second tenet about inconstancy of human purposes and knowledge can be upheld as a general proposition. (1976, 50)

That is,

1. Economic explanations rely on human purposive action. "Purposive" means stemming from an individual decision aiming at an end: a "subjective" decision. Thus, subjectivism is a basic trait of the Austrian conception of economics. Accordingly, Austrian Economics refuses mathematical and mechanical explanations, which are inadequate for dealing with purposive human actions. Summing up, as Lachmann (1979, 65) poses, "Austrian economics rests on subjectivism, a view of the social world in which human action occupies the central place."

2. Individual actions have unintended consequences. The traditionally considered unintended consequence was the tendency toward equilibrium. "Kirzner's inconsistency" has not yet been fully solved and has originated two positions. One position prefers equilibrium over uncertainty, despite relaxing the firmness of equilibrium. The other position prefers uncertainty over equilibrium: the unintended consequences could not be foreseen. In either case, Austrian Economics clearly focuses on market processes.

3. Methodological individualism is the adequate method to analyze those social phenomena "unconsciously" arising from (being caused by) purposeful individual subjective actions and, thus, constituting the method of Austrian thought.

4. A final concept—although arguable—seems to be proper to Austrian Economics: value-neutrality. It was defended by Menger, Mises, and Hayek, and even now, "despite certain murmurings of apparent dissent on this matter within the ranks of contemporary Austrian economists, . . . *Wertfreiheit* is still stoutly upheld as an ideal," (Kirzner 1994, 313).[2]

I'll show that all those traits were considered by Aristotle, even the latter. Moreover, I'll contend that Aristotle can teach us a lot toward understanding those traits in a right and cogent way.

To effectively see this process, we ought to follow the argument step by step.

Freedom as the Link Par Excellence between Subjectivism and Uncertainty

The title of the already classical *The Economics of Time and Ignorance* mentions two causes of uncertainty: thus subjectivism reaches a certain degree. Radical subjectivists have claimed a greater degree. On the grounds of this extended subjectivism "the agent's task is not to estimate or discover, but to create" (Littlechild 1986, 29). According to Shackle, this creation or beginning originates in Imagination and Choice. Freedom explicitly enters the game (cf. Shackle 1979, passim).[3]

James Buchanan has wisely realized the problem with the introduction of this essential element of subjectivism, that is, freedom: it imposes constraints to "positive economics." Hence, he sustains that the *subjective* elements are defined within the boundaries between the positive science and moral philosophy. Buchanan recognizes that there are certain patterns of human behavior in economic interaction that are reactions to stimuli, as if humans were rats. However, he stresses other aspects that are freer. This position calls for a new conception of economics. Let us hear from Buchanan:

> The residual aspects of human action that are not reducible to ratlike responses to stimuli, even in much more complex human variants, define the domain for a wholly different, and uniquely human, science—one that cannot, by its nature, be made analogous to the positive-predictive sciences of orthodox paradigm. There is surely room for both sciences to exist in the more inclusive rubric that we call economic theory. (1982, 17)

Buchanan finally encourages scholars to advance in developing a methodological frame apt to subjective economics. As we will see, Aristotelian practical science offers a fully satisfactory answer to this challenge.

Freedom is also explicitly present in Lachmann's works, as the following quotations show. In his 1950 article, "Economics as a Social Science," he stated some tenets about human action and its sciences. "In choosing ends," he wrote, "we are free. Choice indeed *is* a manifestation of Free Will. . . . It is the possibility of choice which makes (a problem essentially economic)" (1977, 167). Thus, "as human action is governed by choice, and choice is free, there can be no prediction of our actions" (1977, 179). Therefore, "expectations must be regarded as autonomous, as autonomous as human preferences are . . . We cannot predict their mode of change as prompted by failure or success" (1976b, 129). In another place he states: "Human action is not 'determinate' in any sense akin to the one [proper of] . . . natural science" (1971, 36. cf. also 37). In his address to a conference on "Interpretation, Human Agency, and Economics" held at George Mason University in 1986, he stressed "our need for conceptual schemes more congenial to the freedom of our wills and the requirements of a voluntaristic theory of action than anything we have at present" (1990, 137).

Rudy van Zijp has recently explained this question very well:

> In the social sciences, indeterminateness may be due to two "sources." It may arise for epistemological reasons, in the sense that the human mind is incapable of grasping social reality in all its complexity. . . . This position was held by Hayek. . . . In contrast, Lachmann based his methodological dualism on a different argument. He seems to have regarded indeterminateness as part and parcel of social reality. That is, his methodological views seem to be based on an ontological claim. (1995, 423–24)

While Hayek, in a classical passage ([1948] 1980: 44), argued in favor of an empirical tendency towards equilibrium, Lachmann, as van Zijp states (1995, 427), "rejected the importance of the Hayek problem, and instead emphasized man's freedom to choose and to act. In turn, this freedom means that future knowledge, and hence future actions, are indeterminate. . . . Lachmann emphasized the realism of assumptions in order to establish a closer connection between economics and common-sense knowledge."

What has been said may seem to be obvious. Nevertheless it is not so. It is argued that subjectivism and freedom survive behind stochastic models and predictions. The reason why this is partially true is that tendencies rely on both, habits configured by free actions and average free actions. Free options are incorporated into data and into relations established in the model. However, these models are developed according to rational choice theories in which freedom is not denied, but left aside, "iced," "paralyzed."[4] I would call this position a "hidden-freedom reasoning" concept of economics. However, freedom being real and an undetermined openness, real acting economy surpasses possibilities of models. The arising problem is: What kind of science could manage such an indetermination? One that simultaneously owns a broader rationality and also embraces the former. In my opinion, Austrian Economics ought to work in such a frame adequate to a real acting person. That is, I believe that for Austrian Economics to focus on human action, it needs to consider its traits. Thus, it cannot turn back to freedom, as neoclassical theory does. Therefore, it is relevant to manage a full concept of freedom.

As an example of the "matching freedom with rationality problem" I will analyze Mises's concept of freedom in the next section.

Mises on Freedom

Before analyzing Mises's notion, let me clarify "what" freedom I am referring to. This could actually be a nuisance for it supposes that I am taking position in a difficult philosophical discussion: the free will vs. determinism controversy. As I have already stated, I believe that economics supposes engagement with this basic—often hidden—notion, namely freedom. I consider that Austrian Economics should bear a generous notion of freedom. Let me at least assume it. Freedom in this paper is an analogous term: its most inner meaning is a radical openness of mind and will towards reality. The second analogous meaning is *liber arbitrium* or freedom of choice, an inner capacity of will to decide, a power to will. Of course, will is conditioned in its decisions by sociological, psychological, and physiological antecedents as well as by previous habits; however, it is not totally and univocally determined by them. Decisions are not without cause: they are caused by the person who wills conditioned as it were. In the human realm "to be caused" is not equivalent to necessity. (I am adopting a causal indeterminist position which may include agent causation, as Chisholm 1995 sustains.)[5] Choice is, as Shackle sustained, like a beginning. The former kinds of freedom are innate. Acquired freedoms are moral inner freedom—the capacity to act rightly—and external-political and economic freedoms, a power to do. These latter freedoms find their sources and fundaments in the former. I am aware of the oppositions that might arise with such set of definitions. But, let me suppose them as though they were ceteris paribus clauses and let us now analyze Mises's notion of them.

Criticisms against Mises are a proof of Austrian Economics' vitality.[6] Austrian debates essentially follow the paths drawn by the already mentioned tension pointed out by Kirzner. Mises is criticized from different points of view for the results and extent of that tension. For many authors like Lachmann—and even Hayek—Mises was a rationalist. (see Lachmann 1982, 31; 37) To be a rationalist is not in itself a problem. The real problem is to have a narrow scope of the notion of reason. Hence, I would rather say and try to prove that Mises was an intellectualist. As will be shown, he adopted a concept of rationality—formal-coherent with his belief in an active role of reason and a weak role of will.

According to Lachmann's interpretation, Mises's apodictic theory stems from Menger's exact orientation; expectations à la Shackle are left out in both cases: "It is possible for us in 1982," Lachmann says, "to view Mises's neglect of expectations from a Shackleian perspective and find it justified. 'Time is a denial of the omnipotence of reason' (Shackle 1972, 27). Who could blame a stout rationalist for ignoring phenomena concomitant to elusive Time?" (Lachmann 1982, 37) Accordingly, Mises lays out a construct such as the generally criticized[7] "evenly rotating economy," which offers what he was looking for, that is, security; but in this way, his theory runs the risk of losing its principal worth, namely a sound insight into human action, which may finally become denaturalized. In fact, praxeological laws do not leave room for freedom. David Gordon, categorically asserts: "Mises was a determinist,"[8] whereas Mark Addleson states that he was a conductist.[9] Actually, Mises states: "The sciences of human action by no means reject determinism" ([1957] 1985, 93). Addleson (1986, 11) suggests that, "The reason Mises views the market process in deterministic terms is associated with his particular approach to the meaning of action as reflected in his lack of concern with the underpinnings of choice and, especially, in his neglect of ends in the planning and decision-making process."

Plenty of reasons could be argued for such a position. Nevertheless, an important one may be that his determinism was closely related to a denial of intrinsic human freedom. Hence, let us analyze some of Mises's texts from his paragraph on freedom in his magnum opus, *Human Action*, and other related texts, *Theory and History* and *The Ultimate Foundation of Economic Science*.

First of all, for Mises, "Primitive man was certainly not born free." Thus, what is freedom according to Mises? "A man is free," he adds, "in so far as he is permitted to choose ends and the means to be used for the attainment of those ends" ([1949] 1966, 279). Then, he says that "there is no kind of freedom and liberty other than the market economy brings about" (id., 283), and that the individual "is free in the sense that the laws and the government do not force him to renounce his autonomy and self-determination to a greater extent than the inevitable praxeological law does" (id., 281). The reason is that, as he asserts, "a man's freedom is most rigidly restricted by the laws of nature as well as by the laws of praxeology" (id., 279: see also 885), to such an extent that "we may or may not believe that the natural sciences will succeed one day in explaining the production of definite ideas, judgments of value, and actions in the same way in which they explain the production of a chemical compound as the necessary and unavoidable outcome of a certain combination of elements"(id., 18).

Mises's very definition of action states: "Action is . . . the ego's meaningful response to stimuli and to the conditions of its environment, it is a person's conscious adjustment to the state of the universe that determines his life" (id.: 11). From the former quotations we may conclude that Mises clarifies a univocal concept of external freedom as absence of coercion. Since all personal action is rational, there is no room for "irrationality," except for interfering with others' actions, which are themselves praxeologically determined. In sum, according to Mises, freedom consists in avoiding obstructions to acting deterministically. Such a concept is a weak vision of what freedom really is.

The former stems from Mises's intellectualism. What do I mean by "intellectualism"? To assign a predominant role to reason as source of human action. In effect, in *Theory and History* he says that "Choosing means is a matter of reason, choosing ultimate ends a matter of the soul and the will" ([1957] 1985, 15) ;and "Action"—he asserts in *Human Action*—"means the employment of means for the attainment of ends" ([1949] 1966 13). Therefore, "Action and reason are congeneric and homogeneous"(Id., 39). The only thing will should do concerning action is "to behave according to the decision made"(id., 13). This is what Mises calls "activistic determinism": "If you want to attain a definite end, you must resort to the appropriate means; there is no other way to success" ([1957] 1985, 177–8). Either there is no room for freedom "during" action, or for a dynamic consideration of human action. According to classical anthropology, rational will and freedom give origin to and inform all the human action from beginning to end.[10] Meanwhile, for Mises, "the incentive that impels a man to act is always some uneasiness,"[11] a rather sensitive feeling, not a positive will of an end. Neither is freedom present for Mises "before" action. Values and ultimate ends are not freely chosen.

All his [Man's] actions are the inevitable results of his individuality as shaped by all that preceded. An omniscient being may have correctly anticipated each of his choices . . . Actions are directed by ideas, and ideas are products of the human mind, which is definitely a part of the universe and of which the power is strictly determined by the whole structure of the universe. ([1962] 1978, 57)

Every freedom is just appearance stemming from the ignorance proper of individuality.[12] In sum,

The offshoots of human mental efforts, the ideas and the judgments of value that direct the individuals' actions, cannot be traced back to their causes, and are in this sense ultimate data. [The lack of such knowledge generates the epistemological differences between natural and human action's sciences. (see [1962] 1978, 58.)] In dealing with them we refer to the concept of individuality.

But in resorting to this notion we by no means imply that ideas and judgments of value spring out of nothing by a sort of spontaneous generation and are in no way connected and related to what was already in the universe before their appearance. We merely establish the fact that we do not know anything about the mental process which produces within a human being the thoughts that correspond to the state of his physical and ideological environment. ([1957] 1985, 78)

Thus, for Mises, uncertainty ultimately stems from ignorance. Once the former is surpassed, a unique best way of performing actions arises. In that way, his intellectualism (misappraisal of the role of will in human action) slides him into a sort of rationalism: the reduction of all kinds of rationality to technical or instrumental rationality. He reasoned this process in a seminal work, his *Grundprobleme der Nationalökonomie* (see Mises, [1933] 1960, 82). Are we probably only facing a "hidden-freedom reasoning" concept of economics? In my opinion, that is not the case: I think that it is not his notion of economics (/rationality) that is limiting the extent of his view of human action (/freedom), but, on the contrary, that his undervalued notion of human action (/freedom) is limiting the scope of his notion of economics (/rationality). I think that the former is proving that freedom matters, and showing that economics cannot be done without having dived before into the deep waters of anthropology for economics is conditioned by it.

Yet, it may be argued that Mises's *ERE* is only considered as a useful tool. However, broader and more useful types are to be found in order to achieve a more thorough analysis, one which Austrian Economics greatly deserves. Leaving anthropological problems and apriorism aside, Mises's frame is not essentially mistaken. He outlined a fruitful perspective of economy as human action. I think that this perspective should be used, however, as a stepping stone for further developments considering an enriched notion of human freedom and action.[13]

Austrianness and Aristotle's Social, Epistemic, and Economic Thought

We should be extremely satisfied with the praiseworthy Austrian open-mindedness. Some years ago, Louis Spadaro (1977, 210) said that, "As new implications of subjectivism unfold, the conceptual-analytical-methodological framework of Austrian theory may require extensions, and even revisions, for purposes of consistency and coordination." And Mario Rizzo (1996, vii) recently wrote, "Austrian economics *is* broad because it *needs* to be broad in order to be interesting and in order to grow in the knowledge it conveys. Narrow Austrian economics cannot ask interesting questions and cannot give interesting answers." It should be opened to intellectual interaction which may enrich it; for example, in my opinion, with Aristotle's social and economic teaching and with his epistemology of classical practical sciences.

Aristotle on Society[14]

Aristotle argued that reality is ordered. He drew a system for describing this order of reality. According to his physical theory even physical hazard does not impede cosmic order. For Aristotle, order in human affairs is not a deed but a task. This task is to seek happiness through virtues. (He also posed a theory of what happiness is.) As Rasmussen and Den Uyl (1997, 29) state, "effort is needed for reason to discover the goods and virtues of human flourishing as well as to achieve and implement them." Virtues are not isolated, but they are a system. They are coordinated by justice—a personal virtue of the will which regulates the social aspect of the whole system—and prudence or practical wisdom—the personal habit of the mind that discovers and facilitates ordered and just actions. In such a way, a just and wise person naturally seeks a good which (unintentionally) benefits the whole society. Aristotle ends his argument asserting: "Thus it follows that the end of politics is the good for man" (*Nicomachean Ethics* (NE) I, 2, 1094b 6–7).

For Aristotle, the work of prudence is personal, essentially free, and variable according to circumstances. What is prudent for one person may not be for another. However, according to him, the coordination of free, prudent, different actions leads to social coordination. Aristotle coherently thought that economic coordination is also possible when people prudently decide and perform economic actions, in accordance—only when necessary—with social coordination. As expressed by Rasmussen and Den Uyl (1997, 28), for Aristotle, "human beings cannot flourish in isolation. Our fulfillment demands a life with others." As human beings are essentially political, that is, social, a wise agent considers other people: the consequences on their well-being and their possible reactions. Let me remind readers that etymologically, coordination means "to give an order together."

Within this frame, however, it might happen that coordination will never be reached (surely not completely.) Three reasons may be pointed out. Ignorance and time, as mentioned, are signaled in the title of O'Driscoll and Rizzo, already classic book (1996). We struggle against conveying information. But the story does not end at this point. Freedom, the third reason, is intertwined with ignorance and time, stemming interpretations and acts that may not lead to coordination. These misleading interpretations, decisions, and actions are consciously, semiconsciously, or completely unconsciously guided by will. As will is not mind, the solution must be more than merely inform. A teaching-learning process is to be followed so that people individually and freely decide to act in the right way. It is the teaching-learning process of acquiring habits. These are the habits which will facilitate rational action, both in a narrow and in a broad sense. That is, people ought to get used to analyzing their consciences and to freely decide to obey the traditionally called "economic rationality" in the light of this new broader economic rationality informed by virtues through prudence. This teaching process may surpass the classrooms. However, I think that a lot may be done through changes in the way of teaching which I will mention below, and that to achieve anything is better than nothing. I can hear a lot of voices claiming that this is not economics. Call it "political economy" if you like.[15]

In my opinion we are facing a good explanation of how the unintended consequence of individual actions is (or is not) social and economic coordination. If everybody freely acts rationally—in the broad sense that includes the narrow rectified—coordination will be unintendedly achieved. This explanation simultaneously leaves room for uncertainty, even ignorance being surpassed, for freedom is always present. As long as human freedom is radical, the only way by which unintended consequences will lead to coordination will be individually following the corresponding moral standards. I will try to illustrate how this happens in a later section.

In other words, once accepted and supposed the information-conveying requirement, coordination as a result of individual actions is possible because the subjective aspect of prudence is the application of an objective set of socially recognized values to concrete situations and actions. I would like to express my thanks to Israel Kirzner, who gave me permission to quote some of his phrases from a personal letter on this topic (July 23, 1998, emphasis on the original):

> You suggest that "moral coordination is an implicit condition for economic co-ordination." Now I have, in other papers, expressed my agreement with the central idea with which you conclude your letter: "Economy does not run without a common *ethos*." Like you, I do not believe that a market economy (and the economic coordination it is able to achieve) is feasible, as a practical matter, without a shared moral framework. So that I agree that a condition for the *practical achievement* of economic coordination is (what you call, if I understand correctly) "moral coordination."

Kirzner's agreement is important. However, he stresses that a common ethos only conditions a practical fact. He adds that "a condition for the *practical achievement* of economic coordination is (what you call, if I understand correctly) 'moral coordination.'" I agree. But I would like to point out that what precisely Aristotle may contribute is a notion of practical science and of economics as a practical science, as we will see below. In this frame, not only the definition of coordination, but also the know-how to practically achieve it, is a matter of science. This know-how needs a scientific incursion in the field of values that constitutes the mentioned social *ethos*. We have slid to the next section.

Aristotle on Epistemology of Social Sciences

Aristotle and modern practical science supporters precisely maintain that a rational research on values is possible. Practical science is the Aristotelian antecessor of social science.[16] It is an essentially moral or evaluative science. A strong movement of rehabilitation of practical science has recently arisen, mainly in Germany. A collective work edited by Manfred Riedel (1972-1974) entitled *Rehabilitierung der praktischen Philosophie* could be mentioned as a hallmark of this current. They conceive the practical paradigm as a reaction against the modern prevailing requirement of value-neutrality in the realm of the social sciences. For this latter position, scientific reason was only applicable to means. The ends were a matter of private decision which surpassed the limits of science. However, since human action is essentially free and therefore essentially moral (freedom entails commitment, moral responsibility), sciences whose subject is an aspect or sector of human action, have to include, they argue, ethical considerations as well. Some years ago, before theory-ladenness was commonly accepted, Leo Strauss, a predecessor of the above-cited movement, stated:

> It is impossible to study social phenomena, i.e., all important social phenomena, without making value judgments. . . . Generally speaking, it is impossible to understand thought or action or work without evaluating it. If we are unable to evaluate adequately, as we very frequently are, we have not yet succeeded in understanding adequately. The value judgments which are forbidden to enter through the front door of political science, sociology, or economics, enter these disciplines through the back door. (1959, 21)

If these values, which inevitably embed all social thinking, are not rationally found and established, then we are confronted with ideology. The answer to this challenge in our area is an evaluative economics. To my opinion, this proposal may perfectly fit with the Austrian concern with human action. We are in fact returning to Buchanan's challenge. We are dealing with a broader notion of economics that lies closely united to social and political moral thought. The borderlines of these disciplines are diffuse. In this conception, economics is neither exact nor separate.

I'm not alone in this view. Hausman and McPherson surveyed recent work by economists and moral philosophers that borders the two disciplines: "In defending their model of rationality, economists wind up espousing fragments of a moral theory" (1996, 7). "(E)conomics remains partly a moral science" (id., 8). As John Tiemstra (1998) commented, "The values and worldviews that imply certain policy conclusions also form the foundations of the economic analyses that justify those conclusions."[17] We will return to Tiemstra in the discussion of practical teaching suggestions.

If the former is true, what will happen with the value-free requirement? We have to interpret this concept in another way. Value-neutrality will not be "officially" leaving values aside, but "impartially" reasoning about them. Values, I insist, cannot be avoided. Thus, they are to be scientifically considered. In fact, current new revisions of Weber's thought points out that *Wertfreiheit* means "impartiality" in the context of German academic fights.[18]

John Finnis has worked on the concept of value freedom. How could we neutrally describe this concept? Neutrality in the "concept-election" in social sciences is only achievable through scientific definition of the standards of rational practical reasonableness. And he clarifies:

> By "practical" . . . I mean "with a view to decision and action." Practical thought is thinking about what (one ought) to do. Practical reasonableness is reasonableness in deciding, in adopting commitments, in choosing and executing projects, and in general in acting. Practical philosophy is a disciplined and critical reflection on the goods that can be realized in human action and the requirements of practical reasonableness. (1984, 12)

That is, the way to resolve the value-free problem is not to put away values—which is impossible—but to reason about them and thus rationally determine the set of them that are at the roots of economics. We may think, for example, that real concern with human rights supposes a set of attitudes and habits in the economic realm. Further detailed analyses should come after the acceptance of this frame. This is a work and a teaching that, to my opinion, could not be denied to students of economic. But it must be done in the interdisciplinary field in which economics cannot work separated from moral sciences. Even though by another (brilliant) way, Hilary Putnam reaches the same conclusion about overcoming fact/value dichotomy through ethical objectivity (1990, chapter 11).

A last remark on the epistemological frame required by the Aristotelian social theory is that it actually constituted the ancient antecessor of methodological individualism. Social analysis begins in individual actions and ends. Societies, Finnis sustains following Aristotle, cannot be adequately described, explained, justified, or criticized unless they are also centrally understood as the carrying out of free choices. These individual decisions and actions are free and personal but not individualistic, for they consider and are oriented through prudence and justice toward the others within the frame of a social or political conception of human nature.

Up to now, in my opinion, we are meeting the conditions of Austrian Economics, as described in the introduction. In the next section I will offer a systematic summary of the traits of practical sciences, pointing out how they match with Austrianness.

Characteristics of Practical Science

Although we have expanded on the concept of practical science we will now briefly complete the frame by mentioning its main traits.

Firstly, practical science acknowledges the inexact character of its conclusions, due to the contingency of human action, which stems from its freedom and singularity. Aristotle asserts in his *Nicomachean Ethics*:

> Now our treatment of this science will be adequate, if it achieves that amount of precision which belongs to its subject matter. The same exactness must not be expected in all departments of philosophy alike, any more than in all the products of arts and crafts. . . . We must therefore be content if, in dealing with subjects and starting from premises thus uncertain, we succeed in presenting a broad outline of the truth: when our subjects and our premises are merely generalities, it is enough if we arrive at generally valid conclusions. (I, 3, 1094b 11–27)

This belief seems to be extraordinarily coherent with Austrian stress on subjectivism. Science should not be demanded for more than it could say in relation with the nature of its subject. This limitation is not shameful since it does not derive from a weakness of science but, as Aristotle also says, from "the nature of the case: the material of conduct is essentially irregular" (*NE*: V, 10, 1137b 17–9). That is, uncertainty stems from an ontological reason (lastly human freedom) and is an essential feature of economic actions that will be always present. I consider this as a confirmation and extension of subjectivism in a genuine Austrian spirit. This trait is not opposed to an acceptable apodictic certainty of Mises-Rothbard's Praxeology (see Endnote 2), as this apodictic character applies to the formal, not to the material content, and what precisely we are focusing on here is the inexactness of the material subjective content of the conclusions.

Once the former has been established, a second feature directly follows it. Practical science must be closely connected to the concrete case. "Now no doubt," Aristotle says, "it is proper to start from the known. But 'the known' has two meanings—'what is known to us,' which is one thing, and 'what is knowable in itself,' which is another. Perhaps then for us at all events it is proper to start from what is known to us" (*NE*: I, 4, 1095b 2–4). An adaptation to the particular case, considering its cultural and historical environment is necessary. This way of knowing is familiar with the inclusion of factors such as institutions of recent Austrian developments. A wise blending of adequately chosen scientific types and historic, cultural; and empirical elements is the key to a correct interpretation of economic human action.

While inexactness and closeness to reality are features which stem from the freedom and singularity of human action, the ethical engagement of practical science arises as a consequence of its other side, namely, morality. However, let us bear in mind that economics is not ethics. Political economy is a moral science as much as it is a practical science. While ethics studies the ethical problem in itself, political economy studies the economic problem—as politics and law do with their corresponding subjects; however, these problems cannot be isolated from their ethical aspects. Aristotle has smartly distinguished between ethics—which is a science and practical sciences, which are ethical insofar as they consider ethical aspects of the analyzed subject. These ethical aspects are, as I said, essential to human action. In transitive human actions a triple rationality may be distinguished, that is, practical or moral, technical, and logical, but practical *inmanens* rationality embeds the whole action to the extent that the existence of a purely technique *transiens* action cannot be sustained. Whatever may be the action, it is always essentially ethical. Since human action is ethical, and since economic action is human action, therefore political economy has an ethical commitment. Concerning our field of study, Gilles-Gaston Granger (1992, 80) states, "Within the economic area an intertwining between the different perspectives of rationality seems to be necessary in order to attain an effective definition of concepts." I have already laid out my argument for the compatibility of this characteristic with Austrian Economics.

A fourth trait of practical science to be considered is its pragmatic aim. An abusive theoretical intentionality has invaded the realm of the social sciences. This process is connected with the already mentioned modern process and has led economics into a certain sterility which is evident in the mainstream economic journals.[19] A social science may have a theoretical aim, but it is always virtually oriented to action due to the essentially practical character of its subject, which defines its epistemological status. On this point, we share Austrian criticism of mainstream developments.

Last but not least, we ought to mention the methodical devices proper to practical sciences. The bibliography on this topic is abundant and could be summarized in an interesting proposal of methodological plurality. In his *Politics* and *Nicomachean Ethics,* Aristotle admirably combines axiomatic deduction, inductive inference, dialectic arguments, rhetoric suggestions, imagination, examples, topics. In a prudential science of this kind, all these instruments add up. Methodical strategies that have been separately developed in different economic currents are amalgamated in this approach, which takes away from the social and economic sciences any dogmatic methodological reductionism. I consider that this is a trait that greatly coincides with Neo-Austrian recent concern for integrating new methods and epistemological points of view.

Aristotle on Economics

This is the right place to insert a short description of Aristotle's theory of economics. Firstly, we should stress that Aristotle's *oikonomike*—the Greek adjective usually used by him—is more than household management, as many economic historians believe. Aristotle pointed out that oikonomike deals with the house and also with the polis.[20] Secondly, Aristotle considers oikonomike to be the use of the things necessary for good life, that is, the life of virtues. Oikono-

mike can only be aimed at the good; it is essentially moral, because it is an act—
energeia—belonging to the *praxis*, that is, practical category. On the contrary,
according to Aristotle, chrematistics is a technique subordinate to economics
that deals with the acquisition of those things used by oikonomike. It is not essentially oriented toward the good. Therefore, while for Aristotle a harmful
oikonomike is unthinkable, two kinds of chrematistics can be considered: a subordinate, limited, and natural one, and a wicked, unnatural, unlimited one. Thus
oikonomike is an act, the right act of using things in order to achieve the good,
that is, virtuous life. Therefore, virtue is needed as a habit that facilitates the
performance of the former act. In addition to this relevant trait of Aristotle's
oikonomike, that is, its intrinsical morality, what was to be said next is that his
oikonomike was embedded in its political environment.[21] Summing up, Aristotle's oikonomike is an ethical act with an inner relation with the historical,
cultural, social, and political factors that surround it.[22] As Newman (1950, I,
138) stated, "Political economy almost originated with him." "Economic science," adds Peter Koslowski (1985, 2), "is an integral part of the hierarchically
ordered sciences of human action and societal interaction." Aristotle poses an
example of practical analysis of an economic issue by his market analysis in the
Nicomachean Ethics (V, 5). Hereby, he concludes that the principle that rules
demand, and therefore prices and wages, is *chreia*, which means economic necessity. Chreia is relative and subjective, but intrinsically moral. It should not be
forgotten that this chapter on economic exchange belongs to his *Treatise on Justice* and that justice is the main social virtue.

Aristotle's oikonomike approximately corresponds with political economy,
a practical science, and chrematistics with economics, a technical science (cf.
my "Controversy" with P. Boettke; Crespo and Boettke, 1998). However, it
must be pointed out that for Aristotle chrematistics ought to be subordinated to
oikonomike, which embraces and deals with the former. The use of this scheme
and terminology—concepts and relations of economics and political economy—
may be greatly helpful for it is familiar and acknowledges the validity of economics. It also adds, by political economy as a practical and embracing science,
an epistemological framework to manage remaining problems, and thus it com-
plements economics.

I prefer not to discuss here the contributions of O. Krauss, E. Kauder, T. W.
Hutchison, Barry Smith, M. Alter, R. Cubeddu, U. Mäki, and other scholars who
established links between Aristotle and Menger's thoughts. Instead, I would
simply like to say that from the former description of Aristotle's view of economy, an awesome similarity with Austrian perspectives evidently arises. He
considers: 1. a definition of economy as human action; 2. an epistemological
frame both for economics—*chrematistiké*—and to political economy—
oikonomiké; 3. a value-subjective theory where demand has the principal role; 4.
a vision of economy as immersed in a cultural, institutional environment.

The only relevant aspect that would need to be cleared up concerning the relation with Austrian Economics is the moral engagement of the theory. In my
opinion, as already argued, this aspect is precisely a valuable contribution of

Aristotle, for it is the key to understanding the simultaneous play of uncertainty and coordination as an unintended consequence.

How to Acquire Virtues and
How Virtues Foster Coordination

The question is double: how do we develop virtues? and how do virtues collaborate in coordination? Aristotle answered the first "how" but not the second one.

We modern minds tend to look for mechanical, automatic, technical explanations—a mentality that better corresponds to the neoclassical scheme. But, in this field we cannot find concrete mechanisms. The practical area depends on life, and life is always changing. The practical is a field where ends and means are dialectically interacting and changing. We can only know some general ideas, which application depends on the concrete circumstances of a concrete society and time.

Let us speak about the first "how." How do we acquire virtues? Aristotle answers: "We are by nature equipped with the ability to receive them, and habit brings this ability to completion and fulfillment" (*NE*: II, 1, 1103a 24–25). Virtues are good habits. Habits are ways of being, firmly fixed possessions of the mind, established by repeating actions. Thus, people acquire virtues through practice. What are the main means to foster these practices? Education and law. The argument is developed by Aristotle in his *Nicomachean Ethics*. First, education, in the broad Greek idea of *paideia*, the shaping of personal character. This is the reason why Aristotle says that "it is no smaller matter whether one habit or another is inculcated in us from early childhood" (*NE*: II, 1, 1103b 24). Second, law. Let us remember that for Aristotle law has a pedagogical objective:

> To obtain the right training for virtue from youth up is difficult, unless one has been brought up under the right laws. To live a life of self-control and tenacity is not pleasant for most people, especially for the young. Therefore, their upbringing and pursuits must be regulated by laws; for once they become familiar, they will no longer be painful. But it is perhaps not enough that they receive the right upbringing and attention only in their youth. Since they must carry on these pursuits and cultivate them by habit when they have grown up, we probably need laws for this, too, and for the whole of life in general. (*NE*: X, 9, 1179b 31–1180a 4)

Aristotle understands that a set of concrete virtues leads humans to their natural excellence, that this process begins with education on those virtues, and that is convenient to consolidate it by laws.

Let us pass to the second "how": how do virtues improve economic coordination? What is coordination for Aristotle? He never defines this concept; however, we can try to draw it. According to him, the reason why we need economics is that, "It is impossible to live well, or indeed to live at all, unless the necessary conditions are present" (*Pol*: I, 4, 1253b 25). He also contends that "it is therefore the greatest of blessings for a state that its members should possess a moderate and adequate fortune" (*Pol*: IV, 11, 1296a 1). Happiness is an activity in conformity with virtue, and, "Still, happiness, as we have said, needs external goods as well. For it is impossible or at least not easy to perform noble actions if one lacks the wherewithal" (*NE*: I, 8, 1099a 31–3). So, I would say that for Aristotle coordination means that through chrematistic and economic activity all people succeed in possessing what they need to use in order to achieve the good life. This objective has various aspects in which virtues collaborate, as we will analyze.

Austrian Economics has, of course, a more elaborated and concrete concept of coordination. However, this concept is consistent with the "primitive" of Aristotle. Coordination for Austrians is compatibility of individual plans: that everybody could achieve his/her intended ends through his/her plans (O'Driscoll and Rizzo 1996, 80). The problem of coordination is uncertainty, unpredictability. Time and ignorance threaten coordination. Hayek's conveying of information and Kirzner's entrepreneurial alertness attempt to solve these problems, but as O'Driscoll and Rizzo (1996) pointed out, they cannot fully manage them.

However, time and ignorance are not the only problems. Free conscious actors may act in an economically irrational way. Free conscious actors, although provided with full knowledge, may act in an unpredictable way. Human action is always unique, and this uniqueness cannot be overcome. All we can state is that people generally act following some tendencies. Habits, precisely, are patterns of behavior. This is the reason why O'Driscoll and Rizzo spoke about "pattern coordination" (1996, 85), with the limitation of recognition of uniqueness.

This is the point where virtues help. Firstly, because the chance of habits creating stable behaviors is greater if they are morally good habits, that is, virtues. According to Aristotle, the incontinent is unpredictable; on the contrary, the virtuous, continent person, is more predictable because he perseveres. "A morally weak person," he says, "does not abide by the dictates of reason. . . . But a morally strong man remains steadfast and does not change on either account" (*NE*: VII, 9, 1151b 25–7); "A morally strong person remains more steadfast and a morally weak person less steadfast than the capacity of most men permits" (*NE*: VII, 10, 1152 a, 26–7). Thus, the probability of plans coordination is larger among virtuous people for they have a stable character and their conduct may be better foreseen. Therefore, coordination is easier within a people possessing an ethical common *ethos*.

Secondly, virtues foster the process in other ways. Prudence or practical wisdom—an intellectual and ethical virtue—makes people act with an accurate estimation of the real situation, avoiding or at least decreasing errors. And, as Aristotle remarks, "It is not possible for the same person to have practical wisdom and be morally weak at the same time" (*NE*: VII, 10, 1152a 7–8). Justice helps people's will to act in the way prudence indicates. In fact, as we said, for Aristotle, market relations are regulated by justice. In this structure the commercial vices have no place. Free-riding does not appear within persons with a strong commitment to justice.

Aristotle devoted the largest part of his *Nicomachean Ethics* (books 8 and 9) to friendship. This virtue, seed of social cohesion, intervenes in particular temporary situations when justice does not suffice. In fact, justice is not necessary between friends. Liberality or generosity also helps to overcome the problems of disequilibrium, through individual or collective action (volunteering, nonprofit organizations, etc.). I would like to stress that all these virtues are free habits of free people. If not, they are not virtues.

As it has been recently highlighted by Jeffrey Young, as well, for Adam Smith, the market is a social arena of action in which cognizance of the sympathetic feelings of the impartial spectator is an operative factor in understanding market activity, price, and distribution (1997, 56). The paper of the impartial spectator in depersonalized societies and markets is to be "a bond of union and friendship" (61). "Wealth and virtue are complementary in Smith" (157) in the frame of a "benevolent model" (69, 76) and a "virtuous sequence" (184).

In sum, in a world of imperfection, virtues help to reduce error and act as a balm. They both foster coordination and reduce the problems remaining during coordination adjustments. This is the promised explanation of how the unintended consequences of individual persons lead to coordination. However, the Aristotelian conception entails a different meaning of "unintendedness" than is traditionally involved in the economic tradition. Aristotle's vision of humans as political animals implies that a prudent action is an action with an eye out for the good of others. As long as prudence becomes a virtue this attitude becomes "natural," spontaneous, "unintended." But this is not the "unintendedness" of the invisible hand tradition which does not need virtues. For this later position, coordination is something rather "magic." Virtues in the Aristotelian approach replace magic from the invisible hand explanation.

The Teaching of Economics

I have referred during the chapter to better ways of teaching economics. Briefly, I would suggest a more-engaged-with-real-problems way of teaching economics than the current. As Mark Blaug (1998) has asserted: "Economics as taught in graduate schools has become increasingly preoccupied with formal technique to the exclusion of studying real-world problems and issues." He reasoned: "That may be why students are increasingly choosing business management over economics."

On the one hand, I am thinking about a broader curriculum with emphasis in humanities. On the other hand, I propose the use of cases or other pedagogical devices simulating real situations. These are the best ways to teach practical sciences. We should aim at developing practical wisdom and capabilities of synthesis.

Peter Boettke (1996, 34) emphasized the relevance of history: "What economics needs today is an anchor in the world. The educational proposal that I would suggest would be a reevaluation of the history of economic thought (as theory) and economic history (as empirical touchstone) in our curriculum." I fully agree.

Lionel Robbins, who devoted a lot of time to these pedagogical affairs, had a similar mind. Once he stated:

> We must be prepared to study not merely economic principles and applied economics. . . . We must study political philosophy. We must study public administration. We must study law. We must study history which, if it gives rules for action, so much enlarges our conception of possibilities. I would say, too, that we must also study the masterpieces of imaginative literature. (1956, 17)

In another lecture (1955, 582; 587) he insisted on studying political science and economic and general history and he also stated: "I suspect that, in the ideal state, economics would be taken as a second degree after some short experience of practical life."

Ethics should also be included. As J. Tiemstra (1988) expressed, "Students would understand economics better if we connected it with social ethics, at least by acknowledging commonly accepted moral standards at the appropriate points in the discussion." Understanding that personal morals synergically lead to coordination as an "unintended consequence" will also push for taking into account "economic" virtues such as generosity, industriousness, competence, order, initiative, spirit of service, keeping one's word, frugality, and the like. Cases will facilitate the consideration of moral aspects.

In sum, less technique and more enlightenment and training of practical wisdom, a greater intertwining between technical economics and practical political economy. This may be, I think, an answer to James Buchanan's challenge.

Conclusion

In this paper, I tried to show that Aristotelian practical science and notion of economy together with their underlying conception about society, perfectly fit into the aims and characteristics of Austrian Economics and can successfully contribute to its current debates, mainly through a broader concept of freedom. This proposal could actually constitute an updated research program, incorporate some ideas from current epistemological theories, and favor fruitful interrelation with other views.

Summing up, I enumerate some mentioned traits congenial with the Austrian approach: (1) free purposefulness of human action, therefore, (2) subjectivism, and (3) recognition of inexactness and unpredictability, and (4) of the role of institutions, (5) methodological individualism, (6) moral individual effort as the last key for the achievement of coordination as an unintended consequence of individual actions. The former trait finds a solution to the here called "Kirzner's inconsistency." Since it is impossible to fully overcome the lack of information of our ever-changing world and, since evil will never be completely eradicated from earth, we will always be in a process of coordination, and this will be economics' and political economy's concerns.

Finally, the adoption of practical science together with subsequent teaching reforms answers to what here I called "Buchanan's challenge:" to find "a wholly different, and uniquely human, science—one that cannot, by its nature, be made analogous to the positive-predictive sciences of orthodox paradigm," (1982, 17) that can solve the "matching freedom with rationality problem." Economic theory, in the sense of the "inclusive rubric" of Buchanan, would become a synthetical and realistic science, closely oriented toward action, with an original freshness, free from positivist prejudices.

Notes

First published in *Review of Austrian Economics* 14, no. 4: 313–33.

1. The expression "defining work" is from P. Boettke (1994: 601).

2. One anonymous referee suggested that I should pay attention to apodictic certainty, as one trait of Austrian thought. I agree: this is an important feature. However, I think that it is not essential to Austrian Economics in the way that Mises introduces it (as for example, J. Egger 1978, 19ff). Philosophical anthropology is apodictic in some conclusions about human nature. I agree with Mises's apodictic certainty as the extent to which his praxeology picks up some of these conclusions or principles—for example, that human action is teleological. However, these are conclusions of anthropology, not of Austrian Economics. On the contrary, the Austrian School and I cannot accept Mises's conclusions threatening freedom. As I will show, Mises's concept of freedom is poor and this poverty is directly connected with the rigidity and extent of his praxeology. (cf. *Mises and Freedom*, below).

3. I consider it worth noting that, a century before, Carl Menger grasped the centrality of "freedom of the human will." However, he finally left it aside: cf. Menger ([1883] 1985, 214). It must be kept in mind that Aristotelian influences often pointed out in Menger's thinking stem from an Aristotle "unconsciously filtered" by philosophical and cultural currents of that time.

4. For a review of those theories, see R. Sugden (1991).

5. For an expanded exposition of those issues, see O'Connor (1995).

6. This vitality is shown in the new introduction to *The Economics of Time and Ignorance* by M. J. Rizzo (1996).

7. For example, by S. C. Littlechild (1982, 91; 93; 97). Littlechild thinks that Hahn—whose neoclassical version of the general equilibrium model he studies—and Mises share a similar view of the role of general equilibrium (in its timeless sense)" (1982: 91). See also J. High (1986, 112), T. Cown and R. Fink (1985), Lachmann 1976a: 60–1), G. P. O'Driscoll and M. J. Rizzo (1996, 82).

8. D. Gordon (1993, 53). See also his argument in 1994, especially pp. 98–99 and 103–4.

9. See Mark Addleson (1986; 1992, 227).

10. Cf. , 1996b.

11. [1949] 1966, 13. I acknowledge Greg Gronbacher's suggestions about the consequences of the Misesean concept of uneasiness.

12. See, for example, [1957] 1985, 78, 90, 93, 183; [1961] 1978, 58.

13. In another paper—Crespo, 1997a—I praise Mises's praxeology because it is the assertion of the possibility to achieve a scientific knowledge of the basic principles of human action in a different way from the classical positivist one.

14. For an expanded and thorough exposition of this topic, see Rasmussen and Den Uyl (1991; 1997).

15. P. Boettke and I have agreed on this terminology in our "Controversy" (1998).

16. See Yves Simon (1991, 120).

17. See also F. E. Foldvary (1996, 152).

18. See W. Hennis (1988; 1991).

19. See M. Blaug (1998). He affirms: "To pick up a copy of *American Economic Review* or *Economic Journal*, not to mention *Econometrica* or *Review of Economic Studies*, these days is to wonder whether one has landed on a strange planet in which tedium is the deliberate objective of professional publication. . . . To paraphrase the title of a popular British musical: "No Reality, Please. We're Economists."

20. See *Politics*, I, 8, 1256b 12–14; I, 10, 1258a 19–21; I, 11, 1259a 33–36.

21. See K. Polanyi (1968).

22. I analyze the Aristotelian concept of economy and economics at length in some works: R. Crespo (1993–1994) and (1996a), and (1997b, chapters 4 and 5).

References

Addleson, M. "'Radical Subjectivism' and the Language of Austrian Economics." Pp. 1–15 in I. M. Kirzner, ed., 1986.

Addleson, M. Robbins. "Essay in Retrospect: On Subjectivism and an 'Economics of Choice.'" Pp. 507–22 in *Pioneers in Economics* 40, edited by M. Blaug. Aldershot: Edward Elgar, 1992.

Aristotle. *Nicomachean Ethics*, trans. by H. Rackham. Cambridge, Mass.: Harvard University Press, 1934.

———. *Politics*, trans. by E. Barker. Oxford: Oxford University Press, 1958.

Blaug, M. "Disturbing Currents in Modern Economics." *Challenge* 41/3: 11–34, 1998.

Buchanan, J. M. "The Domain of Subjective Economics." Pp. 7–20 in I. M. Kirzner, ed., 1982.

Boettke, P. J., ed. *The Elgar Companion to Austrian Economics*. Cheltenham: Edward Elgar, 1994.

———. "What is Wrong With Neoclassical Economics (And What is Still Wrong With Austrian Economics)?" Pp. 22–40 in F. E. Foldvary, ed., 1994.

———. "Controversy: Is Economics a Moral Science? A Response to Ricardo F. Crespo." *Journal of Markets & Morality* 1/2: 212–19, 1998.

Chisholm, R. "Agents, Causes, and Events: The Problem of Free Will." Pp. 95–100 in T. O'Connor, ed., 1995.

Cowen, T., and R. Fink. "Inconsistent Equilibrium Constructs: The Evenly Rotating Economy of Mises and Rothbard." *American Economic Review* 75/4: 866–69, 1985.

Crespo, R. F. "Aristóteles y la economía." *Philosophia*, 9–84, 1993–1994.

———. "Actualidad de la doctrina económica aristotélica." *Cuaderno de Humanidades*, Universidad Adolfo Ibáñez: 9–22, 1996a.

———. "El acto humano: Aristóteles y Tomás de Aquino." *Sapientia* 51/199: 7–28, 1996b.

————. "Max Weber, Ludwig von Mises, and the Methodology of Social Sciences." Pp. 32–52 in *The Theory of Ethical Economy in the Historical School*, edited by Peter Koslowski. Berlin: Springer Verlag, 1997a.

————. *La Economía como Ciencia Moral. Nuevas perspectivas de la teoría económica.* Buenos Aires: Educa, 1997b.

————. "Controversy: Is Economics a Moral Science?" *Journal of Markets & Morality*, 1/2: 201–211, and "A Response to Peter J. Boettke," id.: 220–25, 1998.

Dolan, E. G., ed. *The Foundations of Modern Austrian Economics.* Kansas City: Sheed & Ward, 1976.

Egger, J. B. "The Austrian Method." Pp. 19–39 in *New Directions in Austrian Economics*, edited by L. M. Spadaro. Kansas: Sheed, Andrews and McMeell, 1978.

Finnis, J. *Natural Law and Natural Rights.* Oxford: Clarendon Press, 1984.

Foldvary, F. E., ed. *Beyond Neoclassical Economics: Heterodox Approaches to Economic Theory.* Cheltenham: Elgar, 1994.

Gordon, D. *The Philosophical Origins of Austrian Economics.* Auburn, Ala.: The Ludwig von Mises Institute, 1993.

————. "The Philosophical Contributions of Ludwig von Mises." *The Review of Austrian Economics* 7/1: 95–106, 1994.

Granger, G. G. "Les trois aspects de la rationalité économique." Pp. 63–80 in *Forme di Razionalità pratica*, edited by S. Galvan. Milan: Franco Angeli, 1992.

Hausman, D. M., and M. S. McPherson. *Economic Analysis and Moral Philosophy.* Cambridge: Cambridge University Press, 1996.

Hennis, W. *Max Weber: Essays in Reconstruction.* London: Allen & Unwin, 1988.

————. "The Pitiless 'Sobriety of Judgment': Max Weber Between Carl Menger and Gustav von Schmoller—The Academic Politics of Value Freedom." *History of the Human Sciences* 4/1: 27–59, 1991.

Hayek, F. A. v. *Individualism and Economic Order.* Chicago: The University of Chicago Press, [1948] 1980.

High, J. "Equilibration and Desequilibration in the Market Process." Pp. 111–21 in I. M. Kirzner, ed., 1986.

Kirzner, I. M. "On the Method of Austrian Economics." Pp. 40–51 in E. G. Dolan, ed., 1976.

————. ed. *Method, Process, and Austrian Economics.* Lexington, Mass.: Lexington Books, 1982.

————. ed. *Subjectivism, Intelligibility, and Economic Understanding.* New York: New York University Press, 1986.

————. "Value-freedom." Pp. 313–19 in P. J. Boettke, ed., 1994.

Koslowski, P. F., ed. *Economics and Philosophy.* Tübingen: J. C. B. Mohr (Paul Siebeck), 1985.

Lachmann, L. M. *The Legacy of Max Weber.* Berkeley, Calif.: The Glendessary Press, 1971.

————. "From Mises to Shackle: An Essay on Austrian Economics and the Kaleidic Society." *Journal of Economic Literature* 14: 54–62, 1976a.

————. "On the Central Concept of Austrian Economics: Market Process." Pp. 126–32 in E. G. Dolan, ed., 1976b.

————. *Capital, Expectations, and the Market Process.* Kansas City: Sheed, Andrews and McMeel, 1977.

————. "Comment: Austrian Economics Today." Pp. 64–69 in *Time, Uncertainty and Disequilibrium*, edited by M. J. Rizzo. Lexington, Mass.: Lexington Books, 1979.

————. "Ludwig von Mises and the Extension of Subjectivism." Pp. 31–40 in I. M.

Kirzner, ed., 1982.
————. "Austrian Economics: A Hermeneutic Approach." Pp. 133–46 in *Economics and Hermeneutics*, edited by D. Lavoie. London: Routledge, 1990.
Littlechild, S. C. "Equilibrium and the Market Process." Pp. 85–102 in I. M. Kirzner, ed.
————. "Three Types of Market Process." Pp. 7–39 in *Economics as a Process*, edited by R. N. Langlois. Cambridge: Cambridge University Press, 1986.
Menger, C. *Investigations into the Method of the Social Sciences with Special Reference to Economics.* New York: New York University Press, [1883] 1985. (*Untersuchungen über die Methode der Sozialwissenschaften und der Politischen Oekonomie insbesondere.* Leipzig: Ducker & Humblot.)
Mises, L. v. *Epistemological Problems of Economics.* Princeton, N.J.: D. van Nostrand, [1933] 1960. (*Grundprobleme der Nationalökonomie.* Jena: Gustav Fisher.)
————. *Human Action: A Treatise on Economics,* 3rd rev. ed. San Francisco: Fox & Wilkes, [1949] 1966.
————. *Theory and History: An Interpretation of Social and Economic Evolution.* Auburn, Ala.: The Ludwig von Mises Institute, [1957] 1985.
————. *The Ultimate Foundation of Economic Science: An Essay on Method,* 2nd ed. Kansas City: Sheed, Andrews and McMeel, [1962] 1978.
O'Connor, T., ed. *Agents, Causes, and Events: Essays on Indeterminism and Free Will.* New York: Oxford University Press, 1995.
O'Driscoll, G. P., and M. J. Rizzo. *The Economics of Time and Ignorance,* 2nd ed. London: Routledge, 1996.
Newman, W. L. *The Politics of Aristotle.* Oxford: Clarendon Press, 1950.
Polanyi, K. "Aristotle Discovers the Economy." Pp. 64–94 in *Primitive, Archaic and Modern Economies: Essays of K. Polanyi,* edited by G. Dalton. Garden City, N.Y.: Doubleday, 1968.
Putnam, H. *Realism with a Human Face.* Cambridge, Mass.: Harvard University Press, 1990.
Rasmussen, D. B., and D. J. Den Uyl. *Liberty and Nature: An Aristotelian Defense of Liberal Order.* La Salle, Ill.: Open Court, 1991.
————. *Liberalism Defended: The Challenge of Post-Modernity.* Cheltenham: Edward Elgar, 1997.
Riedel, R. *Rehabilitierung der praktischen Philosophie.* Freiburg i. Br.: Rombach Verlag, 1972-1974.
Rizzo, M. J. "Introduction: Time and Ignorance After Ten Years." Pp. xiii-xxxiii in G. P. O'Driscoll and M. J. Rizzo, 1996.
Robbins, L. C. "The Teaching of Economics in Schools and Universities." *Economic Journal* 65: 579–93, 1955.
————. "The Economist in the Twentieth Century." Pp. 1–17 in *The Economist in the Twentieth Century and Other Lectures in Political Economy.* London: MacMillan, 1956.
Shackle, G. L. S. *Epistemics and Economics.* Cambridge: Cambridge University Press, 1972.
————. *Imagination and the Nature of the Choice.* Edinburgh: Edinburgh University Press, 1979.
Simon, Y. *Practical Knowledge,* edited by Robert J. Mulvaney. New York: Fordham University Press, 1991.
Spadaro, L. "Toward a Program of Research and Development." Pp. 205–27 in *New Directions in Austrian Economics,* edited by L. Spadaro. Kansas City: Sheed, Andrews and McMeel, 1977.

Strauss, L. *What is Political Philosophy?* Glencoe, Ill.: Free Press, 1959.

Sugden, R. "Rational Choice: A Survey of Contributions from Economics and Philosophy." *Economic Journal*, 101: 751–85, 1991.

Tiemstra, J. "Why Economists Disagree." *Challenge* 41/3: 46–62, 1998.

Van Zijp, R. W. "Lachmann and the Wilderness: On Lachmann's Radical Subjectivism." *European Journal of the History of Economic Thought* 2/2: 412–33, 1995.

Young, J. T. *Economics as a Moral Science: The Political Economy of Adam Smith.* Cheltenham: Edward Elgar, 1997.

14

Praxeology, Economics, and Law: Issues and Implications

Larry J. Sechrest

Introduction

Praxeology has been described as a process of deducing correct, universal, historically invariant principles from one, or a few, axiomatic propositions, that is, from propositions which are self-evidently true (Rothbard 1979, 31–43; Hoppe 1995, 7–27). The emphasis is on the subjective[1] nature of individuals' preferences and values, and on verbal rather than mathematical reasoning. It is an a priori method in that it claims not to rely on specific, concrete observations of external events, which observations then form the basis for quantitative tests of hypotheses. Instead, the praxeologist makes extensive use of the fact that he, the analyst, is himself a member of the set of entities whose actions he wishes to examine and illuminate: individual human beings. Introspection and deductive logic would seem to be the centerpieces of the approach. The use of the following terms certainly can be misunderstood, but one can categorize a praxeologist as a rationalist rather than an empiricist (Hoppe 1995, 27–48).

Alternatively, one could say that the praxeological approach, in sharp contrast to the much more common positivist/empiricist approach, recognizes that teleology and causality fold into one another insofar as human affairs are concerned. He who intentionally causes a particular result does so because he values it. The purposive actor, upon reflection, can find embedded within his actions both motivation and (psychological) justification, on the one hand, and causal relations between himself and the external environment, on the other.

The praxeological method outlined above has long been considered a distinctive, almost defining, feature of the Austrian School of economics. What most mainstream economists are unaware of is that several of the classical economists seemed to view their discipline as being rooted in praxeological insights. For example, Jean-Baptiste Say declared:

> Political economy, in the same manner as the exact sciences, is composed of a few fundamental principles, and of a great number of corollaries or conclusions, drawn from these principles. It is essential, therefore, for the advancement of this science that these principles should be strictly deduced from observation; the number of conclusions to be drawn from them may afterwards be either multiplied or diminished at the discretion of the inquirer, according to the object he proposes. ([1880] 1971, xxvi)

It is quite telling that Rothbard (1979, 46), in a vigorous defense of praxeology, favorably cites this same statement by Say—along with citations from John E. Cairnes and Nassau W. Senior—and concludes that he has found in the Frenchman a kindred spirit. Yet, one should be cognizant of the fact that Say seems simultaneously to have conceived of economics as, in some sense, a broadly empirical, even experimental, science which is not unlike chemistry:

> The science of political economy, to be of practical utility, should not teach what must *necessarily* take place, if even deduced by legitimate reasoning and from undoubted premises; it must show in what manner that which in reality does take place is the consequence of other facts equally certain. It must discover the chain which binds them together, and always, from observation, establish the existence of the two links at their point of connection. ([1880] 1971, xviii, xlvii)

The above quotations are not intended to serve as the touchstone for a detailed analysis of Say and his place in the history of economic thought.[2] The task at hand is quite different from that. The reason for referring to these comments by Say is to suggest that 1) it may be possible for even such a penetrating thinker and dedicated praxeologist as Rothbard to misidentify advocates of praxeology and 2) it is not obvious exactly to what extent—if at all—or in what precise sense, the praxeological method may be said to have an empirical foundation. Certainly it is true that most who embrace praxeology in economics appear to be saying that it is an approach which utterly eschews all that is empirical. The boundaries between theory and history are supposedly drawn with precision. Praxeology deals with necessary, abstract principles. History deals with contingent, particular facts. One of the tasks of this essay is to confront that boundary issue.

The other methodological question of interest here has to do with the "subjective" nature of actors' values, preferences, expectations, and plans. When Austrian economists, or any other practitioners of the praxeological method, invoke such a term, what exactly do they mean to convey? If values, to choose one of the above, are subjective, does that mean that they can exist independently of all external reality, that is, as an arbitrary construct of a metaphysically active consciousness? Or does that mean only that each conscious human mind is epistemologically active? In other words, each person interprets his or her relation to the external world in a (potentially) unique way, but everyone is still ultimately constrained by what is metaphysically real.

Of those who see themselves as working within the "Austrian paradigm," a number have failed to address adequately the above two methodological questions. This has, no doubt, weakened their position and diminished the impact that Austrian ideas might otherwise have had. But these questions are by no means unanswerable. This chapter will first argue that, *properly understood*, praxeology remains a rich and insightful means of analysis. This must be the initial concern, because without a sound methodological base, one cannot safely proceed to the application stage.

If a praxeological approach to economics is a powerful tool, can that tool be applied to other disciplines? If this approach enunciates the abstract principles of human action, are those principles sufficiently general that they can be usefully applied to a wider range of human interests? Or must praxeology be confined to the limits of economics? In particular, can legal theory be explored praxeologically? In partisan terms, is there a uniquely Austrian analysis of legal issues just as there is a uniquely Austrian analysis of economic issues?

To answer that last question is the second major task of the present chapter. The reader will find that the answer is affirmative. Praxeology can indeed serve as the analytical framework for both economic theory and legal theory. That is itself a significant result, but there is something more, something quite remarkable. It will be seen that the consistent application of praxeological reasoning leads one to the same general social system, regardless of whether one's explicit concern is with economics or with law.

Murray Rothbard takes the praxeological road in economics, and, as is well known, it leads him to a pure, laissez-faire, or "anarcho-capitalist" society ([1970] 1977, 203–66). This chapter proposes that anyone who, like Adolf Reinach, adopts a praxeological method in law will be irresistibly led, whether it is intended or not, to a similar anarchistic (or "polycentric") conclusion.

Praxeology may indeed be the one (and only?) unifying framework which reveals the principles that connect all varieties of human decision-making and interaction. Moreover, such analysis holds the promise of stripping away centuries of muddled thinking and demonstrating that all which is essential to a civil human order can be achieved within an anarchistic system.[3]

Methodological Issues

It should be clear from the foregoing that the present writer has high regard for the praxeological method. However, being a proponent of a given approach does not preclude one from suggesting improvements by means of clarifications or modifications.[4] The first item that requires attention is the question: To what extent, if at all, is economics an empirical enterprise?

As will be explained below, the seeming rejection of all empirical elements by Austrians is often more a semantic problem than a substantive one and thus can be dispatched fairly easily. But in order to do so, one must distinguish between "empirical" and "empiricism." Empirical knowledge is that gained by means of observational experience of external reality. Initially, it involves the use of one or more of the five senses. Secondarily, it requires one to interpret the perceptual data provided by that sensory apparatus. In this broad sense, all human knowledge is empirical. Empiricism, on the other hand, is a particular attitude toward verification of that knowledge. The strict empiricist, or positivist, declares that man cannot know the essence of a category of entities, only the concrete entities themselves. Therefore, to reflect on the essential nature of a kind of entity, and how it would interact with an entity of another kind, is pointless.

What one must continually do is *test* to discover whether this particular A reacts to this particular B in the same way that all As have in the past reacted to all Bs.[5]

Austrians certainly do reject empiricism.[6] Do they also deny that theirs is an empirical science? Superficially, yes. Actually, no. It is easy to conclude otherwise, because so many have condemned empiricism so often, and one might equate the (justifiable) rejection of empiricism with the (unjustifiable) rejection of all things empirical. Nevertheless, careful consideration of Austrian thought will reveal that the praxeological method itself is fundamentally empirical. Hoppe states that "(o)bservational experience can only reveal things as they happen to be. There is nothing in it that indicates why things must be the way they are" (1995, 19). What must be added, according to Hoppe, is introspection upon ourselves as acting persons. Then "the gulf between the mental and the real, outside, physical world is bridged. . . . For it is through actions that the mind and reality make contact" (1995, 20). It is the necessary categories of human action which reveal "why things must be the way they are". In short, there do exist prepositional statements which can properly be termed "synthetic a priori," to use the Kantian phrase (Hoppe 1995, 17–27). From the foregoing it may seem that Hoppe has demonstrated that economics is indeed both an a priori and a nonempirical discipline.

Despite the depth of his analysis, however, Hoppe has not gone deeply enough. He himself grants that causality is one of the categories of action. "[E]very actor must presuppose the existence of constantly operating causes. Causality is a prerequisite of acting" (1995, 21). Furthermore, "the validity of the principle of causality cannot be falsified by taking any action, since any action would have to presuppose it" (Hoppe 1989, 195). How do humans gain an understanding of causality and the other categories of action? Causality is apprehended by means of "reflection upon ourselves rather than being in any meaningful sense 'observable'" (Hoppe 1995, 20).

But causality in economics is principally concerned with humans' manipulation of things external to themselves. After all, that is why scarcity plays such a central role. Many Austrians might try to counter with the proposition that, despite the constraints placed upon us by nature, the core of economics is thoughtful reflection, introspection into the functioning of our conscious minds. That claim is true as far as it goes, but it is incomplete. How can we know that we can "cause" a particular desired result if we ignore the external, empirical world? Perhaps we can know "in principle" that actions can effect results even though we may not know that a particular action will effect a particular result. False. We *discover* by means of our actions and our observations of the results that we can, under some circumstances, achieve the goals we seek. Purely in terms of inner mental functioning all we know is that we desire to achieve particular goals and that we choose particular means as the route to those goals. We are not born with an innate understanding of cause and effect. Indeed, there are no innate ideas at all.

And here is the crux of the problem. Austrians such as Hoppe insist that understanding causality is an inescapable part of our consciousness. It is true that causality is axiomatic (Menger [1871] 1976, 51). However, what they overlook is the most fundamental question of all: How does a person know that he possesses the conscious mind he calls "I"? There is only one way to do this. One must differentiate the operations of his mind from external events. To know that A causes B, one must first be able to differentiate A from B. In short, one achieves self-awareness through reflection upon one's *observations*. In that sense, life is ineluctably observational and empirical. This may seem to run counter to the fundamentals of Austrian theory, but this writer is not alone in positing an empirical base for the Austrian school. Murray Rothbard, whose credentials as an Austrian are unimpeachable, states:

> There is considerable controversy over the empirical status of the praxeological axiom. Professor Mises, working within a Kantian philosophical framework, maintained that like "the laws of thought," the axiom is a priori to human experience and hence apodictically certain. This analysis has given rise to the designation of praxeology as "extreme apriorism." Most praxeologists, however, hold that the axiom is based squarely in empirical reality, which makes it no less certain than it is in Mises's formulation. If the axiom is empirically true, then theological consequences built upon it must be empirically true as well. But this is not the sort of empiricism welcomed by the positivist, for it is based on universal reflective or inner experience, as well as on external physical experience. . . . While this sort of empiricism rests on broad knowledge of human action, it is also prior to the complex historical events that economists attempt to explain. (1979, 35–36)

Philosopher Barry Smith agrees with Hoppe about the key role played by the idea of synthetic a priori propositions, but sees this solution as being one which is both non-Kantian and non-Misesian. He relies for insight more on Carl Menger, Edmund Husserl, and Franz Brentano (1986, 2–15). Smith is led thereby to a strongly worded exhortation:

The Misesian vision of economics as an edifice generated entirely by conceptual (logical) analysis of this single [human action] notion. . . has done much to
inhibit the acceptance of the more general aprioristic claims made on behalf of
Austrian Economics. The suspicion has remained . . . that other core notions, in
addition to the concept of action, have been smuggled into his theory. . . .It is
the most important lesson of Husserl's work that Austrian economists, armed
with the conception of synthetic a priori (intelligible) connections between
parts and moments in the world, can properly abandon the official Misesian
conception of their discipline as a part of the analytic theory of human action
and conceive it instead precisely in Menger's terms: as a synthetic a priori theory of the whole family of kinds and connections manifested in the phenomena
of economic life. (1986, 18)

Of the two methodological problems noted earlier, the second is clearly the
thornier and will, therefore, require a more extensive exploration. Austrian
economists typically describe economics as one of a constellation of disciplines,
all of which share the characteristic of being interested in illuminating purposive
human action (Kirzner [1960] 1976, 148–56). Thus praxeology is the broader
category. Economics is one of the subsets of praxeological inquiry. "[T]he
praxeological view sees economic affairs as distinguished solely by the fact that
they belong to the larger body of phenomena that have their source in *human
actions*" (Kirzner [1960] 1976, 148). Yet many Austrians slip into the habit of
equating praxeology with economic theory alone. This is understandable as long
as Austrians think of economics as the science of human action. However, to do
so is an error, since it is praxeology which is the science of human action, not
economics. In other words, it would be preferable to define economics in a narrower fashion, one that does not merely equate it with praxeology. What, then, is
it that distinguishes economics from other, related disciplines?

George Reisman has recently offered an answer that looks very promising.
He insists that economics should be defined as "the science that studies the production of wealth under a system of division of labor" (1996, 15). Indeed, those
economists who focus on choice per se "confuse an aspect of the science with its
totality . . . ; they seek esoteric extensions of the subject that have nothing whatever to do with its actual nature" (Reisman 1996, 42). For Reisman, choices
(human action) are certainly important, but only insofar as they are involved in
the process of producing more wealth.[7]

Why does Reisman concentrate on the creation of wealth? Because, he declares, man's need for wealth is unlimited. This need for ever-greater wealth is
the unavoidable result of the fact that man "possesses the faculty of reason. . . .
The potential of a limitless range of action and experience implies a limitless
need for wealth as the means of achieving this potential" (1996, 43). Man's
unique mode of survival, the dependence on cognition at the conceptual level,
marks him as the only living creature which requires progress. Other animals,
both domesticated and wild, do not possess our conceptual mode of functioning
and, therefore, do not seek always to expand both the magnitude and the variety

of their material goods. Endless repetition is commonplace in the rest of the animal kingdom, but is intolerable to humans (Reisman 1996, 44). We need the new and different. We need both a) tools to further our productive enterprises and b) objects of contemplation and esthetic appreciation to enrich our leisure time. We need not only to survive, but also to flourish.

The endless array of new gadgets which the free market has (blessedly) produced may have often elicited derision from socialists, but are actually a profound reflection of the mental capacities and psychological needs of the human race. To attack capitalism for exhibiting "affluence" and "conspicuous consumption" is to attack man's conceptual faculty.

By the way, if economics is the science that studies the production of material wealth, what about the so-called service industries? Does Reisman mean to claim that the activities of accountants, lawyers, nurses, barbers, bartenders, and so forth are of no consequence and need not be studied by economists? Not at all. But he does point out that, in all such occupations, the services in question either a) are provided "as auxiliaries to the production, distribution, or ownership of goods" or b) "vitally depend on the use of goods in their rendition" (1996, 41). "The rendition of personal services falls within the sphere of economics insofar as the providers of such services render them *for the purpose of acquiring wealth*" (1996, 41–42). In other words, economics should concern itself with services, but only when those services are the means by which the providers generate a monetary income. In contrast, Reisman posits that although identifiable services are mutually provided in a pleasurable personal conversation, this does not constitute a true economic activity.

Reisman's alternative definition of economics should be a refreshing change from certain fashionable trends in economics. In recent decades various economists have expanded the boundaries of their discipline to include discussions of, among other items, monogamous marriage as a kind of bilateral monopoly, the family as a productive enterprise, politics as a subset of catallactics (or market exchanges), and the price system as a semiotic exercise in "embedded meanings." These manifestations of "economic imperialism" are clearly wrongheaded if economics is the science that studies the production of wealth under a system of division of labor. Marriage is not mutual enslavement, families are not business firms, political "exchanges" are not comparable to market exchanges, and prices are not arcane linguistic symbols fraught with multiple layers of explicit and implicit meanings.

Austrians should be particularly concerned with clarifying the proper limits of economics, at least in part because a number of Austrians have been at the forefront of the trend described above. Perhaps the most egregious offenses have been those committed by the hermeneuticians. Inspired by the ruminations of Marx, Heidegger, Gadamer, Foucault, and Derrida, these writers bury the reader under "ponderous and obscurantist verbiage surrounded by a thicket of broad citations to largely irrelevant books and articles" (Rothbard 1989, 52). For hermeneuticians, objective reality fades into the background, and they seem only to be concerned with "maintaining the discourse" upon an endless variety of "inter-pretations" until some sort of "consensus" is achieved. These influences have been felt in literature, sociology, philosophy, political theory, linguistics, and history for decades (Windschuttle 1997; Kimball 1990), but only rather recently have begun to infect economics, even though such ideas are really not new. "It is the ancient tune of skepticism and nihilism, of epistemological and ethical rela-tivism that is sung here in ever-changing, modern voices" (Hoppe 1989, 179). "[T]he economics discipline has been in a state of methodological confusion for over a decade, and in this crisis situation minority methodologies, now including hermeneutics, have begun to offer their wares" (Rothbard 1989, 53).

Of course, another of those minority methodologies is the praxeology of the Austrian school. Are the hermeneutical approaches to economics encouraged in some way—even if only implicitly or by mistake—by the relentless emphasis on *subjective* valuation to be found in the works of Mises, Rothbard, and other ad-vocates of praxeology? Whatever the proper answer, Austrians should not shrink from the question, nor dismiss it. The term "subjective" can easily be miscon-strued in a way that could lead one to adopt the radical irrationality of hermeneu-tics. And in that case, all is lost.

Is economic value essentially subjective or essentially objective? Tradition-ally, Austrians have embraced the former and rejected the latter. Or so most have said. One must try to be clear about what one *ought* to mean by these two terms. Since knowledge should be a seamless continuum,[8] not a series of isolated cubi-cles, the economic meanings of subjective and objective should at least be con-sistent with their proper use in philosophy and other fields. Therefore, this writer takes a truly subjective theory of value to be one which claims that what is of value to an individual is, in a literal sense, *created* by the individual's mind without any necessary reference to the facts of external reality (Runes 1968, 303–4). "The subjectivist school . . . holds that values, like concepts and defini-tions, are creations of consciousness independent of reality. . . . In this view, the consciousness of each individual is the creator of its own reality" (Peikoff 1993, 246–47). To a subjectivist, the human mind is metaphysically active.

In contrast to this is an objective approach to value which, while recogniz-ing that values only have meaning in relation to some valuing consciousness, asserts that that relation is essentially one of *discovering* what maintains, fur-thers, and enhances the life of the individual. This is a process of apprehending reality rather than creating it (Runes 1968, 217). The fact that resources are scarce relative to man's endless need for additional wealth requires individuals to choose among a vast array of possible goals (and goods). Although the indi-vidual chooses a course of action, no act of will can cause entities to possess characteristics inconsistent with their nature. "The particular evaluations a man should make, therefore—both in regard to ultimate purpose and to the means that foster it—do not have their source in anyone's baseless feeling; they are discov-ered by a process of rational cognition" (Peikoff 1993, 242). To an objectivist, the human mind is epistemologically active, but metaphysically passive.

Confusion reigns at the boundaries of objectivity. On the one hand, one en-counters intrinsicism (often mistaken for true objectivity), which recognizes that reality is to be discovered, but ignores the fact that values must be values to an actual human being. Values are contextual. On the other hand, one encounters true subjectivism, which recognizes that values do not float through the cosmos with no relation to human life, but ignores the fact that values are not whimsical concoctions. Values are identified, not created, by one's mind.

What has all this to do with economic theory? Broadly speaking, there have been two approaches to valuation in the history of economic thought. Classical economics is usually portrayed as asserting that labor, in some more-or-less me-chanical way, is the proper measure of value. Adam Smith ([1776] 1937, 30), for example, intoned that "(l)abour . . . is the real measure of the exchangeable value of all commodities." This allegedly objective approach culminated in the dead-end known as Marxism. The Marginal (and Subjectivist?) Revolution of the 1870s, led by Carl Menger, Leon Walras, and William Stanley Jevons, is usually thought to have demonstrated just that, namely that all attempts to found eco-nomics on objective grounds are certain to prove barren and misguided.[9] But this presents economists with a *false dichotomy*: Either goods are intrinsically valu-able because they contain a certain quantity of labor, or they are valuable merely because the buyer believes them to be, irrespective of any characteristics they may actually possess. Both propositions are untenable. Properly understood, an objective theory of valuation is one which recognizes two fundamental facts. The concept "value" presupposes a valuer, a conceptual consciousness. And goods possess specific and identifiable attributes. In short, objective values are *rela-tional*. They result from an individual actor's attempt to achieve certain goals within the limits of external reality.[10]

A long-standing problem in Austrian Economics has been the aggressive declaration by many of its proponents that this is a school of economics which concerns itself wholly with subjective processes. As one can see from the forego-ing, that is not really correct. One may call these processes introspective or idio-syncratic, but they are not, strictly speaking, subjective. The hermeneutical wing of the Austrian school has understood the Austrian paradigm to be literally con-cerned only with the subjective and, therefore, has contributed little if anything to the discipline, other than obfuscation. On the other hand, and somewhat in their defense, a dispassionate observer can see how easily such writers might honestly misperceive the proper task of economics.

Hans-Hermann Hoppe seems to understand the issue at stake here, although he will probably disagree with this writer's conclusions. He grants that much rationalist analysis appears dangerously subjective in that it seems to suggest some form of philosophical idealism (1995, 68–69). However, he believes that the problems can be solved by the realization that knowledge is itself a category of human action:

Understood as constrained by action categories, the seemingly unbridgeable

gulf between the mental on the one hand and the real, outside physical world
on the other is bridged. So constrained, a priori knowledge must be as much a
mental thing as a reflection of the structure of reality, since it is only through
actions that the mind comes into contact with reality. . . . A priori knowledge . .
. must indeed correspond to the nature of things. The realistic character of such
knowledge would manifest itself not only in the fact that one could not *think* it
to be otherwise, but in the fact that one could not *undo* its truth. (Hoppe 1995,
69–70)

Austrians should abandon all talk of subjectivism and, instead, describe their
approach to valuation as being relational and objective. There is no need to
abandon praxeology. However, Austrians do need to defend it as being broadly
empirical and fundamentally objective. These are not concessions to the empiri-
cist/historicist mainstream but merely recognition of the proper basis for the science of human action.

Implications for Law and Economics

It has been argued above that praxeology, although incorrectly portrayed by
many Austrians as having subjective and nonempirical underpinnings, nevertheless remains a potent tool of analysis in economics. Can it also, and with equal
success, be applied to legal theory? Yes, it can. Moreover, the political implications of a praxeological approach to law are the same as those which emerge
from a praxeological approach to economics—anarchy. This is particularly evident with the various rationalist theories of rights that have appeared in recent
years.

The first task is to identify some parallels between the use of praxeology in
law and its use by economists. Special attention will be given to the similarities
with Murray Rothbard's defense of anarcho-capitalism. Adolf Reinach, a prime
exponent of praxeology in law, describes his approach thus:

> Together with pure mathematics and pure natural science there is also a pure
> science of right, which also consists in strictly a priori and synthetic proposi-
> tions and which serves as the foundation for disciplines which are not a priori. .
> . . If one formulates the essential laws of right in such a way that the possibility
> of their being suspended is taken into account, then they hold unconditionally.
> Otherwise their validity depends on those possibilities not being realized. But
> in either case it remains true that the validity of these laws, considered *in them-
> selves*, is free from any exception. . . . There can be no question of a "contradic-
> tion" between the a priori theory of right and the positive law, there are only
> deviations of ought-enactments from the laws governing what is. These devia-
> tions, however, can never be used as an argument against the validity of the a
> priori laws of being. . . . The idea—posing as so scientific whereas it is ulti-
> mately quite simple-minded—that the relations which are grounded in the es-
> sence of social acts and are available to our direct insight could be refuted by

the study of historical facts, proves to be thoroughly untenable and even absurd. ([1913] 1983, 6, 114–15)

Just as with Austrian economists, Reinach's interest is in human *actions*. There is no way to know what another person wants without observing what that person does. If person A desires X, that preference can only be demonstrated by A undertaking a course of action so as to acquire or achieve X (Rothbard [1956] 1977, 2–7).[11] But Reinach focuses largely on actions of a particular kind, what he terms "social acts." These are acts, for example, commanding, promising, or requesting, that are not only spontaneous and intentional, but also "are in need of being heard" ([1913] 1983, 18–19). They are not merely inner mental phenomena such as wishing or intending. For example, to establish an obligation/claim relation between persons A and B, A must demonstrate this by means of a statement in which the obligation is willingly and knowingly expressed. If this has not occurred, B cannot subsequently demand performance of the specified obligation by A. This is a most crucial example, because the greatest part of those human relationships which involve practical legal questions are of an obligation/claim sort. In theory, it might even be said that all legal conflicts can and should revolve around obligations and claims, whether directly or indirectly.

Furthermore, the analysis of social acts reveals certain axiomatic statements which are true everywhere and always (Reinach [1913] 1983, 89). "[E]ssential laws . . . are rather grounded in the essence of the acts and in the essence of relations of right, no matter when and where they are realized. They hold not only for our world but for any conceivable world" ([1913] 1983, 138). As one can see, Reinach frequently refers to the "essence" of a thing, as in the preceding, or in "the essence of legal structures" or "self-evident essential laws" ([1913] 1983, 96). It is not clear whether, to Reinach, the essence of an entity is a metaphysical or an epistemological concept. That is, does a given, concrete entity literally "partake" of the metaphysical essence of the class to which it belongs, or is the essence of an entity merely a reflection of the epistemological processes of integration and differentiation which enable human beings to sort concretes into classes. The first might be called naive realism (or Aristotelian essentialism), and the second contextual realism.[12] In either case, Reinach's mode of reasoning is of the "causal-genetic" sort espoused by Austrian economists[13].

Reinach and Rothbard also share a commitment to methodological individualism. Rothbard categorically declares that "only an individual can adopt values or make choices; only an individual can *act*. . . . This primordial principle . . . must underlie praxeology" (1979, 57). Therefore, groups, nations, and states simply do not exist in a metaphysical sense. All such collective concepts are just linguistic conventions, that is, they are succinct ways to describe various complex interactions of the only real entities—individual, concrete, specific human beings. No attribute of a conscious mind should be associated with those collective concepts, although it is commonly enough done. It is crucial to understand collective concepts correctly, because misapplications of the law of causality will result otherwise. All events are the actions of existing entities, therefore to identify the cause of an event one must identify the entity which initiates the causal chain. Little or nothing has been accomplished if one ascribes causal power to a mere linguistic convention. Positive damage is done if one thinks collectives possess feelings, values, preferences, interests, and so forth. Rothbard understands this very well.

For his part, Reinach refers to "a legal power which cannot be derived from any other legal ability but which has its ultimate origin in the person as such. . . . [This] forms the ultimate foundation for the possibility of legal-social relationships" ([1913] 1983, 81). Or, more bluntly, "only persons can be the holders of rights and obligations" ([1913] 1983, 102).

In comparing Reinach and Rothbard, one finds that both men draw a sharp distinction between the abstract principles of his discipline, on the one hand, and the manifestations of those principles under particular circumstances, on the other hand. For Rothbard, this is the contrast between economic theory and economic history, or alternatively, applied economics. The praxeological principles of economics are valid for all places and times, but they yield no historical laws because each historical event is "the highly complex result of a large number of causal forces, and, further . . . it is unique and cannot be considered homogeneous to any other event" (1979, 42). Economic principles are the result of mental experiments which depend on the ceteris paribus assumption. In history, those "other factors" are rarely if ever actually constant.

For Reinach, the parallel contrast is between the "a priori theory of right" and "positive law." The former identifies the logically undeniable rights and claims of individuals. The latter constructs a legal code that (supposedly) embodies those rights. Reinach elaborates:

> Confusion results when principles of the a priori theory of right are conflated with questions of the positive theory of law. . . . It is the task of positive jurisprudence to investigate in detail how the natural entitlement to a thing is related to obligatory claims, at what point in time it arises—in particular whether it presupposes that one is given possession of the thing in question—how far its sphere of application and its practical consequences extend. Philosophy of right has only to establish the essentiality of the concept of natural absolute rights.[14] ([1913] 1983, 123)

Finally, both Reinach and Rothbard embrace the Lockean homesteading principle as a vital component of praxeological analysis. Reinach the legal theorist refers, for example, to the "case in which someone *produces* a thing out of materials which have never belonged to anyone. Here it seems quite obvious that the thing from its very beginning belongs to the one who produced it. . . . Just as a relation of owning is *not* grounded in the nature of possessing or using, it *is* grounded in the nature of production" ([1913] 1983, 73). Using very similar language, Rothbard the economist declares that "an unowned resource should, according to basic property-rights doctrine, become owned by whoever, through his efforts, brings this resource into productive use"([1970] 1977, 255). Moreover, Rothbard ([1970] 1977, p. vii) contends that employment of the homesteading principle remains "value-free" and thus within the boundaries of praxeology.

In other words, no particular presumptions regarding ethics are involved. What is involved is an analysis of the nature of man, the meaning of the concept "ownership," knowledge of the finiteness of resources, and the necessity therefore of some system of property rights. Any system that does not begin with self-ownership, that is, the right to control one's own actions, will prove self-contradictory. If each man owns himself, then whatever he creates out of unowned raw materials must belong to him. If it does not, then man ceases to be able to function as a causal agent. At that point human action becomes useless and ceases, because it *presupposes* that man can cause the ends he seeks. Without the homesteading principle as the basis for property rights, mankind would eventually die out, albeit slowly. Or equivalently, without the homesteading principle, mankind would be mired in socialism.

It is clear from the foregoing that Murray Rothbard and Adolf Reinach are thinkers committed to the praxeological method. The works of both men are characterized by value-free, a priori reasoning, abstract universal principles, methodological individualism, homesteading as the origin of property rights, and a focus on human *actions* rather than on intentions, wishes, or hopes. Furthermore, as will be discussed below, both men lead the reader to an engagement with anarchistic social systems. One does it quite explicitly, while the other does it implicitly.

Before progressing to the topic of anarchy (or polycentrism), one additional, broad comparison must be drawn. Are there connections between law and economics beyond the particular works of Rothbard and Reinach, connections which may suggest why both disciplines can be explored so profitably by praxeologists? It would appear so, since both are concerned with wealth. If economics is the science that studies the creation of wealth under a system of division of labor, as was argued earlier in this paper, then how might legal theory be defined? Perhaps one could say that it is the study of the *protection* of wealth under a system of division of *property titles*. Of course, what is meant here is law in the abstract—what Reinach calls "the a priori theory of right"—not some specific society's legal code. Legal theory rather than practical jurisprudence. Further, the concept of wealth would have to be extended to include one's self and one's rights. Rothbard ([1970] 1977, 213) says that praxeology as applied to economics is based on three axioms: "the major axiom of the existence of purposive human action; and the minor postulates, or axioms, of the *diversity* of human skills and natural resources, and the disutility of labor."[15] In imitation of Rothbard, one might say that praxeology as applied to law is based on purposive human action plus the minor axioms of the diversity of human interests and the disutility of rights violations.[16]

Even if one's viewpoint is not explicitly praxeological, there are good reasons to consider law and economics to be overlapping fields of study. Those reasons find their basis in the relative scarcity of all resources and the attendant necessity of human choice. "Law consists of both rules of conduct and the mechanisms or processes for applying those rules. Individuals must have incentives to recognize rules of conduct or the rules become irrelevant, so institutions of enforcement are necessary. . . . Clearly the enterprise of law. . . requires scarce resources that must be allocated. Beyond that, economic theory explains human behavior by considering how individuals react to incentives and constraints" (Benson 1990, 2).

Praxeology, Anarchy, and Rationalist Theories of Rights

It is well known that Rothbard devoted much of his career to a spirited defense of what might be called anarcho-capitalism. This he undertook from several perspectives—historical, political, ethical, cultural—but predominantly from the perspective of an economist. Insofar as the last is concerned, his goal was to demonstrate that there exists no legitimate role for the State, because private, free-market enterprises or associations are capable of providing every good or service actually demanded by noncriminal individuals.[17] One may grant that Rothbard is fully successful in this endeavor but still question whether he demonstrates that the free market *must* provide all essential goods and services, or merely that the free market *can* provide all such goods and services. This requires careful elaboration, especially because it is not meant in any way as a diminution of Rothbard's very real contributions. The suggestion is just this: By adopting a praxeological approach to law one can analyze this issue in a way that augments Rothbard's conclusions.

The point of departure is the fact, discussed earlier, that a thoroughgoing application of praxeology requires that the analyst adopt an individualistic methodology. Praxeology examines the actions of humans, living, breathing, thinking, striving, goal-oriented individuals. Collectives, that is, groups of individuals, merely represent the interactions of those individuals. In no meaningful metaphysical sense are they entities in their own right. To treat them as though they are real entities produces serious intellectual errors and dangerous public policies (Rothbard 1979, 57–61). The principal error—though very common—is to forget that the *meaning* or *significance* of any given action is relational. It varies depending upon which particular individual actor one refers to. Therefore, it is mere presumption to ascribe a single, internally consistent meaning to actions undertaken by a variety of individual actors/valuers. Although doing so is not strictly correct, almost all Austrians describe this as the "subjective" nature of individual actions.

If collectives do not really exist, then concepts founded on the premise that they do exist must be invalid. It makes no sense to speak of the attributes, preferences, values, goals, or choices of nonexistent entities. It is an act of fantasy, much like speculating about some characteristic of the mythical unicorn. There are, to put it bluntly, no such things as "public goods," the "public interest," the "public good," the "national interest," or "collective security." These are just empty phrases used by particular persons to manipulate others in order to bring about specific ends. Moreover, this should be obvious to economists. To be a "public good," X must first be an economic good. To be an economic good, X must be relatively scarce, the valuer must have control over X, and there must exist a causal relation between X and the utility of the valuer (Menger [1871] 1976, 52). Otherwise, X cannot be the object of action by the valuer. And acting man is the subject matter of economics. To choose one of these alleged public goods as an example, security is not, and cannot be, collective. Hoppe explains:

> [A]re there any nonarbitrary borders separating different security-risk (attack) zones? The answer is yes. Such nonarbitrary borders are those of private property. . . . The insurance of property against aggression would seem to be an example of individual rather than group (mutual) protection. . . . The correct answer to the question of who is to defend private property owners from aggression is the same as for the production of every other good or service: private property owners, cooperation based on the division of labor, and market competition. . . . The idea of collective security is a myth that provides no justification for the modern state. . . . All security is and must be private. (1999, 9, 15, 1)

Collective notions as applied to human beings are invalid and presumptive. Well and good. But what has this to do with legal theory? A very great deal, because civil law is based on relationships of obligation and claim between individuals, perceives violations as torts, and seeks redress through restitution. Civil law is fundamentally private and individualistic. On the other hand, criminal law is based on the notion of public safety (a variant of the concept of the public good), perceives violations as crimes against the State as the alleged representative of the people, and seeks redress through punishment. Criminal law is fundamentally public and collectivistic. It is revealing to note that even some who otherwise are extremely critical of the depredations of the modern State nevertheless defend both the alleged necessity and the collective nature of public law. For example, law professor Murray Franck[18] asserts:

> [E]ach individual has a *right to a "sense of tranquility,"* against even a threat to the security of his rights, if he is to be free to focus on life-sustaining productive activity and his happiness. Civil as well as criminal trespasses upon rights are public harms, not merely private wrongs. The enforcement of contracts and of other rights is not a "private good" only; it is a "public good" as well, and thus merits and validates taxation. (2000, 153)

One should notice that Franck assumes that the systematic protection of rights, and thus this "sense of tranquility" he quite correctly espouses, are impossible without the State. This writer believes that latter claim to be false.[19] However, that is not quite the issue at hand here. The issue here is the public and therefore collectivistic nature of State law. From a praxeological perspective, all valid law must be individualistic—and therefore private. Law, just like economics, must use as its components the actions of individuals. This is precisely what civil or tort law does. Moreover, those legal systems which have developed without, or even in defiance of, State direction—systems variously described as anarchistic, polycentric, or customary [20] —have been systems based on the principle that "offenses are treated as torts (private wrongs or injuries) rather than crimes (offenses against the state or 'society')" (Benson 1990, 13).

Is this some accident of history? Not at all. In the absence of a centrally-planned, authoritarian legal system, individuals naturally gravitate toward principles of interaction which they perceive as mutually beneficial. "Because the source of recognition of customary law is reciprocity, private property rights and the rights of individuals are likely to constitute the most important primary rules of conduct. . . . Incentives must be largely positive when customary law prevails. Protection of personal property and individual rights is a very attractive benefit" (Benson 1990, 13).[21] The praxeology of law must be built upon the actions of individuals, and thus must consider interpersonal offenses as torts. In short, a praxeological approach to law leads one unavoidably to the promotion and defense of a system of customary, or polycentric, legal principles. Even more bluntly, anarchy is the logical extension of praxeology.[22]

Parallel reasoning leads to parallel conclusions. A close analysis of human interaction for mutual benefit forms the foundation for both private markets and private law. But what if one rejects the whole of praxeology itself? Might there still be an argument on behalf of polycentric law? It turns out that there is.

Tom Bell recognizes that express individual consent—a common feature of such legal structures—is superior to all other methods of justification, because "[o]nly express consent reliably signals that a justification has achieved its objective" (1999, 13). Clearly, for the praxeologist as a strict methodological individualist this requires the direct and explicit agreement of every person involved. However, "[o]ne need not become a methodological individualist to accept this account of justification. . . . One can believe that social organizations exist independent of their members and still agree that a justification succeeds only relative to the individuals who consent to it" (Bell 1999, 15).

Moreover, justification is transitive. So any organization, as long as it is justified as the representative of its individual members, can legitimately act in their names (Bell 1999, 15). Bell then retreats further, suggesting that one may have to invoke "hypothetical consent" in certain "borderline cases." Nevertheless, "[d]espite this more generous view of justification, statist law still fares poorly. . . . Because statist law is only justified relative to its fans, they can only justify inflicting institutionalized coercion on themselves" (Bell 1999, 18). He concludes that "statist law can never be fully justified, and can never be as justified as polycentric law" (Bell 1999, 13).

Granting the point that anarchistic law is in principle more defensible than State law, one still must ask what theory of rights should be the basis for an anarchistic legal system. Reinach offers a theory of rights which are founded on the Lockean concept of homesteading and expressed through "social acts" which create relations of obligation and claim, and therefore the possibility of violations in the form of torts. Reinach's approach may be described as a priori, praxeological, and rationalist. More recently several writers have argued in a fashion reminiscent of Reinach; such rationalist theories of rights can be found summarized in Kinsella (1996).

The first of these is Hoppe's "argumentation ethics", which begins with the observation that "it is impossible to deny that one can argue, as the very denial would itself be an argument" (Hoppe 1995, 65). Thus, the statement that "humans are capable of argumentation and hence know the meaning of truth and validity" is axiomatic (Hoppe 1995, 65). Argumentation, per Hoppe, is both a subset of human action and an independent axiom that exists at the same, or an even higher, level of fundamentality (1995, 66–67). Given that argumentation is the method by which humans search for truth and try to persuade others, both self-ownership and the ownership of scarce resources are implicitly assumed by all who argue. In order to engage in argumentation at all, one must control his own person. Furthermore, to maintain one's existence as a person who argues, one must also be able to own certain nonhuman resources. The alternative to peaceful argumentation is violent conflict. Whether or not they are aware of what they are doing, those who choose argumentation indicate their preference for nonviolent interaction and, therefore, for a structure of property rights which discourages conflict over those scarce resources. Hoppe's train of thought demonstrates that even the most dedicated collectivist, insofar as he tries to persuade others of the superiority of collectivism, *implicitly assumes* the necessity of individual rights and private property. Verbal attacks on capitalism are thus performative contradictions, and, as such, are logically indefensible.

Kinsella is a proponent of an approach remarkably similar in some ways to that of Hoppe: estoppel theory. This is based on the common law principle that "a person may be prevented, or estopped, from maintaining something (for example in court) inconsistent with his previous conduct or statements" if that denial brings harm of some kind to another party (Kinsella 1996, 317). When applied to the issue of punishment,[23] this means that an "aggressor contradicts himself if he objects to his punishment" (Kinsella 1996, 317). By this reasoning, then, individual rights must exist, because individuals, as actual or potential victims of aggression, are fully justified in requiring that violators of those rights be punished. Kinsella's approach shares with Hoppe's the characteristics of being a priori, rationalistic, and devoted to revealing implicit contradictions, but differs from Hoppe's in that it focuses more narrowly on the interaction between aggressor and victim. Hoppe's argumentation theory is meant to be applied broadly to any and all cases of verbal disagreement.

A third approach to rights deals with the self-contradictions committed by those who deny the existence of rights altogether, that is, so-called "rights skeptics" (Kinsella 1996, 319–20). To rebut this position, one must first reflect on exactly what it means to have a right. Whether or not one has a right to a certain course of action hinges on enforceability. Having a right to action X means the holder of the right (A) can use force against anyone (B) who tries to prevent him from doing X. At this point in the proceedings the rights-skeptic condemns A, saying A has no such right because no one has rights of any kind. But to insist that A has no right of enforcement means that B must be justified in using force to stop A. That of course implies that B has a right to stop A. In other words, rights do exist. Dramatically, but appropriately, Kinsella suggests that the proponent of rights should announce that he will shoot the rights-skeptic. If the skeptic objects, he can only do so on the grounds that he possesses a right not to be aggressed against. Otherwise, the proponent of rights must possess a right to shoot the skeptic. Either way, individual rights of some kind do exist. This method of establishing rights—by uncovering the contradictions of the rights-skeptics—"is similar to the estoppel approach outlined above, although the discourse under examination need not involve an aggressor" (Kinsella 1996, 319).

The three approaches Kinsella surveys[24]—argumentation, estoppel, and refutation of rights-skepticism—all achieve something quite important. They establish, by means of clear reasoning from irresistible axiomatic propositions, that a) such things as rights do indeed exist and b) those rights are attributes of an individual human actor, not of a collective. The power of these approaches lies in the fact that "they show that the opponent of individual rights, whether criminal, skeptic, or socialist, presupposes that they are true. Critics must enter the cathedral of libertarianism even to deny that it exists" (Kinsella 1996, 326). For reasons given earlier, this writer would go one step further and suggest that it is specifically the cathedral of anarchism which one must enter.

Conclusion

The praxeological method is an efficacious way to investigate the fundamental theoretical questions at the heart of any study of human endeavor. Unfortunately, however, Austrian economists have often erred in portraying the method as subjective and nonempirical. It is neither. It is rooted in empirical reality and concentrates on valuations that are relational and objective. For some Austrians those distinctions are, more than anything else, just semantic differences. For another branch of the Austrian school, they represent significant conceptual differences, and result in a departure from the foundational work of Carl Menger.

Once praxeology is correctly understood, one can apply it to subsets of human action such as economics and law. Two of the outstanding exemplars of praxeology in those fields are, respectively, Murray Rothbard and Adolf Reinach. There are many interesting aspects to the work of both men, but perhaps the most compelling is the parallelism one finds. Specifically, Rothbard's employment of praxeology demolishes the argument for any sort of government intervention into the economy and produces the explicit conclusion that society and the State are inherent enemies. Therefore Rothbard argues that the only fully free society is an anarchistic society. Working from the homesteading principle as the source of rights, as does Rothbard, Reinach demonstrates that legal principles have their origin in certain "social acts" which create relations of obligation and claim. These are individualistic and private acts which in no way require the existence of the State. Although Reinach apparently does not himself realize it, the implication of his analysis is that all law can be private. In order to see that all truly beneficial law *should and must* be private, one need only reflect on the fact that public law is inescapably collective, while private law is inherently individual. Moreover, when left to their own devices, human beings naturally opt for privately defined and enforced legal principles in preference to public (or statist) law.

Praxeology, when applied to either economics or law, produces the same conclusion: anarchism. Recent rationalist defenses of rights have only served to reinforce that conclusion.

Notes

First published in *Quarterly Journal of Austrian Economics* 7, no. 4 (Winter 2004): 19–40.

1. Some possible dangers that can accompany the focus on "subjectivism" will be discussed later.

2. For an introduction to the work of Jean-Baptiste Say, see Sechrest (1999a)

3. Does this mean that, in a sense, Ludwig von Mises was actually *insufficiently radical* regarding his claims on behalf of praxeology? See, for example, Mises ([1949] 1966, 1–71).

4. The suggestions which follow are meant to strengthen praxeology, not destroy it.

5. Of course that begs the question of how, if the essence of a class of entities cannot be identified, one is able to categorize the entities as "As" and "Bs" in the first place. That is one of the deficiencies in the positivist approach.

6. Hoppe calls empiricism "a methodology suited to the intellectually poor, hence its popularity" (1989, 188).

7. It is interesting to see that in the course of his discussion Reisman draws a distinction between "property" and "wealth" much as did Carl Menger. To Menger, property was "the entire sum of goods at a person's command"; while wealth was "the entire sum of *economic* goods at a person's command" ([1871] 1976, 109).

8. This does not, however, preclude the possibility that the different fields of knowledge may require significantly different technical procedures.

9. To interpret Menger as making this claim may be an error, despite the frequent and favorable use (in translation at least) of the phrase "subjective value" ([1871] 1976, 74–77, 119–21, 226–35). It seems that what Menger objects to should more accurately be termed an intrinsic rather than an objective approach to value. The same *may* be true of

Mises, although Mises, due to the Kantian elements in his thinking, more often sounds like a true subjectivist.

10. For a political philosopher who is very familiar with the Austrian school, and who expresses a similar viewpoint, see Sciabarra (2000, 197 n.16).

11. Rothbard points out that this "demonstrated preference" differs from the "revealed preference" of mainstream economists in that it recognizes that one's ranking of preferences is constantly subject to change.

12. See Kelley, 1986, for an extensive treatment of the appearance of these ideas in the history of philosophy and their meaning, significance, and implications.

13. See Rothbard (1979, 53) for comments on the Aristotelian influence in Austrian economic thought.

14. One should note that Rothbard ([1973] 1985, 42–44), like Reinach, construes natural rights as being absolute.

15. This seems to be a departure from both Hoppe (1989, 199–200; 1995, 22–25) and Mises (1976, 24), who insist that only the core axiom of human action is necessary. Moreover, it supports Barry Smith's contention that axioms in addition to the core axiom are effectively included (1986, 18).

16. These are not Reinach's words, but those of the present writer.

17. This excludes "public goods," which concept Rothbard criticizes and rejects ([1962] 1970, 883–88).

18. Franck is an Objectivist who, like most Objectivists, is a "minarchist" (or defender of limited government) and extremely critical of anarchy in any form.

19. For details, see Sechrest (1999b) and Sechrest (2000).

20. Legal scholar Randy Barnett studiously avoids calling them anarchistic, opting instead for the term "polycentric" (1998, 264–82).

21. Also see Benson (1993, 48).

22. This is the present writer's conclusion. One should not assume that Reinach shares this view.

23. This writer assumes that Kinsella here means generally any method of redress, whether specifically referred to as punishment or restitution. See Kinsella (1997, 608). However, the estoppel principle seems even stronger in the case of private restitution for torts than in the case of public punishment for crimes. With the former, the hypothetical dialogue is with the victim himself (or an unambiguously designated agent of the victim); whereas with the latter, that dialogue is with a public sector employee who presumes to act on behalf of society at large—one member of which is the aggressor himself.

24. He actually mentions several others. However, they are all either some sort of variation on these three, or have little in common with praxeology, and so will not be discussed here.

References

Barnett, Randy E. *The Structure of Liberty: Justice and the Rule of Law*. Oxford: Oxford University Press, 1998.

Bell, Tom. W. "The Jurisprudence of Polycentric Law." Unpublished manuscript. University of Chicago School of Law, 1999.

Benson, Bruce L. *The Enterprise of Law: Justice Without the State*. San Francisco: Pacific Research Institute for Public Policy, 1990.

————. "The Impetus for Recognizing Private Property and Adopting Ethical Behavior in a Market Economy: Natural Law, Government Law, or Evolving Self-Interest." *Review of Austrian Economics* 6:2 (Spring): 43–80, 1993.

Franck, Murray I. "Private Contract, Market Neutrality, and 'The Morality of Taxation.'" *Journal of Ayn Rand Studies* 2:1(Fall): 141–59, 2000.

Grassl, Wolfgang and Barry Smith, ed. *Austrian Economics: Historical and Philosophical Background.* New York: New York University Press, 1986.

Holcombe, Randall G., ed. *15 Great Austrian Economists.* Auburn, Ala.: Ludwig von Mises Institute, 1999.

Hoppe, Hans-Hermann. "In Defense of Extreme Rationalism: Thoughts on Donald McCloskey's *The Rhetoric of Economics.*" *Review of Austrian Economics* 3: 179–214, 1989.

————. *Economic Science and the Austrian Method.* Auburn, Ala.: Ludwig von Mises Institute, 1995.

————. *The Private Production of Defense.* Auburn, Ala.: Ludwig von Mises Institute, 1999.

Kelley, David. *The Evidence of the Senses: A Realist Theory of Perception.* Baton Rouge: Louisiana State University Press, 1986.

Kimball, Roger. *Tenured Radicals: How Politics Has Corrupted Our Higher Education.* New York: Harper and Row, 1990.

Kinsella, N. Stephan. "New Rationalist Directions in Libertarian Rights Theory." *Journal of Libertarian Studies* 12:2 (Fall): 313–26, 1996.

————. "A Libertarian Theory of Punishment and Rights." *Loyola of Los Angeles Law Review* 30:2 (January): 607–45, 1997.

Kirzner, Israel M. *The Economic Point of View.* Kansas City: Sheed and Ward, [1960] 1976.

Menger, Carl. *Principles of Economics.* Translated by James Dingwall and Bert F. Hoselitz. New York: New York University Press, [1871] 1976.

Mises, Ludwig von. *Human Action: A Treatise on Economics.* Chicago: Henry Regnery, [1949] 1966.

————. *Epistemological Problems of Economics.* Translated by George Reisman. New York: New York University Press, 1976.

Peikoff, Leonard. *Objectivism: The Philosophy of Ayn Rand.* New York: Meridian, 1993.

Reinach, Adolf. "The Apriori Foundations of the Civil Law." Translated by John F. Crosby. *Aletheia* 3: 1–142, [1913] 1983.

Reisman, George. *Capitalism: A Treatise on Economics.* Ottawa, Ill.: Jameson Books, 1996.

Rothbard, Murray N. *Toward a Reconstruction of Utility and Welfare Economics.* New York: Center for Libertarian Studies, [1956] 1977.

————. *Man, Economy, and State: A Treatise on Economic Principles.* Los Angeles: Nash Publishing, [1962] 1970.

————. *Power and Market: Government and the Economy.* Kansas City: Sheed, Andrews and McMeel, [1970] 1977.

————. *For a New Liberty: The Libertarian Manifesto.* New York: Libertarian Review Foundation, [1973] 1985.

————. *Individualism and the Philosophy of the Social Sciences.* San Francisco: Cato Institute, 1979.

————. "The Hermeneutical Invasion of Philosophy and Economics." *Review of Austrian Economics* 3: 45–59, 1989.

Runes, Dagobert D., ed. *Dictionary of Philosophy*. Totowa, N.J.: Littlefield, Adams, and Company, 1968.

Say, Jean-Baptiste. *A Treatise on Political Economy, or the Production, Distribution, and Consumption of Wealth*. New York: Augustus M. Kelley, [1880] 1971.

Sciabarra, Chris M. *Total Freedom: Toward a Dialectical Libertarianism*. University Park: Pennsylvania State University Press, 2000.

Sechrest, Larry J. "Jean-Baptiste Say: Neglected Champion of Laissez-Faire." In Holcombe, ed. (1999), 45–58, 1999a.

———. "Rand, Anarchy, and Taxes." *Journal of Ayn Rand Studies* 1:1 (Fall): 87–105, 1999b.

———. "Taxation and Government Are Still Problematic." *Journal of Ayn Rand Studies* 2:1 (Fall): 163–87, 2000.

Smith, Adam. *An Inquiry into the Nature and Causes of the Wealth of Nations*. New York: Modern Library, [1776] 1937.

Smith, Barry. "Austrian Economics and Austrian Philosophy." In Grassl and Smith, ed. (1986), 1–36, 1986.

Windschuttle, Keith. *The Killing of History: How Literary Critics and Social Theorists Are Murdering Our Past*. New York: Free Press, 1997.

15

Reason in Economics versus Ethics

Tibor R. Machan

Reason is not a simple tool for simplifying, nor is rational thought an intellectual monoculture. And this . . . is not a tragedy. The world does not relapse into helpless confusion just because things have more than one aspect and can be correctly described in more than one way. On the contrary, overlapping pictures taken from different angles provide the right way to get a reasonably unified notion of an object.

—Mary Midgley, *The Ethical Primate* (1994)

Misunderstanding Rationality

How has the concept of rationality been used, and also confused, by many economists who, often unbeknownst to them, have been following certain modern philosophers in their understanding of human reason? What the economists have done with and in the name of reason has left us with the very widespread and well-entrenched idea—especially among champions of the free-market economic system—that reason is only useful for purposes of determining what are the most effective means to achieve various ends. As far as ends or goals are concerned—that is, what one ought to pursue, what is good or the right thing to do—that is supposedly to be left to such *arational* elements of our nature as desires whims, instincts, drives, preferences, cultural pressure, etc. By conjoining these two beliefs—instrumental rationality and value-subjectivism—we get the curious and paradoxical result that all persons act rationally, all the time. Furthermore, it also follows that no one does anything wrong.

My discussion will be philosophical, not so much cast in the language of technical economics—in this subject it would be easy to veer off into very complex jargon, even mathematical terminology. I believe, however, that what I plan to say will help us both to understand the problem of rationality and to begin to see a way to its solution.

Rewarding Economic Imperialism

Professor Gary Becker, University of Chicago professor of economics and soci- ology, won the 1992 Nobel Prize in economics, for "having extended the domain of economic theory to aspects of human behavior which had previously been dealt with—if at all—by other social science disciplines such as sociology, de- mography, and criminology." Becker is one of the earliest and perhaps most pro- lific among those economists who believe that what motivates human beings in the marketplace, namely, utility—that is, to make a good deal—is exactly what motivates them everywhere else—when they make love, play with their children, go to church, or develop theories of social science. He is the most unabashedly imperialistic of the neoclassical school of economic analysis in whose view hu- man rationality consists of acting effectively so as to satisfy one's desires or ful- fill one's preferences. Only Gordon Tullock, of the University of Arizona, coau- thor with James Buchanan of the classic *The Calculus of Consent*[1] comes close. (The book, edited by Gerard Radnitzky and Peter Bernholz, *Economic Imperial- ism: The Economic Method Applied outside the Field of Economics*,[2] collects the writings of many supporters of this way of thinking.)

The Nobel committee for the last several years has been rewarding a good deal of the work resting on the economic approach championed by Professor Becker. In 1986 they gave the prize to Professor James Buchanan, who was credited for his pioneering work in applying economic (or "public choice") the- ory to an understanding of the political process. Public choice theory holds, in essence, that we can best understand the conduct of politicians and bureaucrats if we take it that they are all motivated in line with the "utility maximizer" model of human behavior. As Buchanan characterized the approach, "Politicians and bureaucrats are seen as ordinary persons, and 'politics' is viewed as a set of ar- rangements, a game if you will, in which many players with quite disparate ob- jectives interact so as to generate a set of outcomes that may not be either inter- nally consistent or efficient."[3] In some details Buchanan's views differ from the Chicago school's, although it is not possible to distinguish them briefly concern- ing the nature of rationality. (The crux of the difference is that Buchanan seems to locate individual rational action, following Hobbes, at the point of the incep- tion of political society, not at each point of human decision-making.)

A few years ago it was the late George Stigler who received the award for his similarly oriented work in studying government regulation. And earlier, in 1975, Milton Friedman, the head of "the Chicago school," was rewarded for his work along more general lines that many credit for laying some of the foundations for subsequent economic imperialism.

Let's notice at the outset what some of the most prominent participants in the discussion appear to understand by "rational," namely, nothing more than "logically consistent."

Misunderstanding Rationality, A

For example, Amartya Sen tells us: "Rationality, as a concept, would seem to belong to the relationship between choices and preferences, and a typical question will take the form: "Given your preference, was it rational for you to choose the actions you have chosen?"[4]

The term "rational" is to mean such circumstances wherein someone pursues a given objective in a way that he or she reaches it most efficiently—that is, in the shortest possible time, with the least amount of disagreeableness involved.

This is not the only way economists misunderstand rationality. They make another claim that is difficult if not impossible to defend.

Misunderstanding Rationality, B

For example, Ludwig von Mises, former leader of the Austrian school of economics, claimed that, "Human action is necessarily always rational." [5] As Richard McKenzie explains, "Austrian 'rationality' can be captured in the very general notion that people either know, or will learn within tolerable limits, what is best for them and will seek to improve their position in life, with no mention of what it is that is pursued."[6]

Stigler apparently also thought that the economic way of understanding human behavior—to whit, that everyone acts rationally or maximizes utilities, all the time—is accurate: "Man is eternally a utility-maximizer—in his home, in his office (be it public or private), in his church, in his scientific work—in short, everywhere."[7] Gary Becker put it somewhat less directly when he said: "The combined assumptions of maximizing behavior, market equilibrium, and stable preferences, *used relentlessly and unflinchingly*, form the heart of the economic approach as I see it."[8] And Milton Friedman put the position as follows (in his own Nobel acceptance address in 1975): "[E]very individual serves his own private interest. . . . The great saints of history have served their 'private interest' just as the most money-grubbing miser has served his interest. The *private interest* is whatever it is that drives an individual."[9]

This is to say that we are all doing what we do so as to achieve the subjective values we hold: the great saints are acting as they do, so as to attain eternal salvation, the money-grubbing misers as they do, so as to achieve wealth. Which is pretty close to saying that we are all acting rationally (provided we do not slough off in our pursuits—although if our values were to change, that, too, might be the rational thing to do.)

Combining Two Misunderstandings

Is there a connection between the two positions on rationality? If one takes it that rationality is entirely instrumental, and one also holds that the ends of action are entirely subjective, incapable of being evaluated objectively and designated as either rational or irrational, then everyone who pursues any goals at all will necessarily be rational. This is because anyone whose actions might be judged irrational could claim, plausibly, that his or her goals are such that the way one is acting constitutes the rational pursuit of those goals.

We have already seen that economists see rationality in instrumental terms—only *means in the pursuit of ends* can be judged as rational (excepting when we judge some person who uses such means in such terms). But do economists think that the merits of goals or ends of action are subjective? Certainly the Austrian school has many prominent adherents who do.

Von Mises claims, for example, that "When applied to the ultimate ends of action, the terms rational and irrational are inappropriate and meaningless. The ultimate end of action is always the satisfaction of some desires of the acting man. . . . No man is qualified to declare what would make another man happier or less discontented."[10] Don Bellante made the following observation which embraces the subjective value theory about chosen objectives: "The Austrian approach is most distinct from mainstream economics in its thorough emphasis on the individual decision maker as the focus of scientific analysis. Yet with the values and motives of individuals being entirely subjective it is impossible for an analyst to pass judgment on the optimality of the individual's chosen actions."[11]

Neoclassical economists tend, also, to embrace value-subjectivism. As Richard McKenzie explains, for these economists "No agreement is presumed with reference to subjective evaluations of 'goods' because there is no basis for establishing what constitutes agreement. (What is 'satisfaction derived from apples'?)"[12] And Milton Friedman himself suggests this subjectivist take on values when he states, referring to himself, that "The liberal conceives of men as imperfect beings. He regards the problem of social organization to be as much a negative problem of preventing 'bad' people from doing harm as of enabling 'good' people to do good; and, of course, 'bad' and 'good' people may be the same people, depending on who is judging them."[13]

I wish to argue, then, as follows: if the subjectivity of values—that is, of ends sought or goals pursued—is embraced by both the Chicago and the Austrian schools—the two schools supportive of the free market—and both also view rationality as purely instrumental, it would follow that both would have to regard all human action as rational or utility maximizing, exactly as von Mises and Stigler state. Why? Because there is no way to deny that an action is rational if the goals can always be altered, at will, so as to understand the means as efficient for purposes of achieving them.

Say that I set out to get to New York City. Am I being rational in how I do this? That is, do I employ the most economic means within the shortest time? I do as follows: I drive my car and I take numerous detours, make various stops, backtrack now and then, linger and bide my time, as far as getting to New York City is concerned. A friend notices this and claims that I am being somewhat irrational, given how my means are inefficient with reference to my end. But I respond: I want to get to New York City just this way, slowly, biding my time, backtracking, etc. So I am, in fact, being perfectly rational—I am doing what I want to do, what I prefer. If there is no way to assess whether getting to New York City rapidly is itself a rationally superior goal to, say, getting there slowly, any way of getting there will be rational. Indeed, instrumental rationality without the prior determination of the comparative superior rationality of the objective sought is actually indeterminable, unspecifiable.

The Simple Truth of Imperialism

Economic imperialists believe that they are telling us something quite simple and true, namely, that, to use Buchanan's way of putting it, all persons in society "are seen as ordinary persons." And, as they understand it, ordinary persons are driven to advance their own lot on every front. Everyone is, to put it even more plainly, selfish. Greed is no sin but a fact of life, a natural drive. For the economists, however, such terms are misleading, since when pressed they will insist that they "do not assume that people in all parts of their lives are motivated by selfish considerations, but also by 'honesty,' 'justice,' 'love,' and 'friendship.'" And, as Geoffrey Brennan and James Buchanan elaborate the point, "the *homo economicus* model in no sense rules out the possibility that each individual may be motivated by certain ethical or moral concerns, as long as we can take it that such ethical conduct on the part of anyone cannot be presumed to benefit everyone else."[14] Yet, as Becker himself made clear, "the heart of the economic approach [is] to include hatred, love, obligation, etc."[15]

Implied in this position is that rational moral *choice* or *initiative* is absent from human life, as it is from the lives of dogs or giraffes. Everything is set. (Stigler once argued just that point, holding that the world is exactly as it has to be—nothing is wrong or right with it, it merely is.) Furthermore, when reference is made to ethics or morality, what is meant is some form of conduct that benefits other persons than the agent. Thus the economist tends to accept the neo-Kantian characterization of morality, to whit, that no action is morally significant— praiseworthy—if it achieves a purpose of the acting agent. They do not take ethics to be a framework of understanding how to choose to act rightly or wrongly, principles whereby one initiates one's conduct for good or ill to be identified objectively, independently of the current feelings, desires, or preferences of the agent who is acting. Ethics or morality for these economists is, instead, doing whatever benefits other people, period—that is, altruism. But since such conduct is incomprehensible, from the motivational (scientistic) viewpoint, morality does not really make sense as anything other than some people's (e.g., the great saints') private, albeit perhaps unconventional, interests.

While these thinkers are supporters of free markets, I believe on grounds of the *common sense realization* that it has been the most productive in human history, their support is not argumentatively decisive and not what the free market requires, even strategically, in our time. (Scientism might have been in great fashion sometimes in the past, but it isn't today, given all the clamoring for visions and values, except perhaps by computer buffs.) It is insufficient to argue for a political economic system by assuming—and that is all these economists do —that human beings are utility maximizers (even when they benefit others) and that the system of free production and exchange is most hospitable to how they must behave. That is because many criticisms of the free market rest on a far more detailed and complex conception of human behavior, one that includes reference to the basic capacity of human beings to initiate and make choices about what they will do. Furthermore, these criticisms take it that some standard of proper conduct is identifiable and should be followed, regardless of who is to be benefited.

Economic Rationality in Doubt

Despite their winning the Nobel Prize, the reputation of the free market has not gained a great deal from what those economists have said who champion this system from a "scientific" point of view. What little popular support there is now for capitalism in mainstream intellectual circles—for example, Jeffrey Sacks and Janos Kornai at Harvard—comes from the collapse of socialism in Eastern Europe and elsewhere, and even that is waning by now. The economic advocates of free trade and the unregulated marketplace have had a little to do with that, of course, but they have also unleashed a strong backlash. (Stigler even agreed with this, saying in one of his addresses to the Mt. Pelerin Society that ideas have no impact, all that matters is what people desire!)

Outside of the discipline of economics most academicians are hostile to capitalism. They treat the greed that economist praise with disdain—one need but recall the "hero" of Oliver Stone's movie, *Wall Street*, who espoused the doctrine "greed is good" and was roundly seen as a villain for this. One need only consider how the popular press has embraced the largely phony claim that the 1980s, guided by the free-market rhetoric of Ronald Reagan—who many of these economic imperialists advised—was a "decade of greed."

It is my thesis here that extending the approach economists take to understanding human behavior to every area of human life is wrong—people do not simply calculate costs and benefits all the time in terms of certain set preferences or goals. (Indeed, they probably ought to do so more regularly than they actually do.) I will also argue that a rational approach to ethics would give support to such a recommendation, although not to the view that many economists advance, namely, that we necessarily engage in such cost-benefit analysis everywhere in our lives. In short, we would all be better off if people did practice prudence more consistently as they embark upon their economic tasks. But it is by no means automatic that they do, and to pretend it misleads us into complacency. As the late Allan Bloom put it in his essay "Commerce and 'Culture,'" "It is not true, as the moderns appear on the surface to say, that men in civil society are always motivated by utility, by self-interest."[16] To claim otherwise, as these economists do, leaves outsiders incredulous. As Stephen Breyer put it, in his review of Thomas Philipson's and Richard Posner's *Private Choices and Public Health*,[17] a book critical from an economic approach of government spending on AIDS research: "Economics can wisely inform our efforts to attain our goals; but ultimately, if we prefer John Donne to Adam Smith, economists cannot prove us wrong."[18] Should we prefer reading literature to reading economics if we cannot do both at the same time? The economists cannot help us at all with such choices, namely, those we are most troubled by. We find from the economists little to help us with making decisions about the ends we should pursue. All we can get is some measure of wisdom as to how we might pursue the ends we have. And, to add to the difficulty, there really is no "we" here—no consensus—on those ends, in which case we are pretty much at sixes and sevens as to how to proceed.

Now if the case for establishing and protecting the right to individual liberty, including in the marketplace, depends on such economic analysis, then so much the worse for freedom. Economics can, at most, offer suggestions why free markets are useful for purposes of enabling people to strive for prosperity or well-being, but it cannot demonstrate that this is something we ought to foster and place ahead of, say equality, order, or revolutionary progress.

Rationality in Market Behavior

But can anything prove us right or wrong about our preferences? Actually, economic analysis can *contribute* to such a quest, namely, by showing us the limits of the possible or highly probable. Economics can confirm that one cannot get blood out of a turnip, as it were. And this is the beginning to the story of the virtue of prudence.

One reason the market approach to understanding human conduct does make limited sense is that *in markets* people do tend to focus on making a good deal in terms of already-set desires and preferences. They do not deliberate about whether to get food *in* the grocery store but *before* they go there, nor whether to hire a stockbroker once they are investigating who might be the best in their vicinity, or whether to take a plane trip as they are calling their travel agent. Such decisions are made outside of the market and serve as the reasons why the market is entered in the first place.

And even elsewhere, outside the market place, there are economic concerns. It is prudent to pay heed to our economic well-being even while embarking on noneconomic matters such as going to church or getting married to one's beloved.

Once a person has chosen to obtain some good or service via the market process, he or she is likely to take into consideration that there are several options available and search out which of those options will secure the desired good or service at the lowest possible cost and effort. Such instrumental rationality is clearly important and without it there would be a great deal of waste in human life. Adjusting one's available means to the goals one wants to attain is indeed rational, but to understand why, we require more than what the economist gives us, namely, the view that human beings are rational automatically. That view simply does not make sense of even the widespread economic irrationality we witness in the world, not, at least, without making the economic approach entirely vacuous.

Rationality in economics appears, thus, to be purely instrumental. When it appears to include considerations that seem not to be related to economics, the proper scientific approach, as many prominent economists argue, is to bring those concerns within the rubric of economics. At the Hoover Institution, where I was a fellow in 1975–1976, Aaron Director, the somewhat ignored guru at the University of Chicago, argued that "true" has no meaning in economics, only "useful" does. Whether that is itself true was not a polite question to ask, as I found out.

Vacuous Explanations by Preference Satisfaction

To conclude, let me state, in summary, that because there is no provision within the economic perspective to rank preferences in some rational order, except perhaps by reference to some other preference scale that is itself simply given, the claim that the economic approach can give a clear idea of human rationality and can pay adequate heed to virtues or ethics is vacuous. This claim merely advances the imperial ambitions of some members of the discipline.

There is, as Becker makes clear, an effort by many economists to account for seemingly varied human motivation—for example, honesty, justice, love, friendship, etc. But the account states that some people just have a preference for these and when they abandon the quest for efficiency in some economic endeavor—for example, in obtaining a job in an office or factory in favor of letting a less-experienced good friend get it—they do this only because their other preferences make this necessary. Thus if someone foregoes seeking a promotion by means of letting down his best friend, it is only because the person prefers keeping the friend to obtaining the better job. Or if someone refuses to treat an employee unjustly in the course of seeking to obtain some economic objective, that is only because, within his or her preference scale, treating employees justly occupies a prominent position. In the end, then, all decisions are economic decisions, after all, to recall Friedman's point, "[E]very individual serves his own private interest."

This kind of reasoning was explored by Wittgenstein some decades ago. Bousma gives the following account of it:

> The hedonist says: "Men desire nothing but pleasure. . . . Obviously this is no empirical proposition. The hedonist does not find this out by going about asking people what they want. He has no statistics about this. And yet he knows very well that people want all sorts of things. So it isn't at all like: Everybody wants a motorcar. If someone wants a motorcar, then he wants pleasure, and if he wants to smoke or to write a letter, then he wants pleasure. Pleasure is another word for whatever anyone wants. In other words it's a tautology. Everyone prefers the preferable. So pleasure is the desirable, the preferable.

> But there is, of course, the illusion of having discovered something. How does that happen? Perhaps in some such way as this. Freud asked—in his own language: What is the essence of the dream? Then he inspected and noticed that a certain dream was a wish-fulfillment dream. And another, and another. This was it. A man is hungry and dreams of feasting, is thirsty and he dreams of passing water. Some dreams are like this. This comes like a flash, a great light—an *apercu*. . . . Concerning pleasure there is no doubt. Pleasure is desired and there is no question of "Why?" or "For what?" about it. When it is desired, the case is clear. And now the temptation is to say that when you desire an automobile, what you desire is automobile-pleasure, eating-pleasure, writing-pleasure, etc. The generalization, which was mistaken at the outset, compels this manner of speaking. . . . Pleasures are not all of the same kind. There are higher and lower. This is the mistake of the generalization breaking out into curious distinctions, or it proceeds to develop the absurdities of the calculus. We desire nothing but pleasure, but there are qualities of pleasure. Poetry pleasure is better than pushpin pleasure.[19]

To the charge of vacuousness Becker responds by saying that the conclusions of the economic analysis "would not be attacked so much if they were, in fact, vacuous."[20] What can one say to this? Is the criticism most successfully understood to imply that the thesis has powerful substance and is, thus, far from vacuous?

A better explanation is that since such vacuity is put in service of capitalism, as well as some rather disturbing notions (e.g., that crime or suicide or divorce is always rational), and since the prominent economic supporters offer no other support for this odious system, most people find the approach objectionable, not just fruitless. They object to the supposed dirty work that is done by the vacuous thesis, not so much to a vacuous thesis as such.

Becker does not appear to appreciate just how serious the opposition to capitalism is, regardless of how it is given backing. Because in his case the critic can plausibly argue that the economist is embarking on scientism, economic imperialism, at the expense of leaving out some quite reasonable common-sense considerations, not only the economist's method but also his or her preference for a system of free exchange in the marketplace are dismissed as unworthy of support.

Rationality in Ethics

Sen notes that from the economic or instrumental conception of rationality, paradoxes will arise "in a situation where the outcome depends on other people's actions in addition to one's own." More importantly for our purposes, he observes that "Morality would seem to require a judgment among preferences whereas rationality would not."[21] This suggests that if the view of rationality embraced by the economist is left intact, there will be a gap between morality and rationality. Must we accept this? I'll turn to that point in the following pages.

Outside of the marketplace, virtues other than prudence—in the narrow sense of looking out for one's economic well-being—can take precedence. Courage, honesty, justice, generosity, and so forth are also important to practice and at times outweigh prudence or the concern for prosperity. By denying our freedom to make a rational choice as to which of the numerous virtues one needs to practice, economic imperialism is not only false to the facts but also demeans us. It suggests that we are *unable* to pay attention to anything other than the satisfaction of certain built-in desires or preferences. This demeans our humanity and creates the illusion that we carry on as *we must*, *driven* by our preferences, never mind the situation, never mind what is at stake. It is no wonder, then, that some economists have argued that economic analysis can make the best sense of the behavior of laboratory mice!

Let me make clear that, no doubt, nearly all aspects of human living involve some economics—some thought of cost and benefit as determined in the marketplace. But there are values one cannot reduce to such factors—friendship, love, truth, beauty. There is, then, the economic aspect of, say, the purchase of a Rembrandt. But is not the beauty of the work more important?

The way the Beckerian approach manages to cover so much is that it is very open—indeed, vacuous. Every decision a person makes has to do with cost and benefit, but what will count as such for that person is purely subjective. Thus if a criminal prefers to steal Volkswagens instead of Rolls Royces, that is explained by reference to that criminal's preferences. But if another makes the opposite choice, that too is so explained—both wanted to maximize their values, satisfy their preferences, but what they prefer or what actually is of value to them is a mystery as far as the economic approach would have it. So, as I noted before, the economist can say that everyone acts rationally only because the goals of behavior are entirely a matter of subjective-personal choice, nothing that is objectively determinable. Even if someone were to steal the leaves off the front yard of a neighbor, never mind that there are zillions of those everywhere for free, it could be argued, on these grounds, that the thief is rational just so long as he or she prefers those leaves (plus it won't thwart the efficient satisfaction of his or her other desires)! But this is not of much help in understanding thieves and how their kind of life fits in with how human beings ought to live.

Despite the welcome support of free-trade measures in most commercial realms the economist's thinking has generated among these famous economists, to defend and revitalize the concern for individual freedom requires more. The proper approach would be to admit that while economics can shed light on many aspects of human living, other disciplines must also address those areas, lest we be left with a rather incomplete and thus misleading understanding of ourselves. (Of course, they will reply that my motivation for saying this is purely economic —I want to keep my job, to retain its reputation as being useful, so I prefer that their imperialism be rejected. But this tact can be turned against these scientific theorists, so I will not explore it further.)

On How to Proceed

I want at this point to explore what rationality is. I will not employ the time honored method of considering the most recent reflections of prominent contributors to the discussion, such as Robert Nozick's input via his *The Nature of Rationality*.[22] I want, instead, to start—or at least to simulate starting—anew.

Lest we fail at the outset in our exploration of the difference between the economic and ethical ideas of rationality, we need to defend, briefly, a way of going about answering the question "What does 'rational' mean?" This may look like trying to begin without the prospect of getting off the ground, since all beginnings seem to pose the problem of needing support.

But, as Aristotle and Rand have argued, it is just a mistake to believe that no starting point is warranted. Some matters really cannot be questioned or doubted with any hope of being understood, despite what some current schools of philosophy—for example, Richard Rorty's form of pragmatism—suggest.[23]

We (barring funsters and madmen) pose questions when we face problems. Once a language is in use for a significant period of time, an inquiry into the meaning of some term is commonly prompted by the occurrence of incompatible serious usage. The results sought from the inquiry are firm grounds—for example, the truth of the matter for resolving the incompatibility.

Why do we think that such grounds might be found? Because, to start with, we are here asking these questions and doing so by resting (or suspecting that we do already rest) on some grounds in many of our activities. In other words, our mutual presence at the inquiry, our mutual interest in the problem itself, our mutual ability to focus on the issue at hand, and similar factors implicitly affirm that our mutual search is mutually grounded over time (indeed over several generations, considering the history of this inquiry). Denying this would make the search we are mutually conducting unintelligible. Without some common ground, those of us who inquire about these matters, talk to one another about them, write and review proposals on the issues, etc., would not be able to embark upon it.

A discussion such as this one cannot proceed unless most of the terms used in it hold reasonably firm for us, unless the environs are stable, unless we ourselves remain intact over the duration of the exchange, etc. Thus there is an axiomatic common ground that underlies what we do, inasmuch as even to deny that we are discussing the issue in mutually intelligible terms would be to affirm that such terms are indeed at work in the discussion. In this respect we know that we have common grounds because without them we could not even doubt that we have common grounds—exactly the reason that in order to remain consistent, the ancient sophist Cratylus stopped speaking and used mere signs, made with his hands, to express himself. (Of course, even this assumed that such signs could be used successfully to make a common reference for purposes of some measure of communication between interlocutors.)

Once these grounds are uncovered, confusion and conflict in usage are more likely to cease, though no one is justified in expecting final guarantees (because we can go astray in innumerable ways often not anticipated). Accordingly, let us briefly contrast some uses of the term "rationality" with others to see which will yield better results in terms of the standard implicit in our purpose, namely, to discover an unambiguous rendering of what a term means within the context of the rest of our discourse and experience.

On Rationality

"Rational" is a term with diverse and sometimes incompatible usage in both common discourse and philosophical dialogue. The term is used to characterize what we say and do; but, given the different meanings people attach to it, they will disagree about whether the same course of conduct is or is not rational. Some tend to mean by "rational" that, for example, one is "in possession of his (uniquely human) conscious faculties." Actions that are rational are then supposed to involve competent, unimpeded, undiluted use of these faculties or what is sometimes referred to as articulable or intelligible accounts. That, in turn, requires a large array of virtues so as to be guided by competent, alert awareness of the world around us. In this rendition of "rational," both means and ends of action can be subject to evaluation as either rational or irrational. (Some matters, of course, would not be subject to such evaluation, namely, anything not capable of being placed under one's conscious control.) Others tend to mean by "rational" that, for example, some action led efficiently or effectively to satisfactory results, to just what was desired. This, as we have seen, is often designated as the "instrumental" conception of rationality—what counts as rendering some behavior rational is that the most effective (even technically up-to-date) means are employed to get from some starting point to some desired objective. The meaning here is the one I have associated with the economists and that we saw characterized by Mises and Sen. It is to act consistently, being (formally) logical, internally consistent in one's course of conduct, as well as employing the most advanced technical resources in one's carrying out of one's policies as rational.

Some, in turn, hold that "rational" means whatever is widely accepted—conventionally agreed to—in the relevant community as the way to proceed. Or it is argued that this is the most one can expect to mean by the term, given the difficulties with attempts to defend the sense of it indicated above. Rational or, less strictly, reasonable, is that which conforms to the commonly adhered-to standards. (In the law the "reasonable man" standard is sometimes taken to mean this.)

It is clear that in certain contexts some of the conceptions described above will conflict. To take "rational" as meaning both "self-consistent" and "widely accepted in the relevant community" is perhaps plausible, yet it assumes that the relevant community prizes consistency. (Charles S. Peirce verged on assuming this when he proposed his conception of truth as that which an *ideal* community's membership will accept. Richard Rorty seems to take it much further into the realm of intersubjectivity when he construes objective knowledge to be no more than what an actual community agrees to.) The intersubjectivist sense of "rational" we find in the early pragmatists also conflicts with one that takes "rational" to mean: "action flowing from competent use of one's conscious faculties," since the bulk of the relevant group might not use its faculties competently. Now, before going farther, here is a warning we ought to heed from Ayn Rand:

A man's protestations of loyalty to reason are meaningless as such: "reason" is not an axiomatic, but a complex, derivative concept—and, particularly since Kant, the philosophical technique of concept-stealing, of attempting to negate reason by means of reason, has become a general bromide, a gimmick worn transparently thin. Do you want to assess the rationality of a person, a theory, or a philosophical system? Do not inquire about his or its stand on the validity of reason. Look for the stand on axiomatic concepts. It will tell the whole story.[24]

In the present context, however, we have already made clear that any inquiry, any action, and the being of any particular entity or process involved in these presuppose the axiom of existence, of the fact that existence exists, that there is a definite something that exists. So we must grant that our inquiry about the nature of rationality rests on the existence of some common framework arising from this axiom. But at this level the standard is extremely broad and will not help with such special areas of inquiry as economics and ethics.[25]

What we are after in inquiring whether human institutions, policies, goals, etc., are rational is a narrower common standard. That is why the decision theorists' or economists' rendition of "rational" is of little use here. But could we use the other, intersubjectivist sense just discussed?

A common standard implies a framework for evaluating judgments, actions, etc., of such matters as distance, time, size, speed, quality, kind, in all sorts of areas such as the sciences, arts, humanities, and personal life. It presupposes some shared capacity on people's part by reliance on which they can (even if they do not do so) identify the standard as indispensable, binding, and universal within the context of the inquiry or endeavor at hand. In judgments as such, independently of the specific subject matter (but not of any subject matter), the context would be seeking knowledge or learning what exists or ought to be done, or why. Given the purpose of gaining knowledge, therefore, there would be a common standard by which judgments or conclusions could be evaluated (at least concerning a minimum degree of success so that, for example, explicit contradictions are ruled out from the start). "Rational" would thus mean abiding by such a standard.

Clearly, inquiry into the meaning of 'rational' produces at least two (but maybe more) mutually exclusive answers. (These, as we saw, include where rationality is characterized, roughly, as "an intelligent approach to both ends and means," as well as where it means "an intelligent approach only to means, never to ends [since those are beyond reach of intelligent assessment or evaluation].") Why should we select one over the other? (Although we perhaps should, some may still refuse.) Can we give an answer to this question without encountering vicious circularity?

If adopting one of the answers (to "What does 'rational' mean?") implies that it is impossible to make ourselves clear about what exactly the answer is, then the answer should be rejected. At this fundamental level of inquiry, accepting the criterion of internal consistency is necessary, for inquiries as such make no sense without it. Seeking solutions itself presupposes that the standard is fully applicable. (With other terms, such as "pleasure," "love," and "happiness," or "alienation," it may not be so obvious that an internally consistent meaning is a must, but it is no surprise with the term "rational.")

Some conceptions of rationality do allow contradictory procedures in the same context to be rational. When widespread acceptability in the relevant community is used as a substitute for "rational," too many matters are left ambiguous to yield the absence of avoidable conflict.

Therefore, we cannot consistently, reliably make use of the economic nor of the conventionalist idea of rationality. They fail to provide us with any common ground, the main purpose that we appear to expect to be achieved when the term is employed. The economist and the conventionalist can take us closer to settling on common means or methods, but most often what concerns us are goals—for example, in guiding our own lives or, especially, in public policies that are being recommended to an entire nation.

"Rational" as Proceeding from Objective Standards

Since we cannot use the instrumental conception of rationality to make clear and comprehensive sense of the concept, we turn to the conception of "rationality" as meaning "established by reference to common standards for judging choices or decisions in some specific context." We have noted that the instrumental conception leaves us without a solution to the kind of problems the concept is used to address, namely, arriving at common standards where disagreements obtain. This, then, justifies looking for a different account of the concept.

When someone correctly asserts that "'X is right' is the rational evaluation," he must mean that "'X is right' is established by reference to common standards in a given context (e.g., chemistry, metaphysics, ethics, or public choice theory inquiry)." We can already see that within the context of human conduct, the common standard is going to be human nature.

But now we need to consider whether this result begs the question. If one believes that the method for establishing the proper meaning of "rational" is itself employed because it is considered rational, then one will think the result empty. This is especially relevant in ethics, because human nature includes as a central feature the capacity for rationality. Although the concept of "rational" here has a different sense from "rational" as applied to the characterization of specific conduct, the two are not separable, only distinct. That human beings are by nature rational means they have as one of their central, defining aspects their capacity to think conceptually, to form ideas, theories, identify principles, consider long-range plans, etc. And it is this capacity that enables them to detect and assess whether some course of conduct is rational, that is, conforms to principles that are based on relevant facts of reality such as human nature itself.

Reason and Choice

We need now, for a bit, to consider the concept "choice" since it is a central component not only of rationality but also of human nature. First, let me note that the same points concerning methodology apply here as when we examined what "rational" means. Second, the relationship between rationality and a certain kind of (initial) choice has been recognized as a very strong one by many philosophers, beginning with Aristotle (who identified right reason as the central virtue of human life and linked moral virtues to choice quite unambiguously), through Spinoza, Kant, Wittgenstein and Rand. The relationship is worked out in detail by Boyle, Grise, and Tollefson.[26] Third, we should take note of the fact that decision theorists and economists often use the concept "choice" in a way that brings the sense of the term relevant to the above relationship together with its sense when used to mean selecting from among alternatives. For instance, when economists speak of choice, they usually mean revealed preference, that is, the action or behavior of someone who is exposed to an existing range of alternatives. The sense of the term in its strong relationship to rationality, however, concerns *initiating* one's actions—as when we speak of freedom of choice/free will. With the decision theorists' or economists' idea of rationality, so long as a given long- or short-range goal is efficiently achieved, the selection that is made from the available alternatives would be rational. With the conception of rationality developed above, however, the choice of a goal or end, too, could be either rational or not.

Given that a choice can involve both selection from among alternatives and the initiation of some (possible) course of conduct, which sense of the term is appropriate for our purpose? Since we are speaking of rational choice, we are concerned with both possible uses, as well as with uses that indicate both aspects of choice within one particular phenomenon. Thus, if someone chooses to learn to play an instrument, he would both initiate some available (but not existent) course of conduct and select from (existent) alternative kinds of conduct (e.g., learning an instrument, learning skiing, taking a vacation).

Only where the possibility of initiating—that is, being the fundamental or first cause of—one's conduct exists can the possibility of noninstrumental rational choice arise. This explains in part why it does not make sense to speak of a dog making a rational choice, although dogs make many selections. (Again, the prevalent economic conception of rationality would not rule out considering a dog's selection of one dog food over another a rational choice! Nor the behavior of computers. That is one result of the view that many economists embrace, namely, that all internally consistent behavior patterns are rational.) It needs also to be noted that even when a choice is made in the sense that someone makes a selection from among alternatives, there can be initiation involved. To act, as in "George bought the car," involves initiative. The judgment that forms the plan of action, as it were—or the intention—that culminates in the overt behavior, had to have been initiated by a person. Yet, such an initiative is often nearly automatic. For example, when a concert pianist performs, the behavior is guided by a rather grand plan the details of which are not intended one by one. Instead, once the pianist embarks upon the performance, the rest pretty much follows. Yet, even here a difference exists between someone who focuses intensely and someone who is merely drifting along. Certainly this would be evident enough when one pianist is inebriated while the other is sober. But it is just as true when one pianist is lax in his or her concentration, while the other chooses to be in sharp focus.

The free-will position involved here is indispensable for purposes of understanding human action. The exact mechanism of the process is not something I can discuss here in full, although I would wish to draw on the work of Roger

Sperry, who accounts for free will in terms of the human brain's composition as a self-monitoring organ that makes self-governance or self-determination possible.

Keeping all this in mind, we can propose as a definition of the concept "choice": either the initiation of some course of conduct, or the selection from among alternatives, or both. Rational conduct, in turn, would mean: initiation of a course of conduct or selection from alternatives or both in accordance with a common standard appropriate to the context, the broadest of which is human life, that is, the human life of the individual who is the agent.

Accordingly, when we speak of rational action in the context of ethics, we are referring to what someone ought to do based on the best information he or she can obtain about human nature and oneself. It needs to be noted that when we speak of invoking principles in ethics, we are in something of a bind. For the most important ethical step comes before any principles could be known to the agent. This is when the agent embarks upon rational thought, when the agent initiates and sustains his or her thinking process. But one would already have to be thinking in order to become aware of the truth and relevance of principles of living. So the most fundamental principle of living is acted on not from conviction or belief but as a matter of will. It is, as it were, the will to live that is the ignition of the rational process which, in turn, brings to awareness more of what one requires for living and flourishing, namely, ethical principles or virtues. One will not become aware and apply these if one fails to think, other than accidentally, haphazardly. A person, to be ethically good, will require the policy of rational thought to carry himself or herself forward in an integrated fashion.

Economics and Ethics Reconciled

Whereas in economics the sort of rationality that is usually referred to concerns only select virtues, in particular, the virtue of prudence—whereby one, in essence, does not waste one's life on irrelevance—this virtue cannot be sufficient to guide someone to living and flourishing. It can, in fact, misguide one if the practice of other virtues is lacking. One can become, for example, a superbly "rational" profiteer and be guilty of parental malpractice, if one fails to be a rational person vis-à-vis the breadth of one's life. Rationality in ethics has a far broader scope than rationality in any special area of human conduct, be it commerce, art, science, politics, parenting, education, etc. Although there is the likelihood that someone who is narrowly rational will eventually be irrational even within his or her narrow domain, it is at least possible to excel in such a domain, while seriously neglecting others by way of failing to be in focus when confronted by or attending to them.

If, however, one has a balanced or integrated character, and sustains a consistent practice of all virtues, then one may well act exactly as the economist assumes we all act when addressing our commercial concerns. Thus, the economist's assumption that we act rationally is probably not far from the truth, especially when we embark on market behavior, both in the sense in which the economist means "rational" as well as in the sense in which "rational" is best understood within ethics. But now what we face is that actually, once the story is told in full, the economist means (if only implicitly) by "rational" that *if we go to market, then we will most likely seek to make a good deal.* It is false, however, that wherever we are, whatever we do, we are making good deals, since we may very well have other rational objectives that rank making a good deal lower in our hierarchy of values than it ordinarily is when we go to market. If, for example, one is embarking on identifying and acting upon what is true in economics or ethics or politics, that usually would rank as more important than making a good deal in the narrow sense—so that one would not sell out one's convictions in order to receive a higher salary or one would not betray a friend to get a better job.

Yet, it needs also to be noted that very often a rational person, one who is ethical through and through, would act rationally in the sense meant by the economist. An ethical individual does not squander his wealth, tries to enrich himself to the degree that this is conducive with how he ought to live as a human individual. And this could, often, involve very sensible, conscientious attention to making a good deal in the market.

It may help here to anticipate at least one of the objections a champion of economic or instrumental rationality would likely advance against the above discussion. A follower of Milton Friedman might argue that a person who values his or her character has a different preference function from the one who values, say, a higher salary. Is that not all there is to the matter, rather than some kind of objectively demonstrable superiority we are justified in ascribing to the former person over the latter?

In a certain respect, based on the way economics approaches the phenomenon of human behavior, this will be true just because someone does, in fact, act to maintain his or her integrity. Doing it will mean, for the economic imperialist, that the agent places personal integrity very high on his or her preference scale. "Preference scale" means "just what people select first, second, third, and so forth, from among available alternatives as the act."

Yet does this inform us? We already see what the person does, what we need to know is why? It is uninformative to claim, "Well the person prefers doing it," if all this means is that he or she acts accordingly. Asking for an explanation means asking for some set of factors that help uniquely to make sense of why some action rather than some other was taken. As we saw from the remarks from Wittgenstein, it is an illusion to believe that invoking preference talk supplies what is wanted here.

But then what alternative do we have? Something that is more informative? While it is very dangerous to attempt to establish objective values for human beings without knowing of whom in particular and in what sort of case one is speaking, there are some general principles that apply pretty much across the board. This is indeed what ethical theories aim at, namely, to identify some general virtues or principles of action that we ought to choose to guide us as we undertake living our lives.

The rational egoist holds, for example, that an integrated character, in a world that is governed by the laws of identity, noncontradiction, and excluded middle, is evidently of superior value to (nearly) anyone than obtaining a higher salary, if one had to make a choice between these two alternatives. Indeed, it is nearly impossible to consider, without inherent confusion, how it could be better for a person to earn more money, if to do so would require the person to sacrifice his or her honesty, courage, self-respect, sense of justice, or generosity of spirit. Those attributes are part and parcel of the guiding system of human action; so without them the higher salary itself would run the risk of serving hardly any purpose in someone's life. In other words, a disintegrated individual isn't even likely to gain rational advantage from increasing his or her wealth because the use of that wealth to his or her best advantage is itself based on being someone with integrity.

Ethics and Homo Economicus

Indeed, it is arguable that in order to make economic behavior—that is, the pursuit of wealth, good deals, prosperity—morally defensible, this view of the matter would have to be sound. Furthermore, when critics of capitalism and free-market economics reject the homo economicus approach to human behavior, they are hoping that they will have undermined a lot more. They believe, I think, that discrediting the economic approach will have as one of its consequences the discrediting of a rational egoist approach to life as a whole, including the principles of the polity that make it possible for citizens to live the rational egoist tenets, particularly the virtue of prudence.

If the admittedly vacuous selfishness identified, albeit confusedly, with the free market is misguided, then a step has been taken in the direction of rejecting rational egoism. The economist's futile attempt to defend his value-free, economic man approach to understanding human behavior plays into the hands of capitalism's critics who wish to discredit rational self-interest. Only if one first appreciates the soundness of the broader ethics of rational egoism, can the more narrowly focused idea of economic rationality be defended.

For the benefit of those who see value in much of neoclassical and Austrian economics, I should reiterate that from the rational egoist viewpoint it is morally upright to act effectively, prudently in the course of market transactions. There is, of course, no guarantee that we will all do this throughout such voluntary transactions. Yet, because ethics is a matter of individual responsibility, even if one embarks on economic activity in an unbalanced, irrational fashion, so that one neglects other personal responsibilities or virtues, there is nothing that any third party is authorized to do about this, apart from attempting to convince the agent of his or her wrong doing.

Contrary to much that is taught in business ethics courses across the world, attempting to interfere with unethical, irrational conduct in markets removes ethics from the realm of human economic life. To put this in familiar terms, used in economics and public policy discussions, market failures are not remediable by means of regulation and interference. So called remedies are, in fact, nothing less than ways to demoralize the marketplace.

The free society and free market offers no guarantee of ethics and, thus, of rational conduct by its participants. But such a system is most hospitable to rationality, both in economics and in ethics, by placing what Nozick called "side constraints" around individuals, by means, for example, of the instrument of the law of property. By this means the irrationality that does obtain both in economics and in the broader realm of ethics is most likely to impact those who perpetrate it and those who freely associate with the perpetrators. No other system offers this kind of promise for a largely prosperous and ethical human community.[27]

Notes

First published in *International Journal of Social Economics* 22, no. 7 (1995): 19–37.

1. Ann Arbor: University of Michigan Press, 1962.

2. New York: Paragon House, 1987.

3. James Buchanan, "Why Governments 'Got Out of Hand,'" *New York Times*, October 26, 1986.

4. Amartya K. Sen, "Choice, Orderings, and Morality," in Stephan Korner, *Practical Reason* (New Haven, CT: Yale University Press, 1974), p. 55.

5. Ludwig von Mises, *Human Action* (New Haven, CT: Yale University Press, 1952), p. 19.

6. Richard McKenzie, *The Limits of Economic Science* (Boston: Kluwer-Nijhoff Publishing, 1983), p. 8.

7. George Stigler, Lecture 2, Tanner Lectures, Harvard University, April 1980. Quoted in McKenzie, ibid., p. 6.

8. Gary Becker, *The Economic Approach to Human Behavior* (Chicago: University of Chicago Press, 1976), p. 8. (My emphasis.)

9. Milton Friedman, "The Line We Dare Not Cross," *Encounter*, November, 1976, p. 11.

10. Mises, *Human Action*, 19.

11. Don Ballente, "Subjective Value Theory and Government Intervention in the Labor Market," *Austrian Economics Newsletter*, Spring-Summer 1989, pp. 1–2. As should be obvious, the *mainstream* economics being referred to is not that embraced by the Chicago school, including Friedman, Stigler, or Becker, but by contemporary welfare *macro*economists, such as Paul Samuelson, James Tobin, or John Kenneth Galbraith.

12. McKenzie, *The Limits of Economic Science*, p. 44; see also Stigler and Becker's classic paper, "De Gustibus non est disputandum" ("There is no disputing of tastes"), *American Economic Review* 67 (1977), pp. 76–90. Some much harsher versions of the kind of fatalism that we find implicit in (but at times made explicit by) some economists' works is available in Edward O. Wilson's *Sociobiology* (Cambridge, MA: Harvard University Press, 1975) and Richard Dawson's *The Selfish Gene* (Oxford: Oxford University Press, 1976).

13. Milton Friedman, *Capitalism and Freedom* (Chicago: University of Chicago Press, 1962), p. 12.

14. Geoffrey Brennan and James Buchanan, "The Normative Purpose of Economic 'Science,'" *International Review of Law and Economics* (Winter 1981), p. 158.

15. Personal correspondence, March 15, 1993.

16. Allan Bloom, *Giants and Dwarfs* (New York: Simon & Schuster, 1990), p. 288.

17. Cambridge, MA: Harvard University Press, 1993.

18. *New York Times Book Review*, March 6, 1994, p. 24.

19. O. K. Bousma, (J. L. Craft and Ronald E. Hustwit, eds.), *Wittgenstein: Conversations 1949–1951* (Indianapolis, IN: Hackett Publishing Co., 1986), pp. 58–60. The same point, essentially, was made later by Nathaniel Branden in *The Objectivist Newsletter* (I believe) in a contribution to the "Intellectual Ammunition" column on whether everyone is selfish.

20. Becker, Personal correspondence.

21. Sen, "Choice, Orderings, and Morality."

22. Robert Nozick, *The Nature of Rationality* (Princeton, NJ: Princeton University Press, 1993).

23. I have argued this in "Evidence for Necessary Existence," *Objectivity* 1 (Fall 1992), 31–62, and "Some Reflections on Richard Rorty's Philosophy," *Metaphilosophy* 24 (January/April 1993), 123–135.

24. Ayn Rand, *Introduction to Objectivist Epistemology*, 2nd ed. (New York: New American Library, 1990), p. 61.

25. For a detailed treatment of the axiom of existence, aiming to clarify and develop Ayn Rand's account, see Machan, op. cit., "Evidence of Necessary Existence."

26. See their book, Joseph Boyle, G. Grise, and O. Tollefson, *Free Choice* (South Bend, IN: University of Notre Dame Press, 1976). See, also, the essay by Anthony Bertocci, "Personality, Free Will, and Moral Obligation," in William F. Enteman, ed., *The Problem of Free Will* (New York: Charles Scribner & Son, 1967). Finally, see also Mary Midgley, *The Ethical Primate* (London: Routledge, 1994).

27. An earlier version of this paper was presented at the 1994 Institute for Objectivist Studies Summer Seminar at Oberlin College, Ohio.

PART III

THE FUTURE

16

Toward the Development of a Paradigm for a Free Society

Edward W. Younkins

There is little doubt that the most prominent and articulate champions of capitalism are economists. But this reliance on economic defenses has caused problems for capitalism. The reason is that economists are always concerned to retain for themselves the mantle of science. They insist that economics is not committed to any particular values. Yet it is transparently false to claim that an economic system isn't tied to moral and political views that may or may not be correct, sound, or well-founded.

If economists who defend the marketplace admitted that at its base we find certain assumptions about how individuals ought to act and what governments should uphold, they could still carry on with their analysis of how such a system works and why it produces more efficiently than all others. This would leave open the question of whether the moral assumptions on which capitalist market analysis rests are sound.

—Tibor. R. Machan

Ideas rule the world. Especially important are the philosophical ideas that determine conceptions of the human person in relation to the world in which he lives. Throughout history, the philosophy of individualism has played a critical role in man's progress. Each individual is a discrete being with a unique mind and a distinctive set of abilities, desires, and motivations. Each person is a self-responsible causal agent who has the capacity to pursue his well-being through his intellectual and physical actions. By nature, each person has the right to have the opportunity to develop his potential as a free, individual human being. People are happier when their lives are lived in freedom. When people exercise their freedom they enter the arena of morality as responsible free agents.

America was intentionally created based on the following fundamental phi-

losophical ideas: (1) the material world is an orderly, intelligible, natural domain that is open to men's minds; (2) a man's rational mind is able to attain an
objective knowledge of reality that is necessary for the pursuit of his happiness—a man is able to acquire knowledge based on evidence provided by the
senses; (3) the good life is one of personal self-actualization—each person
should strive to attain his own happiness through his own independent thoughts
and efforts; (4) each man has inalienable natural rights to his own life, liberty,
and the pursuit of his own happiness; and (5) a government with limited power
is needed in order to secure these rights. The founding fathers thus advocated
rights, reason, freedom, individualism, capitalism, and the minimal state.

For centuries the philosophy of freedom and individualism has underpinned
the political and economic order that characterized the American way of life.
Unfortunately, beginning in the early 1900s, American society has become more
and more collectivized. Special interest groups have increasingly persuaded the
government to grant them special privileges. People form political coalitions in
order to better obtain government favors. People implore the government for
assistance. As government has become more dominant and has produced programs to meet our needs, it has also corrupted people's values and made them
dependent on government. There has been a growing tendency for government
to expand and undermine personal freedom and responsibility.

We must restore in America the founders' understanding of government as
a necessary evil created solely in order to secure individual rights. In addition,
we need to supply to people in the rest of the world a blueprint for market liberalism rooted in philosophical principles based on an analysis of the nature of
man and the world. The works of Carl Menger (1840-1921), Ludwig von Mises
(1881-1973), and Ayn Rand (1905-1982) go a long way toward providing the
ideas required for the construction of a paradigm appropriate for a free society.
This chapter represents an initial effort to reconcile and extend some of the ideas
of these three great thinkers.

The Nature and Benefits of a Paradigm

A paradigm is a model, symbolic representation, or fundamental image of the
subject matter of reality or some aspect of reality. It is a tool of the intellect that
enables people to survive and prosper. A paradigm that parallels and reflects
reality helps a person to understand and function in the world. Of course, reality
is senior to any paradigm. A paradigm can only approximate reality and needs to
be checked against reality. It is impossible to legislate reality.

A paradigm subsumes, defines, and interrelates the theories, methods, and
exemplars that exist within it. An exemplar is a piece or body of work that
serves as a model for those who work within the paradigm. It is a concrete academic or scholarly achievement which orders and guides research and stands as
a standard for future works. As illustrated in the previous chapters in this book
the works of Carl Menger, Ludwig von Mises, and Ayn Rand are key exemplars

for an Austrian-Objectivist paradigm for a free society.

A paradigm for a free society addresses a broad range of issues in metaphysics, epistemology, value theory, ethics, etc. in a systematic fashion. Such a paradigm requires a sound theory of mind, reason, and free will, and logically grounded doctrines of natural rights and morality. Its derivation of natural rights would be grounded in its view of nature, knowledge, and values.

A conceptual and moral defense of a political and economic system must be grounded on the best reality-based ethical system that a reasoning individual can discover. A true paradigm or body of theoretical knowledge about reality must address a wide range of issues in metaphysics, epistemology, value theory, ethics, and so on in a well-ordered manner. The concern of the system-builder is with truth as an integrated whole. Such a body of knowledge is circumscribed by the nature of facts in reality, including their relationships and implications. When constructing a paradigm, it is legitimate to take a selective approach with respect to existing philosophical positions, because a paradigm's consistency with reality is all that really matters. It is thus appropriate for us to extract what is true and good from the writings of Menger, Mises, Rand, and others and use those components as a basis for a better integration that allows for a deeper understanding of what would constitute a morally right socioeconomic system. By integrating and synthesizing essential elements of the ideas of the Austrian school of economics with those from Ayn Rand's philosophy of Objectivism we can come closer to a comprehensive, logically consistent view of the world and a foundation and justification for laissez-faire capitalism.

The Aristotelian perspective is that reality is objective. There is a world of objective reality that exists independent of human beings and that has a determinate nature that is knowable. It follows that natural law is objective because it is inherent in the nature of the entity to which it relates. The content of natural law which derives from the nature of man and the world is accessible to human reason. Principles that supply a systematic level of understanding must be based on the facts of reality. In other words, the principles of a true conceptual framework must connect with reality. The only way to successfully defend principles and propositions is to show that they have a firm base or foundation.

We need to formulate principles explicitly and relate them logically to other principles and to the facts of reality. A systematic, logical understanding is required for cognitive certainty and is valuable in communicating ideas, and the reasoning underlying them, clearly and precisely.

This chapter presents a skeleton of a potential Austrian-Objectivist philosophical foundation and edifice for a free society. See the enclosed exhibit for an example model or diagram of what an Austrian-Objectivist paradigm might look like. It is an attempt to forge an understanding from seemingly disparate philosophies and to integrate them into a clear, consistent, coherent, and systematic whole. A paradigm should conform with reality and focus on pertinent factors and relationships. It consists of a framework of essential principles that define the system. Understanding the world in terms of general principles permits us to integrate a large volume of information in a condensed form.

The approach of this chapter is expository and does not engage in formal academic debate or argumentation. My approach is simply to search for correct ideas and to promote what is true and right. Because I am not a professional economist or philosopher, my inquiry does not extend beyond a systematic level that relies heavily on logic and common sense. I will defer to scholars in these and other disciplines to evaluate, critique, and extend my systematic understanding. They are better equipped to deal with subtle and deep concerns and the construction of a more detailed, exact, and consistent formulation of principles. Given that a paradigm combining insights from Austrian Economics and Objectivism is possible and desirable, it follows that it may require extensions, refinements, and revisions for reasons of coordination and consistency. This can occur in an atmosphere of open rational inquiry as additional value can be found in the work of many contemporary scholars who engage and extend the notion of combining the doctrines of the Austrian school and Objectivism. Of course, it will be inevitable that there will be opportunities for different interpretations and developments as more work is done on this edifice. Ultimately, it is hoped that the proposed integration and synthesis will preserve Mises's praxeology while maintaining a realistic ethical objectivism. The resulting synergy may provide a superior basis for communicating to the general public why a capitalist society is the best society for human beings.

Frameworks for thinking about reality have long been the basis for organized knowledge. Constructing a set of ideas about real-world objects, events, and occurrences would serve as a framework for a realistic political and economic system. Such a conceptual framework would provide at once both the reasoning underlying society's rules and institutions and a standard by which they are judged.

To construct a conceptual framework, we must be concerned with observed or experienced phenomena. Induction, generalization from perceptual experiences of reality, is used to form axioms, concepts, and constructs. The observational order and the conceptual order must correspond with one another if we are to conceive things properly. It is through the analysis of inductively derived ideas that the appropriate principles of society can be deduced. A correctly constructed internally consistent conceptual framework represents the real world in constructs and language. A conceptual framework should be logically consistent and based on reality so that inferences derived from it can be said to be deductively valid.

From a deductive perspective, philosophy precedes and determines politics, which, in turn, precedes and determines economics. On the other hand, the philosopher must begin by inductively studying the fundamental nature of existence, of man, and of man's relationship to existence. This is the point at which we will begin our review of the conceptual foundations of a free society.

A Paradigm of Human Nature, Human Action, and Human Flourishing

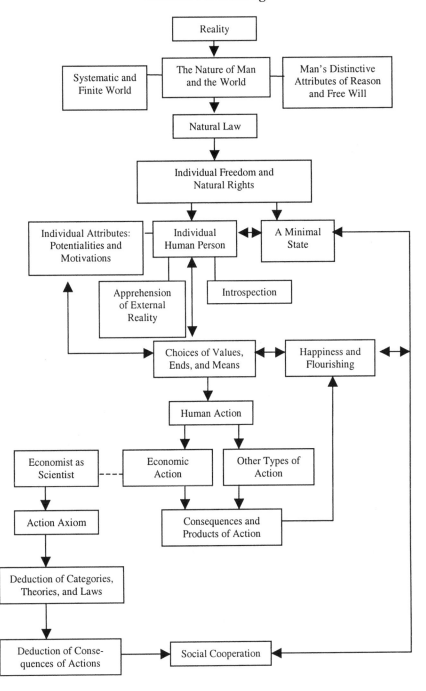

Human Nature

In developing a conceptual framework for capitalism, it is necessary to focus our attention on the enduring characteristics of reality. Men live in a universe with a definite nature and exist within nature as part of the natural order. Using their minds, men have the ability to discover the permanent features of the world. A unified theoretical perspective and potent intellectual framework for analyzing the social order must be based on the constraining realities of the human condition. Reality is not optional.

We live in a systematic universe with an underlying natural order that makes it so. There are discernible regularities pervading all of creation. There is an underlying order that gives circumscription, predictability, and their character to all things. Through the use of the mind, men can discover the nature of things, the laws that regulate or apply to them, the way they now exist, and the ways they can potentially be. To determine the nature of anything, it is necessary to remove all that is unique and exclusive to a thing and examine it in terms of the common characteristics it shares with all others of its type. This is done in order to study the fundamental nature of existence, of man, and of man's relationship to existence. Our goal is to discover the natural order as it applies to man and his affairs. There exists a natural law that reigns over the affairs of human conduct. Natural law theory holds that there is a law prior to man, society, and government. It is a law that must be abided by if each of these is to attain its true character and fulfillment.

To ascertain man's nature, we must, through a process of abstraction, remove all that is accidental to any specific man. What is left must be man's distinctive features and potentialities. It is man's ability to reason that separates him from other vital organisms. Man's rational faculty distinguishes him from all other living species. Conceptualization (i.e., reason) is man's unique and only proper way of dealing with the rest of the natural world. It is in man's nature to use his rational powers, to form concepts, to integrate them, to evaluate alternatives, to make choices, and so on. In order to survive and flourish, men must come to terms with the requirements of reality.

The ability to control one's actions (i.e., natural liberty) is an inborn condition of man. In the nature of things no person can use the mind, senses, or appendages of another. Man is free to use his faculties provided that he does not harm others in his use of them. All thinking and acting is done by individual persons in their own spatiotemporal localities—a society cannot think nor act although men can choose to act in a coordinated manner with one another. Men have the ability to cooperate and achieve through voluntary action.

To properly construct a paradigm for a free society it is necessary to go back to absolute fundamentals in human nature. We need to have a precise understanding of the nature of the human person. Human beings are a distinct species in a natural world whose lives are governed by means of each person's free will and individual conceptual consciousness. Unlike other beings, a person's survival and flourishing depends on cognition at a conceptual level. People are all of one species with a definite nature who are uniquely configured because of their individuating features. There is a biological case for human diversity with the individual as the primary reality. We must respect the condition of human diversity and the fact that people are not interchangeable. Individuality is vital to one's nature. A person is responsible for achieving and sustaining the human life that is his own. Each person has potentialities, is the steward of his own time, talents, and energies, and is responsible for becoming the person he has the potential to become by means of his own choices and actions.

Human beings alone in the world possess a stable nature with certain definite, definable, and delimitable characteristics. Consciousness and free will are essential attributes of man's nature. Reason is man's guiding force. Human activities are self-conscious, purposeful, and deliberately chosen. One's actions are caused by his own volition which is a capacity of human nature. A human being can initiate and make choices about what he will do. Human action involves purposeful, intentional, and normative behavior. Mental action or thinking is the ultimate free action, is primary, and includes the direct willing of the person. Behavior thus takes place after a judgment or conceptualization has been made. It follows that there is a moral element or feature of action because human beings possess free will, which can cause most (or at least some) of what they do.

The distinguishing features of human nature (i.e., rationality and free will) provide objective standards for a man's choice of both means and ends. Man is a volitional being whose reason should guide his selection of both ends and means to those ends. Volition is a type of causation—it is not an exception to the law of causality. Men can think, choose, act, and cause. Human beings act, choose means to achieve ends, and choose both means and ends. In human action, a person's free will choice is the cause and this cause generates certain effects. Causality is a prerequisite of action and is primarily concerned with a person's manipulation of objects external to himself.

Free will is not the negation of causality, but rather is a type of causality that relates to man. Causality is an association between an entity and its mode of action. It is not the relationship between actions and earlier actions. For a human being, a cause can be the change in his assessment of the relative importance of his values. A person uses his knowledge to correlate his values with his various plans. The concept of purpose underlies the idea of causality as motivated action. Action in behavior is directed at attaining a purpose. Human action has a teleological character because it is rational conduct aimed at a goal. A person acts to initiate a sequence of causation by changing or moving an attribute of his body. This act implies that he has a contemplated objective that he wants to attain. This initial change in a person's body is intended to cause other events to take place and to eventually lead to the accomplishment of the desired goal. The success or failure of a person in attaining his objective depends on his ability to isolate correctly the relevant causal features of a situation and to predict the future accurately both in the presence and in the absence of one's own contemplated actions.

The idea of human action depends upon the introspectively valid fact that there is a type of conduct that is peculiarly human. This kind of conduct coincides with the consciousness of volition. Actions are free only if they are controlled by a faculty that functions volitionally. A person knows via introspection that he experiences physical variables and properties, creates concepts, chooses values, and changes physical variables and properties because he constantly does those activities. Introspection supplies the knowledge that we can make metaphysically free decisions to attempt to attain our values.

What is known (i.e., the object) is distinct from, and independent of, the knower (i.e., the subject). Men are born with no innate conceptual knowledge. Such knowledge is gained via various processes of integration and differentiation from perceptual data. For example, a person apprehends that he has a conscious mind by distinguishing between external objects and events and the workings of his mind. Self-awareness is thus attained when a person reflects upon what he has observed.

Reality is what there is to be perceived. Reality exists independently of a man's consciousness. It exists apart from the knower. It follows that empirical knowledge is acquired through observational experience of external reality. People can observe goal-directed actions from the outside. An individual attains an understanding of causality and other categories of action by observing the actions of others to reach goals. He also learns about causality by means of his own acting and his observation of the outcomes. Action is thus a man's conscious adjustment to the state of the world.

It is necessary to provide a realistic foundation for a true paradigm for a free society. Therefore, a comprehensive moral defense of individualism and its political implications is founded appropriately on a naturalistic philosophy. An Aristotelian metaphysics such as those supplied by Menger or Rand would be an excellent starting point for a political and economic framework based on the requirements of reality and of man's nature.

Logic is pivotal to correct human thought because reality corresponds to the principles of logic. Men are capable of comprehending the workings of the world through the application of logic. Logic is the method by which a volitional consciousness conforms to reality. It is reason's method. The method of logic reflects the nature and needs of man's consciousness and the facts of external reality.

Principles such as the laws of identity and noncontradiction underpin the observable fact that there are innumerable distinct types of being in reality. Human beings are a unique class, characterized by the real attributes of reason and free will, that introduce a dimension of value into nature. Human existence represents a distinct ontological realm different from all others. A human being can choose and is thus a moral agent. This moral nature is grounded in the facts of nature. What a thing must be or do depends on the kind of object or entity that it is. The values (and virtues) of life are discovered by means of an understanding of human nature and the nature of the world.

Human Flourishing

Moral values enter the world with human life. There is a close connection between an objective normative structure for understanding human life and economics. Human flourishing or happiness is the standard underpinning the assessment that a goal is rational and should be pursued. This common human benchmark implies a framework for evaluating a person's decisions and actions. It follows that the fundamental ethical task for each man is the fullest development of himself as a human being and as the individual that he is. Human life thus provides the foundation and context of the realm of ethics. The idea of value is at the root of ethics. A man's immediate needs for survival are economic and are values for his life. Economic production is necessary to satisfy these needs or material values. A productive man is a rational, self-interested, and virtuous man. He is doing what he ought to do to sustain his life.

To survive and flourish a man must grasp reality. To do this requires a rational epistemology and an objective theory of concepts. These have been supplied by Ayn Rand. A person needs to observe reality, abstract essentials, and form objective concepts and laws. The objective nature of the world circumscribes the operations that must be accomplished if goals and values are to be attained. Reality is what is there to be perceived and studied. Everyone is constrained by what is metaphysically real. Fortunately, people have the capacity to objectively apprehend reality. A man's mind can identify, but cannot create, reality. Knowability of the world is a natural condition common both to the external world and the human mind.

Ayn Rand's conception of universals (or essences) as epistemological, is arguably superior to the traditional interpretation given to Aristotle's ideas or universals as being metaphysical. Rand explains that knowledge is acquired by an active, conscious agent through the processes of induction and deduction. In order to deduce from axioms and general statements, we must first have inductive inferences. We can know via the senses, inferences from data supplied by the senses, and introspective understanding. Once it is acknowledged that Mises's action axiom could be derived through an inductive process, it will then be legitimate to follow and adopt his logical arguments that all the core principles and relationships of economics can be deduced from that axiom.

Capitalism is the consequence of the natural order of liberty which is based on the ethic of individual happiness. Freedom is connected with morality, ethics, and individual flourishing. Men are moral agents whose task it is to excel at being the human being that one is. In order to be moral agents people need to be free and self-directed. It follows that capitalism is the political expression of the human condition. As a political order relegated to a distinct sphere of human life, it conforms with human nature by permitting each person to pursue happiness, excellence, and the perfection of his own human life through the realization of his rational and other capacities. A free society, one that respects an individual's natural rights, acknowledges that it is an individual's moral responsibility to be as good as possible at living his own life. Of course, such a society cannot guarantee moral and rational behavior on the part of its members. It can only make such conduct possible.

Free will is critical to human existence and human flourishing. A person has the ability to choose to actualize his potential for being a fully-developed individual human being. A man depends on his rationality for his survival and flourishing. He must choose to initiate the mental processes of thinking and focusing on becoming the best person he can be in the context of his own existence. He is responsible for applying reason, wisdom, and experience to his own specifically situated circumstances. Rationality is the virtue through which a man exercises reason.

Rand explains that men know they have volition through the act of introspection. The fact that people are regularly deciding to think or not to think is directly accessible to each person. Each person can introspectively observe that he can choose to focus his consciousness or not. A person can pay attention or not. The implication of free will is that men can be held morally responsible for their actions.

The idea of free will does not imply that a person has unlimited power with respect to the operation of his own mind. Man's consciousness has a particular nature, structure, set of powers, and characteristics. Action can be said to be influenced by physiological, psychological, sociological, and other factors, but there is at least some residual amount of free will behind the action that operates independently of the influencing factors. An action is not totally determined by a man's inheritance.

Although a man's choices are ultimately free, there is, in all probability, some connection to a person's physical endowments, facticity, urges, past choices, articulated preferences for the future, scarcity of a good, acquisition of new knowledge, and so on. None of these deterministically causes value. Something is only of value when some human being has decided to act to gain or sustain it. An object can only become a value by means of a person's free choice. Certainly each person is subject to his unconscious mind, biological constraints, genetic inheritances, feelings, urges, environment, etc. However, none of these denies the existence of free will, but only shows that it may be challenging for a person to use his free will to triumph over them.

Each person shares some attributes with other human beings, such as free will and the capacity to reason. It follows that at a basic level what is objectively moral or ethical is universally the same. In addition, a person's moral decisions depend, to a certain degree, on his particular circumstances, talents, and characteristics. The particular evaluations a person should make are made through a process of rational cognition. A rational ethical action is what a person believes he should do based on the most fitting and highest quality information acquired about human nature and the individual person that one is. When people approach life rationally, they are more likely to conclude that virtues and ethical principles are necessary for human flourishing. They discover that human beings have a profound need for morality.

Human purposefulness makes the world understandable in terms of human action. Human action is governed by choice and choice is free. Choice is a product of free will. A voluntaristic theory of action recognizes the active role of reason in decisions caused by a human person who wills and acts. Choosing both ends and means is a matter of reason. Because human action is free it is potentially moral. It therefore follows that human actions necessarily include moral or ethical considerations. Values cannot be avoided. Free will means being a moral agent.

Mises views social cooperation and coordination as a proxy for happiness, which is similar to the Aristotelian notion of human flourishing. He deduces that the coordination of free prudent different actions leads to social coordination. It follows that virtuous and moral human actions based on freedom and singularity foster the coordination process.

A Life-Centered Metaethics

An Aristotelian self-perfectionist approach to ethics can be shown to support the natural right to liberty which itself provides a solid foundation for a minimal state. This approach gives liberty moral significance by illustrating how the natural right to liberty is a social and political condition necessary for the possibility of human flourishing—the ultimate moral standard in Aristotelian ethics interpreted as a natural-end ethics. A foundation is thus provided for a classical liberal political theory within the Aristotelian tradition. Modern proponents of this approach include Tibor R. Machan, Douglas B. Rasmussen, Douglas J. Den Uyl, and others.

Human flourishing (also known as personal flourishing) involves the rational use of one's individual human potentialities, including talents, abilities, and virtues in the pursuit of his freely and rationally chosen values and goals. An action is considered to be proper if it leads to the flourishing of the person performing the action. Human flourishing is, at the same time, a moral accomplishment and a fulfillment of human capacities, and it is one through being the other. Self-actualization is moral growth and vice versa.

Not an abstraction, human flourishing is real and highly personal (i.e., agent relative) by nature, consists in the fulfillment of both a man's human nature and his unique potentialities, and is concerned with choices and actions that necessarily deal with the particular and the contingent. One man's self-realization is not the same as another's. What is called for in terms of concrete actions such as choice of career, education, friends, home, and others, varies from person to person. Human flourishing becomes an actuality when one uses his practical reason to consider his unique needs, circumstances, capacities, and so on to determine which concrete instantiations of human values and virtues will comprise his well-being. The idea of human flourishing is inclusive and can encompass a wide variety of constitutive ends such as knowledge, the development of character traits, productive work, religious pursuits, community building, love, charitable activities, allegiance to persons and causes, self-efficacy, material well-being, pleasurable sensations, etc.

To flourish, a man must pursue goals that are both rational for him individually and also as a human being. Whereas the former will vary depending upon one's particular circumstances, the latter are common to man's distinctive nature—man has the unique capacity to live rationally. The use of reason is a necessary, but not a sufficient, condition for human flourishing. Living rationally (i.e., consciously) means dealing with the world conceptually. Living consciously implies respect for the facts of reality. The principle of living consciously is not affected by the degree of one's intelligence nor the extent of one's knowledge; rather, it is the acceptance and use of one's reason in the recognition and perception of reality and in his choice of values and actions to the best of his ability, whatever that ability may be. To pursue rational goals through rational means is the only way to cope successfully with reality and achieve one's goals. Although rationality is not always rewarded, the fact remains that it is through the use of one's mind that a man not only discovers the values required for personal flourishing, he also attains them. Values can be achieved in reality if a man recognizes and adheres to the reality of his unique personal endowments and contingent circumstances. Human flourishing is positively related to a rational man's attempts to externalize his values and actualize his internal views of how things ought to be in the outside world. Practical reason can be used to choose, create, and integrate all the values and virtues that comprise personal flourishing.

Virtues are the means to values which enable us to achieve human flourishing and happiness. The constituent virtues such as rationality, independence, integrity, justice, honesty, courage, trustworthiness, productiveness, benevolence, and pride (moral ambitiousness) must be applied, although differentially, by each person in the task of self-actualization. Not only do particular virtues play larger roles in the lives of some men than others, there is also diversity in the concrete with respect to the objects and purposes of their application, the way in which they are applied, and the manner in which they are integrated with other virtues and values. Choosing and making the proper response for the unique situation is the concern of moral living—one needs to use his practical reason at the time of action to consider concrete contingent circumstances to determine the correct application and balance of virtues and values for himself. Although virtues and values are not automatically rewarded, this does not alter the fact that they are rewarded. Human flourishing is the reward of the virtues and values, and happiness is the goal and reward of human flourishing.

Self-direction (i.e., autonomy) involves the use of one's reason and is central and necessary for the possibility of attaining human flourishing, self-esteem, and happiness. It is the only characteristic of flourishing that is both common to all acts of self-actualization and particular to each. Freedom in decision making and behavior is a necessary operating condition for the pursuit and achievement of human flourishing. Respect for individual autonomy is required because autonomy is essential to human flourishing. This logically leads to the endorsement of the right of personal direction of one's life, including the use of his endowments, capacities, and energies.

These natural (i.e., negative) rights are metanormative principles concerned with protecting the self-directedness of individuals thus ensuring the freedom through which individuals can pursue their flourishing. The goal of the right to liberty is to secure the possibility of human flourishing by protecting the possibility of self-directedness. This is done by preventing encroachments upon the conditions under which human flourishing can occur. Natural rights impose a negative obligation—the obligation not to interfere with one's liberty. Natural rights, therefore, require a legal system that provides the necessary conditions for the possibility that individuals might self-actualize. It follows that the proper role of the government is to protect man's natural rights through the use of force, but only in response, and only against those who initiate its use. In order to provide the maximum self-determination for each person, the state should be limited to maintaining justice, police, and defense, and to protecting life, liberty, and property.

The negative right to liberty, as a basic metanormative principle, provides a context in which all the diverse forms of personal flourishing may coexist in an ethically compassable manner. This right can be accorded to every person with no one's authority over himself requiring that any other person experience a loss of authority over himself. Such a metanormative standard for social conduct favors no particular form of human flourishing while concurrently providing a context within which diverse forms of human flourishing can be pursued.

A person's happiness is tied to human nature and to the characteristics of the individual involved. Happiness relates to a person's success as a rational and unique human being possessing free will. A happy person tends to be a good person who makes real the highest potential of his humanity and individuality. A human being has a moral dimension to his nature in that he has the potential to be good as an element of his self-fulfillment. Ethics is based on the need to concern oneself with living a good human life. Moral goodness involves the choice of each individual in determining what will contribute to his own moral goodness.

Given the nature of man and the world, if we want persons to be able to pursue happiness, peace, and prosperity while living with one another, then we must adopt and respect a social structure that accords to each person a moral space over which he has freedom to act and within which no one else may rightfully interfere. The idea of natural rights defines this moral space. Individuals have basic rights because of what they are. In order to uphold each person's sovereignty, men should create a political and legal system that makes it possible for individuals to properly survive, flourish, pursue happiness, and carry on a virtuous life. It follows that the proper role of government is to protect individuals' natural rights through the use of force, but only in response, and only against those who initiate its use.

An Aristotelian life-centered metaethics supports the natural right to liberty, which itself provides a solid foundation for a minimal state. Natural rights are metanormative principles concerned with protecting the self-directedness of individuals, thus ensuring the freedom through which they can pursue their survival and self-perfection.

Of course, it needs to be pointed out that not all libertarians see the state as a necessary evil with minimum functions as do Rand, Mises, and Nozick. Others, such as Murray Rothbard, consider the state to be a totally evil institution that can aggress against individuals through taxation, conscription, and the imposition of its own arbitration and defense services. Both groups agree that the defining characteristics of a state are its ability to acquire revenue by the physical coercion of taxation and its coerced monopoly with respect to the provision of defense services. Both minimal statists and anarcho-capitalists perceive the state as a political entity that, by its nature, involves coercion. In addition, both acknowledge the moral importance and legitimacy of individual liberty.

For anarcho-capitalists, law is a natural outcome of men living and working together that does not assume a coercive monopoly of power. Declaiming the antisocial predatory nature of the state, anarcho-capitalists advocate a natural order with competing security, conflict resolution, and insurance suppliers. Anarcho-libertarians contend that such services can be supplied more efficiently and in greater accord with human freedom on an open market. They propose a system of competing protection agencies in the same territory.

In such a private law society, people would be free to choose among various voluntarily funded protection agencies of a nonmonopolistic nature. There is a controversy between anarcho-capitalists and minimal state libertarians as to who the final arbiter for resolution should be when competing courts arrive at different decisions in a given case. The anarcho-capitalists explain that the competing agencies will have prearranged means for dispute resolution (e.g., arbitration by an agreed-upon third agency. Minimal statists, who tend to be concerned with efficiency, argue that both protection and conflict resolution would be better provided by a minimal state.

Both groups want to leave more space for the free market and tend to agree that there is no such body as a morally legitimate state because all states depend on coercion. Both groups want less government and view the state as their common enemy. They agree in their basic reasoning that freedom is the top priority and that coercion harms freedom. Where they in fact disagree is with respect to the mechanism for final arbitration for conflict resolution.

Value Theory

The preeminent theory within Austrian value theory is the Misesian subjectivist school. Mises maintained that it is by means of its subjectivism that praxeological economics develops into objective science. The praxeologist takes individual values as given and assumes that individuals have different motivations and prefer different things. The same economic phenomena means different things to different people. In fact, buying and selling takes place because people value things differently. The importance of goods is derived from the importance of the values they are intended to achieve. When a person values an object, this simply means that he imputes enough importance to it to be willing to start a chain of causation to change or maintain it, thus making it a thing of value. Misesian economics does not study what is in an object, as does the natural scientist, but rather, studies what is in the subject.

On the other hand, Menger and Rand agree that the ultimate standard of value is the life of the valuer. Human beings have needs and wants embedded in their nature. Both Menger and Rand begin with the ultimate value of human life and determine the values that a man needs. Their respective objective approaches to value hold that value is only meaningful in relationship to some valuing consciousness. A value must be a values to an existing human being. The differences between the ideas of Menger and Rand on value is that Menger was exclusively concerned with economic values whereas Rand was interested in values of all types. For Rand, all human values are moral values that are essential to the ethical standard of human nature in general and the particular human life of who the agent is.

Although Menger speaks of economic value while Rand is concerned with moral value, their ideas are essentially the same. Both view human life as the ultimate value. Their shared biocentric concept of value contends that every value serves biological needs. Value thus has its roots in the conditional nature of life. Life can perish. Objective values support man's life and originate in a relationship between a man and his survival requirements.

Menger was concerned with the many values the pursuit of which is mainly an economic matter. Because anything that satisfies a human need is a value, that which satisfies a man's material needs for food, shelter, health care, wealth, production, and so forth, is deemed to be an economic value. People require a certain degree of prosperity with respect to their needs, desires, and wants.

Rand explains that the idea of value enters the world with the phenomenon of life and that the nature of values depends on the type of life in question. Good and bad are objective relational features of living beings. It follows that the human good is connected to human nature which involves life, the source of value, and free will, the element of responsibility. Of course, a human being can choose to pursue or reject life. Moral judgment is concerned with what is volitional. Moral principles are useful only to beings with conceptual consciences who can choose their actions.

From Ayn Rand's perspective, every human value is a moral value (including economic value) that is important to the ethical standard of man's life qua man. Rand viewed virtually every human choice as a moral choice involving moral values.

Both Rand and Menger espouse a kind of contextually—relational objectivism in their theories of value. Value is seen as a relational quality dependent on the subject, the object, and the context or situation involved. The subject, object, and the situation that combine them are the antecedents of value.

Values come into existence with the emergence of life. Only living things have values. Values are linked to life, and moral values are linked to human life.

The ultimate value is life itself. Whereas all living things pursue values, it is only human beings that hold this ultimate value by choice. The idea of human value presupposes a valuer with a conceptual consciousness. In addition to a valuer for whom a thing is a value, other prerequisites of human value are an end to which the value is a means and man's life as an end in itself (i.e., a final end that is not a means to a further end). Life's conditionality (i.e., the alternative of life or death) makes action necessary to achieve values.

If a person chooses to live, this choice implies that he will attempt to obtain the means or fulfill the requirements and needs of his life. A need is a condition whose presence improves a person's ability to survive or flourish or whose absence hinders that ability. Needs arise from a man's nature and thus have a rational foundation. It is natural to satisfy one's needs. In fact, a person's needs can be viewed as the bridge between the natural sciences (especially biology) and the human sciences. Whatever satisfies a need can be deemed to be a value. Value depends on man's needs.

The act of valuing is one of discovering what maintains, advances, and enhances the life of the individual. Objective values support a man's life and objective disvalues jeopardize it. We can say that values are objective when particular objects and actions are good to a specific person and for the purpose of reaching a particular goal. Objective value emanates from a relationship between a man's conceptual consciousness and existence. Of course, it is possible for a person to value objects that are not actually valuable according to the standard of life. This is because a man is fallible or may choose not to use his capacity to be rational and self-interested. Menger has correctly stated that values correspond to an objective state of affairs when men value what they objectively require to sustain themselves. Value is an objective relationship between a man and an aspect of reality. This relationship is not arbitrary.

Objective value involves a connection between conceptual human consciousness (i.e., reason) and the facts of reality. A specific thing's value is a function of the relationship which it has to a given person's life. Whether or not the relevant relationship exists is a matter of fact. A true objective value must exist in a life-affirming relationship to a man, and it must obtain in a proper relationship to his consciousness.

A person properly starts with the specific needs of human life, examines his own capacities, and then determines what values are proper for him. Next, in order to achieve values, a person needs to gain and use conceptual knowledge. Action is required to reach one's values. However, before one acts in his efforts to gain a value, he should use his reason to identify pertinent causal factors and means-ends relationships. A human being freely chooses to initiate his own actions. He is the fundamental cause of his own behavior.

Some objective values are universal and stem from common human potentialities and characteristics. There are also values that are objective but not universal. Objective values depend on both an individual's humanity and his individuality. A person's individuality is consistent with realism and with an all-embracing consistent explanation of existence. Since individualism is a fundamental feature of the human species, each person is able to employ his unique attributes, talents, and situations in his efforts to do well at living his own individual life. Each person needs to consider his needs, capacities, the nature of the world, and opportunities it offers for human action.

Values are objective when they are based on the facts that are relevant to him as an individual. A person's moral responsibility, from the perspective of ethical naturalism, is to make the fullest possible development of himself as an individual rational being in the context of the world in which he lives. What a person is, together with what the world is, reveals how he should live his life. A person who chooses to live should use reason to satisfy his needs, choose what goals to pursue, and determine what actions will achieve them.

As we have seen, there is an important dissemblance within Austrian value theory between Menger and Mises. However, it is possible for Menger's more objective-value-oriented theory to coexist and complement Mises's pure subjectivism, which is based on the inscrutability of individual values and preferences. Although Menger agreed with Mises that an individual's chosen values are personal and therefore subjective and unknowable to the economist, he also contended that a person ought to be rationally pursuing his objective life-affirming values. Menger thus can be viewed as a key linchpin thinker between Misesian praxeology and Objectivist ethics.

Production and Economic Activity

Production is the means to the fulfillment of men's material needs. The production of goods, services, and wealth metaphysically precedes their distribution and exchange. When a man acts rationally and in his own self-interest, he makes wealth creation, economic activity, and the scientific study of economics possible. To survive and flourish, men have to produce what is necessary for their existence. The requirements of life must be objectively identified and produced. The facts regarding what enhances or restrains life are objective, established by the facts of reality, and based on proper cognition. There are requirements and rules built into the nature of things which must be met if we are to survive and prosper.

Both Austrian economists and Objectivists agree with the French classical economist, Jean-Baptiste Say, that production is the source of demand. Products are ultimately paid for with other products. A man must produce before he can consume. Consumption (i.e., demand) follows from the production of wealth. Supply metaphysically comes before consumption. The primacy of production means that we must produce before we can consume. Demand does not create supply, and consumption does not create production.

The idea that supply comprises demand is true in a money economy as well as in a barter economy. Money is an intermediate good that allows people to buy the things they desire. What ultimately permits men to buy is not the possession of money but rather the possession of productive assets through which they can earn money in the market economy. It follows that when individuals spend money they are demanding from the wealth their production created.

Productiveness is a virtue. People tend to be productive and successful when they are rational and self-interested. Production requires people who practice the virtues of rationality and self-interest. Rationality, a common standard in human nature, is a discerning approach to the selection of both ends and means. Self-interest is also a virtue because living for human beings is ultimately an individual task. Because the maintenance of each person's life is conditional, it is necessary for each individual to choose to think, plan, and produce if he wants to survive and flourish.

As volitional beings, men have the capacity to be rational and self-interested. In fact, it is only to the degree that men are rational and self-interested that they can produce and it is only to the extent that they produce that an objective science of economics can emerge. Economic laws are based on rational, self-interested actions. Economics studies producers whose behavior is predominantly rational, self-interested, and based on the requirements of reality. Regularity (and laws) can be recognized in economic activity because economic actors usually act rationally and in their own interests. If a man is to succeed in his capacity as a producer and exchanger of values, he needs to be rational and self-interested. Because most people are rational and self-interested most of the time, causal explanations in the economic realm can be discovered. This fact generates outcomes that are consistent and regular.

Economic concepts, laws, and theory are concerned with the universal abstract aspects of phenomena. These flow from the nature of man, knowledge, value, and the world itself. Since a man's life is conditional, he needs to acquire economic and other values in order to live. Material wealth (i.e., value) is necessary to maintain one's life. A man has the capacity to choose to produce and exchange values. Most people do choose to live and thus are productive. To be productive, a person must be rational and self-interested. That is a fact of the nature of man and the world. People produce in order to consume (i.e., to live). Economic behavior occurs and is regular when men act rationally and in their own self-interest. Because most people want to survive, they attempt to rationally comprehend the facts of the world and choose to create and trade values. Descriptive and explanatory economic laws are possible because of the regularity that is evidenced in economic activity due to most people acting in their own rational self-interest. A rational self-interested person looks for causal connections in reality. He attempts to cause a specific result because he values it. As an economic agent, he reflects on the goals of his action and the causal relations between himself and various elements of the external environment. Causal connections are thus manifested in the phenomena of economic life. Rational self-interest is the driving force of both production and consumption. It is easy to see why both Menger and Mises viewed the field of economics as one of exact laws and exact inquiry. According to Menger, exact laws assume that men are rational, self-interested, informed, and free. Similarly, Rand saw economic laws as objective laws.

Praxeology

Praxeology is the general theoretical science of human action. Mises grounds economics upon the action axiom that states that men exist and act by making purposive choices. Misesian praxeology refers to the set of sciences that derive by logical inference exclusively from the axiom of human action. Economics is thus a division of praxeology and is made up of apodictically true statements that are not empirically testable. Praxeological laws are universal doctrines whose applicability is independent of any particular empirical circumstances. Praxeology is a unifying framework that unites all types of human decisions, actions, and interactions.

Mises emphasized the central role that "acting man" plays in economics and the necessity to work within a framework conducive for real acting persons. Because axioms expound bedrock metaphysical facts that are self-evident, it is obvious why Mises is in error when he identified action as a primary axiom. Action depends upon a thing's nature. Action is not an irreducible primary. What is primary in studying human action is the nature of man. This leads to a consideration of man's modes of action and their related causal factors. The action axiom is thus more appropriately seen as a secondary axiom to the primary axiom of identity which states that a thing is what it is. The significance of any given action is relational and changes depending upon what or who is performing the specific action.

Rand explains that entities act in accordance with their natures, and the causality is the axiom of identity applied to action. It follows that action cannot be a primary independent of something's nature. In other words, action depends on the underlying characteristics of the thing. This presupposes the axiom of existence which means that "existence exists" and that there is a definite something that exists.

Mises explains that a man's introspective knowledge that he is conscious and acts is a fact of reality and is independent of external experience. Mises deduced the principles of economics and the complete structure of economic theory entirely through the analysis of the introspectively-derived a priori idea of human action. While it is certainly important to understand and acknowledge the useful role of introspection in one's life, it is also necessary to realize that its role is limited, secondary, and adjunct to the empirical observation and logical analysis of empirical reality. It would have been better if Mises had said that external observation and introspection combine to reveal that people act and employ means to achieve ends. Introspection aids or supplements external observation and induction in disclosing to a man the fundamental purposefulness of human action.

Murray Rothbard defends Mises's methodology but goes on to construct his own edifice of Austrian economic theory. Although he embraced nearly all of Mises's economics, Rothbard could not accept Mises's Kantian extreme aprioristic position in epistemology. Mises held that the axiom of human action was true a priori to human experience and was, in fact, a synthetic a priori category.

Mises considered the action axiom to be a law of thought and thus a categorical truth prior to all human experience.

Rothbard, working with an Aristotelian, Thomistic, or Mengerian tradition, justified the praxeological action axiom as a law of reality that is empirical rather than a priori. Of course, this is not the empiricism embraced by positivists. This kind of empirical knowledge rests on universal inner or reflective experience in addition to external physical experience. This type of empirical knowledge consist of a general knowledge of human action that would be considered to be antecedent to the complex historical events that mainstream economists try to explain. The action axiom is empirical in the sense that it is self-evidently true once stated. It is not empirically falsifiable in the positivist sense. It is empirical, but it is not based on empiricism as practiced by today's economics profession. Praxeological statements cannot be subjected to any empirical assessment whether it is falsificationist or verificationist.

Both induction and deduction are required. Initially, the concept of action is formally and inductively derived from perceptual data. Next, the whole systematic structure of economic theory would be deduced from the notion of human action. The categories, theorems, and laws implied in the idea of action include, but are not limited to, value, causality, ends, means, preference, cost, profit and loss, opportunities, scarcity, choice, marginal utility, marginal costs, opportunity cost, time preference, originary interest, association, etc.

There is a dimension of interiority for human beings who have the ability to imagine new futures for themselves and to invent projects and paths for their personal development. Each person is responsible for, and provident over, his own actions and identity. The human person, the acting person, can reflect, deliberate, choose, initiate action, and assume responsibility for his own actions. In addition to Austrians, noted economic personalists such as Pope John Paul II and Michael Novak herald the acting person's interior life of insight, reflection, and decision.

Introspection is a reasonably reliable but ancillary source of evidence and knowledge with respect to what it means to be a rational, purposeful, volitional, and acting human being. Each person knows universally from introspection that he chooses. In other words, observation is introspective in the case of free will. Universal inner or reflective experience is an important adjunct to external, empirical, physical experience.

Free will means that a person is able to perform actions that are not determined by forces outside of his control. This means that at least some choices and actions are not caused by antecedent factors or governed by physical laws or physical events. A human being has the power to reflect, weigh, arrange, and select from among various courses of behavior. In order for an action to be free, it must be because no antecedent factors were enough to make the person carry out exactly that action. A human action is thus not merely a reaction to some prior force or action. We can say that free will exists if a change in a physical variable or property is not due to a prior change in some other physical variable or property. Because a man has reason and free will, he can create concepts, form values, and develop plans aimed at actualizing those values. A person recognizes opportunities to improve his well-being and pursues actions to attain the preferable state of affairs. Actions are intended mainly because of what is desired and thought to be possible. Means-end rationality presumes that people can imagine futures that are different from the present. In devising a plan, a man imagines the future conditions he believes he would experience if he decides to act.

Physical events cannot cause praxeological events. There is a qualitative difference between human actions and deterministic reactions of totally corporeal objects. Action embodies a forward-looking character. Human beings can cause goal-directed, self-generated behavior. Reaction in a determined entity can theoretically and potentially be followed back in time until the beginning of the universe. It follows that, in the natural sciences, the researcher deals with things and the regular relationships that can be discovered to be functioning between them. While we find determinism in physical nature, we discover that a human being possesses specific, delimited control over his consciousness. Every existent is constrained to be what it is and to not be anything else. Men's thoughts and actions are therefore irrelevant to the natural scientist but crucial to philosophers and economists.

A person discovers relationships between his values and his plans. He also strives to learn the relationships between various pertinent causal variables and strives to create those relationships. He must act to acquire the factors or goods he believes are required to accomplish the plans that will achieve his values. Of course, as he gains knowledge, his values may change, which, in turn, may result in a change of his plans. A person is always free to change the significance of his values and plans and may decide to act in a different manner than before. People learn from their experiences, past choices, and discoveries and revise their plans accordingly.

According to Mises, economics is a value-free science of means, rather than of ends, that describes but does not prescribe. However, although the world of praxeological economics, as a science, may be value-free, the human world is not value-free. Economics is the science of human action, and human actions are inextricably connected with values and ethics. It follows that praxeological economics needs to be situated within the context of a normative framework. Praxeological economics does not conflict with a normative perspective on human life. Economics needs to be connected with a discipline that is concerned with ends such as the end of human flourishing. Praxeological economics can stay value-free if it is recognized that it is morally proper for people to take part in market and other voluntary transactions. Such a value-free science must be combined with an appropriate end.

Economics, for Mises, is a value-free tool for objective and critical appraisal. Economic science differentiates between the objective, interpersonally valid conclusions of economic praxeology and the personal value judgments of the economist. Critical appraisal can be objective, value-free, and untainted by bias. It is important for economic science to be value-free and not be distorted by the value judgments or personal preferences of the economist. The credibility of economic science depends upon an impartial and dispassionate concern for truth. Value-freedom is a methodological device designed to separate and isolate an economist's scientific work from the personal preferences of the given economic researcher. His goal is to maintain neutrality and objectivity with respect to the subjective values of others.

Misesian economics focuses on the descriptive aspects of human action by offering reasoning about means and ends. The province of praxeological economics is the logical analysis of the success or failure of selected means to attain ends. Means only have value because, and to the degree that, their ends are valued.

The reasons why an individual values what he values and the determination of whether or not his choices and actions are morally good or bad are certainly significant concerns, but they are not the realm of the praxeological economist. The content of moral or ultimate ends is not the domain of the economist qua economist. There is another level of values that defines value in terms of right preferences. This more objectivist sphere of value defines value in terms of what an individual ought to prefer.

Simply because Mises expounds a value-free science of economics, it does not mean that he believes that a man's behavior lacks moral content. Because a human being is not compartmentalized, economic values and moral values coexist in a man's consciousness, frequently affect one another, and oftentimes overlap. Sooner or later, some moral values must be referred to before the propositions of praxeological economics can be used in men's concrete situations and in service of their ultimate ends. It follows that theories of the moral good are compatible with Austrian Economics because they exist on a different plane.

Knowledge gained from praxeological economics is both value-free (i.e., value neutral) and value-relevant. Value-free knowledge supplied by economic science is value-relevant when it supplies information for rational discussions, deliberations, and determinations of the morally good. Economics is reconnected with philosophy, especially the branches of metaphysics and ethics, when the discussion is shifted to another sphere. It is fair to say that economic science exists because men have concluded that the objective knowledge provided by praxeological economics is valuable for the pursuit of both a person's subjective and ultimate ends.

Advocating or endorsing the idea of "man's survival qua man" or of a good or flourishing life involves value judgments. To make value judgments, one must accept the existence of a comprehensive natural order and the existence of fundamental absolute principles in the universe. This acceptance in no way conflicts with the Misesian concept of subjective economic value. Natural laws are discovered, are not arbitrary relationships, but instead are relationships that are already true. A man's human nature, including his attributes of individuality, reason, and free will, is the ultimate source of moral reasoning. Value is meaningless outside the context of man.

Knowledge of the consequences of alternative social arrangements is necessary and useful in deciding from among different social structures. The choice of the best model of political economy is a value-laden endeavor that is underpinned by the value-free logic of praxeological economics. Given the nature of a human being, it is only he who can decide, and has the right to decide, upon the relative importance of different values and whether or not to act upon them. Since a person has free will, he can choose to cause physical changes to occur without any prior physical causes. Values are metaphysically freely chosen and acted upon when there is an absence of coercion. Man's distinctiveness from other living species is his ability to originate an act of his consciousness. This process of thought is originated volitionally. Freedom is the degree of independence of an individual's plans from the plans of others. Freedom can be assessed by examining the autonomy a man would have under various social arrangements. Praxeological analysis reveals that a free market society results in the optimum amount of freedom, social cooperation, and social coordination.

Praxeological economics and the philosophy of human flourishing are complementary and compatible disciplines. Economics teaches us that social cooperation through the private property system and division of labor enables most individuals to prosper and to pursue their flourishing and happiness. In turn, the worldview of human flourishing informs men how to act. In making their life-affirming ethical and value-based judgments, men can refer to and employ the data of economic science.

A Synthesis of Philosophical Traditions

Austrian Economics and Objectivism can benefit from each other's insights. These two schools have more in common than heretofore has been appreciated. Austrian Economics and Objectivism have more in common than they have in conflict. It is acceptable to mix and match components from different paradigms in our efforts to achieve a deeper understanding of the nature of man and the world. By extracting information from existing paradigms it is possible to create a paradigm that is more reflective of reality. Specifically, it may be desirable to refine and fuse together the following components: (1) an objective, realistic, natural-law-oriented metaphysics as exemplified in the work of Aristotle, Carl Menger, Ayn Rand, and in the more recent works of Murray Rothbard; (2) Ayn Rand's epistemology, which describes essences or concepts as epistemological rather than as metaphysical; (3) a biocentric theory of value as appears in the writings of Menger and Rand; (4) Misesian praxeology as a tool for understanding how people cooperate and compete and for deducing universal principles of economics; and (5) an ethic of human flourishing based on reason, free will, and individuality as suggested in the contemporary works of Tibor R. Machan, Douglas B. Rasmussen, Douglas J. Den Uyl, and others.

An integration and combination of selected doctrines from the Austrian school of economics (as exemplified in the writings of Mises and Menger) and from the Objectivist school can provide a philosophical basis for an appropriate moral and political structure for a free society. A naturalist metaethical perspective provides the foundation for the type of framework that is most supportive and accommodating of the moral nature of human life.

Austrian-Objectivism would be a systematic philosophy that includes a particular view of reality, human nature, human action, the nature of knowledge, and the nature of value and would include a specific code of morality based on the requirements of life in this world. The integration of the tradition of Austrian Economics and the philosophy of Objectivism would enhance both traditions and provide a more solid foundation and a more unified perspective with respect to understanding the nature and workings of the world.

Mises's theoretical system deals with uncertainty that is due to the passage of time and the implications of human ignorance. These are natural dimensions of human existence. There are natural phenomena that act in certain ways under certain conditions. It follows that we can properly relocate Austrian Economics in general and Mises's praxeological axioms in particular into the great coherent natural law traditions of realist analysis and rational epistemology. In fact, the natural-law tradition is not only capable of assimilating and synthesizing the Misesian logic of human action, it is also able to serve as a metatheoretical underpinning for the merger of Austrian thought with Objectivism.

Objectivism's Aristotelian perspective on the nature of man and the world and on the need to exercise one's virtues can be viewed as synergic with the economic coordination and praxeology of Austrian Economics. Placing the economic realm within the general process of human action, which itself is part of human nature, enables theoretical progress in our search for the truth and in the construction of a systematic, logical, and consistent conceptual framework. The Objectivist worldview can provide a context to the economic insights of the Austrian economists. Of course, any paradigm should be open to further intellectual interaction which may enrich it. There is always more to be learned about reality.

Our goal is to have a paradigm or system in which the views of reality, knowledge, human nature, value, and society make up an integrated whole. The suggested synthesis of Austrian Economics and Objectivism can provide an excellent foundation for such a paradigm. Of course the paradigm will grow and evolve as scholars engage, question, critique, interpret, and extend its ideas. This systematic approach and/or its components have been studied by many modern-day thinkers. This is as it should be because our goal is to have a paradigm that accords with reality. As such, it must be viewed as a vibrant, living systematic framework that aims at the truth.

We need to educate the young and attempt to reeducate, persuade, and convert mainstream economists, philosophers, educators, and the general public to the philosophy of freedom. What is needed is a well-articulated, theoretically consistent, and intellectually and morally sound defense of capitalism. An Austrian-Objectivist paradigm for a free society is an excellent candidate for the provision of this defense. Perhaps the best strategy to follow is to bypass the system of formal mainstream education and speak directly to the public via the

Internet and organizations such as the Ludwig von Mises Institute and the Objectivist Center.

Recommended Reading

Badhwar, Neera K. *Is Virtue Only a Means to Happiness?* Poughkeepsie, N.Y.: The Objectivist Center, 2000.

Caldwell, Bruce C., ed. *Carl Menger and His Legacy in Economics.* Durham, N.C.: Duke University Press, 1990.

Ebeling, Richard M., ed. *Human Action: A 50-Year Tribute.* Hillsdale, Mich.: Hillsdale City Press, 2000.

Fuerle, Richard D. *The Pure Logic of Choice.* New York: Vantage Press, 1986.

Herbener, Jeffrey M., ed. *The Meaning of Ludwig von Mises.* New York: Kluwer Academic Publishers, 1992.

Kelley, David. *The Evidence of the Senses.* Baton Rouge: Louisiana State University Press, 1988.

Kirzner, Israel M. *Ludwig von Mises.* Wilmington, Del.: ISI Books, 2001.

Machan, Tibor R. *Capitalism and Individualism.* New York: St. Martin's Press, 1990.

———. *Classical Individualism.* London: Routledge, 1998.

———. *Individuals and Their Rights.* LaSalle, Ill.: Open Court, 1989.

Menger, Carl. *Investigations into the Method of the Social Sciences with Special Reference to Economics.* New York: New York University Press, [1883] 1985.

———. *Principles of Economics.* New York: New York University Press, [1871] 1981.

Mises, Ludwig von. *Epistemological Problems of Economics.* Princeton, N.J.: Van Nostrand, 1960.

———. *Human Action.* New Haven, Conn.: Yale University Press, 1949.

Peikoff, Leonard. *Objectivism: The Philosophy of Ayn Rand.* New York: Dutton, 1991.

Rand, Ayn. *Atlas Shrugged.* New York: Random House, 1957.

———. *Capitalism: The Unknown Ideal.* New York: New American Library, 1965.

———. *Introduction to Objectivist Epistemology.* New York: The Objectivist, 1967.

Rasmussen, Douglas B., and Douglas J. Den Uyl. *Liberty and Nature.* LaSalle, Ill.: Open Court, 1991.

Reisman, George. *Capitalism.* Ottawa, Ill.: Jameson Books, 1996.

Rothbard, Murray N. *The Ethics of Liberty.* Atlantic Highlands, N.J.: Humanities Press, 1982.

———. *Man, Economy, and State..* Mission, Kan.: Sheed, Andrews and McMeel, 1962.

Sciabarra, Chris Matthew, ed. Special Issue on "Ayn Rand Among the Austrians." *Journal of Ayn Rand Studies.* (Forthcoming in Spring 2005).

———. *Total Freedom: Toward a Dialectical Libertarianism.* University Park: Pennsylvania State University Press, 2000.

Smith, Barry. *Austrian Philosophy: The Legacy of Franz Brentano.* LaSalle, Ill.: Open Court, 1994.

Smith, Tara. *Viable Values.* Lanham, Md.: Rowman & Littlefield, 2000.

Yeager, Leland. *Ethics as Social Science.* Cheltenham, UK: Edward Elgar, 2001.

Index

About the Editor

Edward W. Younkins is professor of accountancy and business administration in the Department of Business at Wheeling Jesuit University and the founder of the university's undergraduate degree program in political and economic philosophy. He is also the founding director of the university's Master of Business Administration (M.B.A.) and Master of Science in Accountancy (M.S.A.) programs. In addition to earning state and national honors for his performances on the Certified Public Accountant (CPA) and Certified Management Accountant (CMA) exams, respectively, Dr. Younkins also received the Outstanding Educator Award for 1997 from the West Virginia Society of Certified Public Accountants. The author of numerous articles in accounting and business journals, his free-market-oriented articles and reviews have appeared in *Ideas on Liberty* (formerly *The Freeman*), *The Journal of Markets and Morality*, *The Social Critic*, *Le Québécois Libre*, *Liberty Free Press*, *The Free Radical*, *Free Life*, *The Individual*, *The Journal of Ayn Rand Studies*, *The Autonomist*, *Sense of Life Objectivists*, *The Rational Argumentator*, *The Libertarian Alliance* (working paper), *The Ludwig von Mises Institute* (working paper), and many other publications. He has recently written *Capitalism and Commerce: Conceptual Foundations of Free Enterprise* and has edited a collection of Michael Novak's articles and essays entitled *Three in One: Essays on Democratic Capitalism, 1976-2000*.

About the Contributors

Walter Block is an author, editor, and coeditor of many books which include *Defending the Undefendable*; *Lexicon of Economic Thought*; *Economic Freedom of the World 1975-1995*; *Rent Control: Myths and Realities*; *Discrimination, Affirmative Action and Equal Opportunity*; *Theology, Third World Development and Economic Justice*; *Man, Economy, and Liberty: Essays in Honor of Murray N. Rothbard*; *Religion, Economics, and Social Thought*; and *Economic Freedom: Towards a Theory of Measurement*.

Dr. Block has written more than five hundred articles for various nonrefereed journals, magazines, and newspapers, and is a contributor to such journals as *The Review of Austrian Economics, Journal of Libertarian Studies, The Journal of Labor Economics, Cultural Dynamics,* and *The Quarterly Journal of Austrian Economics.* He is currently the Harold E. Wirth Eminent Scholar, professor and chair of economics, college of business administration, at Loyola University.

Samuel Bostaph is currently associate professor of economics and chairman, Department of Economics at the University of Dallas, where his teaching areas include economic theory, history of economic thought, comparative economic systems, and finance. His Ph.D. and M.S. degrees in economics were awarded by Southern Illinois University at Carbondale, his B.A. in economics by Texas Christian University. Past research publications include articles on Plato's political and social theories, William Stanley Jevons's early intellectual roots and research accomplishments, Friedrich von Wieser's contributions to Austrian and socialist theory, Friedrich von Hayek's theory of social coordination, and this current reprinted article on the Methodenstreit.

Ricardo F. Crespo has an undergraduate degree in both philosophy and economics and a Ph.D. in philosophy. He is currently professor at Universidad Nacional de Cuyo and Universidad Austral (Argentina), where he teaches philosophy of economics. He holds a position of researcher in the Consejo Nacional de Investigaciones Cientificas. Among his research interests are Austrian Economics, ontology of economics, economics and ethics, and epistemology of economics. He has published three books, coauthored another, and published several articles in books and journals of philosophy and of economics, including *The Review of Austrian Economics*, *The Journal of Markets and Morality*, *Theoria*, and *The Journal des Economistes et des Etudes Humaines*.

Jeffrey M. Herbener, a senior fellow of the Ludwig von Mises Institute, has taught economics at Washington and Jefferson College and is now professor of economics at Grove City College. Author of many articles on the microeconomic foundations of Austrian theory, he is associate editor of *The Quarterly Journal of Austrian Economics*, director of the Austrian Scholars Conference, and a lecturer at the Mises University. He is the editor of the book *The Meaning of Ludwig von Mises*.

Richard C. B. Johnsson recently earned his Ph.D. at the University of Uppsala and is on the staff of the Ratio Institute, an independent economic research institution in Stockholm, Sweden. His dissertation included construction and application of a Computable General Equilibrium (CGE) Model.

Tibor R. Machan, Distinguished Fellow and professor at the Leatherby Center of Chapman University, Argyros School of Business and Economics, is also professor emeritus at Auburn University's Department of Philosophy and Research Fellow at the Hoover Institution (Stanford, California). He has written, among other works, *Ayn Rand* (Peter Lang, 1999), *Generosity: Virtue in the Civil Society* (Cato Institute, 1998), and *Classical Individualism: The Supreme Importance of Each Human Being* (Routledge, 1998). His latest book is entitled *Passion for Liberty*. He is editor of the series "Philosophic Reflections on a Free Society" at the Hoover Institution Press.

Douglas B. Rasmussen is professor of philosophy at St. John's University in New York City. He is coauthor of *The Catholic Bishops and the Economy: A Debate* (1987), *Liberty and Nature: An Aristotelian Defense of Liberal Order* (1991), and *Liberalism Defended: The Challenge of Post-Modernity* (1997), and coeditor of *Liberty for the Twenty-First Century* (1995). He has published numerous articles on issues in epistemology, ethics, and political philosophy in various professional journals and books. He guest-edited the January 1992 issue of *The Monist* on the topic "Teleology and the Foundation of Value."

Murray N. Rothbard (1926-1995) was the S. J. Hall Distinguished Professor of Economics at the University of Nevada, Las Vegas. He was the author of twenty-five books, including *America's Great Depression*; *The Panic of 1819*; the four-volume *Conceived in Liberty*; the two-volume set *An Austrian Perspective on the History of Economic Thought*; *Man, Economy and State*; *The Ethics of Liberty*; and more than a thousand articles. Rothbard was also Academic Vice President of the Ludwig von Mises Institute and editor of its *Review of Austrian Economics*.

Chris Matthew Sciabarra, visiting scholar, Department of Politics, New York University, is the author of the "Dialectics and Liberty Trilogy," which includes *Marx, Hayek, and Utopia* (SUNY Press, 1995), *Ayn Rand: The Russian Radical* (Penn State Press, 1995), and *Total Freedom: Toward a Dialectical Libertarianism* (Penn State Press, 2000). He is also coeditor, with Mimi Reisel Gladstein, of *Feminist Interpretations of Ayn Rand* (Penn State Press, 1999). His articles and letters on popular culture and music have appeared in publications as diverse as the *New York Daily News, Billboard, Just Jazz Guitar, Jazz Times*, and *The Free Radical.*

Larry J. Sechrest, is associate professor of economics, Sul Ross State University, and associate professor of economics and director of the Free Enterprise Institute at Sul Ross State University. His research interests include free banking, business cycles, the history of economic thought, economic history, and the philosophical foundations of economics. He is the author of *Free Banking: Theory, History, and a Laissez-Faire Model* (Quorum Books).

Barry Smith is professor of philosophy at the State University of New York, Buffalo, and editor of *The Monist*. He is the author or editor of over a dozen books, including *Austrian Philosophy: The Legacy of Franz Brentano*, and is the coeditor of *Austrian Economics: Historical and Philosophical Background.*

Gloria L. Zúñiga received her Ph.D. in philosophy in June 2000 from the University of Buffalo. She wrote her dissertation, titled *A General Theory of Value: Axiology in the Central European Philosophic Tradition*, under the direction of Dr. Barry Smith. This was an ontological examination of three species of value—economic, moral, and aesthetic—and their relations. Much of her research was conducted in Germany, thanks to a grant from the German government (DAAD). She has published in the areas of applied ontology, moral philosophy, and the philosophy of economics. She has studied with Dr. Kurt Leube, a friend and pupil of Friedrich von Hayek, in the Austrian school economics graduate track at California State University at Hayward. There, she also earned her undergraduate degree in business and economics. Recently, her interdisciplinary work extended to the field of information systems, in which her work concerns the ontology of information systems.